The Illustrated History of
SPORTS
at the
U.S. MILITARY
ACADEMY

Joseph E. Dineen

UPON THE FIELDS OF FRIENDLY STRIFE,
ARE SOWN THE SEEDS THAT, UPON
OTHER FIELDS, ON OTHER DAYS,
WILL BEAR THE FRUITS OF VICTORY.

The Illustrated History of
SPORTS
at the
U.S. MILITARY ACADEMY

Joseph E. Dineen

THE DONNING COMPANY
PUBLISHERS
NORFOLK/VIRGINIA BEACH

The Donning Company/Publishers
Norfolk/Virginia Beach

The Donning Company/Publishers
5659 Virginia Beach Boulevard
Norfolk, Virginia 23502

Edited by Tony Lillis
Richard A. Horwege, Senior Editor

Library of Congress Cataloging-in-Publication Data

Dineen, Joseph E.
  The illustrated history of sports at the U.S. Military Academy.

  Bibliography: p.
  Includes index.
  1. United States Military Academy—Athletics—History.
I. Title.
U410.L1D56   1988   355′.007′1173   88-3903
ISBN 0-89865-629-X

Printed in the United States of America

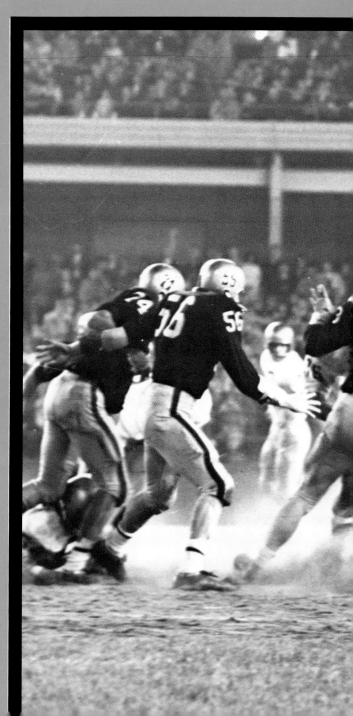

CONTENTS

FOREWORD

"Upon the fields of friendly strife..."

Graduates and friends of West Point have heard those words of Gen. Douglas MacArthur so often. But even those who have memorized the phrase, can miss the depth of meaning in its close:

"...are sown the seeds that, upon other fields, on other days, will bear the fruits of victory."

Victory is not an idle pastime to the profession of arms. There's very little to be said of second place on the battlefield.

Defense of the nation, and of our way of life, is a heavy responsibility—but a responsibility gladly undertaken. It embodies intangibles like spirit and teamwork and belief in a cause that has no limits. At West Point, these intangibles are molded by the experience of sport, because athletics at West Point have a very special meaning.

For graduates and friends of the Academy, it is the spirit of sport that bonds each heart in that Gray Line with the hearts of teammates, classmates, those who went before, and those who will follow after. Sports form a special bond, as well, between individuals and institutions, and between individuals and the nation. Sports can be—and at West Point they are—a crucible in which the stuff needed for life's toughest battles is forged.

More than at any other institution I know of, the "fields of friendly strife" at West Point are the practice fields for the challenges that every graduate will face—whether those challenges are on the battlefield, in business, in education, or in other fields of public service.

Even though this spirited collection of tales and pictures focuses on intercollegiate football and the happier moments in the history of other major West Point intercollegiate sports, it's important to remember that the world of sport at West Point extends far more broadly. Every cadet is an athlete. From intramurals to club sports to minor sports—to the Army-Navy football classic with its international following—every cadet gains a wealth of experience from sport.

The moments shared in this collection are but a small sampling of West Point's contribution to what Grantland Rice so aptly called the "Wonderful World of Sport." I think they do a good job, however, of capturing the spirit. And I hope you enjoy these selected memories as much as I, and thousands of other graduates, profited from making them.

—Pete Dawkins
Rumson, New Jersey
March 1988

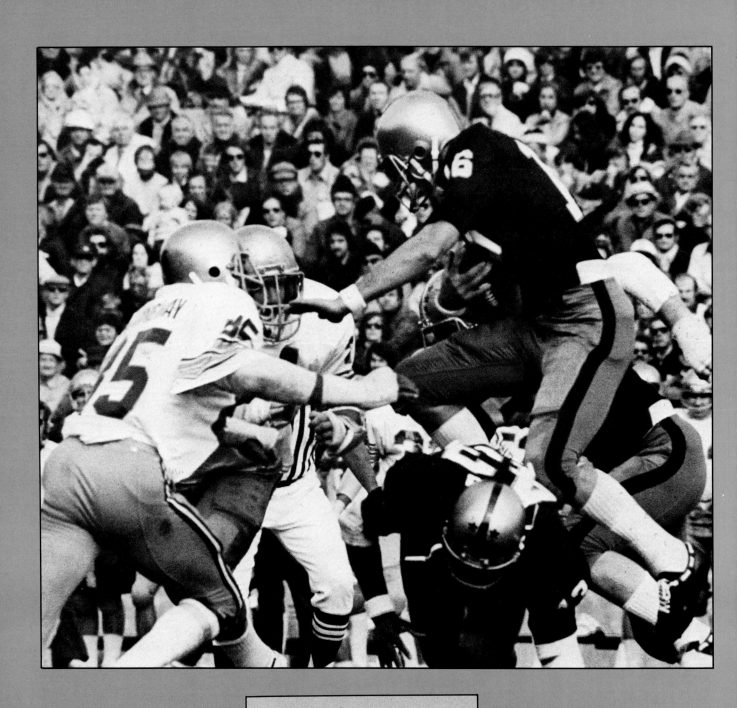

Army quarterback Leamon Hall (16) uncustomarily picks up yardage on the ground against Boston College in 1976. Hall holds all of West Point's passing records in game, season, and career categories, but ran the football only when absolutely necessary.

On the cover of an Army football program during the 1987 season were the artist renderings of Felix "Doc" Blanchard, Glenn Davis, and Pete Dawkins, winners of the Heisman Trophy that is presented each year to an individual who is considered the most outstanding college football player in the nation. Perhaps no other athletes in the history of the United States Military Academy have played such an important role in placing this institution into national focus because of their achievements on the "fields of friendly strife" as Douglas MacArthur referred to it.

Yet, above the din of the crowd and the statistics that are kept, perhaps the reflective words of Glenn Davis are quite pertinent. "The greatest accomplishment I ever had, bigger than ten Heisman Trophies," said Davis, "was graduating from West Point. That still means more to me than everything else."

There is a great deal of truth in that statement. While researching nearly one hundred years of intercollegiate sports competition at the Military Academy, those thoughts have been repeated time and time again by athletes of yesteryear and athletes of yesterday.

West Point has played a critical role in the history of this nation, and it is quite sobering to think that the athletic achievements of its graduates are but a small sliver of the history of this institution.

It has taken this writer nearly two years to chronicle the exploits of West Point's favorite sons and now daughters. It is far from complete, and it is not meant to be because it so encompassing. We have tried to give the reader a condensed pictorial view of the athletic program at the U.S. Military Academy. There is a great deal of emphasis on the football program and its growth to the present day, but the advent of football reversed the thinking of the West Point administration on the positive aspects of athletics and the role it plays in the development of our officer-leaders. That is why we view it in such a voluminous fashion.

The effort to chronicle this athletic history became a labor of love, but it would not have been accomplished without the help and assistance of many friends and associates. I would like to take this space to express my thanks for their professional assistance.

I would like to thank Carl F. Ullrich, director of athletics at West Point, and his staff for providing me the opportunity to undertake this project. His confidence in my professional abilities to accomplish the task proved an inspiration when the days grew to months, and the months into years trying to piece together the segments of this work.

My thanks to Sean Brickell, whose recommendation to the athletic department that such a project was noteworthy and of great value, led to a finished product. There is also a good deal of appreciation for his patience.

I would like to thank Bob Kinney, director of the Sports Information, and members of his staff, Madeline Salvani and Eric Blinderman, for their assistance in providing the records, and research materials that have contributed to a more accurate portrait of this athletic history.

I must note a special thanks to Ms. Salvani for the research assistance she provided during the past two years. This endeavor would never have been completed without her help and dedication.

There are many other members in the athletic department who have contributed in some form or fashion, whether it was finding an old photograph in a storage box or recalling an incident of importance. Thanks goes to Capt. Mike Keough, Jack Ryan, Ray Bosse, Jack Riley, Gene Uchacz, and all of the members of the coaching staff who have provided historical background on their respective sports.

I would like to thank Col. Morris Herbert of the Association of Graduates and his staff for their assistance, and the avenues of research they provided on the origin of sports at the U.S. Military Academy and the tracking of graduates during their service careers.

A special thanks is extended to Ms. Wendy A. Whitfield of the U.S. Military Academy Library Archives department, along with Mrs. Marie T. Capps of the Special Collections department of the library for providing photographic support.

I would also like to thank Col. Pierce A. Rushton, Jr., director of admissions, and my close associate, Capt. Stephen R. Naru, for their support throughout the duration of this project.

Special tribute is paid to all of the athletes, and coaches who made history, and the photographers who have recorded these sports exploits at West Point through their lenses. There are so many contributors: Salvador Palazzo, Al Murphy, the late David Meyer, scores of enlisted photographers in the U.S. Army, the Associated Press, United Press International, International Press Association and other news organizations. A special thanks to Charles Kelley, a New York City based free lance photographer who has provided most recent photographic material, as well as an insight on photography in general.

On a personal note, I would like to thank my wife, Linda, for her understanding and support during the hours, days, and weeks this writer was squirreled away in a small bedroom amid constant clutter, staring at a computer screen while chronicling this pictorial history. And, to my mother, Audrey Crosby, who helped provide the tools so desparately needed to accomplish so extensive a task.

History never stands still however, so we must move on with an open view of what is to come. It is hoped what has been provided in these pages proves beneficial, as well as entertaining.

—Joseph E. Dineen

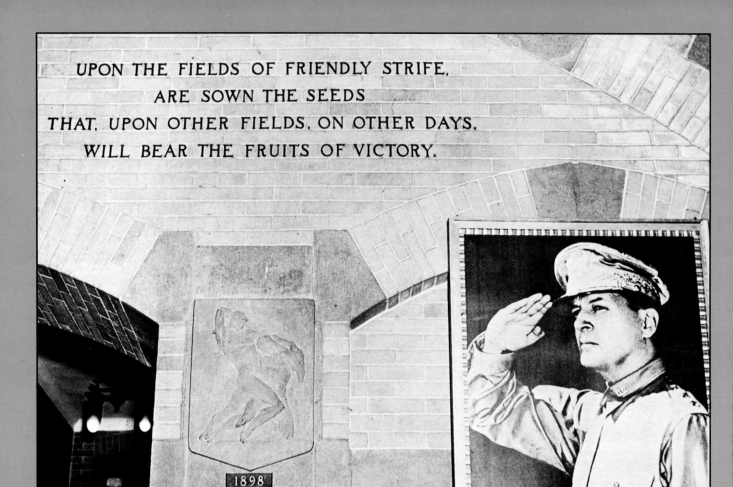

UPON THE FIELDS OF FRIENDLY STRIFE,
ARE SOWN THE SEEDS
THAT, UPON OTHER FIELDS, ON OTHER DAYS,
WILL BEAR THE FRUITS OF VICTORY.

A portrait of Douglas MacArthur displayed in the West Point gymnasium, just below his famous quotation, "Upon the fields of friendly strife..."

CHAPTER 1

WEST POINT ATHLETICS
THE BEGINNING

"Upon the fields of friendly strife are sown the seeds that, upon other fields, on other days, will bear the fruits of victory."

This quotation by the late Gen. Douglas MacArthur provides the foundation and the relevance of athletics at the United States Military Academy. MacArthur felt athletics played an important role in the development of Army officers because athletes were forced to work hard, sacrifice, make instantaneous decisions at critical times, and work together in order to win. Army officers face similar decisions in the midst of battle, so what better place to experience these lessons in leadership than on the athletic field.

Though MacArthur, a 1903 graduate of the Academy, spoke those often-quoted words during his tenure as superintendent at West Point from 1919 to 1922, the meaning holds true for those men who played a significant role in organizing athletics on a formal basis at West Point during the mid to late 1800s.

The U.S. Military Academy was founded in 1802 by an Act of Congress to provide this nation both military specialists and engineers to carve out our expanding borders. West Point graduates served the United States well, building bridges, dams, canals, roads and railroads, in addition to defending our borders in defense of freedom and our democratic form of government.

The history of West Point, its significance as a military fortification during the Revolutionary War, and the heroic efforts of its graduates in times of war as well as peace is well-documented by historians. The names ring familiar to every one of us who has opened a history book. Ulysses S. Grant, Robert E. Lee, John J. Pershing, MacArthur, Dwight D. Eisenhower, George S. Patton, and Omar Bradley are all familiar names, men who fought during the Civil War, World War I, World War II, and the Korean War.

Of course, Eisenhower and Grant made an additional impact on United States history, having both served as President. Other graduates have served as ambassadors, state government leaders, industrialists, as well as leaders in the fields of medicine, education, law, and commerce.

Yet, when one reviews the biographies of these familiar West Point graduates, there is an athletic experience attributed to their days at the Academy. Eisenhower lettered in football in 1912 and was a promising running back until a knee injury ended his playing career. Bradley also lettered in football, but was an outstanding baseball player for the Academy. James Van Fleet, a classmate of both Eisenhower and Bradley, lettered two years in football (1913, 1914). MacArthur lettered in baseball, playing left field for the Army varsity nine, but he also served as manager of the 1902 Army football team, and maintained a special interest in football throughout his military career.

Prior to becoming superintendent, MacArthur always kept track of the plight of the West Point football squad. Whether he was on duty in Europe, Washington, the Philippines, or Japan, he always made certain the football office kept him informed of the squad's progress.

Upon assuming the position of superintendent on June 12, 1919, Gen. MacArthur played a significant role in promoting athletics as a part of the cadets' academic curriculum. In MacArthur's eyes, physical training, as well as competitive athletics, was very important in the development of a cadet as a future military leader.

Those views certainly pleased Lt. Col. Herman Koehler, Master of the Sword at West Point at the time MacArthur became superintendent. Koehler devised a physical education system that was followed in every training camp during World War I. He personally supervised the physical training for over 200,000 troops in France during the war, so MacArthur's interest in athletics and physical training was welcome news.

In 1920, compulsory physical education was integrated into the academic curriculum and a comprehensive intramural program was instituted at West Point. Under this program cadets not only received professional training, but also supervised those intramural sports. Additionally, cadets were required to pass physical training proficiency tests, and were held accountable just as they were with regular academic instruction.

While competitive sports and physical training became an integral part of the daily program at the Academy during MacArthur's tenure as superintendent, it certainly was slow in coming during the historic early years of the Academy.

There was little time for athletics when the Academy was founded in 1802, with a graduating class numbering just two men. Discipline was severe at West Point. Cadets were required to drill and study, a daily routine that left little or no time for such frivolity as sports.

There was little progress in changing the monotonous routine until 1817 when Sylvanus Thayer became superintendent. Thayer, considered the "Father of the Military Academy," developed an academic system that still provides the foundation for today's academic curriculum.

Thayer felt the ideal West Point graduate should be a well-trained, worthy leader. He demanded excellence of knowledge and character. Realizing the nation was in need of engineers, he made civil engineering the core of his academic system.

Sylvanus Thayer wanted cadets to develop mental discipline and high standards of scholarship. He required regular study habits, small classes of ten to fourteen members, and made it mandatory that cadets pass every academic course of instruction.

Although Thayer established an educational system that has endured the test of time, physical training to develop a sound body began in 1817, before any other college in the country. However, there were few strides made in formal athletic competition.

In the 1830s, cadets were instructed in the techniques of riding and fencing, and dancing lessons were given to cadets in 1839, if one considers that a form of athletic activity. That same year, Abner Doubleday of Cooperstown, New York, a young cadet in his second year, supposedly drew up a diamond and a set of rules for the game of baseball.

The game was patterned after a game called rounders which was played by boys and girls in England. The youngsters would hit a thrown ball, drop their bat and run to post (or base). A similar game was played in the United States in the early 1800s, called town ball. Boys would be seen playing the game on the village greens, such as found in a place like Cooperstown.

It was here that Abner Doubleday is credited with creating the original diamond and drawing up a set of rules for baseball. At the suggestion of A. G. Spalding, a famous player and founder of the sporting goods company, a commission was founded in 1907 to determine the origin of baseball. The commission concluded that baseball originated in the United States and that Abner Doubleday invented it in Cooperstown. Later research showed the commission's decision was based more on legend than fact. Consequently, the claim that Doubleday invented the game of baseball may still be rightly debated.

Despite Doubleday's impact on a game we call our "national pastime," baseball did not catch on right away at West Point. In fact, it is written that in 1847 some cricket clubs were formed at the request of Capt. Henry Brewerton, the superintendent. But interest in the sport seemed to vanish within a year.

Midway through the Civil War, a yearling (sophomore) class at the Academy requested permission to purchase baseball equipment. Four years later the Corps of Cadets established some rules and interclass games were held.

Following the Civil War there were reports that rowing competition was held at the Academy, but abuses by some participants ended any thoughts of expanding that sport.

Perhaps one reason why organized sports took so many years to catch on at West Point were the stringent rules of dress. Cadets were always expected to be in uniform—gray trousers, white shirt, and high-neck jacket. While there are many cases of cadets informally participating in athletic activities, it was always in uniform.

Perhaps a key boost to organized athletics came in 1888, thanks to the keen observance of Lt. Col. Hamilton S. Hawkins, Commandant of Cadets from 1888 to 1892. One day while walking by the barracks, Hawkins saw two cadets tossing a ball around. Despite their dexterity and obvious interest in exercising, Lt. Col. Hawkins saw how uncomfortable they were in full uniform. He quickly gave them permission to "lay aside your jackets."

The cadets wasted no time in carrying out the order. Other cadets witnessing the defrocking followed suit, much to the chagrin of several tactical officers who began writing up reports. The commandant shredded the reports and made an appointment to see Col. John G. Parkes, the superintendent.

"These are vigorous young men here," argued Lt. Col. Hawkins during his meeting with the superintendent. "They should have more exercise. But they never in the world can get it wearing those jackets."

The superintendent, perhaps demonstrating the wisdom of Solomon, agreed. From that day on cadets were encouraged to form interclass football and baseball teams.

In 1890, the cadets formed a baseball team that played three outside teams for the first time—the Riverton Club of Philadelphia, the Sylvans of New York, and the Atlantics of Governor's Island.

As typifies the illustrious history of sports at West Point, the Army baseball team was successful in its debut, winning two games while playing to a tie in another. The Army squad was forced to settle for an 8-8 deadlock with Riverton after playing eight innings, but trounced the Sylvans 7-1, and trimmed the Atlantics by a 17-14 margin.

This is a photographic reproduction of a painting of General of the Army Douglas MacArthur. The portrait was painted by Thomas E. Stephens.

Cadet James Van Fleet is pictured here as a member of the class of 1915. He went on to distinguish himself as one of this nation's foremost military leaders.

Cadet Douglas MacArthur, center (6), is pictured with members of the 1902 football squad. MacArthur served as manager of the team and maintained an interest in football throughout his military career. Others pictured who played key roles in Army's early football history include Paul Bunker, far left, the only first team All-America selection for two different positions, Ernest Graves (9) and team captain Robert C. Boyers (with ball), both of whom would later coach at West Point, Ed Farnsworth (13), the only person to play in five Army-Navy games, Charlie Daly, (behind Farnsworth), one of the most successful coaches in history, and Henry Torney (14) a two-time All-America halfback.

Col. Herman Koehler, Master of the Sword at the U.S. Military Academy, was head football coach from 1897 to 1900. He compiled a record of twenty victories, eleven defeats, and three ties. His first and last seasons as head coach were his best. In 1897, Army was 6-1-1, defeating Trinity, Wesleyan, Tufts, Lehigh, Stevens, and Brown. The only loss came against Harvard, 28-0, while the Cadets tied Yale 6-6. Koehler's team in 1900 won seven games, lost three and tied one. Army took the measure of Tufts, Trinity, De La Salle, Williams, Rutgers, Hamilton, and Bucknell. The Cadets lost to Harvard, Yale, and Navy, the last by an 11-7 score.

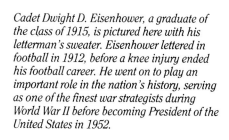

Cadet Dwight D. Eisenhower, a graduate of the class of 1915, is pictured here with his letterman's sweater. Eisenhower lettered in football in 1912, before a knee injury ended his football career. He went on to play an important role in the nation's history, serving as one of the finest war strategists during World War II before becoming President of the United States in 1952.

Omar Bradley, a class of 1915 West Point graduate, takes his turn batting during the 1915 season.

Cadet Dennis Michie, considered the "Father of Army Football," obtained permission to establish football at West Point. He helped set up a challenge extended by the Naval Academy, and then trained, coached and played in the first football game at West Point in 1890.

Here is a photograph of the first football game between Army and Navy in 1890. A young man named Dennis Michie received permission to accept a challenge from the Naval Academy to compete in football for the first time. Only three Army players had played the game before, so the Middies held the upper hand in this skirmish, 24-0.

CHAPTER 2

MICHIE AND THE BIRTH OF FOOTBALL

Football officially came to the United States Military Academy on Saturday, November 29, 1890, when a group of Naval Cadets arrived at West Point. While the skies were gray and foreboding, contrasting dramatically with the gothic structures of the Academy, those who participated or simply observed could hardly understand what this one confrontation would do for athletics at the Military Academy.

Yet, little of this history would be possible without the efforts of Dennis Mahon Michie, who was born at West Point on April 10, 1870. His father, Lt. Peter Smith Michie, was first assigned to the Academy in 1867, and remained there throughout his military career. The elder Michie, who was at Appomattox at the close of the Civil War in 1865, was an assistant professor of engineering at the Academy from 1867 to 1871, and then became professor of natural and experimental philosophy in 1871, remaining in that position until his death in 1901. Lt. Michie also was a powerful member of the Academic Board at West Point.

His young son, Dennis, was very popular with the officers while growing up at the Academy, being a rather friendly sort to all those he would meet on post. Although he was sternly disciplined by his father on occasion, perhaps attributed to Lt. Michie's Scottish upbringing, Dennis still managed to get his way more often than not.

Dennis Michie attended Lawrenceville Prep when of high school age and learned to play the game of football quite well. After entering West Point as a member of the class of 1892, young Dennis contrived a way to bring football to the Academy.

While on summer furlough he met a group of Naval Cadets, and the topic of football came up. The Naval Academy was anxious to challenge West Point to a game of football, but Michie knew a team from the Academy would never be granted permission to leave post. Secondly, he knew any such challenge would have to originate from the Naval Academy. Consequently, such a challenge was issued and young Dennis brought it to the attention of his father, Lt. Michie.

Dennis argued that a challenge from the Naval Academy should never be turned down. The pride of the U.S. Military Academy was at stake, he exclaimed. Under such circumstances certainly the cadets would have to accept the challenge.

Despite some reservations, Lt. Michie agreed and gained the support of Col. John W. Wilson, the superintendent, as well as Col. Hawkins, the commandant. With this type of support in hand, the Academic Board agreed to permit the football contest.

While the political planning and skirmishing to obtain permission to answer the challenge from Navy was now over, Dennis Michie faced the most difficult task, forming a team in a short period of time, obtaining the proper equipment and uniforms, and finding a way to pay for the travel expenses of the Navy team.

The travel expenses were covered by the entire Corps of Cadets, numbering 271. They allowed 52 cents to be charged to their cadet store accounts, an amount that covered half of the Naval Academy's traveling expenses.

The uniforms presented another problem for Michie, who found himself the coach, captain, trainer, and business manager for the first Army football squad. The uniforms consisted of canvas jackets, black socks, white breeches, and a black woolen cap. Team members purchased the uniforms.

Michie scoured the Corps of Cadets for football volunteers. Several of the 271 members of the corps agreed to play, but just three had any previous football experience. Michie was one of them, along with Leonard Prince, a member of Michie's class of 1892, and plebe Butler Ames. Ames had stirred things up somewhat upon arriving at West Point when he requested permission to have a pair of cadet trousers tailored to a pair of shorts, enabling him to work out more comfortably in the gymnasium. Ironically, he received permission to the surprise of many, and despite some outcries, Michie said little because he knew how talented Ames was in football.

Practice sessions also proved difficult. The Cadets normally practiced on Saturday afternoons when the weather was too bad to drill or parade. Michie did get his charges up thirty minutes before reveille for a jog around the Plain and the academic area, and did his best to prepare them for the Navy encounter.

The first Army football team would be characterized by sports reporters as young and inexperienced. The squad lined up with Jim Moore ('92) at left end, Joe Crabbs ('91) at left tackle, Truman O. Murphy ('91) at left guard, Sterling Adams ('92) at center, John Heavey ('91) at right guard, Francis Schoeffel ('91) at right tackle, Leonard Prince ('92) at right end, Kirby Walker ('92) at quarterback, Ed Timberlake ('93) at left halfback, Dennis Michie ('92) at right halfback and Butler Ames ('94) at fullback. Reserves included Leroy Lyon ('91), Tiemann Horn ('91), and Elmer Clark ('93).

The Army team was not particularly big. Adams and Clark weighed 190, while Prince and Timberlake were about 170. Michie and Walker were the lightest players, tipping the scales at 142.

On game day a special ferry boat arrived at West Point and a happy group of Naval cadets disembarked, trudging up the long hill to the parade field. While on the way they passed the home of a noncommissioned officer. Outside was a scrawny but highly spirited goat who kicked up his heels at the sight of the Naval cadets, then walked away.

"Hey, that would make a good mascot," said one of the Naval cadets, according to lore.

"Let's take him," said another. "He ought to bring us good luck." The goat was whisked away and taken to the game. Navy has always had a goat as its mascot since that day.

About two thousand officers, ladies of the post, and Naval cadets attended the first Army-Navy game. After Navy won the toss and when play began it was evident to all that the Army team lacked the necessary experience to turn back Navy. Capt. Red Emrich opened the game by gaining twenty yards and quickly set the tone. While Army turned in some good individual efforts, Navy had the upper hand in working as a team, particularly blocking on the line.

Emrich was almost a one-man show for Navy, scoring four touchdowns, which were worth four points each, and kicking two goals, worth two points each. Moulton Johnson, the only plebe on the Navy squad, accounted for the other touchdown in a 24-0 victory.

A rivalry, which in years ahead would attract upwards of 104,000 people, had begun. It also became, and still is today, one of the most colorful rivalries in college football.

Obviously disappointed with the outcome of the first encounter, young Dennis Michie was not about to throw in the towel. Rather, he took up the challenge, seeking out a coach in order to provide the coaching techniques that were required for such an inexperienced team.

Harry L. Williams, a former Yale football star and hurdler, was teaching at Siglar's Academy in Newburgh, New York, about eight miles north of West Point. In discussing the coaching situation with Lt. Danny Tate, the officer-in-

charge of football at the Academy, Michie felt Williams might be willing to coach the Army team just to keep his hand in the college game.

Michie was correct. After being contacted by Lt. Tate, Williams agreed to coach, making the trip from Newburgh to West Point twice a week. He was not paid for his services, but at Christmas the cadets chipped in for a gift, presenting him a dresser set.

Williams knew his football and was known to participate in practice sessions with the team. He was a hard man to tackle, but his efforts paid quick dividends for Army football.

The Cadets opened the 1891 season with a 10-6 victory over Fordham, then called St. John's. Army tied the Princeton Reserves 12-12, edged Stevens 14-12, bowed to Rutgers 27-6, and then rebounded to blank the Schuykill Navy team 6-0. So, heading into the rematch with Navy the West Point team had compiled a 3-1-1 record.

On November 27, 1891 seventeen cadets, including team captain Dennis Michie, Lt. Tate and Coach Williams departed by train to Annapolis. It was the first time any West Point team gained permission to leave post for an athletic event. Seeking permission for the trip was easy this time, since Superintendent Wilson was upset by the first loss to the Naval cadets and wanted a return match.

The Cadets traveled by train to Baltimore, staying there Friday night. On Saturday morning they journeyed to Annapolis, received a tour of the yard and then sat down to lunch with their counterparts from Annapolis.

Enthusiastic rooters from Washington and Baltimore made the journey to Annapolis to watch the favored Midshipmen take on the Cadets from West Point for the second time. They would be in for quite a surprise.

Unlike the inaugural meeting between the two teams at West Point, the Army team was much more experienced, and developed much more quickly than expected under the tutelage of Coach Harry L. Williams.

Dennis Michie won the toss and Army elected to receive. The Cadets wasted little time, scoring on this very first possession when Elmer Clark, the right guard, scored from five yards out on what was called a "guards-back" play. Michie's goal after touchdown, worth two points, made it 6-0.

Later, Navy tied the score behind the rushing of quarterback Worth Bagley, described as a 155-pound dynamo. Bagley's lugging brought the ball to the Army ten-yard line. On the next play Bagley gained five more yards before being stopped by Michie and Ed Timberlake. However, Martin Trench scampered the final five yards on the very next play, and Navy converted the goal after touchdown for a 6-6 deadlock.

Army took advantage of a Navy miscue to take the lead. Bagley attempted to punt, but the kick was blocked and Army's Bill Smith recovered in the end zone for a touchdown. Michie added the conversion for a 12-6 lead. Later Clark scored his second touchdown to boost the Army advantage to 18-6. The Cadets maintained that momentum throughout the remainder of the contest en route to a 32-16 victory.

Gene Schorr, author of *The Army-Navy Game,* described the Cadets initial victory over Navy in this fashion. "Clark scored for Army once again and the West Pointers led, 18-6. By this time the field was a bedlam—the players on both teams battered, bleeding and groggy.

"Stockings were torn off, five noses were bleeding, one man's ear was split, two Midshipmen were knocked unconscious, recovered, and along with Army's Smith and Prince, managed to stagger and crawl along the edge of the game, until Timberlake's final touchdown put Army ahead, 32-16, and the match was over.

"Army went absolutely wild with joy. The Cadets dashed out into the field and carried off the victorious players, singing, dancing, and shouting, as they marched off the field with a tired but happy Army squad.

"That night both teams attended a dance at the Navy boathouse and the players from both squads danced with all the frenzy and ferocity they had displayed on the gridiron. Before the evening was over, each Army player and each Navy player personally congratulated the other on the fine game, and when the final number of the evening waltzed its slow rhythmic beat across the Severn River, Capt. Dennis Michie, Army's star, and Worth Bagley, Navy's great quarterback, shook hands. 'Till we meet again.'"

Michie and Bagley would meet again on two more occasions, but the results were quite different than this day in Annapolis in 1891. Bagley spelled the difference in a 12-4

Navy win in 1892 as Michie stayed on as Army's coach. It was the only loss the Cadets suffered during a 3-1-1 season. Then in 1893, Bagley led the Midshipmen to a 6-4 win at Annapolis, as Army closed out its season with a record of four victories and five defeats.

Although Bagley and Michie vowed to meet again as a mark of friendship, it would not come to pass. Both men were killed in action during the war against Spain in 1898. Bagley was killed aboard the U.S.S. *Winslow* during patrol duty near Cuba. The ship came under sudden attack, a shell destroying the steering engine. Bagley scrambled to the exposed engine room to try to steer the ship with its propeller, but another shell hit the exposed area, killing Bagley and four other crewmen. Bagley was the first and only Naval officer killed during the Spanish American War.

Michie served with the 17th U.S. Infantry for a five-year period. At the outbreak of the Spanish American War he was stationed at Fort Leavenworth. He was then appointed aide-de-camp to an old West Point friend, Gen. Hamilton Hawkins, the former commandant at the Academy. The regiment then departed on an invasion of Cuba.

During the battle of Santiago, Capt. Michie led a patrol along the San Juan River. He organized his men for an assault on a hill, when he was killed by a Spanish bullet on July 1, 1898. Michie was 28 years old at the time of his death, but he has never been forgotten for his efforts in establishing football at West Point.

Army and Navy meet for the first time in football in 1890 at West Point. The Cadets, in white uniforms and black caps, run downfield *as Navy forms a wedge to return the kickoff. The Midshipmen prevailed in that first encounter, 24-0.*

Army, in white jerseys, tries to top Navy thrust during first game between the two teams in 1890. The more experienced Midshipmen defeated the Cadets in the first game *24-0 to begin one of the most colorful football rivalries in the nation. This first football game at West Point also promoted the expansion of intercollegiate athletics at the Academy.*

After losing to rival Navy in its very first football game in 1890, the Army squad of 1891 came back with renewed dedication to turn the tables around. Coached by Dr. Harry Williams, a class of 1891 Yale graduate, the Cadets won four games, lost just one, and tied another. The team captain was Dennis Michie (holding the ball), long considered the "Father of Army Football" at the Academy. It was Michie who arranged for the Naval Academy to challenge the Cadets for a game, and then he persuaded his father, Lt. Peter Smith

Michie, a powerful member of the Academic Board, to gain approval for the game from the superintendent, Col. John Wilson. While Navy held the upper hand during the first engagement, Army came back to return the favor, defeating the Midshipmen 32-16 at Annapolis. In this team photograph are, front row, Butler Ames, James T. Moore, Willard Gleason, Elmer Clark, Kirby Walker and Sterling Adams; second row, Charles G. Woodward, Dennie Michie (holding ball), Dwight E. Aultman, William J. Barden, and

Fine Smith; third row, Coach Harry Williams, James B. Cavanaugh, Peter W. Davison, Harry Pattison, Edward Timberlake, and Frank A. Wilcox; back row, Lt. Tate, Leonard Prince and George Houle. Lettermen on that Army squad included Adams, Davison, Gleason, Michie, Moore, Prince, Walker, Wilcox, Clark, Houle, Pattison, Edward Timberlake, Butler Ames, and Smith. Michie, Prince, and Ames were the only Army players with football experience prior to the inaugural Army-Navy clash in 1890.

West Football Team – Fall of '94

Members of the 1894 Army football team are pictured here. The fifth varsity football squad in Academy history won three games and lost two. Coached by Harmon Graves, a Yale graduate, the Cadets defeated Amherst, MIT, and Union with shutouts. Army dropped a 10-0 decision to Brown and bowed to Yale 21-5. Edward King served as team captain.

William Nesbitt served as captain of the 1897 Army football team that compiled a 6-1-1 record. Nesbitt lettered two years in football and was one of the finest boxers in the corps. In fact, he had hoped to challenge Jim Jeffries, the world heavyweight champion, but was turned down by the Department of War. They gave Nesbitt approval on the condition that he resign from the Academy.

The 1894 Army football squad pictured here won three games and lost two. Coach Harmon Graves made his coaching debut at West Point, just months after graduating from Yale. His alma mater was one of the teams that defeated Army that year, 12-5. The cadets also bowed to Brown University, but defeated Amherst, MIT and Union College, all by shutout margins. Edward King served as team captain.

The 1897 Army football team, aided by the efforts of Charles Romeyn, compiled a 6-1-1 record. The Cadets, coached by Herman Koehler, the Master of the Sword at the Academy, took the measure of Trinity, Wesleyan, Tufts, Lehigh, Stevens, and Brown. Army's only loss was a 10-0 decision at the hands of Harvard, while the Cadets tied Yale 6-6. Members of that team included Chauncey Humphrey (1), Robert Foy (2), William Wooten (3), William Nesbitt (4) the team captain, Leon Kromer (5), Alexander Williams (6), Malin Craig (7), Wallace Scales (8), Albert Waldron (9), Charles Royeyn (10), Evan Humphrey (11), William Ennis (12), manager Robert Davis (13), and Grayson Heidt (14).

Charles Romeyn, a graduate of the class of 1899, was the first Army football player to be selected for first team All-America recognition as a back in 1898. He lettered four years in football while at the Academy. During those four years the Cadets compiled an overall record of seventeen victories, seven defeats, and three ties.

Herman Koehler, Master of the Sword at the Academy, also coached the football team in 1898, leading the Cadets to a 3-2-1 record. Army defeated Tufts, Wesleyan, and Lehigh. The Cadets and Princeton played to a tie, while Yale and Harvard handed Army defeats. Leon Kromer, holding the ball, was the team captain, while Charles Romeyn, to his left, gained All-America honors as a back.

28

Pictured at left are members of the 1899 Army football team, coached by Herman Koehler, Master of the Sword at West Point. The Cadets won four of nine games during the season.

Brig. Gen. Palmer Eddy Pierce, a graduate of the class of 1891 at the Academy, was the man responsible for the organization and founding of the National Collegiate Athletic Association (NCAA). He was on the original committee of three faculty members appointed to draft a constitution and by-laws for an intercollegiate athletic association, the first of its kind in the country. In 1905, then a captain and associate professor of chemistry, he represented the Academy on that committee. He was elected the first president of the NCAA and influenced the growth of the association from the original 28 colleges to 250 in a quarter of a century. It has been said that the standards of fair play and eligibility rules established by Pierce's committee did much to save the American game of football from being abandoned by colleges.

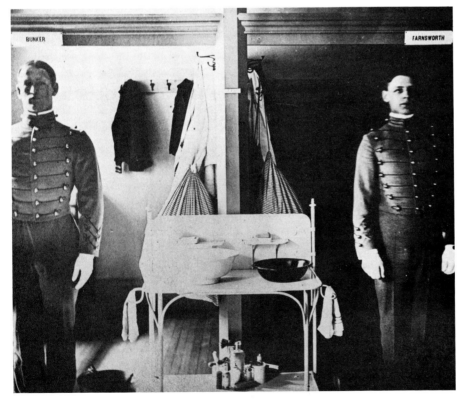

Cadets Paul Bunker and Ed Farnsworth are pictured here as plebes at West Point, standing room inspection. Bunker would eventually become the only player in history to gain first team All-America recognition at two positions, tackle and halfback. Farnsworth is the only player in history to participate in five Army-Navy games.

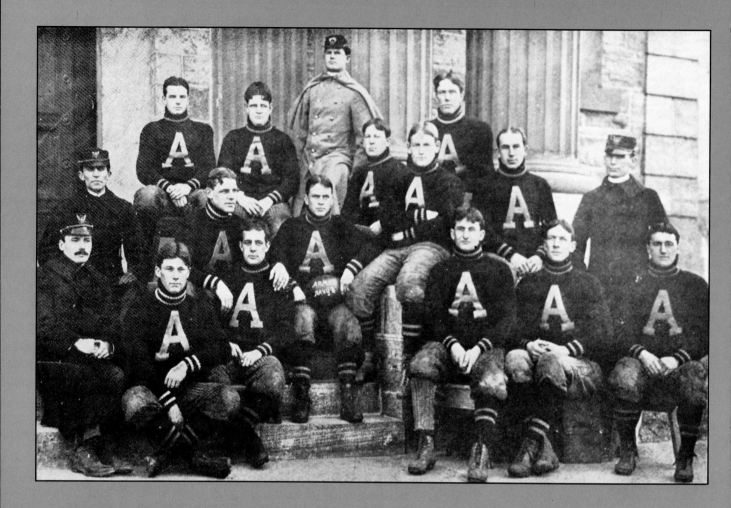

The 1901 football squad, led by Charlie Daly, Ernest Graves, Paul Bunker, and Robert Boyers, won five games, lost one, and tied two. Army shut out Franklin & Marshall, Trinity, Williams, and Pennsylvania before trimming Navy, 11-5. Pictured are front row, left to right, Coach Leon Kromer, Joseph McAndrew, Frank H. Phipps, team captain Adam F. Casad (holding ball), Paul Bunker (arms folded), Henry Nelly, Nelson Goodspeed, and Horatio Hackett; standing, assistant coach Smither, Charles Daly, Edward Farnsworth, Ernest Graves, manager William A. Mitchell, Thomas B. Doe, Napoleon Riley, Robert Boyers, and assistant coach Dennis Nolan.

CHAPTER 4

SUCCESSFUL SEASONS

Army football teams enjoyed immeasurable success during their second decade of intercollegiate competition. From 1900 until 1904, Army posted winning records, while whipping rival Navy in four of five encounters. And in 1905 the Cadets still managed to break even during the season with a 4-4-1 mark. Ironically, the deadlock came in the Army-Navy clash. In 1906, the West Point squad suffered its only losing campaign, but rebounded to post winning seasons for thirty-two consecutive years.

All-America honors were bestowed eight times during that span. Paul Bunker gained All-America honors in 1901 and 1902 at two different positions, tackle and halfback, the only player ever cited by Walter Camp as an All-America in two different positions.

Charles Daly, who gained All-America honors twice quarterbacking the Harvard team, received similar honors at West Point. He earned first team All-America in 1901, a year in which he almost singlehandedly defeated Navy, 11-5.

Daly scored all of Army's points, kicking a field goal in the first half, and dashing one hundred yards with the second half kickoff for a touchdown. He also added the goal after touchdown.

Born on October 31, 1880, Daly was small, wiry, and tough. However, he sometimes rubbed people the wrong way.

"Charlie wasn't very well liked," said one veteran Boston sportswriter. "A lot of people said he was uppity. He had a habit of walking with his hands in his pockets and his head down. He didn't mean anything by it. But it made some people say he was stuck up. Of course, Charlie had to stop walking with his hands in his pockets when he got to West Point."

Daly graduated from Harvard in 1901 and received an appointment to the Military Academy from Congressman John F. "Honey" Fitzgerald's Ninth District. He entered West Point on June 12, 1901, and immediately made an impact on the Army football program.

Following graduation from West Point, Daly served for three months at West Point, then was transferred to Fort Totten, New York, before resigning his commission in 1906. He became a bond broker in New York and Boston before taking over as fire commissioner in the Bay City.

Daly returned to active duty and served as head football coach at West Point for two periods, from 1913 to 1916 and 1919 to 1922. During that time his Army teams won fifty-eight games, lost just thirteen, and tied three opponents, making him the second winningest coach in Academy history. During his second stint as head coach during Gen. MacArthur's tenure as superintendent, Daly played a role in founding the American Football Colleges Coaches Association and served as its first president. He also was the first West Pointer to be named to the College Football Hall of Fame, achieving that honor in 1951.

Charlie Daly married the former Beatrice M. Jordan of Boston in 1912. The Dalys had three sons and two daughters, and West Point was in the hearts of the entire family. All three sons—Charles Jordan Daly, John Harold Daly, and Robert Charles Daly—graduated from the Military Academy. His daughters, Beatrice and Ellen, married West Pointers.

One of Daly's classmates was Ernest "Pot" Graves, who played fullback for three years at the University of North Carolina. That is also where he got the nickname "Pot," and it followed him to the banks of the Hudson River.

Graves played fullback at West Point during the 1901 season, but then was shifted to tackle where he was one of the best of his time. He also was one of the smartest players, graduating second in his West Point class. Graves lettered all four years at the Academy.

The *Howitzer* yearbook described Graves' athletic and academic abilities in this fashion: "...a gentle, graceful, winsome lad, who never knew a harsher tone than a flute note and who runs amazingly to neck. In football, he stands high, plays low, slugs hard and never gets caught. He made an annual habit of eating young Navies alive until they begged to have him muzzled. He doesn't give an ogre-faced damn for anybody that he ranks. He can jump the highest, fall the hardest, yell the loudest and eat more railroad iron and more spikes than any man in the class."

Others who earned All-America honors during this six-year period (1900-1905) were end Walter Smith (1901), center Robert Boyers (1902), center Arthur Tipton, and back Henry Torney (1904, 1905).

Edward Farnsworth, captain of the 1903 Army team, also is the only player in West Point history to play in five Navy games.

The 1903 season also brought a bit of controversy to the forefront between officials of the Naval Academy and the Military Academy. Navy wanted West Point to limit the eligibility of its athletes, claiming the Military Academy held an advantage by permitting cadets to enter up to the age of twenty-one, while Midshipmen were only allowed to enter up to age twenty. That allowed students who had graduated from other colleges to enter the Military Academy, and led to situations where players of the caliber of Charlie Daly and Ernest Graves immediately helped Army's football program. The Military Academy countered by saying the Naval Academy had twice as many men to draw from to form a football squad, and stood firm.

Charlie Daly's talents as a quarterback primed the controversy between Army and Navy officials, and consequently he elected not to play again at West Point. With Daly on the sidelines, Army still thrashed the Midshipmen 40-5 in 1903, spotting Navy a 5-0 first half lead before storming back with forty unanswered points. However, West Point later signed a three-year agreement with the Naval Academy, limiting participants in the Army-Navy game to those who had not played more than three years of college football.

The 1904 Army team coached by former All-America Robert Boyers won seven games and lost just two. The Cadets shut out Navy 11-0 for their fourth straight victory over their archrivals.

The 1905 squad was 4-4-1, defeating Tufts, Colgate, Trinity, and Syracuse before closing out the season with a 6-6 tie against Navy. The clash between the two service academies, witnessed by President Theodore Roosevelt, was one of the most brutal in the series. Eleven players were injured and sidelined for portions of the contest. Roosevelt said the two teams played well, but the rules of football should be changed to avoid the excessive injuries.

Roosevelt got his way as the rules of football were changed for the 1906 season under a Presidential threat to abolish the sport. The length of the game was changed from seventy minutes with a ten-minute halftime break to four fifteen-minute quarters with a fifteen-minute halftime. The field was cut to one hundred yards, and a neutral zone was established on the line of scrimmage. Additionally, the forward pass was permitted, with restrictions.

In 1906, the Army football squad finished with a 3-5-1 record, closing out the season with a 10-0 loss to Navy. Henry Smither handled the coaching before being relieved of duty following a 12-0 loss to Tufts in the opening game, and Ernest Graves took over the coaching chores. George S.

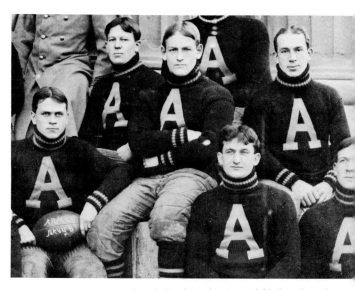

Army's Paul Bunker (arms folded) is the only player in history to be named an All-America by Walter Camp in two positions, tackle and halfback. Robert Boyers, standing to the right of Bunker, gained All-America honors in 1902 at center.

Patton, Jr., then in his second year at the Academy, was a member of that football squad until being sidelined with two broken arms. Army learned its lessons well from that 1906 season, and would not suffer through another losing campaign for the next thirty-three years.

Henry Smither returned in 1907 to guide the Cadets to a 6-2-1 season. Rodney Smith served as team captain, while William Erwin gained first team All-America honors at guard.

In 1908, the Army team finished at 6-1-2, its only loss a 6-0 decision to Yale. The Cadets did trim Navy 6-4, avenging a 6-0 loss to the Middies the previous season.

In 1909, the Army season was cut short by the tragic death of Cadet Eugene Byrne during the Harvard encounter at West Point. Byrne was one of thirty players killed playing football that year, and that brought additional cries to abolish the sport.

Army had won three of its first four games in 1909 before Harvard journeyed to West Point. The Crimson led 9-0 late in the game when they ran the "flying wedge" directly over Byrne's position. When the play was over Byrne remained motionless on the ground. He suffered a broken neck and died before the weekend was out.

His death brought calls for the academies to drop football. Others called for the game to be abolished altogether. Byrne's untimely death did not bring an end to football at the academies, although it played a big role in changing the rules of football once again. The flying wedge was outlawed. Freer substitution was allowed, and restrictions were lifted on the forward pass to further open up the game.

Army closed out its first decade of the 1900s with a 6-2 record in 1910, defeating Tufts, Yale, Lehigh, Springfield, Villanova, and Trinity. The Cadets fell to Harvard by a 6-0 margin and bowed to Navy 3-0 on a field goal by Jack Dalton.

Coach Robert Boyers, an Army All-America center in 1902, was the tenth man to hold the position of head football coach at West Point. He took over in 1904 and coached for two seasons, compiling a record of eleven victories, six defeats, and one tie. During his first season, Boyers guided the football squad to a 7-2 record, defeating Tufts, Dickinson, Yale, Williams, New York University, Syracuse, and Navy, by an 11-0 count. The only Army losses came at the hands of Harvard, 4-0, and Princeton, 12-6. A 1903 graduate of West Point, Boyers posted a 4-4-1 record during his final year in 1905. The tie came against Navy, 6-6. He served with the American Expeditionary Forces during World War I and was wounded. He returned to active duty in 1919 and served until 1922. Boyers then became superintendent of the Florida Military Academy, holding that position until 1930, when he retired at the rank of lieutenant colonel. He died in 1949.

Coach Charles Daly appears here in uniform. The former All-America quarterback at Harvard and West Point went on to become the second winningest coach in Army football history.

Leon B. Kromer, a graduate of the Class of 1899 at West Point, lettered two years in football while at the academy, 1897-1898. During those two seasons the Army team won nine games, lost three and played to a tie twice. Kromer also served as head coach during the 1901 season, compiling a record of five victories, just one defeat and two ties. The Cadets shut out Franklin & Marshall, Trinity, Williams and Pennsylvania and trimmed Navy 11-5. The only loss was a 6-0 decision to Harvard, while Army fought to a deadlock against Yale and Princeton.

In 1905, the football team at the Academy, coached by Robert Boyers, a class of 1903 graduate, won four games, lost four, and tied one. The Cadets trimmed Tufts and Colgate to open the 1905 season, then suffered through a four-game losing streak, bowing to Virginia Polytechnic Institute, Harvard, Yale, and Carlisle. The Cadets came back to shut out Trinity and Syracuse, before battling Navy to a 6-6 deadlock in a game played at Princeton. Alexander Gillespie served as team captain, while Henry Torney gained All-America honors as a back. Pictured are, front row, left to right, Daniel I. Sultan, Wentworth H. Moss, Rodney H. Smith, team captain Gillespie, Charles G. Mettler, and Enoch B. Garey; second row, Roy C. Hill, William L. Moose, William W. Erwin, Henry W. Torney, Walter M. Wilhelm, William C. Christy, and Clyde R. Abraham; third row, team manager George M. Morrow, Edwin S. Greble, Henry J. Weeks, and team captain Palmer E. Pierce. Pierce, an 1892 West Point graduate, was a chemistry instructor at West Point, as well as an instructor and assistant professor of philosophy. He was one of the original founders of the National Collegiate Athletic Association (NCAA), serving as the organization's first president from 1905 to 1912. He also was the NCAA head from 1916 to 1930. From 1931 to 1934 he served as president of the Association of Graduates.

The 1906 Army squad was just 3-5-1. One member of the team, George S. Patton, Jr., was sidelined early in the season with two broken arms. The rules of football also were changed this year to help avoid the thirty deaths and nineteen critical injuries that were sustained by players in the United States.

Cadet Eugene Byrne suffered a broken neck late in the 1909 Harvard game and later died, the first Army fatality in football. Byrne's death brought protests to abolish the sport at the service academies. However, football remained very much a part of the athletic program. Byrne's death did help spur a drastic change in college football rules, including lifting restrictions on the forward pass and banning the "flying wedge," a play which led to Byrne's untimely death.

The football team under Coach Ernest Graves compiled a 5-3 record in 1912. Graves, a 1905 West Point graduate, guided his squad to victories over Stevens, Rutgers, Colgate, Tufts, and Syracuse. The Cadets, who were captained by Leland Devore, dropped 6-0 decisions to Yale and rival Navy, and also lost to Carlisle. Graves coached football at West Point for two years, compiling a 7-8-1 record. Devore earned All-America honors as a tackle at the conclusion of the 1911 season. Pictured are, front row, left to right, Frank Milburn, Vernon Prichard, Walter Wynne, team captain Leland Devore, Geoffrey Keyes, Louis Merillat; second row, Charles C. Benedict, William Hoge, Leland S. Hobbs, Paul A. Hodgson, Thomas B. Larkin, Thomas G. Lamphier, and William E. Coffin; back row, Woodfin Jones, assistant manager Lumas, James B. Gillespie, Charles C. Herrick, Alexander Weyand, Joseph O'Hare, manager Robert Perkins, Hamner Huston, and John P. Markoe.

CHAPTER 5

A COLORFUL SERIES BEGINS

Army football enjoyed a splendid decade of success from 1911 to 1920, compiling winning records throughout that span. Additionally, two Cadet football squads coached by Charlie Daly posted undefeated records, marking the first time in West Point history that the football squad completed its season unscathed.

The 1914 squad won all nine of its encounters, parlaying outstanding offensive and defensive play. The Cadets held six teams scoreless and capped the season with a 20-0 victory over rival Navy.

Two years later the 1916 squad also posted a 9-0 record, including a one-sided 69-7 thrashing of Villanova, and a 53-0 victory over Trinity. The Cadets also trimmed Navy by a 15-7 count.

During this decade four Army players gained first team All-America honors, topped by halfback Elmer Oliphant, who gained All-America honors two consecutive seasons, 1916 and 1917. Leland Devore received All-America honors for his outstanding play at tackle in 1911. Louis Merillat was named a first team All-America in 1913 for his play as an end, and John McEwan received All-America recognition in 1914 as a center.

One of the most colorful football rivalries was inaugurated during this decade. Almost by accident, the Army-Notre Dame encounter in 1913 may have changed the course of football. The Irish unleashed an unexpected passing attack which featured the throwing arm of Gus Dorais and the catching of Knute Rockne. Notre Dame's offense not only surprised the Army squad and its followers, but the rest of the football world as well. It wasn't the first time the pass was used with such aplomb in football, but coming when it did from a relatively unknown school—Notre Dame—against a strong opponent such as Army, it opened some eyes in Eastern football circles. It may have also worked in Army's favor eventually, since the Cadets utilized the pass much more effectively that season during a victory over Navy.

Coach Joseph Beacham, an 1897 graduate of Cornell University, guided the Army football squad to a 6-1-1 record

in 1911. The Cadets, led by team captain Robert Hyatt, won their first four encounters easily, defeating Vermont, Rutgers, Yale, and Lehigh with shutouts. Army then played to a scoreless tie against Georgetown, and bounced back with victories over Bucknell and Colgate before Navy handed the Cadets their only loss when Jack Dalton booted a field goal for the only points in the game. Dalton had more than enough opportunities in this encounter, missing his first six field goal attempts before finally connecting.

Leland Devore and Bob Littlejohn were key performers on Army's line during the 1911 season at the tackle positions. However, on the eve of the Yale encounter, Littlejohn sustained a leg injury and couldn't play. Coach Beacham elected to start a gangly young man named Alexander Weyand in Littlejohn's position. There were some protests about this move, but Weyand performed admirably and established himself as a solid line performer. Weyand, who failed to make his Jersey City, New Jersey, high school football team, lettered five years in football at West Point.

Weyand also was one of the most resilient Army players. He played in thirty-seven games at West Point, never missed a scrimmage, and finished every big game he played except his final Navy game, when he dropped out in the final minutes to permit a teammate to win a varsity letter. Weyand was an outstanding wrestler at West Point and won a spot on the 1920 Olympic team. While he may not have gained first team All-America honors, Weyand received plenty of All-America recognition during his career, and in 1974 was inducted into the National Football Foundation Hall of Fame for his play as a guard and tackle.

The 1912 Army team, which finished with a 5-3 record, opened the season with victories over Stevens Tech and Rutgers, before dropping a 6-0 decision to Yale. The Cadets bounced back with an 18-7 win over Colgate, but then dropped a 27-6 decision to the Carlisle Indians, who were led by Jim Thorpe. Thorpe scored twenty-five touchdowns during the 1912 season and accounted for 198 points to earn All-America honors for the second straight year.

He played an outstanding game against the Cadets in 1912. Army's fine tackle, Devore, had a difficult time stopping Thorpe, while another outstanding young Army player, Dwight Eisenhower, played very well on defense and offense. However, even Eisenhower was unable to stop Thorpe all the time. On one occasion during the game, Thorpe ran for a touchdown, only to have it called back because of a penalty. On the ensuing play he scampered for another long touchdown, and this time it counted.

One week later, Army edged Tufts 15-6, but lost the services of young Eisenhower, who sprained his knee. Unfortunately, the promising young halfback would never again play football at West Point. He reinjured his knee while vaulting a horse in the riding hall and was unable to return to the gridiron. Nonetheless, Eisenhower remained close to the football squad, becoming a cheerleader.

The Cadets closed out the 1912 campaign with another tough loss to Navy, bowing 6-0 on two field goals by Babe Brown. The loss was the third straight to the Middies and concerned Academy officials. The Cadets played well defensively, but simply could not muster much offense against their rivals. Consequently, West Point brought back Charlie Daly as head football coach.

Daly, who had assisted his friend, Pot Graves during the 1912 season, accepted a position of first lieutenant of artillery, and coached the Army football team during the fall.

Graves, an Army captain, remained at the Academy, coaching the line. He and Daly made quite a coaching combination. Daly always relied on Graves for advice when he was installing a new formation. If Graves thought little of the formation, he made his opinion known to Daly immediately.

Despite the difference in personalities, Daly and Graves teamed up very well. Daly occasionally became volatile, while Graves continually maintained his poise, regardless of the circumstances. He was considered an outstanding line coach, opting to teach rather than antagonize his players.

Coach Daly's 1913 squad turned in an outstanding effort, winning eight of nine games, including a 22-9 victory over Navy. The one loss was a 35-13 decision to Notre Dame, at the time an unknown team from a little town called South Bend in Indiana.

In those days the West Point football schedule was drawn up by the team manager, with some guidance from the football officer. It wasn't a difficult task since teams normally played each other on the same date each year. However, Yale elected to give up its date at West Point in 1913. Thus, Cadet Harold Loomis, the team manager, was tasked with the responsibility of filling a November first date. He wrote to every school in the East, but was unable to book the date. Then he tried schools in the Midwest, receiving a positive reply from Jesse Harper, the athletic director and football coach at Notre Dame.

Harper said his team would agree to travel to West Point for a one thousand dollar guarantee. Loomis was authorized to offer only six hundred dollars. When the manager reported the guarantee Notre Dame requested to Lt. Dan Sultan, the football officer, Sultan called a special meeting to obtain approval and scheduled the Notre Dame game.

Army officials reluctantly agreed to the guarantee, although some football fans could not understand why such an unknown school was scheduled. They felt Yale and Harvard should be rescheduled. Even Cadet Loomis was stung by these protestations, only to have the last laugh late in the afternoon of November 1.

Gus Dorais, Notre Dame's fine quarterback, and team captain Knute Rockne, who would later become one of the most revered coaches in Notre Dame history, made the journey to West Point one that would long be remembered. This unknown school made a shambles of the favored Army team, rallying to take a 14-3 halftime lead, before pulling away with three second-half touchdowns. Rockne pulled in a twenty-five-yard Dorais pass for Notre Dame's first touchdown. Dorais, the outstanding Notre Dame quarterback, completed 13 of 17 passes for 243 yards.

Despite the loss to Notre Dame, Army still turned in a strong effort, and a few weeks later took the measure of Navy, 22-9. Vernon Prichard, one of Army's finest quarterbacks, led the Cadets to the victory, hooking up with his favorite receiver, Louis Merillat. Merillat dropped a Prichard pass in the end zone in the first quarter, but then came back in the second quarter, pulling in another Prichard pass for a touchdown to give the Cadets a 9-6 halftime advantage.

After Navy tied the score again on another field goal, a sixty-yard run by Merillat set up Army's second touchdown. Early in the fourth quarter, John Jouett took a pass from the center, flipped it to Prichard, who fired another touchdown pass to Merillat to close out the scoring.

For his efforts that season, Merillat gained first team All-America recognition, while Weyand was a second team choice by Walter Camp.

The victory over Navy in 1913 was the first of five straight for Army against its most hated rival. It is a feat Cadet squads have been unable to duplicate.

In 1914, Coach Daly's squad finished with a perfect 9-0 record, outscoring its opponents by a 219 to 20 margin. John McEwan, the center on that squad, gained first team All-America honors. Ten years later he returned as head football coach, compiling an 18-5-3 record in three seasons. He also was named to the National Football Foundation Hall of Fame in 1962.

The 1915 Army squad, led by team captain Babe Weyand, fashioned a 5-3-1 record. The Cadets got off to a rocky start by playing a 14-14 tie against Holy Cross. Army rebounded to beat Gettysburg, but then dropped a 13-0 decision to Colgate.

Coach Daly's squad blanked Georgetown, but then dropped a 16-13 decision to Villanova and a 7-0 game to Notre Dame. However, the Cadets righted themselves by winning their final three games, including a 14-0 triumph over Navy.

One problem with the 1915 squad was at quarterback. With the graduation of Vernon Prichard, Coach Daly had a hard time filling the position. He finally called for help from baseball coach Sam Strang, asking if there was anyone capable of playing quarterback. Strang recommended Charlie Gerhardt. Although Gerhardt failed to make his prep school football squad, Daly molded him into an adequate quarterback.

Gerhardt was good enough to help the Cadets blank Navy, as Elmer Oliphant scored all of the points. After Bill Redfield recovered a Navy fumble on the Middie five in the first quarter, Oliphant plunged over from the two on fourth down and kicked the extra point. Then in the third quarter, McEwan intercepted a Navy pass and returned it to the Middie thirty. Oliphant accounted for the second touchdown on a sensational run and booted the extra point.

In 1916, Daly's squad again posted an undefeated 9-0 record, led by the running and kicking of Oliphant. The Army back could do just about anything that was asked of him—run, pass, kick, tackle, and block. His West Point athletic career was one of the finest in history. He won four letters in baseball, three in football, three in basketball, and one in track. He also earned monograms in boxing, hockey, and swimming.

Oliphant received solid support in the Army backfield during the 1916 season. A plebe, Gene Vidal, played fullback and Gerhardt continued to improve at quarterback. The line featured team captain and All-America center John McEwan, tackle Biff Jones, who later coached at West Point, and ends Ed House and Ed Shrader.

The Cadets outscored their opponents, 235 to 36, and Oliphant was honored as a first team All-America.

A year later Army finished 7-1, with Oliphant earning All-America honors for the second year in succession. The lone defeat was a 7-2 decision to Notre Dame.

World War I played havoc with the football schedule at West Point in 1918, and the Cadets were limited to just a single game. Capt. Eugene Vidal's squad defeated the Mitchell Field team 20-0.

In 1919, Army finished with a 6-3 record and saw their five-game winning streak against Navy halted, 6-0. The Cadets compiled a 7-2 record in 1920, but once again failed to score against Navy, dropping a 7-0 decision. One member of that disappointed 1919 squad was Earl Blaik, who would return to the banks of the Hudson in 1941 as head football coach, and put together the most successful coaching record in West Point history.

Leland Devore lettered five years in football at West Point and earned first team All-America honors as a tackle following the 1911 season. He also served as captain of the 1912 Cadet eleven, which won five games and lost three.

Here is the cadet portrait of Alexander "Babe" Weyand, who lettered five years in football at West Point and was named to the National Football Foundation Hall of Fame in 1974. When he broke into the program as a plebe in 1911, there was some criticism because of his inexperience, but Weyland performed admirably.

Alexander "Babe" Weyand served as captain of the 1915 Army football team, which finished with a 5-3-1 record and defeated Navy 14-0.

Coach Ernest Graves served as head football coach at West Point in 1906 and 1912. His record during those two seasons was seven victories, eight defeats, and one tie.

Army's 1916 football team was the second to complete a season undefeated, winning nine straight encounters. Among the Cadet gridiron victims were Lebanon Valley, Washington & Lee, Holy Cross, Trinity, Villanova, Notre Dame, Maine, Springfield, and Navy. The squad was coached by Charles Daly, considered one of the finest Army coaches in history. John McEwan served as team captain. Members of the squad who lettered include,

first row, left to right, Eugene Vidal, Charles Gerhardt, team captain McEwan, Elmer Oliphant (an All-America selection), Edwin House, and Cornman Hahn; second row; Matthew Ridgway, team manager, Lawrence McC. Jones, Elbert Ford, O'Ferrall Knight, Laurence Meacham, and Joel Holmes; back row, Royal Place, George Hirsch, William Butler, Edwin Shrader and Francis March.

The Army-Notre Dame football rivalry began in 1913 when the Cadets attempted to fill an open date on their schedule. A manager wrote to a small school in Indiana—Notre Dame—and they agreed to play. This one game may have changed the complexion of football because the Fighting Irish unleashed a vaunted passing attack and trounced the favored Cadets by a 35-13 margin. Here are some photographs that capture the beginning of this football series. The game was played at Cullum Field from 1913 through 1922.

Col. Louis A. Merillat, Jr., a graduate of the class of 1915 at West Point, helped revolutionize the game of football in the East during his four years. He lettered from 1911-1914 and was named an All-America end in 1913 by Walter Camp. He was the receiving end of Army's famed passing combination at that time, "Pritchard to Merillat." That 1913 Army team compiled an 8-1 record, its only loss a 35-13 decision to that little unknown school in the midwest called Notre Dame, in the very first meeting between the two teams.

Some members of Army's 1913 football team that met Notre Dame for the first time included, left to right, Walter Wynne, Alexander Weyand, Alfred Forabee, Dwight Eisenhower, Charles Benedict, and Benny Hoge, the team captain. The boy between Benedict and Hoge is Richards Vidmer, son of the post adjutant, Capt. George Vidmer. He later became a sportswriter and editor.

41

Army grinds out yardage in the inaugural game against Notre Dame held at West Point in 1913. The Cadets' ground game was hardly enough, as the Irish used forward passes by Gus Dorais to dominate the hosts, 35-13.

John J. McEwan won All-America honors as a center for Army in 1914 as a mere sophomore, leading the Cadets to their first undefeated season in history under Coach Charley Daly. McEwan was captain of the grid squad as a senior, once again helping the Cadets put together an unblemished 9-0 record. McEwan returned to the Military Academy as head football coach in 1923, succeeding his old coach, Daly. During his three-year reign Army compiled a record of eighteen victories, eight defeats, and three ties. McEwan was the center for Army when they met Notre Dame for the first time. History recalls that it was a team manager looking to fill an open date on the Army schedule which began the famed Army-Notre Dame series. However, when McEwan was elected to the College Football Hall of Fame in 1962 he claimed he started the Cadet-Irish series. "If the truth must be told," said the broad-shouldered McEwan in a sports column penned by New York Times scribe Arthur Daley, "I started the series. Army won the toss and elected to kick off. I was the kicker. It was as elemental as all that. When my toe struck the ball the series started. Since the toe was attached to me, the burden of responsibility is mine." That game revolutionized football because of the use of the forward pass by quarterback Gus Dorais and

Knute Rockne. "We had a good pass combination ourself in Vern Prichard and Louis Merrillat," said McEwan, "but Charley Daly wouldn't permit our quarterback to call for a pass. However, we used it against a Navy team that was a three-to-one favorite and scored a victory over Navy that was the greatest of my lifetime."

Notre Dame, an unknown in the football world in 1913, stormed into West Point and quickly became a name by trouncing the Army 35-13. Leading that Fighting Irish eleven was team captain Knute Rockne. Rockne would eventually become head football coach at Notre Dame and establish a winning tradition in football that is still expected today in the 1980s at South Bend.

The Corps of Cadets staged a review on The Plain prior to the first Army-Notre Dame football game. In addition, an Artillery Company at West Point also paraded during pre-game activities.

A football Saturday at the U.S. Military Academy attracts many visitors because of the activities that go along with the football game. One of those activities is watching the Corps of Cadets in review. Even in 1913 prior to the inaugural Army-Notre Dame encounter, there was a cadet review on The Plain.

The Notre Dame football team stopped at nearby Kingston, New York, prior to completing their trip to West Point. A photo was taken of that group and they are pictured above. They are, left to right, Gus Dorais,

Eichenlaub, George Hull, Tom Williams, Larkin, Jones, "Goat" Anderson, Pliska, Gushurts, Finegan, Curley Nowers, Lathrop, Mike Calnon, Knute Rockne, and Elward.

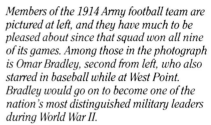

Members of the 1914 Army football team are pictured at left, and they have much to be pleased about since that squad won all nine of its games. Among those in the photograph is Omar Bradley, second from left, who also starred in baseball while at West Point. Bradley would go on to become one of the nation's most distinguished military leaders during World War II.

Notre Dame football coach Jesse Harper required West Point to provide a one thous- and dollar guarantee before he would agree to meet Army at the Academy in 1913. The Army- Notre Dame series developed into one of the top football series in the country, drawing nationwide interest during the 1920s, 1930s and 1940s.

The class of 1915 is sometimes considered the class of stars since several of those graduates went on to distinguish themselves as military leaders during World War II. Pictured left are the varsity lettermen from the class of 1915. Among them is Dwight D. Eisenhower, third from left in middle row, Omar Bradley, fourth from left in top row (who also starred in baseball), and James Van Fleet, first from left, top row.

The 1915 Army coaching staff are pictured here, left to right, Lt. Cuthbert P. Stearns, Lt. John H. Jouett, Lt. Benjamin Hoge, Lt. Walter Wynne, Capt. Daniel I. Sultan, Head Coach Lt. Charlie Daly, and Capt. Ernest Graves.

Charles Daly is pictured here as coach of the Army football team.

Army halfback Elmer Oliphant gained All-America honors during the conclusion of the 1916 and 1917 seasons. He helped lead the 1916 squad to an unblemished 9-0 record, while the 1917 squad finished with a 7-1 mark. Oliphant shared the duties of team captain during his final season, stepping in for Biff Jones who graduated early because of World War I.

46

This is a photograph of the 1917 Army football team that finished with a 7-1 record. The only loss was a 7-2 decision to Notre Dame. Geoffrey Keyes, a 1913 West Point graduate who lettered in football for three years, served as coach. Elmer Oliphant and Lawrence Jones served as co-captains.

This is another photograph of Army's undefeated 1916 football squad, coached by Charles Daly, a 1905 West Point graduate, that compiled a 9 0 record. Halfback Elmer Oliphant won All-America honors at the conclusion of that season, while Lawrence McC. "Biff" Jones lettered. Jones would become head football coach at West Point in 1926. Other lettermen from the 1916 team included William Butler, John Cole, Elbert Ford, Charles Gerhardt, Ernest Harmon, Joel Holmes, Laurence Meacham, Charles Mullins, William Redfield, George Hirsch, Edwin House, Royal Place, O'Ferrall Knight, Francis March, Edwin Shrader, and Eugene Vidal. The photograph of the entire squad was taken on Cullem Field.

The 1919 Army football squad won six games and lost three tough decisions under Coach Charles Daly. The Cadets blanked Middlebury, Holy Cross, Maine, Boston College, and Villanova, while edging Tufts 24-13. However, Army dropped tough decisions to Syracuse 7-3, Notre Dame 12-9, and Navy 6-0. The team captain was Alexander George. Pictured are, front row, left to right, Waldemar Breidster, Earl "Red" Blaik, Claude McQuarrie, team captain Alexander George, Maurice Daniel, Clarence Schabacker, and Herman Lystad; second row, team manager Lawrence Schick, Gustave Vogel, Homer Kiefer, Clovis Byers, Charles H. Swartz, Francis Greene, Walter White, and Elias Gregory; third row, Harrison Travis, Louis Storck, Park Herrick, Howard Davidson, and Garrett Bolyard.

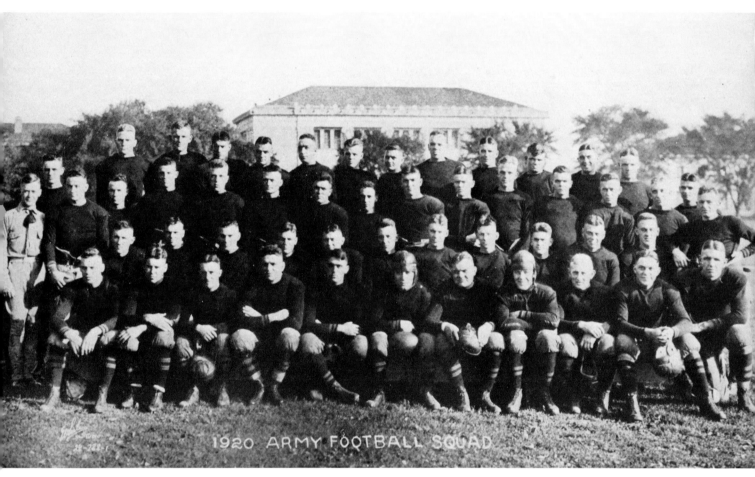

1920 ARMY FOOTBALL SQUAD

The 1920 football squad set an Academy record by destroying Bowdoin College by a 90-0 score. Coach Charles Daly's team won seven games and lost two, bowing to Navy 7-0 and Notre Dame 27-17. Glenn Wilhide served as team captain. Pictured are, front row, left to right, Donald Storck, Francis Dodd, Walter C. White, Howard Davidson, Louis J. Storck, team captain Glenn Wilhide, Waldemar Breidster, Francis Greene, John Stewart, Edwin Clark, and Samuel Strohecker; second row, Denis J. Mulligan, George W. Smythe, James S. Stowell, Charles G. Pierce, Edward J. Doyle, Charles W. Lawrence, Ralph Tibbets, Russell P. Reeder, Robert Perkins, Sanford Goodman, Loren Appleby, and Frank Spettel; third row, Leland Richards, team manager George H. Olmsted, Herbert Enderton, Gustin Nelson, Alfred Kessler, Frederic Henney, John Pitzer, Reginald Dean, William Cornog, John Evans, Patrick Timberlake, Charles Davis, Edward Ebersole, Walter French, and Charles Dasher; back row, Wilson, Ture Larson, Samuel Smithers, Robert Donahue, William Schaefer, Theodore Butler, and Joe Loutzenheiser.

This photograph sets the scene for the 1921 Army-Navy football game played in New York City. The Midshipmen prevailed 7-0 in this encounter.

CHAPTER 6

AN ERA OF NATIONAL PROMINENCE

The era of the twenties brought national prominence to Army football, and rightly so. The Cadets won seventy-one games, lost just seventeen, and tied eight from 1921 until 1930. Their games with Notre Dame, Navy, and Yale drew capacity crowds in New York City and New Haven, Connecticut.

Coach Charlie Daly closed out his coaching career at the start of the twenties, posting a 6-4 record in 1921 and an 8-0-2 record during the 1922 season.

Former All-America center John McEwan followed his former coach and guided the Army eleven to an 18-5-3 record during his three seasons as head coach, 1923-1925. Lawrence McCheney "Biff" Jones took over the coaching reins in 1926 and was even more successful, leading Army teams to thirty victories against just eight defeats and two ties during his four years at West Point, 1926-1929. Ralph Sasse then closed out the twenties, making his debut a memorable one as Army compiled a 9-1-1 record in 1930.

Many of Army's outstanding players gained first team All-America recognition during this decade, led by none other than Christian Keener "Red" Cagle, who gained All-America honors three consecutive years at halfback, 1927-1929. Ed Garbisch earned All-America honors in 1922 and 1924 at center, and was an outstanding kicker for the Cadets. Mortimer Bud Sprague was another two time All-America selection at tackle, receiving those honors in 1926 and 1927.

Gus Farwick, an outstanding guard, was named a first team All-America in 1924 and joined Garbisch as the first two Army players to be selected to participate in the East-West Shrine game in San Francisco. It marked the first time Army players participated in post-season games.

Chuck Born was an All-America end in 1925, while Harry "Lighthorse" Wilson gained All-America honors at halfback in 1926.

The 1921 season was somewhat of a disappointment for Coach Daly. His squad won four of their first five games, claiming victories over Springfield, Middlebury, Lebanon Valley, and Wabash. However, Army managed to win but two of their final five games to settle for a 6-4 record. One of those four losses was a 28-0 decision to Notre Dame in New York City, while Navy nipped the Cadets 7-0 in the season finale in New York City. A seven-yard touchdown run by Bennie Koehler in the fourth quarter provided Navy the margin of victory.

Army did set a team scoring record in 1921, thrashing Bowdoin College 90-0, a record that still stands today. This season was also significant because it marked the first time a Cadet eleven was permitted to play an opponent, other than Navy, off post. Army traveled to New Haven to tangle with Yale and attracted 74,000 fans. The athletic department received a third of the receipts from this encounter, totaling $65,000.

The Corps of Cadets also was permitted to travel to the game, and marched through the streets of New Haven to the Yale Bowl. According to legend, a few weeks after the game a plebe was asked the reason for the left oblique movement in marching.

"Sir," he replied, "it is designed to keep the Corps from being run over by the one-man trolley cars on Chapel Street in New Haven."

Yale's captain Mac Aldrich passed for one touchdown and set up the second by intercepting an Army pass in a 14-7 victory. Walter French tossed a scoring pass to Ed Johnson for the Cadets' only score.

Assistant coach Pot Graves also resigned after the 1921 season, disputing Charlie Daly's decision to install new formations prior to the Navy game. Prior to the 1921 Navy encounter, Daly decided to use Notre Dame's shift from a T-formation to a box. The Cadets did not master it well enough and bowed to the Middies.

When asked why he was quitting, Graves responded quickly. "It's putting in these systems before the Navy game," he grumbled. "Last year it was the Princeton 'Three out and W.' Now it's the Notre Dame shift. I don't blame Charlie Daly. I think he is getting these ideas from

MacArthur. You know, Mac. MacArthur is the smartest man in the United States Army. But he doesn't know a damned thing about football!"

Army continued to use the Notre Dame shift in 1922 with a great deal more success. In fact, Daly's eleven finished 8-0-2. The Cadets tied Yale 7-7 in New Haven and played a scoreless deadlock against Notre Dame. Ed Garbisch missed a field goal for Army during the Notre Dame encounter, while Ed Crowley damaged Notre Dame's hopes when he fumbled on the Cadet three-yard line and Charlie Lawrence recovered for Army.

This marked the last time Army and Notre Dame would meet on The Plain at West Point. In 1923, the game was played at Ebbets Field in Brooklyn. In 1924 it was held at the Polo Grounds and then moved to Yankee Stadium a year later.

The season finale against Navy was one of the most exciting in history. George Smythe set up the winning touchdown with a 50-yard whirling punt return. Then on fourth down at the Navy seven, Bill Wood took the snap from center and handed it to Smythe. He ran to his right as if to sweep around right end. Suddenly he stopped, cocked his arm, and fired a pass across field to Pat Timberlake in the end zone. Smythe kicked the extra point for the 17-14 victory.

In 1923, McEwan made his coaching debut and guided the Cadets to a 6-2-1 record. Army dropped a 13-0 game to Notre Dame, and also was trounced by Yale, 31-10. The Cadets then battled Navy to a scoreless deadlock. Ed Garbisch missed a thirty-five-yard field goal for Army, and Steve Barchet also missed his thirty-five-yarder for Navy during a game played at the Polo Grounds.

In 1923, contruction began on Michie Stadium, the home of the Army football team today. Originally a frog pond, Michie Stadium was dedicated during a game against Columbia in 1924.

The 1924 season was somewhat better for Coach McEwan after his squad finished at 5-1-2. The one loss was a 13-7 decision to Notre Dame, a game in which sportswriter Grantland Rice made Notre Dame's veteran backfield of Don Miller, Elmer Layden, Jim Crowley, and Henry Stuhldreher famous. He penned one of the most colorful sports leads ever written: "Outlined against a blue-gray October sky, the Four Horsemen rode again. In dramatic lore they are known as Famine, Pestilence, Destruction and Death. These are only aliases. Their real names are Stuhldreher, Miller, Crowley and Layden."

Army's only touchdown was set up by Harry Wilson's forty-yard run. He picked up another five, and then Neil Harding took a handoff and went the remainder of the way for the touchdown.

Army tied Yale 7-7 when Wilson galloped sixteen yards for a touchdown and Garbisch added the extra point. A week later Wilson ran forty-five yards for the deciding touchdown during a 14-7 victory over Florida, a team coached by Maj. James Van Fleet, another former Army player.

The 1924 season came to a dramatic close when Garbisch

drop-kicked four field goals to provide Army a 12-0 victory over Navy. The Army team captain booted a thirty-two-yard field goal in the second quarter. In the third quarter he converted two attempts, from forty-two yards and twenty yards for a 9-0 Army lead. Then he completed the virtuoso act with a thirty-yarder during the fourth quarter.

McEwan's final season as head coach, 1925, brought more success for Army. The Cadets were 7-2. Among those seven victories was a 27-0 triumph over Notre Dame at Yankee Stadium, the first win over the Irish since 1916. The Cadets also trimmed Navy 10-3, but dropped encounters to Yale and Columbia at the home fields of the victors.

Army dominated Notre Dame in 1925. Wilson ran for one touchdown and Harding tossed a touchdown pass to team captain Henry Baxter. Bud Sprague recovered an Irish fumble and rambled forty-five yards for another touchdown. Chuck Born blocked a Navy kick and LaVerne "Blondie" Saunders picked it up and ran thirty-nine yards for another touchdown.

Although the losses to Yale and Columbia were upsetting after the way Army manhandled Notre Dame, they were forgotten with a 10-3 victory over Navy. A sixteen-yard touchdown pass from Harding to Baxter provided more than enough points. Wilson added the extra point, and then Russell "Red" Reeder drop-kicked a field goal from the nine-yard line for Army's final points.

In 1926, Biff Jones made his coaching debut at the Academy, and a halfback named Christian Cagle made his varsity debut. Both were highly successful. Jones opened his head coaching career with a 7-1-1 record. Army opened with six consecutive victories before Notre Dame stopped the Cadets 7-0. Army rebounded to trim Ursinus, but then was forced to settle for a 21-21 deadlock against Navy.

Red Cagle was born in De Ridder, Louisiana, in 1905 and starred in football at Southwestern Louisiana Institute. However, he had received little football recognition while playing for such a small school, and received an appointment to West Point. At the Academy, Cagle gained All-America honors three times, the first Army player to achieve that during his career.

Yet, Cagle was very humble about his success. This trait is described succinctly in the 1929 *Howitzer* yearbook: "Great in victory, but with that added characteristic that marks a real leader—great still in defeat; modest and reticent to a fault; happy-go-lucky, but always sincere—that is Red Cagle."

In his first Navy game he played before 110,000 spectators at Chicago's Soldier Field as a substitute halfback. During the final moments all he did was run forty-three yards for a touchdown to provide the Cadets a 21-21 deadlock.

A year later Cagle would dominate the Navy team again, overshadowing team captain Harry Wilson. However, the two Army players were friends and Cagle refused to score, leaving that to Wilson when Army drew within striking distance. "This is Harry's game," said Cagle, and Wilson scored all of Army's points as the Cadets put the finishing touches on a 9-1 season.

Cagle didn't realize it, but that would prove to be his final Navy game. The Naval Academy adopted a three-year varsity rule and Army refused to go along, so the superintendent of the Naval Academy cancelled the game for the next two years.

Biff Jones continued his coaching success during the 1928 and 1929 seasons, guiding Army to respective 8-2 and 6-4-1 records. Cagle led the way, but suffered through perhaps his toughest year while serving as team captain in 1929. Despite his individual effort, Army dropped three of its final five games, including a 7-0 decision to Notre Dame.

Jones went on to further coaching success at Louisiana State, Oklahoma, and Nebraska. He eventually returned to the Academy in 1942 as a colonel and served as graduate manager of athletics until 1948.

Perhaps one of Jones' and Cagle's finest afternoons came in 1927 during an 18-0 victory over Notre Dame. Cagle ran fifty-three yards for one touchdown and caught a pass for another as Army handed the Irish their only loss of the season.

Cagle's good luck turned to bad during the final months of his West Point career. While recovering from a tonsilectomy in the West Point hospital, he made an announcement that he was going to resign his commission shortly after graduation. There was an immediate uproar, although other graduates had resigned for financial reasons before Cagle. However, before that uproar settled down, a report surfaced from Louisiana that Cagle was married.

Cagle admitted he was married to Marion Haile and resigned from the Academy. He later coached at Mississippi A&M, played professional football for the New York Giants, and then became co-owner of the Brooklyn Dodgers professional football team in 1933. A year later he sold his interest in the team and went into the insurance business.

On December 23, 1942, Cagle was found unconscious at the foot of the stairs of a New York subway station. He suffered a fractured skull and died three days later.

Ralph Sasse took over as head coach in 1930 and guided Army to a 9-1-1 record. After tying Yale 7-7 midway through the season, Sasse's squad dropped a tough 7-6 game to Notre Dame before whipping Navy 6-0 in the season finale.

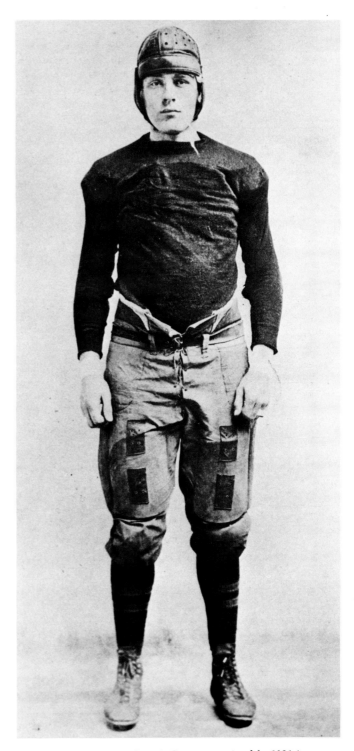

Francis Greene, captain of the 1921 Army football team that compiled a 6-4 record under Coach Charlie Daly, lettered three years in football at West Point, 1919-1921.

"ARMY FOOTBALL SQUAD 1921"

In 1921 the Army football squad, coached by Charles Daly, won six games and lost four. The Cadets defeated Springfield, Middlebury, Lebanon Valley, Wabash, Susquehanna, and Villanova, allowing just a touchdown in the Springfield game during the victorious efforts. The four losses were in games against New Hampshire, Yale, Notre Dame, and Navy, the latter by a 7-0 count. In this team picture are, front row, left to right, Charles W. Lawrence, Leland S. Richards, Walter C. White, Washington M. Ives, Howard G. Davidson, Edgar Garbisch, Waldemar Breidster, Glenn Wilhide, Francis Greene, the team captain, Denis J. Mulligan, Louis J. Storck, Donald G. Storck, John E. McLaren, and George W. Smythe; second row, team manager George H. Olmsted, August W. Farwick, an All-America guard in 1924, William B. Woods, Blackshear M. Bryan, Austin F. Gilmartin, John A. Stewart, William M. Gillmore, John H. Pitzer, Harry O. Ellinger, Bordner F. Ascher, Edwin L. Johnson, John W. Warren, Harvey R. Ogden, and Francis T. Dodd; back row, Patrick W. Timberlake, Samuel W. Smithers, Edward J. Doyle, William S. Triplet, Herbert B. Enderton, Ralph I. Glasgow, Wallace E. Whitson, Phillip R. Dwyer, Frank G. Fraser, Fremont. S. Tandy (Thompson), and Charles T. Myers.

Notre Dame may have had its "Four Horsemen" in the 1920s, but Army's offense counted on center Edgar Garbisch to help open the way for its backs. Garbisch earned a great deal of respect as a center and kicker, gaining All-America honors in 1922 and 1924. He joined teammate Gus Farwick in 1924 as the first Army players to participate in a post-season All-Star game. Garbisch and Farwick competed in the East-West Shrine Game in San Francisco in 1925.

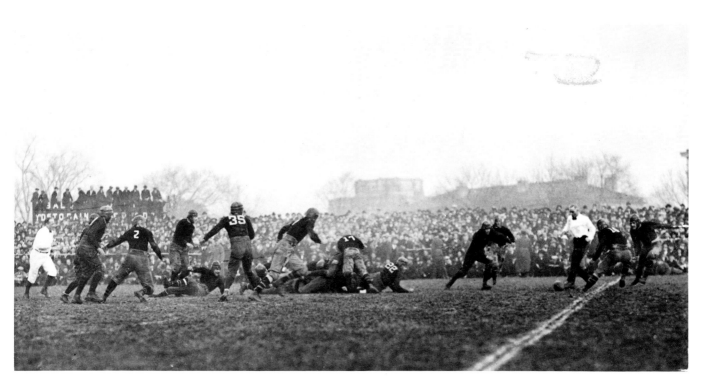

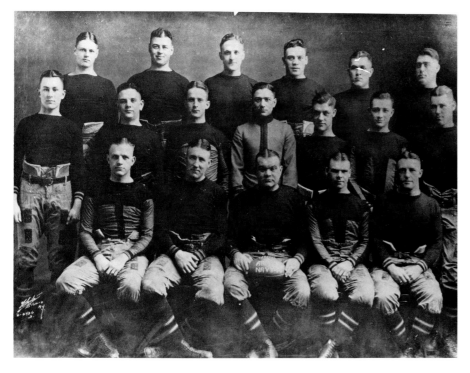

Army and Notre Dame met for the ninth time in 1922 at West Point's Cullum Field, and the two teams played to a 0-0 deadlock. One of the most critical plays occurred when Notre Dame's "Sleepy" Jim Crowley fumbled near the Army goal line. Charlie Lawrence recovered for Army to thwart the biggest scoring opportunity for Notre Dame.

Coach Charles Daly's 1922 football squad completed an undefeated season, winning eight games, while tying in two others. Among those eight victories was a 17-14 win over Navy. The team captain was Waldemar Breidster, while center Edgar Garbisch earned All-America honors. Among the lettermen from that squad were Breidster, Francis Dodd, Charles Lawrence, Charles Myers, John Pitzer, Louis Storck, Patrick Timberlake, Walter White, Sanford Goodman, Washington Jones, Denis Mulligan, George Smythe, Donald Storck, Harry Ellinger, August Farwick, Garbisch, William Gillmore, William Wood, and Leslie Prichard.

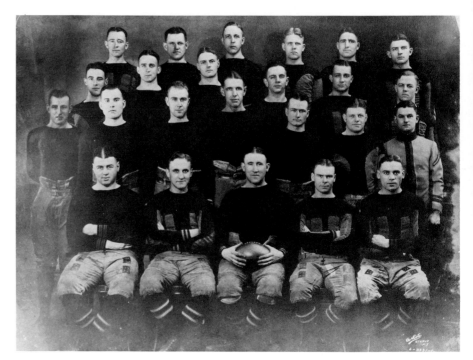

August "Gus" Farwick, a guard on the Army football team from 1922-1924, lettered three years and was a teammate of two-time All-America center Edgar Garbisch. Farwick gained All-America honors himself at the conclusion of the 1924 season.

During the three years in which he lettered in football at West Point, Army compiled an overall record of 19-3-5, including two victories and a tie against rival Navy. In 1922, his first year with the varsity, Army posted an 8-0-2 record, beating Navy 17-14, while tying Notre Dame 0-0, and Yale 7-7. In 1923, the Cadets were 6-2-1, dropping decisions to Notre Dame and Yale. In 1924, Army was 5-1-2, beating Navy in Baltimore 12-0. The Cadets also tied Yale 7-7 and Columbia 14-14. Farwick is considered one of the finest defensive linemen in Army history.

The Army All-America served in the Air Service, Cavalry, and Finance Department, achieving the rank of lieutenant colonel in 1942. He returned to duty in 1950, attending the Army Finance Center as a student. Later, he served as Finance Officer of V Corp in Europe. He retired from active duty in 1955 at the rank of colonel.

In 1925, he was selected to Knute Rockne's All-Time All-Opponent Team. Farwick and teammate Edgar Garbisch were the first Army football players ever invited to play in a post-season All-Star game. Farwick and Garbisch played in the East-West Shrine game in San Francisco in 1925. Farwick was invited to participate in the same charity game in 1928.

In 1923 the Army football team, coached by John McEwan, won six games, lost two, and tied one. Army defeated Tennessee, Florida, Auburn, Lebanon Valley, Arkansas State, and Bethany. Notre Dame trimmed the Cadets 13-0 in a game played at Ebbets Field in Brooklyn, New York, while Yale whipped Army in New Haven, Connecticut. The deadlock came against Navy in New York City. Team captain Denis Mulligan is holding the ball, while All-America Edgar Garbisch is in the first row, second from left, next to Mulligan.

Knute Rockne, who visited West Point for the first time as captain of the Notre Dame team in 1913, appears here as head coach of the Fighting Irish.

In the 1920's Notre Dame had a fearsome backfield that proved almost unstoppable. In 1924, a sportswriter, Grantland Rice, nicknamed the backfield the "Four Horsemen of Notre Dame." They included, left to right, Don Miller, Elmer Layden, Jim Crowley, and Henry Stuhldreher.

Col. Lawrence McC. "Biff" Jones, a class of 1917 West Point graduate, served as head football coach at the Academy from 1926 to 1929. He compiled a record of thirty victories, just eight defeats, and two ties. He also was head football coach at Louisiana State University (1932-1934), Oklahoma University (1935-1936), and the University of Nebraska (1937-1941). He returned to active duty in 1942 and served as graduate manager of athletics at West Point, retiring in 1948 at the rank of colonel. Jones, who lettered two years in football as a cadet, was named to the College Football Hall of Fame in 1954 and the Helms Foundation Hall of Fame in 1964. He died February 12, 1980.

This is a general view of the Army-Notre Dame clash at Yankee Stadium in 1924. The Irish prevailed in this encounter 13-7. Edgar Garbisch served as team captain for Coach John McEwan's squad which compiled a 5-1-2 record.

Army rebounded from a 13-7 loss to Notre Dame in 1924 by blanking the Irish 27-0 in 1925. Army's "Light Horse" Harry Wilson made good on a conversion attempt during the encounter.

Coach Biff Jones guided the 1926 Army football squad to a 7-1-1 record, defeating Detroit, Davis and Elkins, Syracuse, Boston University, Yale, Franklin & Marshall, and Ursinus. The Cadets opened the season with six consecutive victories before Notre Dame knocked Army from the ranks of the unbeaten with a 7-0 victory in New York City. West Point also was forced to settle for a 21-21 deadlock against Navy in a game played in the windy city of Chicago. Pictured are, front row, left to right, Maurice F. Daly, Harry E. Wilson, Orville M. Hewitt, Ernest G. Schmidt, and Thomas J. H. Trapnell; second row, team manager Jeremiah P. Holland, Louis A. Hammack, Samuel R. Brentnall, Garrison H. Davidson, Joseph H. Gilbreth, Norris B. Harbold, and Charles F. Born; third row, Clyde A. Dahl, Paul Elias, John H. Murrell, Arthur W. Meehan, and Neil B. Harding; fourth row, LaVerne G. Saunders, Christian Cagle, Mortimer E. Sprague, Lyle E. Seeman, and George W. Perry.

Army halfback Christian Cagle became the first three-time All-America in West Point history, earning those honors in 1927, 1928, and 1929.

Mortimer "Bud" Sprague received first team All-America honors in football at West Point in 1927 as a tackle. He played an instrumental role in leading the Cadets to a 9-1 record under Coach Biff Jones. Sprague lettered four years in football (1925-1928) and was captain of the 1928 Army squad. He was named to the National Football Foundation Hall of Fame in 1970.

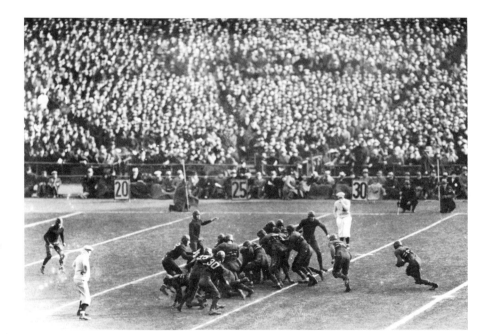

Army-Note Dame 1929

Army running back Christian Keener "Red" Cagle, a three-time All-America at halfback during his football career at West Point, picks up short yardage against Notre Dame in 1929.

With 76,000 fans watching at Yankee Stadium, Army, behind the efforts of Chris Cagle, defeated Notre Dame 18-0 in the fourteenth meeting between the two teams. Cagle, a halfback, was the first three-time All-America selection in Army history.

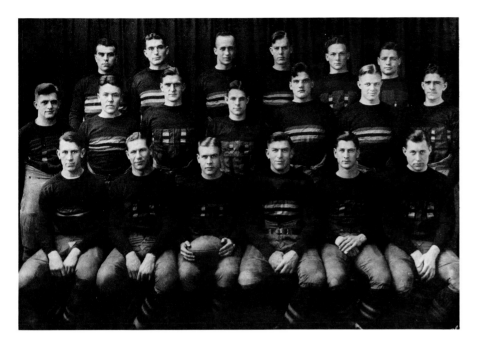

Coach Biff Jones' Army football squad was 9-1 during the 1927 season, bowing only to Yale 10-6 in New Haven. The Cadets, led by team captain "Lighthorse" Harry Wilson, trimmed Navy 14-9 in New York City and also took the measure of Notre Dame by an 18-0 margin. Lettermen from that team included Charles Born, an All-America end in 1925, Bud Sprague, a two-time All-America at tackle, and Christian Cagle, a three-time All-America at halfback, and Wilson, an All-America halfback.

Army and Notre Dame met in 1928 at Yankee Stadium for the fifteenth time in the series. The results were reported in the Herald Tribune *sports section in this fashion.*

Section **IV**   SPORTS MARINE   NEW YORK **Herald Tribune**   SPORTS MARINE   Section **IV**

TEN PAGES   SUNDAY, NOVEMBER 11, 1928   * * *   TEN PAGES

Notre Dame Beats the Army, 12 to 6, in Big Upset Before 90,000;
Maryland Surprises Yale by 6 to 0; Penn Downs Harvard by 7 to 0

Maryland Upsets Yale Eleven, 6-0

Snyder, Last Year's Star, Scores Only Touchdown in 3d Period After Madigan Drops on Loose Ball

Break Comes When Hoben Misses Punt

Southerners Outgain, Outpass and Make More 1st Downs Than Eli Eleven

Special to the Herald Tribune

NEW HAVEN, Conn., Nov. 10—An underized crowd of about 30,000 spectators disregarded pre-game warnings of the Yale walk-away over Maryland and came to Yale's big Bowl to-day to be rewarded by one of the most surprising upsets of the 1928 season in which the University of Maryland eleven trampled upon the Elis, 6 to 0. Yale, rated with the best and conquered only by the Army, was about to enter the annual Princeton and Harvard series a decided favorite.

Penn Defeats Harvard, 7-0, On Early Slip

Fumble by Guarnaccia in First Minute and 15-Yd. Penalty Let Scull Cross Line on 4-Yd. Plunge

Captain Completes Scoring With Kick

Backfield Punch Gives Quakers Edge; Celebration Stopped by Police

By W. B. Hanna

CAMBRIDGE, Mass., Nov. 10—Harvard to-day paid a big price for two mistakes when the football game with Penn was yet so young it had no more than begun. One of these mistakes was a fumble, the other was a foul which brought a penalty. Both counted in the touchdown which Penn made on top of them and Penn won the game, 7 to 0.

The Deciding Touchdown as Notre Dame Defeated the Army, 12 to 6

Jack O'Brien receiving forward pass from John Niemiec in the fourth period, three yards from the goal line. He fell over the final mark with deciding score

Herald Tribune photo—Studin

Forward Pass to O'Brien Gives Notre Dame Victory In 4th Period at Stadium

Niemeic's Long Throw in Final Minutes Breaks Deadlock After Murrell Makes Army Score and Chevigney Ties; Cagle Then Thrills Crowd With Great Runs, Ending Game on Rival 1-Yard Line

By W. O. McGehan

In one of the most dramatic battles ever fought between these traditional rivals Notre Dame beat the Army, 12 to 6, at the Yankee Stadium yesterday before something like 90,000 crowded into the stands and something like 5,000 dangled from roofs, fire escapes, elevated platforms and any point of vantage. The game had everything in the nature of a thrill.

Ga. Tech Downs Vanderbilt in Atlanta, 19-7

Thomason, Lumpkin, Mizell Golden Tornado Stars; Brown Scores on Long Run

By Grantland Rice

Georgetown Is Beaten, 13-0, by Carnegie Tech

Victors Outplay Rivals Until Final Period in Battle of Unbeaten Elevens

By Kerr N. Petrie

ALBANY, N. Y., Nov. 10—Remembering its opponents relentlessly for three-fourths of the game, Carnegie Tech settled one momentous question in the football world to-day and stirred up trouble anew for the followers of New York University by conquering Georgetown by a score of 13 to 0 in Lindenkarr 1924 here before a thin crowd.

College and School Football

Michigan and Navy Elevens Play Tie, 6 to 6

Gannon's 78-Yard Run Leads to Middies' Touchdown; Hozer Scores for West

By Don Skene

BALTIMORE, Nov. 10—The Navy's football team and Michigan's desperately clashing Wolverines clashed on the sunny turf of Baltimore Stadium this afternoon before about 35,000 picturesque partisans and left the field of battle deadlocked in a scoreless 6-6 tie.

61

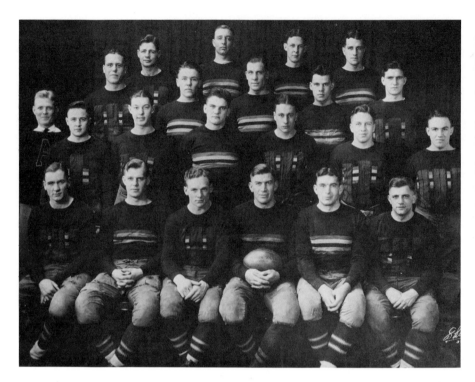

Coach Biff Jones guided the 1928 Army football team to an 8-2 record. The Cadets dropped a 12-6 decision to Notre Dame and a 26-0 verdict to Stanford. Both of those games were played in New York City. Members of the Army team included, first row, left to right, Charles Allan, William E. Hall, Christian Cagle, team captain Mortimer Sprague, Louis A. Hammack, and William L. Nave; second row, Harold Hayes, Richard O'Keefe, Edwin Messinger, George Perry, Carl Carlmark, Herbert Gibner, and Clark Piper; third row, Thomas Lynch, Birrell Walsh, Paul Elias, Benjamin Wimer, and Richard Hutchinson; fourth row, John Murrell, Charles Humber, Winston Maxwell, and Eugene Kenny.

In 1929 the stock market crashed, and so did the Cadets of Army in their classic encounter with Notre Dame at Yankee Stadium. Above, Chris Cagle gains three yards on a run, but his efforts were not enough to avoid a 7-0 defeat.

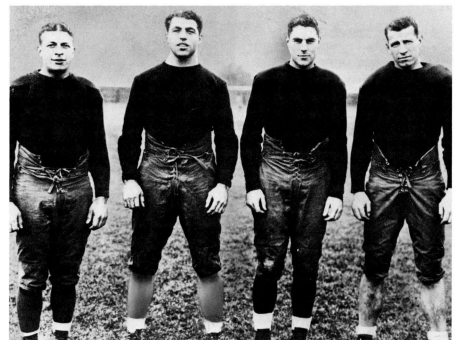

Army met Yale in New Haven in 1929 and suffered a 21-13 defeat against the Elis. The game hardly went unnoticed as shown in this aerial photograph of the Yale Bowl just prior to kickoff.

The Fighting Irish of Notre Dame trimmed Army 7-0 at Yankee Stadium in 1929 thanks in part to the efforts of a backfield combination that included, left to right, quarterback Frank Carideo, and backs Joe Salvoldi, Marchy Schwartz, and Marty Brill.

Notre Dame's outstanding quarterback, Alex Cariedo, goes around Army's right end for nine yards in the 1930 gridiron battle played in the rain and cold at Chicago's Soldier Field. Carideo would convert the extra point following Marchy Schwartz' fifty-four-yard touchdown run with just five minutes to play to provide what proved to be the margin of victory in a 7-6 win over the Cadets. More than 100,000 fans braved the rain and cold to watch the game. The loss was the only setback Army would suffer during the 1930 season.

CHAPTER 7

A NETWORK OF DEFENSE

Defensive football came to the forefront during the 1930s at the U.S. Military Academy, highlighted by the successful coaching tenures of Ralph Sasse and Garrison Davidson.

Sasse, an emotional and forceful coach, molded exceptional defensive teams during his three years, 1930-1932 at West Point. The Cadets shut out twenty opponents and defeated rival Navy three consecutive times. The tragic death of Cadet Richard Brinsley Sheridan in the Yale game in 1931 sapped the enthusiasm of coaching from Sasse, who requested a transfer. He stayed on another year as head coach at the wishes of West Point, but left after the 1932 campaign.

Gar Davidson took over for Sasse and compiled a record thirty-five victories, just eleven defeats, and one tie in five years, the longest coaching tenure at the Academy since Charlie Daly served as head coach for eight years. Davidson would return to West Point later in his military career to serve as superintendent.

Coach William Wood succeeded Garrison as head coach in 1938 and guided Army to an 8-2 record during his first season. However, early success ended quickly for Wood in 1939 and 1940 as the Army team suffered through successive losing campaigns, including two straight defeats at the hands of Navy. The 1940 season was particularly disastrous as the Cadets managed only a 20-19 victory over Williams College in the opener before losing seven and playing to a tie during the final eight games.

That result forced West Point officials to search for a strong successor. The choice was a good one, tabbing Earl Blaik, a graduate and former assistant coach, for the head coaching responsibilities starting in 1941. It would be the beginning of the most prominent era of success in West Point football history.

The 1930s not only marked the success of two outstanding coaches, Sasse and Garrison, but also demonstrated the talents of some outstanding football players. Leading the way was tackle Jack Price, a two-time first team All-America at tackle in 1930 and 1931. Price was followed by another outstanding lineman and team captain, Milt Summerfelt, who received All-America recognition in 1932.

Halfback Jack Buckler gained All-America honors in 1933, while end Bill Schuler and tackle Harry Stella were selected for first team All-America recognition in 1935 and 1939, respectively.

Sasse, a 1916 graduate of West Point, failed to earn a letter in football because he sustained a knee injury which occurred while leaping a wire fence. Following graduation Sasse was the first American combat officer to land on French soil in World War I, commanding a heavy tank battalion. Troops in his command idolized him and he rose to the rank of major.

Sasse returned to the United States in 1919 and served a variety of assignments at Fort Meade, Fort Myer, Fort Riley, and Fort Leavenworth. He then returned to West Point as an assistant professor of drawing. Sasse also had additional duties as assistant football coach, serving under John McEwan for three years and Biff Jones for an additional four years.

When he succeeded Jones as head coach in 1930, he spoke to the Corps of Cadets. "I promise you fireworks!" he said. It was a promise he would keep.

During his first season Army compiled a 9-1-1 record. The only loss was to Notre Dame in the rain, sleet and cold that hit Chicago's Soldier Field. The Cadets also settled for a 7-7 tie against Yale.

Sasse's eleven opened the 1930 season with four consecutive shutouts, taking the measure of Boston University, Furman, Swarthmore, and Harvard. The Cadets played to a 7-7 tie against Yale in New Haven, then posted three more shutouts against Illinois, Ursinus, and Navy.

Sasse's team captain that year was Charles Humber, a young man who inadvertently found himself in hot water when a report leaked out in 1929 that the Army team captain was married. Academy officials thought the report referred to the new team captain, and Maj. Gen. William R. Smith, the superintendent, summoned Humber to his office.

"Cadet Humber," said the superintendent. "It is reported

that you are married. Is that true?"

Humber turned pale. "No, by God, sir," he replied. "It is not true! Nor do I ever expect to be married."

The report actually referred to Christian "Red" Cagle, three-time All-America and captain of the 1929 squad. Cagle later admitted to being married and eventually resigned. Humber went on to lead the 1930 team.

Army carried its 8-0-1 into the 1930 Notre Dame game at Soldier Field. More than 100,000 packed the stadium, despite weather unfit for most mortals. Rain, wind, sleet, and snow played havoc with any pre-game football strategy. It became a matter of survival.

Coach Knute Rockne's football squad was exceptionally strong, having beaten the likes of Southern Methodist University, Navy, Carnegie Tech, Pittsburgh, Indiana, Pennsylvania, Drake, and Northwestern. It didn't faze Sasse.

"Let's pull up our socks and get going," he told his Army squad. They did just that, battling Notre Dame to a scoreless tie during the first fifty-four minutes. Then Notre Dame's diminutive halfback Marchy Schwartz broke off tackle and rambled fifty-four yards for a touchdown and Frank Carideo converted the extra point for a 7-0 lead.

Later in the fourth quarter Carideo dropped back to punt deep in his own territory. Army end Dick King broke through to block the kick. The ball skipped back to the end zone where Harley Trice recovered for an Army touchdown. Charlie Broshous then came off the bench to attempt the extra point, but he missed with his dropkick and Notre Dame won 7-6.

Army bounced back on December 13 against Navy. President Herbert Hoover ordered the two service academies to meet in football to raise money for the needy during the Depression. The two teams had not met for two years, after a disagreement erupted over eligibility rules.

However, neither team thought about that during their 1930 meeting in Yankee Stadium. A crowd in excess of 70,000 flocked to see the encounter and raised $300,000 for charity.

Army decided the issue in the fourth quarter when halfback Ray Stecker rambled fifty-six yards for the game's only touchdown. The Cadet defense took care of the rest.

The year 1931 proved to be tragic for Coach Sasse. In March he mourned the death of Notre Dame coach Knute Rockne, who was killed in a plane crash in Kansas. Rockne and Sasse had become close friends after settling an earlier disagreement about an Army-Notre Dame encounter. The two normally had dinner together after the two teams met, building a lasting friendship.

When Sasse attended Rockne's funeral, Bonnie Rockne thanked him for coming and expressed how much the Army-Notre Dame game meant to Rockne. "It meant so much to him," said Mrs. Rockne. "More than once he said, 'While I'm here and after I'm gone nothing must ever happen to the Army game.'"

Sasse's 1931 Army team was 8-2-1. The tie occurred against Yale in New Haven, a game in which Cadet Sheridan was fatally injured in the fourth quarter.

Sasse was very fond of Sheridan, a slim 149-pounder from Greenville, South Carolina. Prior to the Yale encounter, he informed Sheridan he would not be in the starting lineup. The Army coach decided to start Pete Kopcsak, who was considerably bigger than Sheridan. Sasse wanted to wear Yale down, but nonetheless told Sheridan he still would see plenty of action.

Although disappointed at the news, Sheridan still prepared for when he would be needed against Yale. The Army back always battled back. When he failed to receive an appointment to West Point, he enlisted in the Army and took a competitive exam to gain admission, and finished with the best mark. Now against Yale he saw some action, but late in the fourth quarter he raced downfield on a kickoff, the first Army man there. Yale's Bob Lassiter took the kickoff and began his return. Sheridan met him head on. Lassiter's knee caught Sheridan in the back of the head and he fell to the ground. He did not move, and x-rays later proved that he suffered a fractured fourth vertebrae and a partial fracture of the fifth. Two days later Sheridan died, with Sasse and his parents at his bedside.

Sheridan's death and the death of a Fordham University player brought additional rule changes to football, one of which was banning the flying tackle. Yet, this tragic accident was difficult for Sasse to accept and he seemed to lose interest and enthusiasm for coaching at West Point. He agreed to stay on for a third year, but then moved on.

Army closed out its 1931 season by beating Notre Dame 12-0 and Navy 17-7. Ray Stecker caught a thirty-five-yard pass to set up the Cadets' first touchdown and then scampered sixty-six yards for the second touchdown against the Irish. The Army-Navy game again was held for charity and Buckler had another good day to lead his squad to a 17-7 win.

In 1932, Army finished with an 8-2 record, dropping a tough 18-13 decision to Pittsburgh and a 21-0 game to Notre Dame. These two teams were the only ones to score on the Cadets. Army registered eight shutouts including a 20-0 victory over Navy.

The Navy game was interesting because of its pre-game antics. The two schools had signed a three-year contract to play, eliminating the disagreements on eligibility. So, the Middies came out for their normal pre-game warmups, but the Army squad failed to appear on Franklin Field. Some thought the Cadets had been delayed by a traffic accident, but such was not the case. Sasse held his squad in the locker room, challenging them by saying "We don't need practice to play the boys from Crabtown."

In 1932, Sasse was correct. Felix Vidal put the finishing touches on a fifty-four-yard scoring march in the second quarter by plunging over from the two. Jack Buckler passed to William Frentzel for a forty-yard touchdown and later scored himself during the 20-0 triumph. Thus, Sasse closed out his West Point coaching stint in successful fashion.

Davidson assumed the head coaching position in 1933 and enjoyed immediate success. His Army team was 9-1, thanks to some superlative efforts by team captain Harvey

Jablonsky and All-America halfback Jack Buckler.

Army opened the season with a 19-6 victory over Mercer College, and then followed with seven straight shutouts to move into the Navy game undefeated, 8-0. The Cadets took the lead 6-0 against their counterparts from Annapolis, but Navy countered with a touchdown of their own and converted the extra point for a 7-6 lead. It marked the first time Army had trailed during the season, but the Cadets responded very well. Before the end of the first half Jack Buckler scampered twenty yards for what proved to be the winning touchdown.

Consequently, Army was now 9-0 heading into the Notre Dame encounter, trying to be the first squad to finish with an unblemished record since 1916. Unfortunately, it was not to be.

The Cadets started off well enough. Buckler ran twelve yards for a touchdown after Army recovered a Notre Dame fumble. Then Army intercepted an Irish pass and quarterback Paul Johnson plunged over for the score to make it 12-0.

Notre Dame scored in the third quarter and converted the extra point to trail 12-7. Then Nick Lukats punted seventy-five yards deep in Army territory. Two plays later Wayne Milner broke through to block Ossie Simmons' punt and recovered it in the end zone for what proved to be the winning touchdown.

Coach Davidson's 1934 team won seven and lost three. Gone from the football staff were Earl Blaik and Harry Ellinger. Blaik accepted the head coaching position at Dartmouth College and Ellinger followed him to Hanover.

Army opened with four consecutive shutouts and then trimmed Yale 20-12 for a 5-0 record. The Cadets then dropped a 7-0 decision to Illinois, but bounced back with victories over Harvard and The Citadel. However, Army closed out by dropping a 12-6 decision to Notre Dame and a 3-0 game to Navy. Slade Cutter's twenty-yard field goal provided Navy with the winning margin, their first win over Army since 1921.

In 1935, Army compiled a 6-2-1 record. One loss came at the hands of Mississippi State 13-7, a team coached by an old friend, Ralph Sasse. The Cadets also bowed to powerful Pittsburgh, 29-6. Following the loss to the Panthers, Army played Notre Dame to a 6-6 deadlock, and then closed out the season with victories over Vermont 34-0, and Navy 28-6.

Charles R. "Monk" Meyer played an instrumental role in Army's success during the 1935 and 1936 seasons. Although small by most standards at 143 pounds, Meyer was an exceptional runner, solid kicker and a better than average passer. He lettered two seasons and received All-American recognition in some quarters, although no first team selections.

One of Meyer's favorite receivers was Edward A. "Whitey" Grove. Grove had a great knack as a receiver, perhaps helped by his talents as an outfielder on the Army baseball team. Meyer connected with Grove and team captain Bill Shuler for touchdown passes to whip Harvard 13-0 in 1935 at Michie Stadium.

Coach Ralph Sasse was head football coach at West Point from 1930 to 1932, succeeding Biff Jones. During his three-year stint, Army was 25-5-2. In his first year at the helm the Cadets were 9-1-1, losing only to Notre Dame by a 7-6 margin. Army also whipped Navy 6-0. His second season West Point was 8-2-1, defeating both Notre Dame, 12-0, and Navy, 17-7. Army dropped a tough 14-13 decision to Harvard, tied Yale 6-6 in New Haven, and bowed to Pittsburgh 26-0 in the "Steel City." There was one tragic note during his second season. Cadet Richard Sheridan was killed during the Yale game in New Haven. During Sasse's final year Army was 8-2.

Notre Dame running back Marchy Schwartz is in front of the pack as he races fifty-four yards for the only Notre Dame touchdown during the 1930 game in Chicago. Notre Dame converted the point after touchdown and that proved to be the margin of victory in a 7-6 win over Army.

This photograph shows a portion of the 100,000 fans who trooped to Chicago's Soldier Field to watch the 1930 Army-Notre Dame clash. The weather may have been the worst in the series history with rain, wind, and cold. Despite the elements, the Irish prevailed by a 7-6 margin, blocking Charles Broshous' drop kick attempt that would have tied the score.

Meyer and Grove hooked up again in the first quarter of the Notre Dame game for a touchdown, and the Cadets protected that lead until the final minute of play. Then Army was called for pass interference on their own two-yard line, and Notre Dame plunged over for the tying points seconds later. The Irish missed the extra point.

Army battled back to trounce Navy 28-6, scoring three times in the first quarter. Grove ran eighty yards for the first touchdown, and then Meyer tossed touchdown passes to Grove and Clint True. Bill Grohs accounted for the other touchdown.

In 1936, when Army compiled a 6-3 record, Meyer dueled Columbia's fine quarterback Sid Luckman and came out a winner 27-16. Trailing 16-15 going into the final period, the Cadets scored twice as Meyer closed out by completing 11 of 15 passes for 172 yards.

Army dropped a 14-7 decision to Colgate, bowed to Notre Dame 20-6, and suffered a 7-0 loss to Navy when another pass interference call in the final minutes set up the winning touchdown. The 1936 Army-Navy game was notable for another reason. It marked the first time the game was played in Philadelphia's Municipal Stadium where over 102,000 watched.

Meyer went on to a distinguished military career, rising to the rank of brigadier general before retiring in 1967. He served in the Pacific during World War II and also fought in the Vietnam War. Meyer won numerous citations, including the Distinguished Service Cross, two Silver Stars, two

Notre Dame coach Knute Rockne, left, is joined by Irish team captain Tom Yarr and assistant coach Hunk Anderson during practice before Army game in 1931.

Army end Richard Sheridan is pictured here. Sheridan was tragically killed during the Yale encounter in New Haven in 1931.

Legion of Merit awards, two Bronze Stars, two Purple Hearts, and two Distinguished Service Medals.

Gar Davidson's head coaching tenure ended after the 1937 season, when Army compiled a 7-2 record, including a 6-0 victory over Navy. The Cadets dropped a 15-7 decision to Yale in New Haven and a 7-0 game to Notre Dame. The Navy game was decided in the first quarter when Jim Craig plunged over from the two-yard line for the only points of the game.

Bill Wood took over the coaching reins in 1938 and opened with an 8-2 season, including a 14-7 victory over Navy. Unfortunately, that would be the last time a Wood-coached Army team would compile a winning record. In 1939, the Cadets slipped to 3-4-2 and were shutout by Navy 10-0. Then in 1940 Army was 1-8-1.

Coach Wood's lack of success was not entirely his own making. Army officials did little to promote the Academy, its football program, and the value of an Army career during the 1930s. Additionally, there was a crackdown on height-weight regulations whereby no waivers were granted for overweight cadets. Consequently, entering cadets could be no taller than 6-foot-4 and weigh no more than 198 pounds. If you were six feet tall you could weigh no more than 176.

Another factor in the demise of Army football in 1939 and 1940 was the effect of the three-year ruling in which no cadet could play who had more than three years of varsity football experience. Previously, Army had held fast to its tradition that any upperclassman had the right to play for any Army team, regardless of previous experience. Thus, two

outstanding football players, Carl Hinkle, an All-America center at Vanderbilt, and John Guckeyson, an oustanding back at Maryland, both graduated from West Point in 1942, but were unable to play any football.

Coach Wood graduated from West Point in 1925. He earned twelve varsity letters during his four years at the Academy, four each in football, basketball, and baseball. He was considered one of the best punters in the East in football, and captained the Cadet basketball squad. Wood served as an assistant coach at Army from 1925 through 1928 and from 1932 through 1937, before being elevated to the head coaching position.

After watching Army's football fortunes slip further down the ladder in 1940, Brig. Gen. Robert L. Eichelberger, the new superintendent, decided something must be done. He quickly did it. Wood was out and Earl Blaik was in. With Blaik as head coach, Army began the most successful period in its illustrious football history.

The Army Rabble Rousers, Navy cheer-leaders, and mascots get together for a photograph prior to the start of the 1931 Army-Navy game at Yankee Stadium in New York City. Later the Army mule had more to kick about since the Cadets posted a 17-7 victory.

Army tackle Jack Price received first team All-America honors in 1930 and 1931. He served as captain of the 1931 football squad and earned three varsity letters in football at West Point.

Notre Dame back Marchy Schwartz attempts to go through the Army line in the first quarter of the 1931 game at Yankee Stadium. Schwartz was the lone Notre Dame threat, but his efforts were far from enough as the Cadets pounded out a 12-0 victory.

Coach Ralph Sasse guided the 1932 football squad at West Point to an 8-2 record, including a 20-0 victory over Navy. Ironically, all eight wins over Furman, Carleton, Yale, William & Mary, Harvard, North Dakota State, West Virginia, and Navy were by shutouts. The Cadets bowed to Pittsburgh 18-13 and to Notre Dame 21-0. The team captain was Milt Summefelt (holding ball) who earned All-America honors as a guard.

Notre Dame football coach Hunk Anderson chats with Lt. Garrison Davidson during the annual meeting of the American Football Coaches Association at the Pennsylvania Hotel in New York City on December 27, 1932. Davidson was attending the meeting after being named head football coach at the Academy, succeeding Ralph Sasse.

Milt Summerfelt, captain of the 1932 Army football team, gained first team All-America honors as a guard. Summerfelt lettered in football from 1930 to 1932.

Coach Gar Davidson was the twenty-first head football coach at the U.S. Military Academy. He coached four seasons at West Point, 1933 to 1937, compiling a record of thirty-five victories, just eleven defeats, and one tie. He also served as superintendent at West Point from 1956 to 1960.

Notre Dame defeated Army by a one-sided 21-0 margin in 1932 at Yankee Stadium. The Cadets provided an assist on this play, when Kenneth Fields was unable to hold a center pass in the Army end zone. Jim Harris (44) recovered the loose ball for a Notre Dame touchdown.

Harvey Jablonsky, captain of the 1933 Army football squad, was enshrined in the National Football Foundation Hall of Fame in 1978 for his play as a guard. Jablonsky lettered three years in football, 1931 to 1933.

Army team captain Harvey Jablonski, left, greets Notre Dame captain Hugh Devore at Yankee Stadium prior to the 1933 encounter. The Irish, trailing 12-0 going into the fourth quarter, scored twice during the final minutes to trim the Cadets 13-12. Notre Dame blocked an Army punt in the end zone and recovered for the winning touchdown.

Notre Dame quarterback Buddy Bonar converted a drop kick with seven minutes to play to lift them to a 13-12 victory over Army in 1933 at Yankee Stadium before more than eighty thousand fans. Nick Lukats scored the fourth-quarter touchdown to set the stage for Bonar's drop kick, which he made without a helmet. A Press Association, Inc. photograph.

Halfback Jack Buckler of Army was selected a first team All-America following the conclusion of the 1933 season. Buckler won three letters in football from 1932 to 1934.

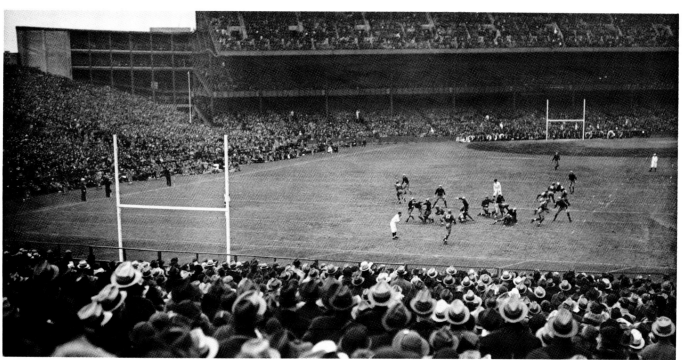

This International News photograph sets the scene of the Army-Notre Dame clash at Yankee Stadium in 1934. It was dark and dreary for football fans, but they were entertained with a spirited 12-6 Irish victory over the Cadets.

This is an aerial photograph of Franklin Field in Philadelphia during the 1934 Army-Navy Classic.

Army halfback Jack Buckler, left, gains three yards during play in the second quarter of the 1934 Army-Navy game at Franklin Field. Navy won the game 3-0 on Slade Cutter's field goal in the first quarter.

Navy back Fred "Buzz" Borries, left, gains some yardage while trying to go around the right end during the 1934 encounter against Army at Franklin Field in Philadelphia. Borries had to high step it through the mud. The Middies won 3-0 despite the weather.

Mud spattered Army players leave the field at the end of the first half of the 1934 Army-Navy Classic at Franklin Field.

Ed "Whitey" Grove, right, pulls in a pass from halfback Charles "Monk" Meyer and crosses the goal line for Army's only touchdown during the 1935 encounter against Notre Dame. The Cadets were forced to settle for a 6-6 tie against the Irish. Notre Dame's Bill Shakespeare attempts to make the tackle, but he is a bit too late.

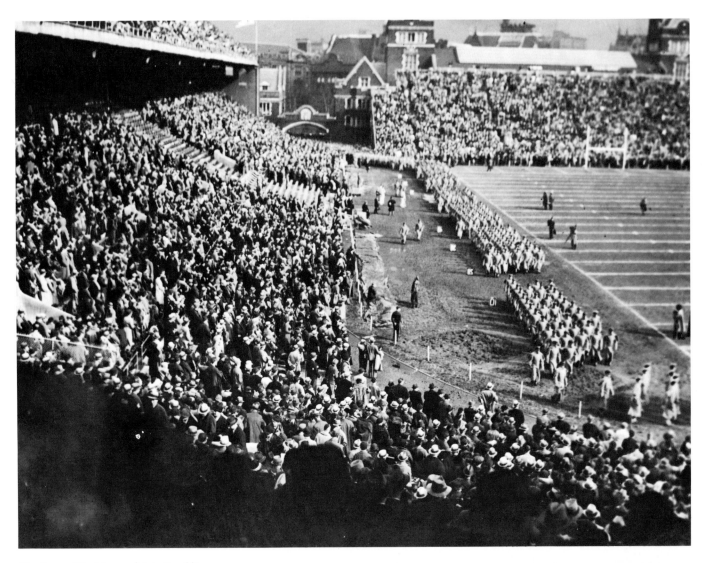

The Corps of Cadets march into Franklin Field in Philadelphia prior to the start of the 1935 Army-Navy clash.

Army built up a 28-0 lead in the 1935 encounter against Navy, but lost a shutout when the Middies fullback John Schmidt plunged over for a touchdown on the first play of the fourth quarter.

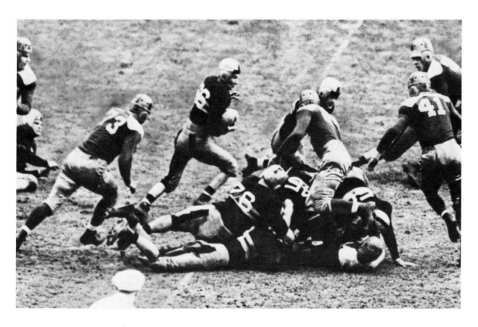

Army running back Charles "Monk" Meyer gains short yardage against Notre Dame during the 1936 encounter. Meyer returned a Notre Dame punt sixty yards for the Cadets' only touchdown during a 20-6 loss to the Irish. Meyer earned two letters in football while at West Point, despite his small stature (5-10, 145 pounds). Meyer also lettered three years in basketball and was team captain in 1937. He also lettered in lacrosse and distinguished himself as an officer in World War II, earning the Distinguished Service Cross, the Legion of Merit, two Silver Stars, the Bronze Star, and two Purple Hearts. He also served in Vietnam and attained the rank of brigadier general before retiring from the U.S. Army.

Andy Puplis (1) of Notre Dame makes a one-handed interception of an Army pass in the end zone during the 1936 game at Yankee Stadium.

Army and Notre Dame fans showed a variety of emotions during the 1936 encounter which was won by the Irish 20-7. There was concern exhibited by a female fan, and some dis-agreement shown by another fan, bottom.

Army's James Craig (12) is about to arc a pass to his teammate during the 1938 Notre Dame game in New York City. The Irish prevailed by a 20-6 margin.

Notre Dame's Ed Simonich tumbles over goal line, extreme right, to score the game's only touchdown during a 7-0 win over Army at Yankee Stadium in 1937. Simonich smashed through the middle and cut to the right to go into the end zone at rain-drenched Yankee Stadium.

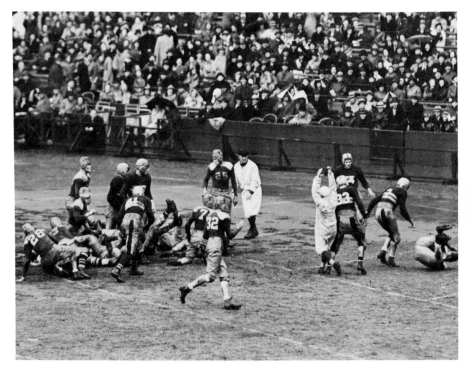

The Army-Navy Classic is more than just a football game for the Corps of Cadets and Brigade of Midshipmen. Here they join forces for some fun and frolic after the game, doing the ''Big Apple,'' the dance craze in 1937.

Army coach William Wood, right, is joined by team captain James Schwenk as the Cadets open football drills in 1938. Wood was making his debut as head football coach and guided the Black Knights to an 8-2 record during his first season. However, Army's football fortunes slipped dramatically in 1939 and 1940. The 1940 squad was 1-7-1 and Wood, a Class of 1925 West Point graduate, was replaced by Earl ''Red'' Blaik.

Traffic was heavy on Broad Street in Philadelphia in 1937 as fans make their way to Municipal Stadium for the Army-Navy Classic. The Bellevue Stratford Hotel, headquarters of the Naval Academy, is in the upper right corner of the photograph.

In this sequence photograph of the 1938
Army-Notre Dame football game in New York
City, the Cadets score their only touchdown.
Charles Long (2) looks for receiver (photo 1),
cocks his arm after spotting Riggs Sullivan
(27) heading toward the end zone and then
lets a pass fly (photo 3). Sullivan is wide open
and grabs Long's pass (photo 4), juggles it
(photo 5) before finally tucking the ball away
for the touchdown.

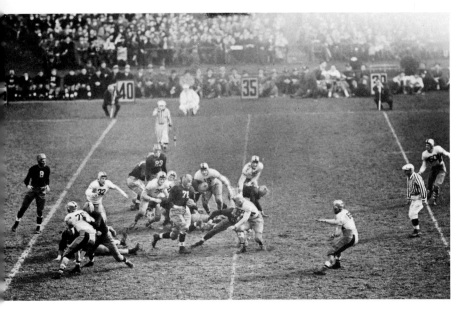

Big Milt Piepul (74) of Notre Dame breaks
through the Army line for a gain of twelve
yards during the 1938 encounter in New York
City. Piepul helped the Irish pin a 19-7 loss
on the Cadets.

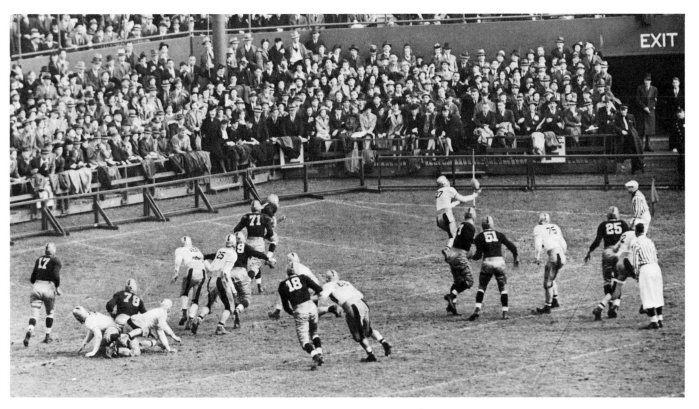

H. Riggs Sullivan (27) corrals a pass thrown
by Charles "Huey" Long (2) to account for
Army's only touchdown in a 19-7 defeat
against Notre Dame in 1938 at New York City.

Army's "do-or-die" effort was exhibited
during the 1938 encounter when Ben Bailey
(10) of the Cadets leaped to block a punt by
Ben Sheridan (12) of Notre Dame. Also in the
picture is Notre Dame's right halfback Louis
Zontini (23), while John Samuel (6) and
tackle James Lotozo (21) apply pressure for
Army.

Army's football team compiled a solid 8-2 record in 1938 under the guidance of Coach William Wood. Among those eight victories was a 19-7 decision over Princeton at the loser's field. In this photo a Princeton back is stopped on a kick return by an aggressive Army defense.

Connie Mack, owner of the Philadelphia Athletics, and Mrs. Mack enjoy a hot dog during the 1938 Army-Navy Classic in Philadelphia.

The Corps of Cadets complete their march-on at Municipal Stadium prior to the start of the 1938 Army-Navy Classic. A crowd of more than 102,000 attended in the bitter cold. Army won 14-7.

Four Army-Navy game fans, Kay Schneider, Barbara Rucker, Peg Sweeney, and Anne Rucker, are decked out for the bitter cold weather prior to the 1938 service academy clash at Philadelphia's Municipal Stadium.

Army tackle Harry Stella was named a first team All-America in 1939. Stella won three varsity letters in football at West Point and served as captain of the 1939 squad.

Navy fullback Wood breaks through to gain seven yards on a reverse during the 1938 Army-Navy Classic in Philadelphia. Army's Harry Stella (15) attempts to move in for tackle, but is warded off by a Navy lineman.

Running back Harry Steveson (32) bolts over for a Notre Dame touchdown in the second quarter of their clash with Army in 1939. The Irish prevailed 14-0 in this encounter.

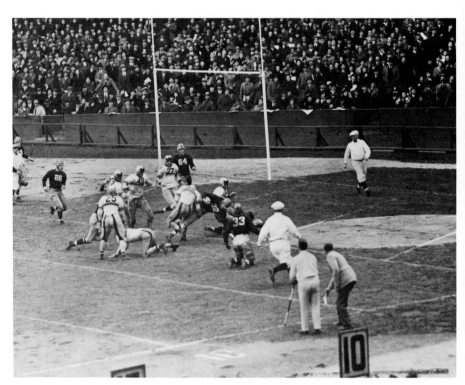

Workers at the Ben Franklin Hotel in Philadelphia hang bunting in preparation for influx of Army cadets, families, and fans attending the 1939 Army-Navy Classic.

Two members of the Bellevue Stratford Hotel staff, Lillian Crane and Margaret Harper, decorate a bouquet with Army-Navy pennants in preparation for the Army-Navy Classic festivities in 1939.

The Army-Navy Classic always attracts friendly bets from those men in uniform and the 1939 encounter was no exception. Here Harry Krieger, first class Navy signalman, Army Sergeant Bill Moran, Navy Chief Machinist's Mate A.H. Jones, Army Sergeant Selig Rosenbloom, and Navy Chief Bosun's Mate T.V. Robbins, agree to terms on one friendly wager.

Navy back Cliff Lenz picks up five yards during 1939 Army-Navy Classic at Philadelphia's Municipal Stadium which the Middies won 10-0. Army players whose numbers are visible are team captain Harry Stella (15) and end Carl Helmstetter (36).

Mr. and Mrs. Robert Frazier and daughter Ellen battle the elements, rain, and cold, while attending the 1939 Army-Navy Classic in which the Middies posted a 10-0 triumph.

*Army's Hank Mazur (89) rambles for twelve
yards against Notre Dame at Yankee Stadium
in 1940. Army tackle Paul O'Brien (7) is
following Mazur, while teammate John Harris
(46), a tackle, is in the middle of the line play.
The Irish prevailed 7-0.*

CHAPTER 8

BLAIK YEARS UNVEIL CHAMPIONSHIP GLORY

There has never been a more glorious period of nationwide success in Army football than occurred during the 1940s. The Cadet football squad simply was elevated from the pit to the pedestal by Earl Henry "Red" Blaik.

The Army football program fell to its lowest ebb in history during the 1940 season when the Cadets managed to win but one game, the season opener against Williams College, 20-19. Seven losses and one tie followed to the dismay of everyone at West Point.

Brig. Gen. Robert L. Eichelberger began his tenure as superintendent on November 18, 1940. He had just witnessed the University of Pennsylvania dismantle the Army team 48-0 at Franklin Field. On his first day of duty he called a meeting of the athletic council, a group that oversees the athletic program at the Academy. Brig. Gen. Eichelberger wanted a change in direction for the football program—an immediate change.

"I was impressed, Saturday, by the way the cadets cheered our team right to the end of that 48 to 0 beating by Pennsylvania," said Eichelberger in an account provided in Tim Cohane's *Gridiron Grenadiers*. "It looks as if we are developing the finest bunch of losers in the world. By the Gods, I believe the cadets deserve a football team which will teach them how to be good winners!"

The Academy selected graduate officers to serve in coaching positions at West Point for many years. It had been successful, but Eichelberger now felt that system was outmoded. He believed the Academy should seek the best football coach available, and his choice was Earl Blaik, who served so successfully as an assistant before accepting the head coaching position at Dartmouth College in 1934.

But Blaik was a civilian, having resigned from the Army in 1922. Consequently, selecting him as the new head coach would be a break in tradition. Eichelberger decided to offer Blaik the head coaching position nonetheless. He wrote a letter to Blaik shortly after the athletic council meeting, offering Blaik the position.

After receiving Eichelberger's letter, Red Blaik agreed to meet with the West Point superintendent prior to the Army-Navy game in 1940. Yet, he could not help ponder the difficult position in which he was now placed. Blaik had enjoyed seven happy and successful seasons at Dartmouth and had the confidence and support of Ernest M. Hopkins, president of Dartmouth College.

Blaik's success in leading the Big Green did not come easily. He demanded sacrifice, hard work, and some sweat and tears from everyone associated with the program. That included players, coaches, and all support personnel. There were no exceptions.

Blaik gathered his first Dartmouth team together for a team meeting early in 1934. "I'll be as successful as you men will allow me to be," he told the squad. "If there is anybody in this room who is not ready to do some strong sacrificing, I hope we've seen him for the last time tonight. Because we're going to bring home the bacon."

Blaik's coaching techniques demanded perfect physical condition and discipline. He was errorless in his judgement of individuals. His attention to detail was monumental, and primarily a key ingredient to his success.

An example of his success came in 1935 at Dartmouth. The Big Green had never won a football game in Yale Bowl in seventeen tries during a span of fifty-two years, but that November Dartmouth prevailed 14-6.

Blaik's success and his work ethic can be traced to his parents. His father, William D. Blaik, was from Glasgow, Scotland. He moved to Canada at the age of sixteen, and then to Detroit. There he met his future wife, Margaret Purcell, a Canadian by birth. The Blaiks had three children, Douglas, Earl, and Mabel.

The Blaiks moved to Dayton, Ohio and opened a hardware store. Earl Blaik attended Hawthorne elementary school and later Steele High School where he played football, basketball, and baseball. Following graduation he entered the University of Miami in Oxford, Ohio, where he blossomed as an athlete. He also met his future wife, Merle McDowell, and became interested in West Point.

His interest in the Academy was generated by a fraternity brother who had gone to West Point, only to be dismissed because of academic difficulties. However, his enthusiasm for the U.S. Military Academy and its challenge attracted Blaik, and he entered the Academy in June, 1918. While at West Point Blaik earned All-America notice in football, and also lettered in baseball and basketball. He received the Army Athletic Association trophy for service to athletics at graduation.

After being commissioned in 1920, Blaik served at Fort Riley, Kansas, and then at Fort Bliss in El Paso, Texas, with the Eighth Cavalry. He resigned in 1922 and returned to Dayton to work in real estate and contracting. He eventually joined businesses with his father.

Blaik's first taste of coaching came during the summer of 1926 when he journeyed to the University of Wisconsin to help coach the ends for his former coach at Miami, George Little. Later that fall, Biff Jones talked to Blaik about coaching at West Point. That came to pass when Blaik became a civilian assistant in 1927, holding that assignment through the 1933 season.

Blaik, now forty-three, faced perhaps the most difficult career decision of his life after discussing the head coaching offer at West Point with Gen. Eichelberger. He asked for more time to consider the proposal, and to confer with President Hopkins and his family. Leaving picturesque Hanover in the New Hampshire hills was far from an easy turn of events for Blaik.

Late in December Blaik again met with Eichelberger at the Ritz Carlton Hotel in New York. He had decided to return to West Point and contracts were agreed upon for both him and his assistants. Later that week, after the announcement that Blaik would take over as head coach, a press luncheon was held to introduce the new coach. Blaik was somewhat diffident during the luncheon.

Col. Charles Danielson, the adjutant general at the Academy, recalled Blaik's actions following his decision to return. "I have never seen a less happy man than Blaik was the morning after the signing," said Col. Danielson. "He was a man in a deep fog. All of us, simply by observation, realized how much of a wrench it was for him to leave Dartmouth."

Blaik's success at West Point began immediately. He took a team that had finished 1-7-1 and carved out a 5-3-1 mark in 1941. Captained by Ray Murphy, the Cadets opened with victories over The Citadel, VMI, Yale, and Columbia, and then played a scoreless tie against Notre Dame.

The Notre Dame squad was the first under Coach Frank Leahy and was led by quarterback Angelo Bertelli. However, the game was played under miserable, wet conditions at Yankee Stadium, and the two teams settled for the deadlock.

There was immediate euphoria at the Academy, but Blaik knew there would be a rough road ahead. He was correct. There was a slight letdown and the Cadets suffered two straight losses, bowing to Harvard in Cambridge 20-6, and to Penn in Philadelphia 14-7. Army rebounded to trip West Virginia 7-6, but then bowed to rival Navy 14-6 in

Philadelphia.

The Cadets were stung by crucial injuries as team captain Murphy and Robin Olds, two outstanding guards, were sidelined. Although Army suffered defeats, the margin against Penn was forty-one points less than the previous year. Additionally, Notre Dame had fielded one of its strongest teams, and the Cadets led Navy 6-0 at the half before going down to defeat.

Hank Mazur led the offensive attack that season, proving a solid runner and passer. Bob Evans was an outstanding linebacker for the Cadets, while Jim White was very strong at tackle.

Mazur helped set up Army's touchdown against rival Navy. It was a punt-reverse to Ralph Hill that set up the touchdown and Jim Watkins plunged over for the score. In the second half, Coach Swede Larson's Navy squad exhibited its power to post its third straight triumph over Army.

Coach Blaik's 1942 squad compiled a 6-3 record, led by team captain Hank Mazur. Once again the Cadets got off to a fast start, whipping Lafayette, Cornell, Columbia, and Harvard while allowing just fourteen points. However, Penn and Notre Dame dimmed the Cadet hopes. The Quakers shut out Army 19-0 in Philadelphia, while the Irish pinned a 13-0 loss on the Cadets.

Victories over Virginia Polytechnic Institute and Princeton followed, only to have the season end on somewhat of a low note with a 14-0 loss to Navy.

Although there were some concerns about de-emphasizing football following the bombing of Pearl Harbor by the Japanese and the United States' declaration of war, it did not occur. During World War I, football was more or less eliminated at West Point. But officials at the Academy felt this would be ridiculous now during World War II. Maj. Gen. Francis B. Wilby, who succeeded Gen. Eichelberger as superintendent at West Point, made those feelings known while testifying before the House Appropriations Committee. Athletics were important to the training of a soldier the superintendent told the committee. Consequently, athletics were not discontinued during the heat of World War II.

The site of the 1942 Army-Navy game was moved to Annapolis at the direction of President Franklin D. Roosevelt. Attendance was limited to the Brigade of Midshipmen, the Army team, newsmen, and West Point personnel required to support the football team, and residents within a 10-mile radius of the city of Annapolis. Thus a crowd of less than twelve thousand attended the encounter.

Navy won 14-0 as Joe Sullivan plunged over from the one for the first Middie score, and Hal Hamberg tossed a touchdown pass to Ben Martin for the final points. Despite the loss to Navy that ended the 1942 season, two Army players, Robin Olds and Frank Merritt, received first team All-America recognition. Olds and Merritt were both selected for their play as tackles.

Their selection for All-America recognition marked the start of a string of honors the Army football program would receive through 1949. Twenty-four times Army players would receive first team All-America recognition during that span, and Glenn Davis and Felix "Doc" Blanchard received the Heisman Trophy, symbolic of being selected as the top college football player in the nation. Blaik's teams won three consecutive national championships, 1944-1946, won the Lambert Trophy as the top football team in the East five times during the forties, and finished unbeaten three times, and unbeaten with a tie one other time. Army also put together a twenty-five-game winning streak from 1944 to 1946, a record that still stands. Army also recorded the longest undefeated streak, thirty-two games (including two ties) from 1944 to 1947.

During the war years colleges suspended the eligibility rule for freshmen. Consequently, Blaik's 1942 team benefited from this and established a solid foundation for the future. Plebes Doug Kenna, Ed Rafalko, Tom Lombardo, Dale Hall, Joe Stanowicz, and Bob St. Onge all saw action during the 1942 season and would play key roles when Army won its national championship in 1944.

Preparing for the 1943 season, Blaik and his offensive coach Andy Gustafson installed the T-formation. That put an end to the single wing attack Army had used under Blaik, and also opened up the offensive attack.

The biggest addition to the Army team in 1943 was Glenn Davis, a young halfback from LaVerne, California. Davis set all types of offensive records at Bonita High School, scoring 256 points during his senior year of football.

Red Blaik corresponded to Davis' parents, Mr. and Mrs. Ralph Davis, about an appointment to the U.S. Military Academy. Davis was interested, but he wanted his twin brother, Ralph, to join him. Consequently, the Davis brothers visited West Point in the spring of 1943, studied for the validating examination, and entered the Academy on July 1, 1943.

Glenn Davis ran into academic difficulties at West Point, and the Army coaching staff was concerned he would not pass mathematics. He received tutoring from Lt. Col. Francis Pohl, but still was found deficient. The Academic Board permitted Davis to re-enter the Academy as a "turnback," and this time he mastered the math courses and went on to be commissioned in 1947, a year after his brother Ralph completed his four-year tour at West Point.

Before failing his mathematics course, Davis gave West Point a preview of what was to come on the gridiron during his career.

The 1943 squad opened with shutout victories over Villanova 27-0, Colgate 42-0, Temple 51-0, and Columbia 52-0. Davis scored his first touchdown against Villanova on a four-yard run, tossed a touchdown pass to Carl Anderson in the victory over Colgate, and scampered eighty-two yards for a touchdown against Columbia. When Army rolled to its fifth straight victory, a 39-7 win over Yale, Davis helped by returning a kick seventy-five yards. His running also was a key factor as Army tied Pennsylvania 13-13 in Philadelphia.

Notre Dame provided the next challenge for Army. The Irish went into the game undefeated, having routed

Pittsburgh, Georgia Tech, Michigan, Wisconsin, Illinois, and one of Navy's best teams in history. Quarterback Angelo Bertelli led the way, but he would be unavailable for the Army game after being drafted into the service.

Notre Dame coach Frank Leahy inserted Johnny Lujack as Bertelli's replacement. Lujack responded dramatically by tossing two touchdown passes to lead the Irish to a 26-0 victory over Army. Davis ran well, but his fumbles proved costly, and kept the Cadets off the scoreboard.

Army rebounded with victories over Sampson, U.S.N., and Brown to raise their season mark to 7-1-1, and set the stage for the season finale against Navy. The 1943 encounter was played at West Point. Once again, attendance was limited and only 12,692 attended. After a scoreless first half, the Middies took command when Bob Jenkins ran for the first touchdown and Jim Pettit added another during a 13-0 win, marking the fifth straight year Army had bowed to their rivals from Annapolis.

As the 1944 football season approached, Army football followers were bullish on the prospects for Red Blaik's fourth West Point team. After all, the Cadets had excellent personnel returning, such as Glenn Davis, Doug Kenna, team captain Tom Lombardo, Ed Rafalko, Joe Stanowicz, and Bob St. Onge, to name just a few. The plebe prospect list also looked promising with tackle DeWitt Coulter, ends Barney Poole and Hank Foldberg, and quarterback Arnold Tucker, considered an excellent passer.

However, the best prospect of the lot was Felix "Doc" Blanchard, who was a punishing six feet and 210 pounds from Bishopville, South Carolina. Blanchard could run, block, and catch. He complemented the talents of Glenn Davis so well that they became the most fearsome running combination in Army history.

Blanchard attended Bishopville High School one year, getting his first taste of football. He was a substitute fullback at the outset, and learned the hard knocks of the game. In the summer of 1938, his father, Dr. Felix Blanchard, enrolled him at St. Stanislaus School in Bay Saint Louis, Mississippi. The elder Blanchard was keeping a promise to Brother Peter, an old friend that ran this boys school, who had guided him through his formative years at St. Stanislaus. Blanchard's father developed as an athlete while there, went to Tulane for three years, and then transferred to Wake Forest where he graduated. After considering a professional baseball career, the senior Blanchard returned to Tulane to earn a medical degree. Prior to receiving his degree, he married Mary Elizabeth Tatum, and the Blanchards settled in Bishopville to begin his medical practice.

Felix Blanchard Jr., was outstanding at St. Stanislaus, leading his football squad to an undefeated season during his senior year in 1941. He attracted the attention of some of the top football schools, Frank Leahy of Notre Dame, and Jim Crowley of Fordham, then a football power. However, North Carolina, Duke, and Tulane had the best chance of landing him because "Doc" wanted to go where his father could see him play.

Army and Notre Dame met for the twenty-seventh time at Yankee Stadium in New York City in 1940, with the Irish prevailing 7-0 on an eighty-one-yard interception return by Steve Juzwik. The pass thrown by Hank Mazur, far right, was intended for end Lou Smith, but Juzwik intercepted at the Notre Dame nineteen-yard line in the first quarter, and rambled for the game's only touchdown. Notre Dame players are in the dark jerseys.

Blanchard decided on North Carolina, but after completing his freshman year he tried to enlist in the Navy's V-12 program unit at North Carolina. He was turned down because he was considered overweight and had a vision problem.

Blanchard then enlisted in the Army, took basic training in Miami, and was assigned to the Army Air Force's ground school in Clovis, New Mexico. His father was working to obtain an appointment to West Point, and finally succeeded. The younger Blanchard studied for the validating exam at Lafayette College, passed it, and entered West Point on July 2, 1944.

Army's 1944 team was unbeatable and succeeded in becoming the first unbeaten and untied team at West Point since 1916. Glenn Davis and Doc Blanchard were instrumental, but the Cadets were solid throughout, and fielded two outstanding units.

Army began the 1944 season with a 46-0 victory over North Carolina. Brown fell 59-7 and Pittsburgh was a 69-7 victim. The Coast Guard Academy suffered a 76-0 loss, while Duke bowed to the Cadets 27-7 in New York City.

Blanchard demonstrated his future talents during the victory over Pittsburgh. He scored two touchdowns, one on a pass from Tom Lombardo. He also intercepted a pass and returned it twenty-one yards for a touchdown. He kicked off four times into the end zone and his only punt traveled forty-four yards. He also gained forty-five yards rushing on just four carries, and pulled in four pass receptions for another 108 yards.

Davis also proved instrumental in this win over Pitt. He gained 161 yards on nine carries, and completed two passes for 118 yards. He also scored a touchdown on a sixty-three-yard run.

Following the Duke game, which saw Army rally from a 7-6 halftime deficit to win, Coach Blaik's eleven thrashed Villanova 83-0 and then set sights on Notre Dame. It had been thirteen years since Army had defeated the Irish, and that is what was on the mind of Earl Blaik and his West Point squad. Notre Dame entered the Army clash with a loss to

Navy, but also claimed victories over Pittsburgh, Tulane, Dartmouth, Wisconsin, Illinois, Northwestern, Georgia Tech, and Great Lakes.

Notre Dame received the opening kickoff, but gained only two yards on their first series, and was forced to punt away. Army took over on the Irish forty-four and drove in for their first touchdown. It took fourteen plays with Doug Kenna capping it with a bootleg for the touchdown. Dick Walterhouse added the conversion for a 7-0 lead.

Notre Dame went to the air twenty times, completing ten of those for 102 yards. But Army picked off eight passes, setting up their second, third and fourth touchdowns. Kenna picked off an Irish pass and Max Minor scored on a twenty-five-yard run for the second Army touchdown. Kenna tossed a thirty-four-yard scoring pass to Ed Rafalko after a Blanchard interception. Then Davis intercepted a Notre Dame pass and later scored from the eight as the Cadets romped 59-0.

Following the one-sided victory over the Irish, Army prepared for Pennsylvania. The Cadets did not suffer a letdown and thrashed the Quakers 62-7, the worst defeat to a Pennsylvania team since Yale whipped them 60-0 in 1890.

Army opened the scoring when Max Minor scampered sixty-six yards for a touchdown. After Penn tied the score, Dale Hall rambled forty-five yards for a touchdown to give the Cadets the lead for good. Blanchard boosted the Army lead with an eight-yard touchdown run in the second quarter, and then Davis countered with a three-yard touchdown run. In the second half, Davis scored twice on runs of forty-five and eight yards, while Blanchard accounted for a second touchdown, taking a pass from Lombardo.

Army, now 8-0, prepared for the season finale against Navy. The Cadets were ranked No. 1 in the country, and the Middies were No. 2. Navy had lost to North Carolina Pre-Flight 21-14, and to Georgia Tech 17-14, but had rolled over Notre Dame, Penn, Purdue, Duke, Penn State, and Cornell. The game, originally scheduled for Thompson Stadium in Annapolis, was switched to Municipal Stadium in Baltimore and seventy thousand jammed in to see this service academy confrontation.

After a scoreless first quarter, Ug Fuson ignited the Army attack by intercepting a Navy pass. The Cadets drove to the Navy sixteen, but the drive stalled there. However, when the Middies were forced to punt moments later, Army launched a sixty-six-yard scoring drive.

Dale Hall, the captain of Army's record-breaking basketball team, scampered twenty-three yards for a touchdown after spelling Davis. Dick Walterhouse added the extra point for a 7-0 lead.

Army boosted its advantage to 9-0 early in the third quarter when Joe Stanowicz blocked a kick for a safety, but Navy was not about to call it quits. The Middies stormed back, driving seventy-two yards in sixteen plays to cut the margin. Fullback Clyde Scott plunged over from the two, and Vic Finos converted the extra point to make it 9-7.

Army failed to move after taking over on the ensuing kickoff as the third quarter came to an end, and Navy began to move once again after returning a punt to the Army forty-six. But just when it appeared that momentum had shifted to the Navy side, Glenn Davis picked off a pass by Bob Jenkins on the Army thirty-five and returned it to the forty-eight. Then Blanchard went to work.

The big Army fullback rambled around right end for twenty-five yards and a first down at the Middie thirty-two. Then it was Blanchard for three, Davis for three, and Blanchard for five and a first down at the twenty-one. Max Minor gained one yard, and then Army gave the ball to Blanchard three consecutive times for a first down on the ten. On the next play, Blanchard slashed off left guard and went into the end zone standing up for the touchdown. Walterhouse added the extra point for a 16-9 Army lead.

Blanchard had been the difference, carrying seven times for forty-eight yards and the touchdown during the critical fourth quarter drive. The Cadets put the finishing touches on the victory the next time they had the ball as Davis scampered fifty yards for the final touchdown. Walterhouse converted the extra point and the script read 23-7.

With Army's 1944 season now history, Coach Red Blaik's squad couldn't help but take a moment to bask in the glory. Hundreds of wires came into West Point, but none more cryptic than this one: "The greatest of all Army teams—stop—We have stopped the war to celebrate your magnificent success. MacArthur."

The 1944 Army team averaged fifty-six points per game. Davis averaged 11.1 yards per carry, a record. Walterhouse converted forty-seven extra point attempts, another record. Army won its first national championship, while first team All-America honors were accorded to Blanchard, Davis, guard Joe Stanowicz, guard John Green, quarterback Doug Kenna, and end Barney Poole.

Perhaps one of the most inspirational tributes to the 1944 team came from Coach Blaik. "Seldom in a lifetime's experience is one permitted the complete satisfaction of being part of a perfect performance. To the coaches, the 23-7

is enough. To the squad members, by hard work and sacrifice, you superbly combined ability, ambition, and the desire to win, thereby leaving a rich athletic heritage for future Academy squads. From her sons West Point expects the best—you were the best. In truth, you were a storybook team."

The Army squad was not about to end the story after the 1944 season. Coach Blaik made sure of that in preparing for the 1945 season. Graduation stripped Blaik of many key performers, but there was still a formidable nucleus remaining. All one had to do was tick off the names: Barney Poole, DeWitt "Tex" Coulter, team captain John Green, Herschel "Ug" Fuson, Art Gerometta, Al Nemetz, Hank Foldberg, Arnold Tucker, Glenn Davis, Doc Blanchard, and newcomer Thomas "Shorty" McWilliams.

With Tucker at quarterback Army blended its attack with the pass more often in 1945, whereas the 1944 squad relied mainly on the run. The backfield of Davis, Blanchard, McWilliams, and Tucker was undoubtedly one of the finest in West Point history. The Cadets scored sixty-one touchdowns, twenty-three of them on plays exceeding forty yards. The 1945 squad scored 412 points, 92 fewer than the previous year, but certainly not a true indication of their domination.

Blanchard and Davis played just 56 percent of the time in 1945, but caught enough attention from the news media that George Trevor of the New York Sun nicknamed them "Mr. Inside" (Doc Blanchard) and "Mr. Outside" (Glenn Davis).

Football was not the only sport in which Blanchard and Davis succeeded. Blanchard tossed the shotput for the track team. During the Army-Navy meet during his senior year Blanchard won the shotput event with a toss of 51 feet, 10¾ inches. Track coach Leo Novak said he had the potential to be an Olympic competitor if he put his effort into it. He also ran the one-hundred-yard dash in ten seconds flat, winning the event during the Cornell meet.

Likewise, Davis was successful in other sports while at West Point. He competed in basketball, track, and baseball, proving to be one of the finest athletes ever to attend the Military Academy. His exploits are well documented during his four-year career.

"Mr. Outside" played center field on the baseball team, possessing the arm, speed, and bat power to earn a spot in the major leagues. The Brooklyn Dodgers' Branch Rickey was interested in Davis and might have offered a contract if he had been available.

Davis also competed in track and basketball during the winter. He was an outstanding sprinter, and during his senior year at West Point set Eastern records outdoors in both the 100- and 220-yard dash events.

One of the most talked about accomplishments by Davis was his performance in the physical training test given by the physical education department at West Point. In the forties, it consisted of ten events, a vertical jump, a bar vault, a run and dodge course, a standing broad jump, a three-hundred-yard run, sit-ups, dips, a rope climb, chins, and a softball throw. The Academy record was 865 points out of a possible 1,000. Davis piled up 926½ points, registering

Army coach Bill Wood, center, is flanked by members of his Army football team on their arrival at Haverford Station en route to the Merion Country Club prior to the 1940 Army-Navy Classic in Philadelphia.

Fred Evans (23) of Notre Dame is shown just before Army's Ted Lutryzkowski throws him for a loss during this gridiron classic at Yankee Stadium.

Harry Smith, a souvenir vendor, shows his assortment of wares to youngsters in Philadelphia on the corner of Broad and Chestnut Streets prior to the 1940 Army-Navy Classic. Scenes like this continue although the prices are somewhat higher.

perfect 100 scores in four events.

The respective talents of Blanchard and Davis carried the 1945 squad to another perfect season and a second successive national championship. Coach Red Blaik's team opened the season by blanking Louisville, AAF 32-0, and Wake Forest 54-0, but then faced a tough Michigan team coached by Fritz Crisler.

Army opened the scoring against Michigan in the second quarter when Shorty McWilliams scampered six yards to finish a twelve-play, sixty-seven-yard drive. Army boosted the lead to 14-0 when Blanchard rambled sixty-eight yards the next time they gained possession.

Michigan could have folded its tent, but instead rallied to cut the margin in half 14-7, with a seventy-five-yard scoring march to start the second half. However, the pressure of stopping Blanchard and Davis was awesome and the Wolverines failed. Blanchard plunged one yard for the third Cadet touchdown and then Davis closed out the scoring with a sensational seventy-yard run to end Army's 28-7 victory.

Coach Blaik's squad slipped somewhat in registering its fourth and fifth victories over the Melville Naval School and Duke, allowing thirteen points in each of those encounters. However, Army's offensive show continued, piling up fifty-five points against Melville and forty-eight against Duke.

The Cadets then smashed Villanova 54-0 to set up another confrontation with Notre Dame. The Irish entered the game undefeated, following a 6-6 deadlock against a heavily favored Navy team the previous week. However, Notre Dame was no match for Army, although they played well during a 48-0 loss to the Cadets.

Once again, the Blanchard and Davis combination was too difficult to handle for the Irish. Davis ran twenty-seven yards for the first touchdown and pulled in a scoring pass from Arnold Tucker for the second TD. Blanchard accounted for the third Army touchdown by plunging over from the three. In the second half, Davis ran off tackle for twenty-one yards and a touchdown, while Blanchard picked off a Notre Dame pass and returned it thirty-four yards for another score. The Army second unit then added two more touchdowns to complete the scoring.

The second straight victory over a Notre Dame team did not diminish Army's intensity as they riddled a Pennsylvania eleven, 61-0. It was Penn's worst setback since 1888 when they bowed to Princeton, 63-0.

The only stumbling block that remained between Army and another perfect season was rival Navy. The Middies also were undefeated, but did not possess the power of Army's squad, even though they defeated Michigan 35-7, a margin greater than the Cadets' win over the Wolverines.

Blaik drove his squad relentlessly to prepare them for all eventualities in the Navy game. The hard work paid off. Army broke the game open in the first quarter by scoring three times. After the opening kickoff Blanchard capped a fifty-five-yard drive by plunging over from the two. Blanchard accounted for the second touchdown on a sixteen-yard scamper, breaking a tackle by Clyde Scott of Navy. Davis

notched the third touchdown by slipping off tackle and rambling forty-nine yards to the end zone.

Navy cut the margin to 21-7 before the end of the first half, but Blanchard halted any thoughts of an upset early in the third quarter. He intercepted a Navy pass and ran it back fifty-two yards for the fourth touchdown. After Navy worked hard to notch a second touchdown, cutting the Army lead to 26-13, Davis closed out the scoring by breaking loose on a thirty-three-yard touchdown run for the final 32-13 margin. It was his eighteenth touchdown of the season, while Blanchard accounted for nineteen touchdowns.

Once again, the 1945 squad was a unanimous national champion. Blanchard won the Heisman Trophy, the Maxwell Cup, and the Walter Camp Trophy as the outstanding college football player in the nation. Blanchard also became the first football player to ever win the Sullivan Award as the outstanding amateur athlete in America. Davis was second in the Heisman voting. Both earned All-America honors, along with tackle DeWitt Coulter, guard John Green, end Hank Foldberg, and tackle Al Nemetz.

The only disappointment associated with the 1945 season came when West Point turned down a bid to play in the Rose Bowl.

The 1946 Army squad faced another difficult challenge, despite the fact that Blanchard, Davis, and quarterback Tucker were back in the fold. The line suffered heavily through graduation and resignations. John Green and Al Nemetz graduated and Tex Coulter fell victim to mathematics, and was forced to resign. Additionally, the backfield was sapped of its depth when Shorty McWilliams resigned amidst a great deal of controversy to return to Mississippi State.

McWilliams' resignation brought charges by West Point officials and countercharges by Mississippi State officials. Maj. Gen. Maxwell Taylor, superintendent at the Academy, claimed McWilliams was offered a large sum of money to resign. Coach Allyn McKeen of Mississippi State claimed McWilliams was denied the right to resign on two occasions because of his football ability.

McWilliams had played one year at Mississippi State, 1944, before entering the Military Academy. However, following his summer leave in 1946, McWilliams vacillated between staying at the Academy or returning to Mississippi State.

Finally, on September 2, 1946, McWilliams was dropped from the squad after the War Department accepted his resignation. Despite the controversy, Red Blaik said little publicly about the incident. He did speak with McWilliams and his parents during the summer regarding his intentions to leave the Academy. When McWilliams resigned in September, Blaik made this statement: "McWilliams has been an exemplary cadet and it is regrettable that this young man has become so hopelessly involved."

With the McWilliams controversy now over, Red Blaik and his staff went about the business of preparing for the 1946 season, knowing full well the challenges they faced. The Army staff would have to deal with Oklahoma,

Two football fans decide on the final decorative touch before making their way to Municipal Stadium in Philadelphia for the 1940 Army-Navy Classic.

Michigan, Notre Dame, and Navy, to name just a few. But those challenges became even greater following the season opener against Villanova.

A sellout crowd of over sixteen thousand journeyed to Michie Stadium for the Army-Villanova season opener. The Cadets took an early 14-0 lead, converting two Wildcat fumbles into scores. Blanchard notched the first touchdown on a ten-yard run, and then Davis scampered three yards later in the period for another touchdown.

Later in the opening quarter, Army appeared to be moving toward a third touchdown. Blanchard broke loose and scampered to the Villanova fifteen, brushing aside a tackle by Sylvio Yanelli, Villanova's center. However, that slowed Blanchard down and he was hit from behind by end Francis Kane. Blanchard's knee buckled and he fumbled the ball. He had suffered a torn ligament in his knee. Such an injury would have sidelined most players for the season, but Blanchard's leg strength enabled him to return to the lineup, although he was never again 100 percent.

Oklahoma provided Army's next test at Michie Stadium. Blaik had decided he would not use Blanchard against the Sooners, but had him dressed-out to keep Oklahoma wondering. Another sellout crowd, which included President Harry Truman (the first chief executive to attend a game at Michie Stadium), watched the Sooners take a 7-0 lead by recovering a blocked punt in the end zone.

Oklahoma nursed that advantage through most of the first half, before Army quarterback Arnold Tucker guided the Cadets on a six-play, sixty-one-yard scoring march to tie the score. Tucker hooked up with Hank Foldberg on a four-yard touchdown pass to tie matters up.

Early in the third quarter, Barney Poole blocked an Oklahoma punt and the Cadets recovered on the Sooners' fifteen. Tucker hit Davis with a nine-yard pass and moments later Ug Fuson plunged over from the one to give Army the lead for good.

Tucker also played well on defense. When Oklahoma threatened to tie the score, it was a Tucker interception that ended the drive. Then the Army quarterback picked off a fumble in mid-air and returned it eighty-six yards for the final touchdown in a 21-7 victory.

The Cadets posted their third straight victory over Cornell 46-21, and then traveled to Ann Arbor, Michigan, to meet the Wolverines. Army was ranked No. 2 in the country behind Notre Dame, while Michigan was No. 4. Eighty-eight thousand people flocked into Michigan Stadium for the encounter.

The partisan crowd had much to cheer about as the Wolverines jumped out in front quickly. Michigan drove forty-one yards for the first touchdown, capped by a scoring pass from Bob Chappuis to Howard Yerges.

Although injured, Blanchard still tried to play, but was kept at bay. The Cadets also suffered another injury when Tucker suffered a shoulder separation after being forced out of bounds on a punt return. He still stayed in the game, throwing short passes.

It was Davis who took up the slack and saved the day for Army. Late in the first quarter, Army took over on its own

Three Army supporters show their allegiance at the Ben Franklin Hotel in Philadelphia during the festivities for the 1940 Army-Navy Classic.

nineteen after a punt. Runs by Rip Rowan and Tucker gave the Cadets a first down at the forty-one. Then Davis broke loose and rambled fifty-nine yards for a touchdown to tie the score 7-7.

Late in the second quarter Davis set up Army's second touchdown, firing a forty-four-yard pass to Blanchard for a first down on the Michigan twenty-three. The Cadets moved backward, and faced a fourth down on the thirty-one. Tucker called for a Davis pass, but the Michigan line broke through and the ball got away from Davis. A Michigan lineman attempted to pick it up but missed, giving Davis another opportunity. He grabbed it and fired a pass into the end zone, hitting Bob Folsom for the touchdown, and a 13-7 halftime lead.

The Wolverines stormed back and marched eighty-three yards after the second half kickoff for a touchdown. Paul White scored on a reverse from six yards out, but Army's Shelton Biles blocked the conversion attempt to keep the score tied, 13-13.

Late in the fourth quarter Army drove in for the winning touchdown, marching seventy-six yards for the score. Davis tossed a twenty-four-yard pass to Blanchard to key the drive. Faced with a fourth down and two, Tucker fired a seven-yard pass to Foldberg for a first down at the eighteen. Davis gained three, and then Blanchard took a pitch from Tucker and rambled eight yards to the Michigan seven. On the next play, Tucker gave Blanchard the ball again, and he broke through for the touchdown. Army preserved the advantage to record a 20-13 win.

Army whipped Columbia handily, but had to work hard to shut out Duke and West Virginia by identical 19-0 scores, to raise their record to 7-0. Now they faced the challenge of top-ranked Notre Dame in New York City. The buildup for this matchup was as intense as the 1944 Army-Navy game. The Cadets were placing a twenty-five-game winning streak on the line *and* their national championship.

Frank Leahy's Notre Dame team was looking for revenge after suffering through two consecutive one-sided losses to the Cadets. His squad stayed at the Bear Mountain Inn and some of his players toured the Academy grounds.

There were even predictions by both coaches, waxing any psychological advantage. "Army will defeat Notre Dame, four touchdowns to two," said Leahy. Blaik countered, "With the preparation that has gone into this one game, there is no excuse for his (Leahy) not winning it. But I'm not conceding he will win it."

However, the game did not live up to its billing as a potential high scoring affair. The two football powers struggled to a scoreless deadlock. Notre Dame drove eighty-three yards in the second period to the Army four, but were thrown back. Johnny Lujack was smothered on a quarterback sneak, and Bill Gompers was stopped on a sweep around right end. Notre Dame managed to get past midfield only on two other occasions during the game.

Army missed a scoring opportunity when Gobel Bryant recovered a Notre Dame fumble on the Irish twenty-four in the first quarter. Tucker tossed a six-yard pass to Davis, but Blanchard was stopped on two cracks and the ball went over.

Late in the third quarter Blanchard broke loose on a thirty-one-yard run to the Notre Dame thirty-seven. Tucker fired a pass to Foldberg for a first down on the Irish twenty, but Notre Dame's Terry Brennan intercepted Tucker's next pass to end the drive.

The day ended with both teams disappointed, but still undefeated. It marked the first time that Blanchard and Davis had been stopped, but the Army defense distinguished itself by stopping a Notre Dame attack that had crushed everyone in its path.

Army rebounded with a 34-7 victory over Penn to raise their record to 8-0-1, but then faced another tough challenge from rival Navy.

The Cadets were heavily favored against the Middies, who had won just one game that season. However, Blaik knew how difficult Navy would be in this game. Once again, he was right.

Municipal Stadium in Philadelphia was filled to capacity with 104,000, primarily to watch the final Blanchard and Davis show. Surprisingly they would also see one of the grittiest performances ever by an underdog Navy squad.

Army opened quickly with a 7-0 lead. Tucker passed to Davis for a thirty-yard gain. Moments later "Mr. Outside" broke loose for a fourteen-yard touchdown run, and Jack Ray converted the extra point. Those conversions proved crucial in the outcome.

Navy fought back to score, but missed the extra point. Army retaliated as Blanchard broke through the middle of the line and raced fifty-three yards for the second touchdown. Ray added the extra point to boost Army's lead to 14-6.

Army added its third touchdown when Davis fired a twenty-seven-yard scoring pass to Blanchard and Ray added the extra point for a 21-6 halftime advantage.

In the second half, the underdog Navy team caught fire. Defensively, they stopped Blanchard and Davis. Navy drove seventy-eight yards for a touchdown with Bill Hawkins going over from the two. The Middies missed the extra point and trailed 21-12.

Early in the fourth quarter, Navy stopped Army and drove in for another touchdown. This time quarterback Reaves Baysinger tossed a two-yard scoring pass to Leon Bramlett, but Hawkins missed the conversion, leaving the Navy three points shy, 21-18.

However, the Middies had gained the momentum. With 7:30 to play in the game, Coach Tom Hamilton's Middies began a drive from their own thirty-three-yard line. The Middies, with Pete Williams passing and running, and fullback Lynn Chewning piling up more yards, moved to the Army twenty-four. The Cadets stiffened, and Navy was faced with a fourth down. Chewning took the ball, circled around right end, and rambled twenty yards to the three and a first down.

Just 1:30 remained on the clock when Chewning went up the middle, but Goble Bryant and Hank Foldberg stopped him for no gain. Chewning tried again, but Barney Poole stopped him without giving up an inch of turf. Navy then was penalized five yards for delay of game by taking a fifth

time out, thus pushing them back to the eight.

On third down, Bill Hawkins took the snap from center, faked a buck up the middle, and then lateraled to halfback Pete Williams. Williams skirted around the left flank for a gain of four yards before Barney Poole dragged him down. Only seven seconds remained on the clock. Coach Hamilton sent in a substitute to try to stop the clock, but the officials did not see the substitute and time ran out on the Navy.

Thus the Blanchard-Davis era ended on a high note, a hard fought 21-18 victory over Navy. The Cadets again won a national championship, while Davis captured the Heisman Trophy. Blanchard and Davis both were accorded first team All-America recognition for the third straight year, while teammates Arnold Tucker and Hank Foldberg joined them as first team All-America selections. Tucker also was the recipient of the Sullivan Award as the outstanding amateur athlete of the year, while Red Blaik was acclaimed "Coach of the Year" in an annual poll of college football coaches by the New York *World-Telegram*.

Blanchard, Davis, and Poole requested a four-month furlough following graduation in order to play professional football, but the War Department turned down the request. The Detroit Lions of the National Football League selected Davis, while the Pittsburgh Steelers claimed Blanchard. In the All-America Conference, the San Francisco 49ers claimed both Blanchard and Davis. Major league baseball also made tempting offers to Davis, with the Brooklyn Dodgers, New York Yankees, Cincinnati Reds, Philadelphia Phillies, and the Philadelphia Athletics expressing interest.

Blanchard and Davis were permitted to appear in a movie, "The Spirit of West Point," during their summer leave. Both earned twenty-five thousand dollars for their efforts, but not one Academy Award nomination. During the filming, Davis injured his knee, aggravated the injury in a charity football game, and was later forced to have an operation.

A new era was beginning in Army football, an era minus Blanchard and Davis. The "Mr. Outside" and "Mr. Inside" story is but a happy and unmatched memory. In 1947 there were new names and faces to carry the lead, such as backs Rip Rowen and Bobby Jack Stuart, Winfield Scott, and Rudy Cosentino. Tucker was gone, leaving Bill Gustafson as the most experienced returnee and Arnold Galiffa a promising prospect. Team captain Joe Steffy, Bryant, and Bill Yeoman played instrumental roles on the line, and were ably supported by Ben Davis, Phil Feir, Joe Henry, Frank Barnes, and Tom Bullock.

Army opened the 1947 season by struggling to a 13-0 victory over Villanova to keep their unbeaten string alive. The Cadets followed with a 47-0 win over Colorado, and then fought a heavily favored Illinois team to a scoreless deadlock. A 40-0 victory over V.P.I. followed before Army traveled to New York City to meet Columbia in front of a crowd of thirty-five thousand at Baker Field.

Army scored first, marching fifty-five yards for a touchdown, capped by a two-yard run by Galiffa. Jack Mackmull converted the extra point for a 7-0 lead. Army scored again in

Pancho, the Army mascot, seems to be keeping the peace between his handler, Jack Kelsey, left, and Navy cheerleader Neil Eastabrook before the start of the 1940 Army-Navy Classic.

the second quarter when Rowan smashed off the right guard from the one and Mackmull added the extra point for a 14-0 lead. Bill Gustafson's twenty-eight-yard run brought the ball to the Lions' one before Rowan took it in.

Columbia came to life behind the arm of quarterback Gene Rossides. On a sixty-nine-yard touchdown drive, Rossides had three completions, two of them going to end Bill Swiacki. Swiacki's second reception put the ball on the Army six where halfback Lou Kusserow took it in for the score moments later. Ventan Yablonski converted the first of three critical extra point attempts to cut the Army lead to 14-7.

Rowan got that touchdown back for the Cadets right before the end of the first half when he rambled eighty-four yards for a score. However, Mackmull missed the extra point, leaving the Cadets in front by a 20-7 margin.

After a scoreless third quarter, Columbia cut the lead again when Rossides tossed a twenty-eight-yard scoring pass to Swiacki in the end zone. Swiacki tried to pull the ball in with one hand, but he failed to hold onto it and it hit the ground. John Shelley, defending against Swiacki, grabbed the ball as the Columbia end tried to wrestle it away. As Swiacki twisted, the field judge raised his hands signifying a touchdown despite the protests from Army players. Yablonski kicked the extra point to leave the Lions trailing 20-14.

Later in the fourth quarter an Army drive was halted on the Columbia thirty-nine. The Lions rolled sixty-one yards in just six plays, five of them runs, to tie the score. A key play on the drive was a twisting reception by Swiacki on the Army four-yard line. Two plays later Kusserow went off left tackle for the touchdown, and Yablonski converted the extra point for a 21-20 lead.

That lead would stand and Army's string of unbeaten, untied games would end. Swiacki was the primary ingredient in the upset, pulling in nine receptions for 148 yards. Rossides was far from a slouch either, completing eighteen of twenty-seven for 239 yards and one touchdown.

Army rebounded to thrash Washington & Lee 65-13, and then traveled to South Bend, Indiana, to meet Notre Dame. It would be the last meeting between these two intersectional rivals until 1958, Blaik's final season at West Point.

The Irish got off the mark quickly when Terry Brennan took the opening kickoff and raced ninety-seven yards for a touchdown. Later in the opening quarter, Brennan plunged three yards for a touchdown to put the finishing touches on an eighty-yard march to boost the lead to 13-0. That is the way it remained until halftime.

Notre Dame scored two more times in the second half, while Army put together a fifty-five-yard scoring march, capped by Rowan's one-yard plunge.

Army traveled to Franklin Field the following week and battled a favored Pennsylvania team to a 7-7 deadlock. The Cadets began a seventy-eight-yard scoring march during the final minute of the first quarter, scoring early in the second period when Stuart ran ten yards for the touchdown.

Penn came right back after the kickoff to drive sixty-eight yards in ten plays for the tying points. Ray Dooney, a powerful fullback took it in from the three for the touchdown. That was all the scoring in this encounter as the Cadet defense managed to keep the Quakers off the scoreboard.

Army put the finishing touches on the 1947 season with 21-0 victory over a Navy team that had played a murderous schedule. Rip Rowan enjoyed one of the finest days of his Army career. He carried eighteen times for 148 yards, including a ninety-two-yard touchdown scamper in the second quarter. He also accounted for the first Army touchdown by tossing an eighteen-yard strike to Bill Kellum in the first quarter. The Cadets closed out the scoring when John Trent picked off a Navy pass and returned it eighteen yards for a touchdown in the third quarter.

Cadet Henry Barker of Cambridge, Maryland, finds himself in good company with Mary Jane Daniell, left, and Jean Hughes, both of Lynchburg, Virginia, prior to the start of the 1940 Army-Navy Classic.

While Army finished with a 5-2-2 record, team captain Joe Steffy won first team All-America honors at guard and also received the Outland Trophy as the "Outstanding Lineman" in the nation.

Coach Earl Blaik completed another page in his illustrious coaching story at West Point, although he would lose one of his most valued assistant coaches prior to the start of spring practice in 1948. Herman Hickman, the mammoth line coach from Tennessee, left to become head coach at Yale. Shortly after the announcement of Hickman's appointment, Blaik saw his trusted offensive assistant, Andy Gustafson, named head coach at the University of Miami in Florida.

Two other Blaik assistants, end coach Stu Holcomb and assistant line coach Bob Woodruff, accepted head coaching jobs at Purdue and Baylor, respectively. It is obvious Red Blaik not only was an outstanding teacher and leader of young men, but was an important influence on his assistant coaches, an influence valued throughout the country.

The 1948 football season proved to be another Blaik masterpiece as the Cadets compiled an 8-0-1 record under the direction of team captain Bill Yeoman. Arnold Galiffa continued to improve as a quarterback, while Bobby Stuart reached his peak as a back, and gained first team All-America honors. Guard Joe Henry also played an instrumental role and received first team All-America recognition.

Galiffa, one of West Point's finest athletes, completed 44 of 95 passes for 701 yards during the 1948 season. Five of those passes went for touchdowns.

The Cadets opened the season by blanking Villanova, 28-0, and then reeled off consecutive victories over Lafayette, Illinois, Harvard, Cornell, V.P.I., Stanford, and Pennsylvania. Only Navy stood in the way of another perfect effort.

Army was ranked third in the nation heading into the season finale, and was favored by three touchdowns. However, the Cadets found themselves in the midst of a struggle, and then fought for their lives just to save pride and a 21-21 deadlock.

The underdog Middies opened the scoring when Slats Baysinger plunged over from the two in the first quarter, capping an eighty-eight-yard march. Army evened things up in the second quarter with a fifty-five-yard march with Harold Schultz going in from the six. A twenty-four-yard pass from Galiffa to Davis Parrish set up the touchdown.

Later in the quarter, the Cadets crossed the goal line again when Rudy Cosentino went over from the three and Bill Yeoman converted the extra point attempt for a 14-7 lead.

Navy tied the game early in the third quarter, driving eighty-three yards for a touchdown. Bill Hawkins accounted for the score, going over from the two. The extra point was made to give the Middies a tie.

Once again, Army retaliated to regain the lead when Galiffa broke loose for a ten-yard touchdown scamper. Yeoman made the extra point for a 21-14 advantage. Yet, Navy was not finished, as Hawkins spearheaded another drive to tie the game, taking it into the end zone himself. The Middies, losers of thirteen straight games, stopped another Army drive inside the Navy thirty during the final five minutes. Hawkins batted away a Galiffa pass to Parrish which appeared to be a sure touchdown. The Middies took over, began a drive of their own, but the clock ran out before they could score, and they settled for a tie.

Army ended the season ranked sixth in the nation and earned the Lambert Trophy as the East's best football team, but Navy held its head up high following that historic deadlock.

The 1949 Army football team ended the era of the forties in just the opposite way the decade began. In 1940, the Cadets struggled to win a single game. In 1949 they compiled a 9-0 record, the last Army team to go undefeated and untied. Coach Blaik's eleven was ranked fourth in the nation by the Associated Press and won the Lambert Trophy as the outstanding team in the East for the second straight year, and the fifth time during the forties.

Galiffa played a key role in the outstanding season. He completed 50 of 97 passes for 887 yards and 12 touchdowns. Only five of his passes were intercepted. He also gained 201 yards on 51 carries and scored four touchdowns. Named to five different All-America teams, Galiffa closed out his career with 119 completions for 1,926 yards. During the season he set an Army record for the longest pass play, hooking up with Jim Cain for an eighty-three-yard reception against Columbia.

During his four years at West Point, Galiffa won eleven varsity letters. He played first base on the Army baseball team and was captain and a starting forward on the basketball team. He was presented the Army Athletic Association Trophy prior to graduation, given to the cadet who has done the most for Army athletics. He was the "Most Valuable Player" on the football team, receiving the Hughes Trophy, and was the recipient of the Eber Simpson Memorial Trophy as captain of the basketball team.

The Cadets opened the 1949 season with one-sided victories over Davidson College 47-7, and Penn State 42-7. The Cadets then edged Michigan 21-7 in Ann Arbor before ninety-seven thousand mostly partisan fans.

Army opened the scoring with an eighty-nine-yard scoring drive, consuming ten plays. Galiffa completed all three of his passes, hitting Bill Kellum twice for gains of twenty and fifteen yards, and Dan Foldberg for eighteen yards. Frank Fischl then skirted left end for five yards and a touchdown.

Army boosted the lead to 14-0 when Jim Cain scored on a ten-yard run and Mackmull added the extra point. This touchdown was set up when Bruce Ackerson recovered a Michigan fumble on the fifteen and returned it to the Wolverine ten-yard line.

In the fourth quarter, Michigan cut the Army lead in half, taking advantage of a bad snap on a punting situation. However, the Cadets closed out the scoring later, thanks to a fine punt return by Schultz, putting the ball on the Michigan thirty. Vic Pollock raced twenty-three yards to the seven, and then Karl Kuckhahn took it the remainder of the way, and a 21-7 victory.

Coach Blaik's team maintained pressure during the next four encounters, blasting Harvard, Columbia, V.M.I., and Fordham, before meeting another tough Pennsylvania team at Franklin Field. This match-up would be the toughest for the Cadets.

Despite being heavily favored, Army found itself behind 6-0 in the second quarter. The Cadets battled back to take the lead on a sixteen-yard run by Cain and Mackmull added the extra point for a 7-6 lead. Midway through the third quarter, Army drove sixty-seven yards for another touchdown, with Floyd Stephenson plunging over from the two.

Penn came back during the final moments of the third quarter, driving seventy-eight yards for a touchdown to close the margin to 14-13. Then in the fourth period, with time running out, Penn moved to the Army five after recovering a fumble. Harold Loehlein helped preserve the Army lead by blocking a Penn field goal attempt.

Navy was the final hurdle for Army's undefeated season, and there would be no stopping the Cadets this time. Before a crowd of 102,000 at Municipal Stadium, the Cadets ran roughshod over the Middies in a 38-0 win. This was the largest margin of victory between these two rivals in the series up to that point.

Galiffa scored one touchdown and passed to Dan Foldberg for another. Stephenson scored three times on runs of eight, five, and thirty-five yards.

The perfect season was now history. It was also satisfying for another reason. Coach Earl Blaik's son Bobby earned a letter as a quarterback, and appeared to have the potential to play an important role in Army's success in the 1950s.

"After the 1946 season the press and college coaches agreed, that Army football had seen its day," said Blaik in recalling the success of the forties during a homecoming visit to West Point in 1977. "No longer would we have the success that came with the era of those legendary players Blanchard-Davis. But the record shows they underestimated the Cadets. West Point lost but two games in 1947, and during the span, 1944 through 1950—seven years—the Army lost three games and tied three out of 63 played."

Earl "Red" Blaik greets his offensive prospects after taking over as head football coach at West Point in 1941. Blaik, who was head coach at Dartmouth prior to accepting the Army coaching position, met his players in the Army Field House prior to the start of spring practice.

Coach Earl "Red" Blaik, the most successful head football coach in Army football history, is pictured at his desk beneath a photo of Gen. Douglas MacArthur, the man most responsible for developing the athletic program at the U.S. Military Academy to its prominence. Blaik left Dartmouth College to accept the head coaching position at West Point in 1941. He succeeded William Wood following a disastrous 1940 campaign when the Cadets posted a 1-7-1 record. During Blaik's first year at the helm, Army compiled a 5-3-1 record. Blaik recorded an overall record of 121 victories, just 33 defeats, and 10 ties during his tenure at West Point from 1941 to 1958.

Army coach Earl H. "Red" Blaik as photographed on the practice field at West Point. A similar portrait of Blaik was dedicated and is displayed in the Army 'A' Room at Michie Stadium.

Coach Red Blaik's first Army squad met Notre Dame in Yankee Stadium and, playing in dismal weather, fought to a scoreless deadlock that snapped a five-game losing streak against the Irish. In this photograph, a pass thrown by Notre Dame's Angelo Bertelli deep in Army territory is intercepted by the Cadets' Ralph Hill. Hill returned the interception a few yards before being tackled by Bernard Crimmins, an Irish guard. Notice the Notre Dame rooters who resorted to umbrellas while sitting on the bench.

The Corps of Cadets marches into Municipal Stadium prior to the start of the 1941 Army-Navy game. There was much enthusiasm by the Corps since this would be the first time a Coach Blaik Army team would meet their rivals from Annapolis.

The Army starting lineup poses for a photograph prior to departing West Point for Philadelphia and the 1941 Army-Navy Classic.

Navy's Howard Clark sweeps around right end for a gain of four yards against Army in the 1941 matchup at Municipal Stadium. Richard Opp (76) runs interference for Clark, while Army guard Raymond Murphy (69) is in hot pursuit. The Middies prevailed 14-6.

Four Army tacklers swarm around Navy's Howard Clark while stopping him for a short gain during the second period of the 1941 Army-Navy game in Philadelphia. In the foreground is Army back Theodore Lutrzykowski (38).

Army's Hank Mazur loops a pass to Ralph Hill for a gain of eighteen yards in the fourth quarter of the 1941 Army-Navy game. Other Army players identified are James Watkins (33), Robin Olds (75), Louis Seith (86), and James Kelleher (85). Despite this successful effort, Navy posted a 14-6 victory.

Coach Red Blaik is joined by team captain Hank Mazur in 1942, his second Army team. Mazur lettered three years in football at West Point, 1940-1942. The 1942 squad compiled a 6-3 record. Two players·from that team, tackles Frank Merritt and·Robin Olds, earned All-America honors.

Army and Notre Dame clashed for the twenty-ninth time in 1942 at Yankee Stadium, and the Irish had the upper hand by a 13-0 count. Notre Dame broke a scoreless deadlock in the third quarter when halfback Dick Creevy of Chicago scampered fifteen yards for the first touchdown. This photograph shows Creevy outdistancing the last Army pursuer to score. Notre Dame players in the photo are guard Bob McBride (47), back Russ Ashbaugh (55), team captain George Murphy (18), an end, and back Corwin Clatt (69). The Army players who can be identified are end Dean Crowell (82), back John Roberts (28), and back Ralph Hill (17).

With the United States at war, the 1942 Army-Navy game was played in Annapolis at Thompson Stadium. Less then twelve thousand attended the game, which was limited to residents of Annapolis and suburbs. The Navy Band is in the foreground. The Middies had much to cheer about later after posting a 14-0 victory.

Frank Merritt earned All-America recognition for two consecutive years while at the Academy as a tackle. Merritt earned those honors in 1942 and 1943. Two other teammates gained national recognition during Merritt's career. Robin Olds joined him as an All-America tackle in 1942, while Casimir Myslinski gained All-America honors in 1943 as a center. Marritt would later serve as an athletic director at the United States Air Force Academy.

The 1942 Army-Navy game was played in Annapolis for the first time since 1893. This photograph sets the scene as less than twelve thousand fans watch on the grounds of the Naval Academy.

Army kicks off to Navy at the start of the 1942 clash in Annapolis. Navy won this confrontation during the midst of World War II by a 14-0 margin.

Navy's Hillis Hume, right foreground, is piled up six inches short of the goal line during second quarter action of the 1942 Army-Navy game at Annapolis, Maryland. The ball popped loose, but the whistle ending play already had blown. Army players in on the action include John Hennessey (84), Willard Wilson (6), a guard, and center Casimir Myslinski.

Notre Dame head coach Frank Leahy congratulates Irish quarterback Angelo Bertelli after an early season game in 1943. Bertelli left Notre Dame to enter the service prior to the Army encounter.

Brig. Gen. Robin Olds, a 1943 graduate of West Point, lettered two years in football for the first two teams Earl "Red" Blaik had at the Academy. He earned All-America honors as a tackle on the 1942 squad that posted a 6-3 record, claiming victories over Lafayette, Cornell, Columbia, Harvard, V.P.I. and Princeton. Olds also was elected captain of the 1943 Army team, but elected to graduate early because of World War II, giving up his final year. Olds served thirty years in the service before retiring in 1973 at the rank of brigadier general. During World War II he served in the European Theater with the 479th Fighter Group, earning two Silver Stars, two Distinguished Flying Crosses, and eighteen Air Medals. He served in Vietnam as commander of the Eighth Tactical Fighter Wing from 1966 to 1967. While there he received the Distinguished Service Medal, four Distinguished Flying Crosses, two Silver Stars, the Air Force Medal, the Legion of Merit, and twenty Air Medals. He was Commandant of Cadets at the United States Air Force Academy from 1967 to 1970, and then was assigned as Director of Aerospace Safety until his retirement. Olds was named to the College Football Hall of Fame in 1985.

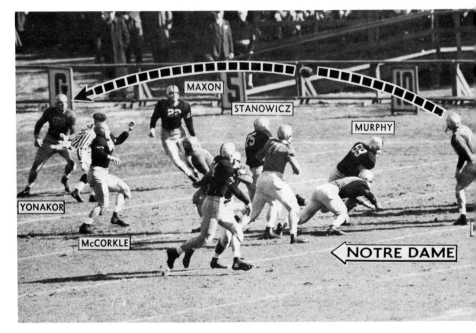

Army and Notre Dame met at Yankee Stadium in 1943, but it was Irish quarterback Johnny Lujack who spelled the difference by rolling up most of Notre Dame's 182 yards passing. Here Lujack connects with end John Yonaker for a gain of fourteen yards to the Army eleven-yard line in the first period. Lujack's performance led the Irish to a 26-0 victory. Other Army players in on the action included guard Al McCorkle, halfback George Maxon, tackle Joe Stanowicz, and tackle Ed Murphy.

Notre Dame end Johnny Yonakor grabs a John Lujack pass in the end zone for the first Irish touchdown during a 26-0 victory over Army in 1943 at Yankee Stadium. It was an auspicious debut for Lujack as he took over the quarterbacking chores from Notre Dame's Angelo Bertelli, who was called up to the Marines. Lujack piled up 176 yards passing during the victory. At left is Carl Anderson (42) of Army and Paul Limont (30) of Notre Dame.

Quarterback Johnny Lujack, left, clutches the ball tightly after scoring the third of Notre Dame's four touchdowns in the fourth quarter against Army in 1943 at Yankee Stadium. He scored on a quarterback sneak from the one-yard line. Army players who can be identified are Glenn Davis (34), George Maxon (22), and Tom Lombardo (10). Notre Dame players identified include Ed Krupa (33), and John Zilly (56).

Army running back Max Minor (41) picked up yardage against Navy during the 1943 game at Michie Stadium. Unfortunately, the Cadets were unable to cross the goal line in absorbing a 13-0 defeat. Navy's George Brown (82) and Bob Jenkins (18) pursue Minor on the play.

Army halfback Carl Anderson (42) finds a gaping hole in the Navy line during the 1943 encounter. Cadet guard Alfred McCorkle provides additional blocking assistance as the play develops. Unfortunately, Army was unable to capitalize on opportunities like this and Navy posted a 13-0 victory at Michie Stadium.

The Army-Navy game was played at Michie Stadium in 1943 and the Cadets proved to be generous hosts, bowing 13-0. Here Army end Ed Rafalko picks up yardage before being stopped by a Navy defender. Army end John Hennessy (84) is at right, along with Navy's Bill Crawley.

Army coach Earl "Red" Blaik is flanked by fullback Felix "Doc" Blanchard (35) and halfback Glenn Davis (41) prior to the 1946 Army-Navy game. Blanchard and Davis were co-captains of the 1946 squad.

George B. "Barney" Poole (89) played a key role for Army's national championship football teams in 1944, 1945, and 1946. He also started on the 1946 Cadet eleven that completed a 9-0-1 season. Poole gained All-America honors in 1944 as an end. He caught nine passes for 100 yards during the 1945 season and had thirteen receptions for 181 yards and three touchdowns in 1946.

Doug Kenna, who quarterbacked Army's national championship team in 1944 that posted a 9-0 record, was enshrined in the National Football Foundation Hall of Fame in 1984. Kenna, hampered by injuries throughout his career, nonetheless lettered in 1942 and 1944 under Coach Red Blaik. He earned All-America honors in 1944, guiding a team that averaged fifty-six points per game. Kenna was a guard on the Army basketball team which was nationally ranked in 1945, and which fashioned a twenty-seven-game winning streak from 1944 to 1945. During his four years at the Academy the Army hardwood squad won four straight games over the Midshipmen, and Kenna gained All-America honors as well during his last year. He also captained the tennis squad during his senior year, leading that team to an undefeated 14-0 mark. Following graduation in 1945, Kenna saw action in Europe during World War II before returning to West Point where he was an assistant football coach. He left the service in 1949 and began a successful business and professional career.

109

Glenn Davis (41) follows some key blocks en route to a sixty-four yard gain against Notre Dame in 1944 at Yankee Stadium. This sequence photograph by International News demonstrates how elusive Davis was during this most one-sided encounter. In the top photo, he takes a handoff from quarterback Tom Lombardo (10), the Army team captain, and breaks up the middle. He breaks through a hand tackle by John Glaab (64) of Notre Dame, and avoids an official in the second photo. At the bottom he breaks clear and looks for blocking help from end Hank Foldberg (81). At top right Davis sees Foldberg move in to take Steve Nemeth (20) of the Irish. Nemeth lunges, middle right, but fails to bring Davis down and the Army halfback breaks free.

Glenn Davis (41) breaks loose for another one of his patented runs against Notre Dame, avoiding an attempted tackle by Notre Dame's Joe Kelly (70) during the 1944 encounter. Stephen Toczylowski (33) and Martin Wendel (58) of the Irish are in pursuit. William Webb (76) of Army is trailing the play. Coach Red Blaik's Cadets trounced the Irish 59-0.

Army halfback John Minor gallops twenty-six yards for the Cadets' second touchdown during the 1944 clash with Notre Dame at Yankee Stadium. Minor took a handoff from quarterback Doug Kenna and sprinted off left tackle. The Army juggernaut prevailed by a 59-0 margin.

Army halfback Dale Hall (42) pulls in a pass from quarterback Doug Kenna in the first quarter of the 1944 Notre Dame clash at Yankee Stadium. Arthur Fitzgerald (56) of Notre Dame stops Hall on the Irish five-yard line. The Cadets went in to score following Hall's reception en route to a 59-0 victory. Bill Chandler (45) of Notre Dame is also in on the play.

A Dough Kenna pass intended for Glenn Davis (41) in the 1946 Army-Notre Dame clash is broken up by Bill Gompers. Army's All-America end Barney Pool (89) and Johnny Lujack (32) of Notre Dame watch the action.

After going twelve years without a victory over Notre Dame, Coach Red Blaik's fabulous 1944 Army eleven recorded its biggest victory in history over the Irish, winning 59-0 at Yankee Stadium. In this photograph, halfback John Minor (25) scored the Cadets' second touchdown in the first period. Army end Ed Rafalko (83) is about to throw a block on Notre Dame defensive back Bill Chandler (45).

Fullback Felix "Doc" Blanchard (35), Army's first Heisman Trophy winner, picks up yardage before being hauled down by a Navy defender during the 1944 skirmish. The Cadets took the measure of the Middies 23-7, snapping a five-game Navy winning streak in this annual gridiron clash.

Glenn Davis (41) and Felix "Doc" Blanchard (35) are photographed together in 1945. The two provided Army perhaps the finest backfield combination in West Point history, leading the Cadets to three national championships. Blanchard won the Heisman Trophy in 1945, while Davis won the same award a year later.

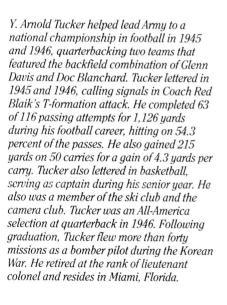

Y. Arnold Tucker helped lead Army to a national championship in football in 1945 and 1946, quarterbacking two teams that featured the backfield combination of Glenn Davis and Doc Blanchard. Tucker lettered in 1945 and 1946, calling signals in Coach Red Blaik's T-formation attack. He completed 63 of 116 passing attempts for 1,126 yards during his football career, hitting on 54.3 percent of the passes. He also gained 215 yards on 50 carries for a gain of 4.3 yards per carry. Tucker also lettered in basketball, serving as captain during his senior year. He also was a member of the ski club and the camera club. Tucker was an All-America selection at quarterback in 1946. Following graduation, Tucker flew more than forty missions as a bomber pilot during the Korean War. He retired at the rank of lieutenant colonel and resides in Miami, Florida.

John F. Green, a 1946 graduate of West Point, earned All-America honors in 1944 and 1945 for Army's football team. He lettered three years in football, 1943-1945, and was a virtual unanimous All-America selection as a guard in 1945, while serving as Army's team captain. Green, a native of Shelbyville, Kentucky, also competed in wrestling. He served as an assistant line coach at West Point for four years.

Army's backfield pauses during practice at Yankee Stadium prior to their clash with Notre Dame in 1945. The backfield includes, left to right, right halfback Tom "Shorty" McWilliams, quarterback Arnold Tucker, fullback Doc Blanchard, and left halfback Glenn Davis.

Tom Lombardo, nicknamed "Lombo" during his cadet days at West Point, won three letters in football, playing with the 1942, 1943, and 1944 squads under Coach Earl "Red" Blaik. A native of St. Louis, Missouri, Lombardo was elected captain of that Army football juggernaut in 1944, a team which won all nine of its games, the national championship, and the Lambert Trophy, symbol of Eastern football supremacy. Tom's ability as a football strategist was further reflected when Blaik chose him to be one of his assistant coaches in 1946 and 1947. Lombardo also played baseball for three years while at the Academy. He was killed in action during the early days of the Korean War.

Army halfback Glenn Davis, top left, pulls in a pass from quarterback Arnold Tucker (17) and romps thirty-one yards for the Cadets' second touchdown against Notre Dame in 1945. Other Army players are DeWitt Coulter (70), John Green (62), Herschel Fuson (22), Al Nemetz (75), and Felix "Doc" Blanchard (35). Notre Dame players in the photo include Fred Rovai (42), Dick Cronin (38), Bob Skoglund (18), and John Mastrangelo (75).

Army routed the Fighting Irish of Notre Dame 48-0 at Yankee Stadium in 1945 and this sequence photograph demonstrates why Coach Earl "Red" Blaik's crew was so successful. In photo one, top left, quarterback Arnold Tucker cocks his arm as Glenn Davis, with the ripped jersey, rounds right end into the clear. Bob Stuart (42), another Army back, takes a position to protect Tucker from Notre Dame's guard John Fallon in photo two. Photo three shows Davis taking Tucker's pass while spinning toward the goal line at the Irish twenty-five. In photo four, at top middle, Davis runs into his first opposition, Phillip Colella (20), but he uses a straight arm to avoid being tackled. In photo five, Davis is clear of Colella, but faces trouble from back Frank Ruggerio (40). The Army halfback reverses field to avoid Ruggerio's tackle, bottom. Davis heads for the goal line in photo seven, top right, with only one Notre Dame defender to beat, quarterback George Ratterman (9). But Barney Poole (89) of Army trailed Ratterman on the play and Davis cut behind Poole at just the right moment. Poole not only dumped Ratterman, but also Terry Brennan (37). Davis then went in for the score at bottom.

Army halfback Glenn Davis (41), scampers twenty-seven yards to score the Cadets' first touchdown during a 48-0 rout of Notre Dame at Yankee Stadium in 1945. The touchdown was set up when Art Gerometta recovered a Notre Dame fumble shortly after the kickoff on the Notre Dame thirty-one-yard line. Phil Colella (29) of Notre Dame makes a futile attempt to catch Davis.

Army's starting unit lines up for photographers prior to the 1945 Navy encounter at Municipal Stadium in Philadelphia. On the line are Hank Foldberg, Albert Nemetz, Arthur Gerometta, Herschel Fuson, team captain John Green, DeWitt Coulter, and Richard Pitzer. The backfield includes Robert Chabot, Arnold Tucker, Felix "Doc" Blanchard, and Glenn Davis. This lineup proved to be a formidable one as the Cadets trounced the Middies 32-13.

The Army-Navy game is considered the most important sporting event of the year at West Point and Annapolis. The tradition is boundless in this rivalry, and cadets and midshipmen alike all have their favorite "war" stories about the Army-Navy game weekend. For years, the Ben Franklin Hotel in Philadelphia was the official headquarters of the Army party. In this photo, chambermaids at the Ben Franklin prepare cots in the ballroom of the hotel for 225 cadets who will make use of them during the weekend. This work was done in preparation for the 1945 Army-Navy encounter.

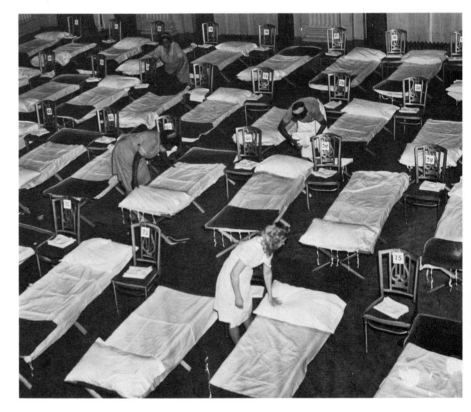

War was on the minds of American citizens in 1945, but Army and Navy still squared off in Philadelphia in their annual skirmish. In this photo, the Corps of Cadets leaves the playing field following the march-on prior to the start of the game.

During the 1945 Army-Navy game the Corps of Cadets enjoyed their version of getting Navy's goat. The football squad also got the Middies' goat by producing a 32-13 victory.

President Harry S. Truman, third row, second from left, attended the 1945 Army-Navy game in Philadelphia. At his right is his wife, Bess Truman, and daughter Margaret.

The Army mascots rest prior to the start of the 1945 Army-Navy game in Philadelphia. The mule riders enjoyed the action as the game progressed, since the Cadets defeated the Middies handily, 32-13.

Felix "Doc" Blanchard picks up eight yards from a kick formation during the 1945 Army-Navy clash. The Cadets prevailed in this game by a 32-13 count to complete their 1945 season with an unblemished 9-0 record, and a second straight national college football championship.

President Harry S. Truman, hand extended at center, changes sides during the 1945 Army-Navy football game in Philadelphia. At the President's immediate left is Gen. Maxwell Taylor, superintendent of the U.S. Military Academy.

Coach Earl "Red" Blaik taps Elwyn "Rip" Rowan, a running back from Memphis, Tennessee, on the head while talking to members of his 1946 football squad on the first day of practice at West Point.

Army's 1946 squad completed a 9-0-1 season to win another national championship. The Cadets played Notre Dame to a scoreless deadlock and trimmed rival Navy 21-18 in the season finale in Philadelphia. In this photo, Coach Earl "Red" Blaik chats with his two backfield stalwarts, Felix "Doc" Blanchard, center, and Glenn Davis, right, prior to a practice session before the Army-Columbia encounter.

Several cadets requisitioned some crosses from the Corps of Engineers at West Point to dedicate a mock cemetery for some members of the Notre Dame football team prior to their 1946 encounter at Yankee Stadium. The crosses include the names of the Notre Dame starters. Unfortunately, Army was unable to bury an equally tough Notre Dame eleven, and settled for a scoreless deadlock.

The Army-Notre Dame clash in 1946 not only pitted two of the finest teams in college football, but it also ignited a good deal of support from the Corps of Cadets during pre-game festivities. This barracks display at West Point was one of many during the week of the game in which the two gridiron powers played to a scoreless deadlock.

Plebes at the U.S. Military Academy fall-in at attention outside the barracks, which are covered with signs proclaiming the Army football team's superiority over Notre Dame prior to their 1946 clash at Yankee Stadium.

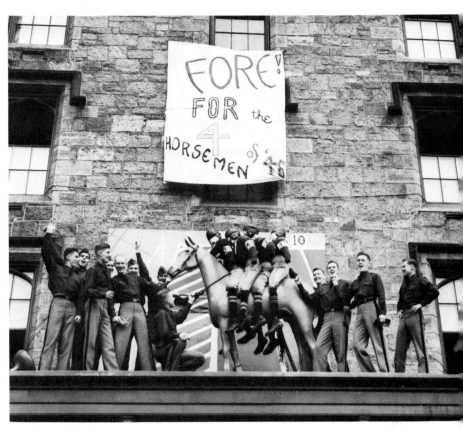

The Army football team received more solid support from the Corps of Cadets prior to their historic meeting with undefeated Notre Dame in New York's Yankee Stadium. This is the Army version of Notre Dame's famous "Four Horsemen."

Notre Dame's undefeated football team relaxed at Bear Mountain in 1946 prior to their clash with undefeated Army. From left to right are left end Paul Limont, right end Jack Zilly, right tackle George Sullivan, quarterback Johnny Lujack, left tackle George Connor, and left end Jim Martin.

Notre Dame coach Frank Leahy talks to six members of his squad during practice at the Bear Mountain prior to their 1946 encounter against Army at Yankee Stadium. Those squad members in the photo included center George Strohmeyer, quarterback Johnny Lujack, Coach Leahy, guard Bob McBride, right tackle Zigmont Czarobski, halfback Floyd Simmons, and halfback Terry Brennan.

Members of the Notre Dame football squad receive communion at Blessed Sacrament Chapel in Fort Montgomery on the eve of their 1946 encounter with Army. The Irish squad was housed at the Bear Mountain Inn. Rev. Charles McCarragher of Notre Dame gives communion to Frank Dancewicz, the team captain, Ed Fay, Bill Leonard, and Bill Walsh.

Members of Army's football team line up during a practice at Yankee Stadium prior to the 1946 encounter with undefeated Notre Dame. Members of that starting unit include Hank Foldberg, Bill Webb, Art Gerometta, Herschel Fuson, Shelton Biles, DeWitt Coulter, and Barney Poole. In the backfield are Dick Walterhouse, team captain Tom Lombardo, Felix "Doc" Blanchard, and Glenn Davis.

Army running back Herschel "Ug" Fuson, center, sidelined with an injury, watches his Army teammates work out at Yankee Stadium prior to the 1946 encounter against undefeated Notre Dame. Joining Fuson are teammates Elwyn "Rip" Rowan, left, and William West, who served as replacements for Fuson.

Here is a view of the pre-game ceremonies in 1946 at Yankee Stadium before Army and Notre Dame clashed for the thirty-third time. The Corps of Cadets are standing at attention while in formation. The Notre Dame team stretches and warms up at bottom left.

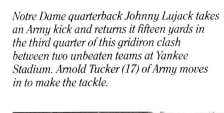

Notre Dame quarterback Johnny Lujack takes an Army kick and returns it fifteen yards in the third quarter of this gridiron clash between two unbeaten teams at Yankee Stadium. Arnold Tucker (17) of Army moves in to make the tackle.

Notre Dame's Bill Gompers is stopped at the Army three-yard line during the second quarter on a fourth and two situation as the Cadets thwarted the most serious scoring threat by the Irish in the second quarter in 1946. Hank Foldberg (81) of Army makes the stop.

Glenn Davis (41) of Army gains fifteen yards returning a Notre Dame kick before being stopped by an Irish defender. The two undefeated teams battled to a scoreless deadlock before a sellout crowd at New York's Yankee Stadium.

Notre Dame back Terry Brennan (37) is all alone waiting for quarterback Johnny Lujack's pass during the 1946 Army-Notre Dame clash at Yankee Stadium. Brennan gained ten yards on the play late in the third quarter of a game that ended in a scoreless tie between the two undefeated gridiron powers. Army players identified in the photograph are Shelton Biles (79), Art Gerometta, Jim Enos, Jim Rawers, Barney Poole, and Goble Bryant.

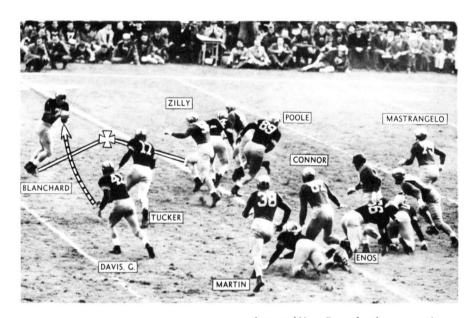

Army and Notre Dame fought to a scoreless deadlock in 1946 at Yankee Stadium and this play diagram demonstrates why both teams had difficulty moving the ball. In this play, Doc Blanchard (35) takes a lateral pass from halfback Glenn Davis (41), but shortly after catching the ball, Notre Dame end Jack Zilly (56) drops him for a two-yard loss. The Army quarterback is Arnold Tucker (17). End Barney Poole (89) appears to be going out for a pass, while Jim Enos (56) throws a block.

Army quarterback Arnold Tucker (17) breaks loose for short gain against Notre Dame in 1946. Tucker's passing arm and the running of Blanchard and Davis were not enough to topple the Irish.

Army's football machine was not as smooth running as Coach Blaik would have liked against Notre Dame in 1946. Here the Cadets fumble. It appears Martin (38) of Notre Dame is about to recover the ball, but Glenn Davis (41) beats him to it.

The scene at Yankee Stadium following the conclusion of the 1946 Army-Notre Dame encounter was one of pandemonium. Fans tore down the goal posts before exiting the stadium. The two teams fought to a scoreless deadlock.

This appears to be a picture from perhaps the ballet of football. Jim Rawers of Army (88) misses Arnold Tucker's pass in the second quarter against Notre Dame at Michie Stadium in 1946. Johnny Lujack and William Gompers, nearest camera, were ready to make the tackle if Rawers had made the catch. Army and Notre Dame tied 0-0 at Yankee Stadium.

Army co-captains Felix "Doc" Blanchard (35) and Glenn Davis (41) meet at the center of the field for the pre-game coin toss prior to the 1946 Army-Navy clash. The Cadets outlasted the Middies 21-18, marking the third successive victory for Army in this annual rivalry with Blanchard and Davis installed in the Army backfield. Coach Red Blaik guided Army to a 9-0-1 record in 1946 and was acclaimed "Coach of the Year."

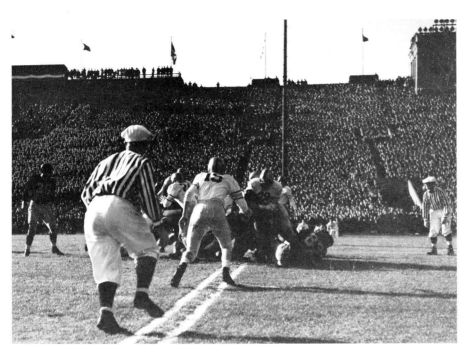

In 1946, Army and Navy met in what proved to be one of the classics of this service rivalry. In this photo of game action, Army is wearing the white jerseys.

The 1946 Army football team were, front row, left to right, Shelton Biles (64), Thomas Hayes (87), Jack Ray (63), Herschel Fuson (22), Glenn Davis (41), Felix "Doc" Blanchard (35), co-captain Arnold Tucker (17), co-captain Barney Poole (89), James Enos (56), and Harold Tavzel (74). Second row, Charles Galloway (60), Bobby Vinson (44), Milton Routt (68), Goble Bryant (73), Hank Foldberg (81), John Shelley (21), Joe Steffy (61), Art Gerometta (65), Joseph Green (28), and Rudolph Cosentino (34). Third row, Robert Lunn (60), Elwyn Rowan (24), Jack Gillette, Raymond Drury, Thomas Bullock, Alfred Anderson, John Burckart, James Irons, Jack Mackmull, and John Lindeman. Fourth row, Russell Dobelstein, Salvatore Fastuca, William West, Harvey Livesay, Frank Barnes, Bennie Davis, Harold Shultz, Philip Feir, and William Yeoman. Fifth row, equipment manager Rogers, William Gustafson, Charles Gabriel, John Trent, Arnold Galiffa, Bert Aton, James Rawers, Winfield Scott, R. W. Summerhays, Robert Means, and Brent Scowcroft, manager.

Army's football team, led by team captain Joe Steffy (61), emerges from the gymnasium at West Point to start fall drills in August of 1947. Coach Red Blaik's squad would go on to post a 5-2-2 record. Despite the so-so record for Army after dominating during the war years, Steffy earned All-America honors as a guard.

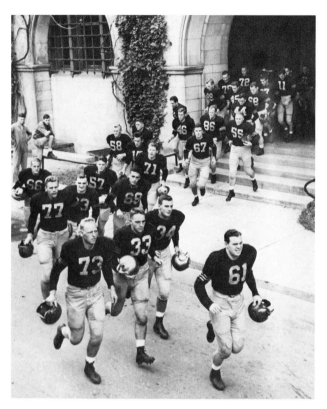

Members of the Army football team pose in the mess hall at West Point prior to departing for South Bend, Indiana, for their encounter with Notre Dame in 1947. Those seated include guard Joseph Henry of Clearfield, Pennsylvania, running back Elwyn Rowan of Memphis, Tennessee, guard Joseph Steffy of Chattanooga, Tennessee, tackle Goble Bryant of Dallas, Texas, and running back Robert Stuart of Shawnee, Oklahoma. Standing are back Charles Gabriel of Lincolnton, North Carolina, guard Charles Galloway of Bristol, Tennessee, guard Sal Fastuca of Pittsburgh, Pennsylvania, and running back Winfield Scott of Winchester, Virginia.

The Army mule runs rampant over the Fighting Irish of Notre Dame in this poster displayed at the Academy prior to the 1947 Army-Notre Dame game at South Bend, Indiana. Unfortunately, the Army squad came up short following its journey to the Notre Dame campus, bowing 27-7.

Notre Dame halfback Terry Brennan (37) skirts around left end for a gain against Army during the 1947 clash at South Bend.

Notre Dame snapped a three-game winless streak against Army in 1947, beating the Cadets 27-7 at South Bend, Indiana. In this photo, Bill Wightkin of the Irish throws a key block to spring ball carrier Larry Contre. This was the thirty-fourth meeting between the two teams and the first in South Bend since Army traveled to Chicago in 1930 to meet Notre Dame.

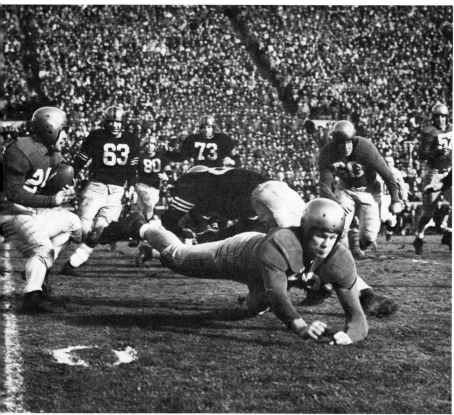

Army halfback Elwyn "Rip" Rowan plunges through a maze of players to score the Cadets' lone touchdown during a 27-7 loss to Notre Dame in South Bend in 1947. Number 60 is Notre Dame guard Bob Lunn.

Notre Dame tackle Ziggy Czarobski (76) chats with Army back Elwyn "Rip" Rowan (33) following the 1947 encounter between the two teams at South Bend. At left is Army center Tom Bullock.

Army coach Earl "Red" Blaik joins cadet
John Trent, captain of the 1949 Army football
team. The Cadets were 9-0 during the 1949
season and were ranked fourth in the nation
by the Associated Press. Army also thrashed
Navy by a 38-0 count. Trent was killed in
action during the Korean War.

John C. Trent, a 1950 graduate of the
Academy and captain of the undefeated 1949
Army team, was killed in action in Korea. He
was the second football captain to be killed in
the line of duty since the early days of World
War II. Thomas Lombardo, captain of the
national championship 1944 squad, also was
killed in the Korean War. Trent proved to be a
very versatile player for Coach Blaik,
performing equally well on offense and
defense. During the 1948 season, All-America
Dan Foldberg broke his collarbone in a game
against Stanford. Trent moved over from
defense to replace Foldberg and caught a
touchdown pass from Arnold Galiffa in the
last thirty seconds to lift Army to a victory
over Pennsylvania. Trent served as a Blaik
coaching assistant for a month prior to being
assigned to Korea. Trent was posthumously
awarded football's "Man of the Year" trophy
presented by the Football Writers Association
of America.

After a cheating scandal at West Point in 1951 destroyed the makings of a solid football team, Coach Blaik rebuilt Army's football squad, completing the turnaround in 1953 when the Cadets were 7-1-1. For his efforts Blaik was singled out as "Coach of the Year" by the Touchdown Club of Washington, D.C. The Cadets also were awarded the Lambert Trophy as the outstanding team in the East. In this photograph Army halfback Freddie Attaya (48) follows the blocking of Tommy Bell (46) to pick up yardage against Duke in a game played at the Polo Grounds in New York City. The Cadets edged the Blue Devils, 14-13. Army's only setback in 1953 was a 33-20 decision to Northwestern. They also played a scoreless tie against Tulane. Duke players identified are tackle W. D. Fesperman (50), guard Jim Logan (73), and Bob Pascal (30).

CHAPTER 9

HEARTBREAK AND COMEBACKS

During the fifties era the automotive industry brought us the submarine-shaped Studebaker, and the Indian Chief hood decoration on the Pontiac. The fifties provided us a Bobby Thompson home run that was heard round the world, propelling the New York Giants into the World Series against the Yankees, after knocking off the Brooklyn Dodgers in a playoff to determine the National League pennant. The victim of Thompson's shot into the upper deck of the Polo Grounds was Ralph Branca.

It was business as usual in 1951 for Charles Dillon "Casey" Stengel, who led the New York Yankees to their third consecutive World Series championship, whipping the Giants in six games, en route to a record five straight World Series triumphs. Stengel, who became the manager of the Bronx Bombers in 1949, led the Yanks to ten American League championships and seven World Series triumphs through 1960. It was a record perhaps as successful as Army's resident genius, Earl "Red" Blaik.

The year 1950 brought business as usual in the Army football program. Blaik demonstrated that Army would be successful on the gridiron after the departure of Blanchard and Davis during the national championship years, 1944-1946. And, the start of the fifties was anything but the exception.

The Cadets compiled an 8-1 record in 1950, losing a chance for another perfect season during a 14-2 upset loss to Navy. Although there were no soothsayers within earshot of the Army coach following the defeat, it certainly was a harbinger of Blaik's most tragic memory at West Point.

Months after the stunning upset to Navy, a total of ninety cadets were dismissed from the Academy for cheating. Among those were thirty-seven football players, including three All-America players, and a member of the Blaik family, son Bobby, who had lettered as a quarterback during the 1949 and 1950 seasons.

Not only was Red Blaik heartbroken because his son was one of those cadets dismissed, but he deeply felt the system was in error this time because of the loss of so many fine young men. After the decision was made on the expulsion of those ninety cadets, Blaik spoke of the incident to members of the press at Leone's Restaurant in New York City.

"These young men," said Blaik, "came to West Point as respected, honorable youngsters, many of them the idols of their communities. It would be considered an indictment of leadership at West Point, if after two or three years of Academy character building, they are returned branded in the eyes of the public as no better than common criminals."

In 1977, when Blaik was honored at the U.S. Military Academy with a special day at Michie Stadium and a dinner at the Hotel Thayer, the 1951 cheating scandal was the focus of a portion of his remarks.

"In 1951, the second best academy squad in Army football history departed," said Blaik in his address. "I would not be in character if I failed to add, the accomplishment of these men in civil life has justified my then known view that those misguided cadets were leaders and fundamentally men of good character.

"At that time of fixed opinion, had authority searched in depth for the truth, the problem would have been internally resolved and the Academy spared the travail of the past twenty years, climaxed by the plague of 1976.

"With the departure of the entire varsity squad, for the coaching staff, September, 1951, was a terribly distressing month. Perhaps a few lines from Tennyson's *Ulysses* will set the scene for those years in which the Army teams never stood more erect—1951-1958.

"Though much is taken—much abides
and though we are not that strength
which in old days moved earth and heaven—
"That which we are—we are—one equal temper of heroic
    hearts—made weak by time and fate, but strong in will.
"To strive—to seek—to find and not to yield!"

Blaik followed his own sage advice back then by following Tennyson's thoughtful verses. At first he seriously considered resigning as head football coach, and spoke of that possibility with Gen. Douglas MacArthur.

"Earl, you must stay on," said MacArthur. "Don't leave under fire."

Blaik followed MacArthur's advice and rebuilt the Army football program, reaching another pinnacle in 1958 when his Cadet team, led by Pete Dawkins, Bob Anderson, and "Lonely End" Bill Carpenter, completed an undefeated 8-0-1 season, and was ranked third in the nation. It also put the finishing touches on Blaik's illustrious coaching career at the Academy.

Yes, the fifties might be characterized as a Greek tragedy for Earl Blaik, but he nonetheless rose from the ashes to, once again, reach the pinnacle of success.

Earl Blaik's anguish over the expulsion of ninety cadets in 1951 is understandable. Thirty-seven of those young men were recruited by Blaik for their talents as athletes and students. One of them, his son Bob, was at West Point because of a strong personal desire to attend the Academy.

The bond between the senior Blaik and the younger Blaik was special, but also somewhat difficult. Bobby Blaik's success on the football field was based on sheer determination to succeed. He refused to allow his parents to attend his high school games at Highland Falls. Red Blaik only managed to capture glimpses of his son's games until he joined the Plebe football squad at West Point.

When Bob gained a spot on the varsity during his second year at West Point, the senior Blaik kept his distance. Red Blaik treated his son just like any other football player on the squad. When the quarterbacks met with the coaching staff, the senior Blaik would do the talking. The younger Blaik would ask questions.

The late Stanley Woodward, a sportswriter for the *Herald Tribune,* wrote an article on the Blaiks for the *Saturday Evening Post* in 1950. He called it "Football's Greatest Father and Son Act." In the article, which was reprinted in Gene Schoor's *The Army-Navy Game,* Woodward said Bobby Blaik was a far more outstanding hockey player than he was a football player, but he developed well enough to be considered a top prospect for the 1951 season.

Vince Lombardi, then an assistant backfield coach for Blaik, was responsible for Bobby Blaik's improvement at quarterback. "Bob doesn't make the same mistake twice," said Lombardi. "I regard him as an exceptionally intelligent football player. He knows the assignment of every man on every play. If any player, even a lineman, gets mixed up, Bob is capable of straightening him out. He took up golf during his leave last summer and I think it did him good. He was so tense last year (1949), he did not execute properly. On plays requiring that he hand off the ball, then fake a pass, he was so stiff and hurried that he didn't fool anyone. Golf taught him the value of proper relaxation. Now, when he fakes a pass, he carries it out just as if he had the ball."

Lombardi considered Bobby Blaik an excellent prospect, but that promising forecast would go unfulfilled because of an academic cheating scandal.

Looking back at the 1950 season Army rolled to eight straight triumphs, holding five of those opponents—Colgate, Harvard, Columbia, New Mexico, and Stanford—scoreless. The Cadets also defeated Penn State, 41-7, Michigan, 27-6, and Pennsylvania, 28-13.

Navy was the only hurdle left for the Cadets to complete their sixth unbeaten season in seven years. Army was considered one of the finest teams in the country in 1950, having won seventeen consecutive games. The Middies had lost six of eight previous games heading into the season finale.

The odds favored the Cadets, but the spirits favored the Middies. Consequently, another one of those sports miracles was recorded for posterity. Quarterback Bob Zastrow, a 209-pounder from Algoma, Wisconsin, ran seven yards for the first Navy touchdown early in the second quarter, and then fired a thirty-yard scoring strike to end Jim Baldinger right before the end of the first half. The Middies won a 14-2 triumph before a capacity crowd of over 100,000 at Municipal Stadium in Philadelphia.

The Navy defense was invincible in the second half, particularly in the fourth quarter when they turned back the Cadets three times inside the Middie twenty-yard line to preserve the victory.

Despite the loss in the season finale, the Army team was ranked second in the nation by the Associated Press and fifth in the country by United Press International. Additionally, four Army players earned first team All-America recognition—end Dan Foldberg, center Elmer Stout, and tackles Charles Shira and J. D. Kimmel.

With the bulk of the varsity football squad being dismissed because of the cheating scandal, the 1951 season was a disaster. The Cadet squad, made up of junior varsity players and welcome volunteers, finished at 2-7. Army dropped its first four games before managing to trim Columbia, 14-9. After another loss, this one to Southern California, the Cadets edged The Citadel, 27-6. However, two more defeats followed, including a 42-7 thrashing at the hands of Navy.

Blaik's 1952 squad demonstrated signs of revitalization by posting a 4-4-1 record. The Cadets defeated South Carolina, Dartmouth, V.M.I., and Penn, and dropped a tough 7-0 decision to Navy.

Army's football program completed its turnaround during the 1953 season when Blaik's squad posted a 7-1-1 record, defeated Navy 20-7, and won the Lambert Trophy as the best team in the East. Blaik was also selected "Coach of the Year" by the Touchdown Club of Washington, D.C., for the way he masterfully reversed the fortunes of the football program at the Academy following the disastrous 1951 season.

Army's success in 1953 was paved by such performers as Tommy Bell, Ralph Chesnauskas, Don Holleder, team captain LeRoy Lunn, Bob Mischak, Bill Purdue, Freddie Attaya, and many others.

"Where, I suggest, in our football history is there a more resolute example comparable to this cadet comeback," said Blaik, recalling the tragedy of '51 with the success of 1953.

Army coach Red Blaik is pictured with his son Bobby Blaik (15) in 1950. Months later his son was dismissed from the Academy following a cheating scandal that rocked West Point and decimated the football squad. Blaik, embittered by the tragic event, refused to resign although he seriously considered it. He remained at the Academy, rebuilt the football program, and retired in 1958 after guiding the Cadets to an 8-0-1 record. Army also was ranked third in the nation in 1958 by both the Associated Press and United Press International, the last team to be ranked in the Top 20 by the two national news wire services.

Dan Foldberg, above, a class of 1951 West Point graduate, gained All-America honors in football as an end in 1950. He lettered three years in football while at the U.S. Military Academy, serving as team captain during the 1950 season. Foldberg also lettered one year in lacrosse. His football career at West Point was outstanding. He was credited with fifty-seven pass receptions for 824 yards and three touchdowns during three years of play. He was a member of the undefeated 1949 Army football team and captained the 1950 squad which won eight of nine games. In 1948 he gained second team All-America honors from United Press International. He also earned second and third team All-America honors during the 1949 season before putting the finishing touches on an outstanding career in football by gaining first team All-America honors in 1950 from the Associated Press, United Press International, Look, and Colliers magazines. Col. Foldberg, above, chats with Army coach Tom Cahill in 1972 while assigned at West Point.

135

In 1954, the Army team compiled a 7-2 record. The Cadets opened with a 34-20 loss to South Carolina, but then reeled off seven straight triumphs over Michigan, Dartmouth, Duke, Columbia, Virginia, Yale, and Pennsylvania. The season came to an end with a 27-20 loss to Navy. The Middies rallied from a 20-14 deficit behind quarterback George Welsh, winning the Lambert Trophy and a berth in the Sugar Bowl against Mississippi. Coach Eddie Erdelatz' Navy squad also went on to whip Ole Miss, 21-0, on New Year's Day 1955.

Despite the loss the Cadets earned Top Ten billing in both college football polls. Associated Press and United Press International both had Army ranked seventh in the nation. Three members of the squad—end Don Holleder, halfback Tommy Bell, and guard Ralph Chesnauskas—all gained first team All-America honors.

One crucial loss came at the quarterback position where Pete Vann departed after passing for 2,915 yards and completing 174 passes during his three seasons with the varsity. Vann still ranks fourth among Army's career passing leaders.

During spring practice in 1955, Red Blaik was desperate in his attempts to fill the quarterback position. He decided to take his All-America end, Don Holleder, and convert him to a quarterback.

"It was a move made in desperation by what the post and press considered a stubborn old coach," recalled the Army mentor. "In retrospect, perhaps they were right, especially as to the 'old' part."

Holleder didn't make things any easier for the coaching staff. He promptly dislocated his shoulder during spring practice, so the experiment had to be carried to September. Holleder was an excellent defensive safety and an outstanding leader. He was not particularly efficient as a lefthanded passer.

Army opened the 1955 season with decisive victories over Furman and Penn State with Holleder at quarterback. However, Michigan dominated the Cadets in the third game at Ann Arbor, posting a 26-2 triumph. Holleder had a miserable afternoon, fumbling several times to allow the Wolverines opportunities for easy touchdowns. It was Army's first loss to Michigan in six games.

On Sunday afternoon following the Michigan debacle, Lt. Gen. Blackshear M. Bryan, the Academy's superintendent, visited Blaik in the football office. General Bryan, a teammate of Blaik's, wanted to know whether the Army coach was aware of the criticism from the officers and cadets on his decision to make Holleder the quarterback.

"Babe," said Blaik, "if it isn't Holly, whom do you suggest?"

"I don't know," the superintendent replied.

"Neither do I," said Blaik. "But I guarantee the only way to beat the Navy is with Holly at quarterback."

Shortly after the superintendent left, Holleder walked into Blaik's office. "I know what the officers and cadets are saying," said a downcast Holleder. "All the way up here I expected you to return my old number 83, but I prayed that you would not give up on me. Now, I'll show them I am your quarterback."

In the first half of the Navy game that year the Middies darn near ran the Cadets out of Municipal Stadium. However, Army drove sixty yards during the final minutes of the half, only to have time run out. In the second half, Coach Blaik's squad took command, piled up over two hundred yards and trimmed Navy, 14-6.

Blaik recalled the circumstances of that game vividly. "Now the night before the game when I took the squad for a walk, I had remarked to them, 'This season I have taken several walks across the field to congratulate coaches. It has been a trying season and I am a bit weary from those walks. Tomorrow before 100,000 spectators, and fifty million television viewers, I want you to know it would be the longest walk of my coaching career if I cross the field to congratulate the Navy coach.'"

There was silence, then a firm voice spoke out. It was Holleder. "Colonel, you're not taking that walk tomorrow."

Holleder and team captain Pat Uebel helped spearhead that victory, closing the pages on the 1955 season with a 6-3 record. Uebel scored three touchdowns to lead the way, the fourth player in Army history to accomplish that in an Army-Navy encounter.

In 1956, Army was 5-3-1, the tie coming against Navy. After a scoreless first half, the Cadets drew first blood with a touchdown in the third quarter, but the Middies battled back with a fourth quarter touchdown.

During the 1957 season a strong Army squad, led in the backfield by Bob Anderson and Pete Dawkins, posted a 7-2 record. The Cadets dropped a tough 23-21 decision to Notre Dame on Monty Stickles field goal in the final moments of play. Then Navy blanked the Cadets 14-0 in the season finale.

Anderson was the most important cog in the backfield for Blaik in 1957. He gained 983 yards, including 214 yards against Utah, and earned first team All-America honors at halfback.

In 1958, Red Blaik introduced a formation that Stanley Woodward described as "the lonely end." Bill Carpenter earned the illustrious assignment during spring practice. When the formation was first installed Carpenter would break from the huddle and rush to his spot, split fifteen yards wide of the offensive line. After six or seven plays he required a break. Consequently, Coach Blaik developed signals and Carpenter remained out of the huddle by himself.

The new formation caught the imagination of football fans throughout the nation, but Army had more than just "the lonely end." Pete Dawkins came into his own that season, leading the offense with able support from Bob Anderson. Both players earned first team All-America honors, while Dawkins also received the Heisman Trophy as the "Outstanding Player in the Nation" and the Maxwell Club Award as the "Outstanding Player of the Year."

Dawkins exceled off the football field as well. He was First Captain of the Corps of Cadets, the highest cadet military position at West Point, the president of his class, and a

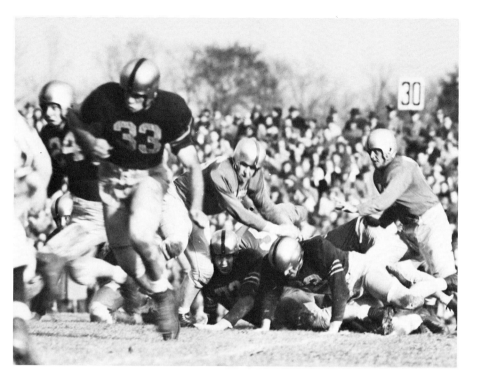

In 1951, Army compiled an 8-1 record, including a 51-0 victory over New Mexico in a game played at Michie Stadium. In this photograph Al Pollard (33) leads the blocking for backfield mate Jack Martin (24). Army tackle Lewis Zeigler (73) and guard Richard Roberts (63) opened the hole in the New Mexico defense for Martin.

Don Holleder is pictured here with his number 84 which he wore while gaining All-America honors in 1954. A year later Coach Blaik pressed Holleder into service as Army's quarterback. Although it was an extremely difficult challenge, Holleder guided the Cadets to a 14-6 victory over Navy to finish 6-3. A class of 1956 graduate, Maj. Holleder was killed in action in Vietnam in 1967.

Tom Bell, a running back who provided the foundation for Coach Red Blaik's rebuilding efforts following the famous cheating scandal at the Academy in 1950, lettered four years in football, 1951-1954. During the 1954 gridiron campaign, Bell gained 1,030 yards on just 96 carries to become the first back to gain 1,000 yards in a season in West Point history. Army compiled a 7-2 record that year. He remained the season rushing leader until 1968 when Charlie Johnson gained 1,110 yards on 208 carries.

Rhodes scholar. He also was an outstanding defenseman on the Army hockey team.

The 1958 Army team opened the season with solid victories over South Carolina, 45-8, and Penn State, 26-0. Then it was off to South Bend, Indiana, to meet Notre Dame before a hostile crowd of sixty thousand. The Cadets were still stinging from a 23-21 loss in 1957 and vowed to return the favor. Blaik's squad was successful, defeating the Irish 14-2 in a punishing game.

Following the victory over Notre Dame, the Cadets romped over Virginia, but then fought to a 14-14 tie against Pittsburgh in the "Steel City." Army rebounded with victories over Colgate, Rice, and Villanova, before handing Navy a 22-6 setback to put the finishing touches on another undefeated season, 8-0-1. The Cadets won the Lambert Trophy as the best team in the East and were ranked third in the nation by both the Associated Press and United Press International.

Dawkins recalls his final Navy game rather vividly. "On the kickoff, because of a masterful play by me, it looked as if our chances were nil. I remember waiting for the whistle, just praying that they would kick it to me, for if they did, I was going all the way. Well, there it came, right down to the goal line, and off I went, the happiest guy on the field. The blocking was good and I was beginning to move and things were opening up over toward the left—at least I sensed daylight over that way. So I cut to the left, with a Navy tackler bearing down on me from the right front, and Bill Rowe, our center, cut across to nail him. My elbow bumped Bill and the ball squirted up in the air, and the whole Navy team fell on it.

"But we still had a football game to play, so I called a quick huddle and said that we were in a hole, and it was my fault, but we could hold these people and beat them. And we held, and we did beat them, 22-6. I didn't score, but it was the happiest day I ever knew, I guess—a fitting end to a wonderful season, and I had almost a feeling of reverence for having had the privilege of associating with such a group as that Army team."

Likewise, Blaik recalls his final Army squad with fondness for the way they developed within the football program at the Academy. "The 'lonely end' squad had talent," said Blaik, "but it was essentially developed talent that paid the price for success in the crucible of rugged preparation—preparation so essential to this game of bodily contact."

Earl Blaik stunned the football world by announcing his retirement after the 1958 season. He closed out a head coaching career in which his teams at Dartmouth and West Point won 166 games, lost just 48, and tied 14 times. During his seven years at Dartmouth, his record was 45-15-4. At West Point he guided the Cadets to a record of 121-33-10.

Football was important to Earl Henry "Red" Blaik, but education was even more important to the Army coach.

"If the school and the coach start out from the correct premise," said Blaik prior to his retirement in 1959, "there will never be any question about football's place. Football is incidental to education. It's secondary. What worries me about the attempts to de-emphasize football is the way it's done. You can't tell the youngsters, 'Now this game isn't as important as you have been led to believe, and winning isn't everything, you know.' When you do that you strip football of its essential ingredients—the importance of the game and the will to win. Now it's true that fifty minutes or fifty months after a game is over, it may no longer seem very important. But for those minutes on the field, the youngsters must feel that the game is the most important thing in the world and that their job is to win it."

In his biography, *You Have to Pay the Price*, penned by Tim Cohane, Blaik spoke of a problem when he first took over at Dartmouth and how it affected his coaching career.

"Our major problem at Dartmouth was to replace the spirit of good fellowship, which is antithetical to successful football, with the Spartanism that is indispensable," said Coach Blaik. "I believe there is a place for good fellowship. I also believe that good fellows are a dime a dozen, but an aggressive leader is priceless.

"I suspect my players, at West Point, as well as Dartmouth, considered me not only serious but severe," added the Army coach. "It may be that some who did not understand what I was trying to do thought me a martinet, and a few may have hated me for it. I also believe that most of them, anyhow, after they left school and assumed more and more of the responsibilities of life, appreciated with increasing clarity what I tried to do—what I had to do. I was not heartless, but any revelation of the slightest sympathy was out of key with the mood I considered urgent if Dartmouth was to regain its lost football respect."

When Blaik closed out his coaching career, he had developed twenty-nine All-America players, and fifteen of his coaching assistants went on to become head coaches. In 1964, Blaik was named to the National Football Foundation Hall of Fame, and two years later he was the recipient of the foundation's Gold Medal Award. Upon accepting that honor Blaik explained what the game of football meant to him, and to those who played under him.

"It is a game played in some form by over a million young Americans, a game uninhibited by social barriers," said Blaik. "It is a game that in early season requires exhaustive hard work, often to the point of drudgery. It is a game of violent body contact that demands a personal discipline seldom found in our modern life. It is a game of team action wherein the individual's reward is that total satisfaction returned by being part of successful team play.

"It is a game that is 100 percent fun when you win, and exacts 100 percent resolution when you lose. And if it is the game most like war, it is also the game most like life, for it teaches young men that work, sacrifice, selflessness, competitive drive, perseverance, and respect for authority are the price one pays to achieve goals worthwhile."

While Earl Blaik, the winningest coach in Army football history, bowed out with optimum success, Dale Hall stepped into what was perhaps an impossible challenge. Filling the

A gaping hole on Navy's right side allows Army fullback Pat Uebel (34) through for eight yards and a Cadet first down during the 1955 encounter in Philadelphia. Quarterback Don Holleder (16), a converted end, just handed the ball off to Uebel, while halfback Bob Kyasky dumped a Navy linebacker.

Army closed out its 1955 season with a hard-fought 14-6 victory over Navy. In this photograph, Navy's Paul Gober (47) takes the kickoff and begins his return. Closing in on him are Army tackle Flay Goodwin (70) and center Ed Szvetecz (54). Other Army players identified include tackle Loren Reid (74), Bob Kyasky (42), Don Holleder (16), Pat Uebel (34), Ralph Chesnauskas (63), Stan Slater (62), and Pete Lash (24).

The color guards from the U.S. Naval Academy, left, and the U.S. Military Academy come to attention during the playing of the national anthem during the 1957 Army-Navy game in Philadelphia. The Middies won that encounter 14-0 as the Cadets closed out their season with a 7-2 record.

shoes of Red Blaik after an illustrious eighteen years at the Academy, might be similar in nature to replacing the king of late night television today, Johnny Carson. There is simply no way to match the captivation and success of those giants of men with immediate comparison.

Hall, a native of Parsons, Kansas, fell victim to that situation, although he accepted the challenge and position as head football coach at the U.S. Military Academy with great anticipation.

Hall was a 1945 graduate of West Point who lettered two years in football as a halfback (1943-1944), playing in the shadows of Blanchard and Davis. It was on the basketball court that Hall made his own mark, becoming Army's first All-America in that sport. He played a key role as the 1944 team compiled a 15-0 record, and then served as captain of the 1945 team that finished with a 14-1 record. In 1971, Hall's achievements in basketball during his four years at the Academy were recognized when he was selected to the Naismith Basketball Hall of Fame.

Hall separated from the service in 1948 following a tour in Germany, and began his college coaching career as an assistant at Purdue. There were also stops at the University of New Hampshire and Florida before he returned to West Point as a defensive backfield coach in 1956.

Hall's 1959 Army team still had team captain Bill Carpenter, the "lonesome end," quarterback Joe Caldwell, halfback Bob Anderson, Don Usry, Frank Gibson, Al Vanderbush (currently Deputy Athletic Director at West Point), and newcomers George Kirschenbauer, Al Rushatz, and Tom Blanda. Anderson was hampered by a knee problem and never regained his All-America form in 1958, so the offense suffered.

Hall's first football squad opened with a solid 44-8 victory over Boston College, but then dropped decisions to Illinois and Penn State. The Cadets rebounded with victories over Duke, Colorado State, and Villanova, sandwiched around a 13-13 tie against Air Force in the first meeting between the two schools. However, Army ended Hall's first season at the helm with a thud, dropping a 28-20 decision to Oklahoma in Norman before suffering a 43-12 thrashing at the hands of Navy.

The Middies unleashed halfback Joe Bellino of Winchester, Massachusetts. Bellino became the first Navy player to score three touchdowns in an Army-Navy game. Midway through the first quarter Bellino galloped sixteen yards for a touchdown. Less than three minutes later he broke loose for a forty-six-yard touchdown scamper before closing out his feat with a one-yard plunge.

While scouting Navy in 1958, Dale Hall predicted Bellino could be one of the finest halfbacks in the country. His prophecy was fulfilled during the 1959 Army-Navy skirmish, ending his first season as head coach at West Point on a particularly low note.

Bob Novogratz, a 1959 graduate of West Point and an outstanding guard on Coach Red Blaik's last and undefeated Army team (8-0-1), received the Knute Rockne Award as the nation's outstanding lineman, given by the Touchdown Club of Washington, D.C. Novogratz, who hails from Northampton, Pennsylvania, turned in his finest performances against Army's most difficult opponents, Penn State, Pittsburgh, Notre Dame, and Navy. Novogratz, an All-America selection, won the Rockne Award over such outstanding linemen as center Bob Harrison of Oklahoma, guard John Guzik of Pitt, tackle Ted Bates of Oregon State, end Buddy Dial of Rice, and guard Zeke Smith of Auburn. He is only the second Army lineman to win the trophy. The other was Casimir Myslinski, a center on the 1943 Army team.

It was a sign of the times at the U.S. Military Academy prior to the 1958 Army-Navy football game. The barracks and academic buildings normally are redecorated by the Corps of Cadets in preparation for the annual clash in Philadelphia.

Bill Carpenter, an All-America end in 1959, received much notoriety as Army's "Lonely End" in 1958. Coach Earl H. "Red" Blaik installed the offense and baffled opponents when Carpenter flanked very wide on the line of scrimmage and never returned to the huddle, receiving signals from the quarterback on just what the upcoming play would be. This photo is Carpenter's cadet portrait.

Heisman Trophy winner Pete Dawkins is seen here in a posed shot prior to the opening of the 1958 season. Dawkins served as captain of the Army football team in 1958, helping lead the Cadets to an 8-0-1 record.

Halfback Bob Anderson teamed with Pete Dawkins to provide the Army football team with its best backfield combination since the Blanchard-Davis days. Anderson is a two-time All-America, gaining those honors for his performance during the 1957 and 1958 seasons. He ranks ninth on Army's career rushing list with 1,887 yards on 355 carries. He gained 983 yards during the 1957 season, which places him seventh on the season rushing list. Anderson's best single game effort came against Utah in 1957 when he gained 214 yards.

The Corps of Cadets stand at attention at the conclusion of the pre-game march-on in 1958. The Corps had much to celebrate later as Army trimmed Navy, 22-6.

Army halfback Pete Dawkins accepts the Lambert Trophy during an awards ceremony in New York City. The Cadets completed the 1958 season with an 8-0-1 record, the last unbeaten football team at West Point. Dawkins was the recipient of the Heisman Trophy that year as the "Outstanding Player in the Country." Joining Dawkins to accept the award on behalf of the Academy is Brig. Gen. Gerald A. Counts, dean of the Academic Board.

Army's "Lonely End" Bill Carpenter posed prior to the start of the 1959 football season. Carpenter served as captain of that 1959 squad which posted a 4-4-1 record under first-year coach Dale Hall.

Cadet Bill Carpenter, center, served as a regimental commander during his final year at the Academy He is pictured with other members of his staff.

143

The Army-Air Force football rivalry began on October 30, 1959. Prior to the game the team mascots met for the first time and unabashedly posed for this historical photo, along with their respective handlers.

Army's "Lonely End" Bill Carpenter (87) catches a pass between Navy defenders Joe Tranchini (16) and Dick Pariseau (47) during the 1959 service clash in Philadelphia. The Middies prevailed 43-12. Other players identified included Don Usry (89) of Army and Navy's Joe Bellino (27) and Ronnie Brandquist (49).

Army football coach Dale Hall had the challenging task of stepping into the shoes of Earl "Red" Blaik after the winningest coach in Army history retired following the 1958 season at West Point. Hall, a 1945 West Point graduate who played under Blaik in 1943 and 1944, took over the reins in 1959. He coached for three seasons, compiling a record of sixteen victories, eleven defeats, and two ties.

Army quarterback Joe Caldwell lettered in 1958 and 1959. He closed out his career with 159 completions for 2,440 yards, currently sixth on Army's career passing list. Caldwell had 105 completions in 1959 and 1,343 yards, the fourth best effort among the Cadets' quarterbacks. One of his finest games came against Oklahoma in 1959 when he passed for 297 yards.

Some former Army football coaches gathered in 1959. They are, left to right, Col. Biff Jones, former head football coach and athletic director, Gen. Garrison Davidson, former head football coach and superintendent at the Academy, Gen. Gerald A. Counts, former dean of the Academic Board at West Point, Brig. Gen. Charles J. Barrett, former professor of foreign languages at the Academy, Col. Earl H. "Red" Blaik, the winningest football coach in West Point history, and Coach Dale Hall, a former basketball All-America who succeeded Blaik as head coach. Barrett distinguished himself in sports, earning a spot on the Modern Pentathlon Team that competed in the 1928 Olympics.

Army halfback Ray Paske (37) leaps high to catch a pass during the 1961 Army-Navy encounter. Defending on the play is Bill Ulrich (40). Also identified in the photograph are Tom Culver (23) of Army and Jim Stewart (21) of Navy. The Middies won 13-7.

CHAPTER 10

CAHILL'S SURPRISING SUCCESS

The sixties era brought change to the Army football program, changes in personnel, changes in the service commitment following graduation, and changes in society where challenging authority in all walks of life was common.

The sixties brought the emergence of a strong following for professional football, primarily because this sport, more than any other, lends itself to television coverage. The introduction of the slow-motion camera and instant replay provided production techniques that helped popularize the sport. It now challenges baseball as the national pastime.

With professional football gaining prominence and individual stars such as "Broadway" Joe Namath commanding higher contracts than anyone ever dreamed of, college football reaped some of the benefits with an increased following of its own. However, student-athletes began to choose the college of their choice by measuring their future prospects in the National Football League, rather than their future career in business or industry. Student-athletes began shopping for colleges and universities based on the school's success in placing graduates on the NFL draft list and on pro rosters.

The service academies began to feel the effects of the popularity of professional football. It was simply detrimental to their recruiting efforts. Athletes who felt they had a chance to play in the National Football League knew such dreams would go unfulfilled at a service academy because of the five-year service commitment following graduation.

Despite the difficulties of his first year as head coach, Dale Hall completed two more years at the helm after taking over in 1959. He enjoyed two winning seasons, but bowed to Navy three straight years to fall in disfavor with the West Point administration. Paul Dietzel, a former Blaik assistant coach who was serving as head coach at Louisiana State University, succeeded Hall in 1962. Academy officials had considered Vince Lombardi, Murray Warmath, and Dietzel, but made the first offer to Dietzel.

Many comparisons were made between Blaik and Dietzel in 1962. Both were graduates of Miami of Ohio. Both took over as head coach at West Point when the football program hit hard times. Both were very successful at their previous head coaching assignments, Blaik at Dartmouth and Dietzel at Louisiana State University. But the new head coach found the challenge of filling Blaik's shoes far more difficult than expected. He stayed at West Point four years before leaving in 1966 for the position of athletic director and head football coach at the University of South Carolina.

Academy officials, caught somewhat in a quandary with Dietzel resigning right before spring practice in 1966, failed to agree on another big name football coach and elevated Tom Cahill, the plebe football coach, to the head coaching position. Cahill, a dedicated soldier, accepted a one year contract, perhaps thinking he was merely an interim choice to give West Point additional time to select a true successor to Dietzel.

However, Cahill did what no one else had been able to do since Blaik's 1958 team—win eight games. Cahill guided the Cadets to an 8-2 record, defeated Navy 20-7, and earned national "Coach of the Year" honors. That effort forced Academy officials to extend his contract. This former New Jersey high school coach carried the fortunes of the Army football program through the remaining years of the sixties and into the seventies with a great deal of success.

Yet, where Cahill enjoyed instant and surprising success, Dale Hall found continuing frustration during the 1960 and 1961 seasons. In 1960 the Black Knights were 6-2 heading into the final two games of the season, but Hall's squad tied Pittsburgh, 7-7, and then bowed to Navy, 17-12, to finish 6-3-1.

Army got off to another good start during Hall's final season in 1961, winning four of five games. The Cadets then bowed to West Virginia 7-3 before whipping Detroit and William & Mary to run their season mark to 6-2. But once again, Dale Hall's Army squad fizzled at the tail end by dropping consecutive games to Oklahoma and Navy.

President John F. Kennedy attended the season ending classic at Municipal Stadium in Philadelphia in 1961, along with 100,000 other interested partisans. A Navy veteran himself, Kennedy participated in the coin toss ceremony to start the game, and then sat back to watch the Middies rally for a 13-7 victory. Kennedy, a P.T. boat skipper during World War II, was the first president to attend the Army-Navy game since Harry Truman joined the football throngs in 1952.

Navy placekicker Greg Mather provided the impetus to lead the Middies past Hall's Army squad. In the second quarter he booted a thirty-two-yard field goal to put Navy on top. After Bill Ulrich matched Army's third period touchdown, Mather converted a thirty-six-yard field goal in the fourth quarter to lift the Middies to a 13-7 victory.

That victory, the third in succession by Navy, proved to be Hall's last hurrah at West Point. Academy officials selected the affable Dietzel as his replacement. Dietzel coached L.S.U. to the national championship in 1958 and he was "Coach of the Year" during his tenure in the Bayou state. When he received the offer to coach at West Point his L.S.U. squad was beating Colorado in the Cotton Bowl.

Dietzel utilized three platoons at Louisiana State, calling his defensive unit the Chinese Bandits. The nickname caught the imagination of the public at that time because they were very successful in their defensive efforts. However, the three platoon system did not work as well at West Point.

Lack of depth and injuries forced Dietzel to curtail use of the West Point branch of the Chinese Bandits. His first Army squad compiled a 6-4 record, dropping its final three games, including a 34-14 decision to Navy. John Ellerson, a three-year letterman, was team captain and Joe Blackgrove and Dick Eckert handled the quarterbacking chores.

In 1963, Dietzel put together his strongest Army squad. Junior Carl "Rollie" Stichweh was the quarterback, a capable passer and an excellent runner. Ken Waldrop, a three-year letterman, junior Ray Paske, and Don Parcells handled the backfield chores. Other three-year veterans among the seniors included Dick Heydt, Chet Kempinski, Tom Kerns, team captain Dick Nowak, Dick Peterson, Ed Schillo, and Gwynn Vaughan.

The Cadets opened the season with victories over Boston University and Cincinnati before dropping a 24-8 decision to Minnesota. Dietzel's squad bounced back with five straight victories, taking the measure of Penn State, 10-7, Wake Forest, 47-0, Washington State, 23-0, Air Force, 14-10, and Utah, 7-0. Pittsburgh ended the winning streak, 28-0, before a heavily favored Navy team with Roger Staubach at quarterback, struggled for a 21-15 victory over the Cadets. The Navy win was the fifth straight over Army, but it was a classic football battle, even though it was postponed one week in deference to national mourning following the assassination of President Kennedy.

Pat Donnelly scored three touchdowns, equaling a Navy record first set by Heisman winner Joe Bellino. Roger Staubach demonstrated why he was considered one of the most exciting quarterbacks in the country, completing six of eleven passes and running the offense superbly. He was named the Heisman Trophy winner shortly thereafter.

However, despite the loss, the Cadets put together a heroic effort, led by Stichweh. Only some confusion in the final seconds halted Army from pulling off a major upset when time expired with the Cadets trying to call another play on the Navy two-yard line.

After a 7-7 standoff in the first half, Donnelly scored twice in the third quarter and Fred Marlin converted all three extra points for a 21-7 lead. However, Stichweh, from Williston Park, New York, brought the Cadets back during a fourth quarter rally. He put the finishing touches on a fifty-two-yard scoring drive, skirting around right end for the touchdown. Seconds later he plunged over for a two-point conversion to cut the lead to 21-15.

Dietzel then pulled off a trick play, calling for a special onside kick. The Cadets lined up normally, but Heydt stood next to the ball sideways as if to give his squad the "go" sign. Ray Hawkins approached the ball, but before he reached it, Heydt booted it across the field and Stichweh recovered at the Navy forty-nine.

The Cadets, with 6:13 remaining to play, had plenty of time to score. Waldrop and Paske pounded away on offense, picking up valuable yardage while moving toward the Navy goal line. With 1:38 to play, Stichweh hooked up with Parcells in the flat, giving Army a first down at the seven.

On first down Parcells gained two yards, the clock ticking down to 1:22. Waldrop went up the middle to the four before being stopped with fifty-eight seconds to play. The Cadets huddled and then lined up, but Stichweh backed off the line because of the crowd noise. Barney Finn, the referee, stopped the clock. The Army players didn't know the clock was restarted after the crowd noise died down and they huddled, using up twelve more seconds. Now there were but twenty-four seconds left when Waldrop rammed to the Navy two. It was fourth and goal, but the Cadets never got enough time to run off a final play.

So, Navy was the victor over Army for the fifth straight time, equaling a record set by the Midshipmen from 1939 through 1943. Stichweh, though, completed an outstanding season, leading Army in rushing with 622 yards on 133 carries for a 4.1 average. He also completed 46 of 94 passes for 454 yards.

In 1964, Army finally ended the Navy jinx because of more inspired play by Rollie Stichweh, trimming the Middies 11-8 during Roger Staubach's final game. It left the Cadets with a 4-6 record, the first time Army suffered a losing season since 1951.

Things went from bad to worse in 1965 when Dietzel's squad compiled a 4-5-1 record, the tie coming against Navy. It was Army's second straight losing season. So, when Dietzel was offered the position of director of athletics and head football coach at the University of South Carolina, he didn't waste much time calling the moving van.

Despite the disappointing season, there were several outstanding veterans, including three-year lettermen Pete Braun, John Carber, Sam Champi, and Charles "Sonny" Stowers, the team captain. Champi was the recipient of the

Army coach Paul Dietzel watches the action during his West Point coaching debut in 1962. Army halfback Dick Peterson (40) awaits to enter the game against Wake Forest. The Cadets won the opener 40-14, and finished with a 6-4 record during Dietzel's first year at the helm.

Army's starting backfield in 1962 on what was called the "Go" squad included quarterback Dick Eckert (10), fullback George Pappas (38), halfback John Seymour (43), and wingback Don Parcells (31).

Army defeated Penn State 9-3 in 1962 at Michie Stadium. In this photograph, Dick Peterson (40) grabs a pass and looks for running room upfield. Closing in to make the tackle is Pete Liske (24). Also pictured is Junior Powell (40) of the Nittany Lions.

National Football Foundation Scholar-Athlete award and an NCAA Football Scholarship winner.

When Dietzel left right before the start of spring practice, West Point officials asked Tom Cahill to run the show on a temporary basis. He would be in charge of spring drills. During that time he also escorted some of those gentlemen who sought the head coaching position, but West Point could not make up its mind. Thus, Cahill was offered the top spot for the 1966 season.

Cahill, 46, had coached the plebe team for seven years and was guaranteed the plebe job even if things did not go well as head coach during the 1966 season. However, Cahill threw West Point an untouchable curve when he guided his first squad to an 8-2 record and was acclaimed national "Coach of the Year."

Cahill, a graduate of Niagara University, could not help but comment on how things can change after being named West Point's head football coach. "Life can change so quickly," he said. "For twenty years I put my shoes on the same way, then all of a sudden people want to know, 'How does it look, Tom?'—people who never asked me anything before."

Linebacker Townsend Clark was captain of Cahill's first Army team, a three-year letterman and one of the finest at his position in the country. Yet, even Clark had to prove himself all over again to Cahill's football staff.

"They let you know in no uncertain terms if we weren't doing our job," said Clark. "And the captain was no special person, either. I was playing on the second team for a while."

Yet, Clark really didn't have to prove himself to anyone. He was a veteran who played a key role in Army's 20-7 victory over Navy in 1966. With the score tied at 7-7, Clark broke in to block a field goal attempt on the last play of the third quarter. Four plays later Army scored the go-ahead touchdown en route to the victory. For his efforts, Clark gained first team All-America recognition at the conclusion of the 1966 season.

Cahill not only defeated Navy in his first season, but the Cadets also took the measure of Kansas State, Holy Cross, Penn State, Rutgers, Pittsburgh, George Washington, and California. The only defeats were to Notre Dame at South Bend, and to Tennessee in Memphis.

In addition to the efforts of All-America linebacker Townsend Clark, senior leadership was provided by three-year lettermen Don Dietz, Mark Hamilton, David Rivers, and Tom Schwartz. Other seniors who lettered in 1966 included Dean Hansen, Claude Herman, John Montanaro, Mike Neuman, and Hank Uberecken.

Cahill guided Army to an 8-2 record in 1967 and a 7-3 mark in 1968. He closed out the sixties with a 4-5-1 mark, unfortunately a signal for the difficult times that were ahead in the seventies.

Bud Neswiacheny captained the Cadets in 1967, another one of Army's outstanding linebackers. He received support from four other three-year lettermen, John Nerdahl, John Peduto, Don Roberts, and Carl Woessner. Peduto and Woessner did yeoman work in the backfield for the Cadets.

Quarterback Steve Lindell, a three-year letterman, played a key role throughout Coach Cahill's first three years at West Point. Lindell set a career record for total yards gained, 3,672, a mark which was broken in 1977 by quarterback Leamon Hall, who played four years with the varsity. He currently ranks third on Army's career list for passing yardage (2,921) and completions (228).

Lindell led the offense during the 1968 season when the Cadets won seven and lost three, while team captain Ken Johnson of nearby Newburgh, New York, led the defense at his linebacker position. Johnson, a three-year letterman, gained first-team All-America honors. It would be seventeen years before another Army player would receive first team All-America recognition.

In addition to Lindell and Johnson, the class of 1969 had four other three-year lettermen who played key roles in Army's success—Charlie Jarvis, a bruising runner, Jim O'Toole, Steve Yarnell, an outstanding lineman, Terry Young, who lettered from 1965-1967, and Gary Steele, who lettered from 1966-1968. Young and Steele were outstanding receivers for the Cadets. Young became the career leader in receptions (95) and yards receiving (1,239), but currently ranks third on the career reception list. Steele is fifth in yards receiving with 1,111 and seventh in receptions with 66.

Jarvis was one of Army's outstanding runners. He ranks fourth in rushing at West Point with 2,344 yards. He still holds the single game record for rushing yards with 253, coming against Boston College in 1968. He set a season rushing record in 1968 with 1,110 yards. That mark was surpassed by Doug Black in 1984 when the Cadet fullback piled up 1,148 yards rushing.

Losing the talents of Lindell, Jarvis, Young, Steele, Johnson, and others did not make things easy for Cahill and his staff in 1969. Team captain Lynn Moore provided hard running in the backfield, but a challenging schedule and lack of depth hurt Army during the fall.

Moore gained 983 yards during the 1969 season, an effort which leaves him seventh on the career list among Army's season rushing leaders. He saved his best effort for last, however, rolling for 206 yards against Navy to spearhead a 27-0 victory.

Army's defensive unit in 1962 was called the Chinese Bandits. In this photograph, the Corps demonstrates their support of the Chinese Bandits. Unfortunately they were not very effective during the Army-Navy encounter which the Middies won by a 34-14 margin.

The Corps of Cadets cheers Army's defensive unit, nicknamed the Chinese Bandits, during the season opener at Michie Stadium against Wake Forest. The Bandits held Wake Forest in check, 40-14.

Army halfback Paul Stanley (20) picks up short yardage in traffic during a 9-2 win over Syracuse at the Polo Grounds in New York City in 1962. Army's Ray Paske (37) and quarterback Cammy Lewis (12), on ground, lead the blocking. Syracuse players identified include defensive end Walt Sweeney (89), guard Henry Heuttner (68), guard Dave Meggyesy (63), and halfback Bill Schoonover (44).

Halfback Paul Stanley (20) looks for some running room against Syracuse during the 1962 encounter at the Polo Grounds. Guard Weynn Vaughan (63) of Army moves in to support. The Cadets won, 9-2.

John Seymour (43) pulls in a pass reception during a 40-14 victory over Wake Forest during the 1962 season opener.

Army quarterback Joe Blackgrove (16) scores a touchdown during the 1962 season opener against Wake Forest. The Cadets prevailed 40-14. It was the coaching debut of Paul Dietzel.

It proved to be Rollie's revenge during the 1964 Army-Navy game. Rollie Stichweh, the Army quarterback, follows the blocking of Sonny Stowers while gaining good yardage against the Middies. Stichweh led Army to an 11-8 victory over Navy during Roger Staubach's final game in Philadelphia. A year earlier Stichweh just missed upsetting Staubach and his teammates.

Army quarterback and team captain, Carl "Rollie" Stichweh, follows the blocking of Sonny Stowers (61) while picking up yardage during the 1964 Army-Navy game. Stichweh led the Cadets to an 11-8 victory over Roger Staubach and the Middies.

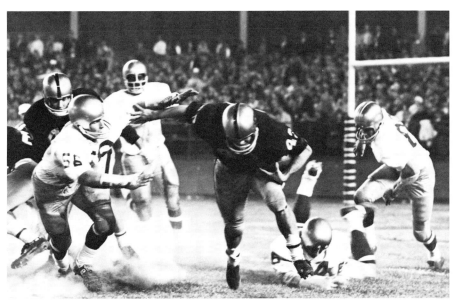

Army halfback Sonny Stowers (43) gains short yardage against Notre Dame in 1965 at Shea Stadium in New York City. Irish linebacker Dave Martin (56) moves in to make the tackle.

Army coach Paul Dietzel watches the action while talking to his assistant coaches in the press box during the 1965 Army-Navy game in Philadelphia. The Cadets and Middies played to a 7-7 deadlock in this encounter. It proved to be Dietzel's final game as Army head coach. Just prior to the start of spring practice in 1966 Dietzel accepted the position of athletic director and head football coach at the University of South Carolina.

Mark Hamilton (40) of Army picks up yardage against Navy during the 1966 clash in which the Cadets prevailed 20-7 during Tom Cahill's first year as head coach. Terry Young (87) tries to block for his teammate.

Army end Terry Young leaps high in the air for a pass reception during the 11-0 victory over Penn State in 1966. Young was one of Army's finest receivers. He had 37 receptions in 1966 for 539 yards, currently ninth on Army's career list for season catches. During his West Point career Young had 95 receptions for 1,239 yards (1965-1967).

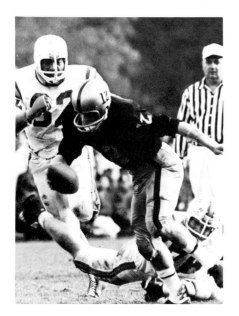

Army quarterback Steve Lindell (12) breaks a tackle to gain yardage against George Washington in 1966. Coach Tom Cahill's squad trimmed George Washington 20-7 at Michie Stadium.

Army running back Lynn Moore (44) bolts over from the one-yard line for the go-ahead touchdown against Pittsburgh during the fourth quarter in 1967. The Cadets posted a 21-12 victory at Pitt Stadium, the final game before its clash with rival Navy. Coach Tom Cahill's squad dropped a tough 19-14 decision to the Middies that year, but nonetheless finished with an 8-2 record.

Steve Lindell (12), Army's fine quarterback during the late sixties, breaks a tackle during the 1967 Army-Navy game. The Middies hung on for a 19-14 victory, but Lindell came back the following year to post a 21-14 victory over the Middies to close out his football career at West Point.

Army linebacker Ken Johnson earned All-America honors in 1968 when the Cadets posted a 7-3 record. Johnson, from Newburgh, New York, lettered three years in football, 1966-1968. During those three seasons the Cadets compiled an overall record of 23-5. Following Johnson's selection for All-America recognition, the Army program waited seventeen years for another first team All-America selection.

Army quarterback Steve Lindell closed out his career as Army's career passing leader with 228 completions for 2,921 yards. During the 1966 and 1968 seasons, Lindell passed for over 1,000 yards. He also ranked third in total offense among Army's career leaders with 3,672 yards. Only Glenn Davis and Chris Cagle accumulated more total yardage.

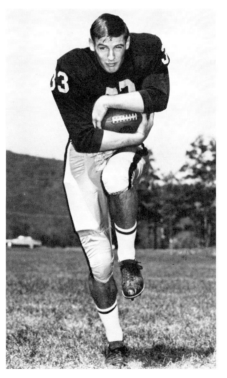

Charlie Jarvis, a brilliant Army fullback from Cornwallis Heights, Pennsylvania, shattered single game and season rushing records in 1968. He ranks fourth on the all-time career rushing list with 2,344 yards. His season record of 1,110 yards was surpassed in 1984 by fullback Doug Black, but his single game mark of 253 yards against Boston College still ranks as the best in Army history. When the Army fullback broke this record, he eclipsed the record of Heisman winner Glenn Davis who had rushed for 230 yards in 1945. Jarvis won three letters in football and two more in lacrosse while at West Point. The 1969 graduate also received the Army Athletic Association Trophy for most valuable service to athletics at the Academy.

Col. Jerry G. Capka, director of athletics, accepts the Coaches and Captains Trophy presented to the Military Academy by John Geist of Harrisburg, Pennsylvania (at Capka's right), during halftime of the Army-Virginia game in 1967. In the background are former Army football captains, left to right, Al Vanderbush (1960), Al Paulekas (1953), Alexander George (1919), Pete Dawkins (1959), Joe Steffy (1947), Bob Farris (1954), Jack Price (1931), Mort Sprague (1928), Dennis Mulligan (1923), Alexander Weyand (1915), Army coach Earl H. Blaik (1941-1958), and Eugene Vidal (1918).

Army coach Tom Cahill walks off Michie Stadium turf with some members of his 1967 Cadet squad. Cahill took over the head coaching responsibilities at West Point in 1966 after Paul Dietzel left to become athletic director and head football coach at the University of South Carolina. Cahill promptly guided Army to an 8-2 record during his first year at the helm, and was acclaimed national college "Coach of the Year." He followed up with an 8-2 record in 1967 and 7-3 in 1968. His overall record during eight seasons at the Academy was 40-39-2.

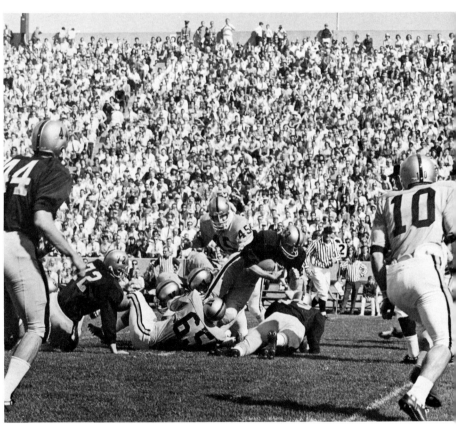

Army halfback Charlie Jarvis (33) gains yardage through the middle against Vanderbilt during the 1968 season. Vanderbilt trimmed Army 17-13 in the second game of the fall campaign. The Cadets went on to compile a 7-3 record that year. Other Army players are Lynn Moore (44) and tackle Carl Oborski (72).

Army halfback Hank Andrzejczak (43) gains short yardage during the 1968 Army-Navy game. The Cadets trimmed the Middies, 21-14. Linebacker Bill McKinney (70) makes the tackle for the Middies.

Halfback Lynn Moore (44) plunges over for a touchdown against Navy in 1969. The Cadets blanked the Middies, 27-0.

Army fullback Ray Ritacco (46) takes a handoff from quarterback Bernie Wall (10) and gains short yardage during the 1969 clash with Navy in Philadelphia. Also in on the action for Army are tackle Robert Johnson (75), tight end Mike Masciello, and guard Paul Watkins (64).

Army placekicker Arden Jensen is seen with holder Bernie Wall in 1969. Jensen was one of Army's finest placekickers.

Army quarterback Steve Lindell lettered from 1966 to 1968, leading the Cadets to three outstanding seasons, 8-2, 8-2, and 7-3. Lindell held Army's career passing record with 2,921 yards, but that mark was broken twice, first by Kingsley Fink and then by Leamon Hall. In 1968, Lindell passed for 1,043 yards.

Army coach Tom Cahill discusses things with Bud Neswiacheny in 1967.

Army football coach Tom Cahill observes his football squad during a 38-7 victory over Boston College in 1969. The Cadets posted a 4-5-1 record in 1969, but closd out the campaign with a satisfying 27-0 triumph over Navy.

The Army-Navy game not only brings out the best in both teams, but ignites the Brigade of Midshipmen and the Corps of Cadets to properly prepare for the annual gridiron clash. In 1958, when Army trimmed Navy 22-6, Company B-1, below, pointed out how success was just eleven easy steps. In 1960, the Corps prepared for a goat barbecue, but the Middies stifled their appetite with a 17-12 victory. In 1962, Col. Sylvanus Thayer, the "Father of the Military Academy," was ready, but it was to no avail as Navy won by a 34-14 margin. There were additional hijinks exhibited in 1962 with this wall montage from the New York Times. In the final photograph, the message was very clear: "Sink Navy." That is exactly what the Army football team works for each year above all else.

The Corps of Cadets provides an appropriate send-off for the Army football team in 1960, in preparation for its encounter with Syracuse at Yankee Stadium. The send-off was well received by the squad, which was coached by Dale Hall, and the Cadets went on to post a hard-fought 9-6 triumph over the Orangemen.

Army defensive coordinator John McCauley instructs his starting unit in 1972. At left is Tim Pfister and Gary Topping (53).

CHAPTER 11

SUICIDE SCHEDULES AND COACHING TURMOIL

There has never been a more difficult period in Army football history than during the seventies. From 1970 through 1979, the football program recorded just three winning seasons from three coaches, Tom Cahill, Homer Smith, and Lou Saban.

Whereas professional football made its impact on service academy football during the sixties, the unpopular Viet Nam War proved devastating to athletic recruiting in the seventies. To make matters worse, the schedule makers provided Army coaches with the most difficult tests in history. At times it was not just a matter of winning, but a matter of survival.

During the 1970 season, Coach Tom Cahill prepared his squad to face four straight road games, traveling to such friendly surroundings as Lincoln, Nebraska, to meet the nationally ranked Cornhuskers; to Knoxville, Tennessee, to meet the Volunteers, a perennial Southeastern Conference power; to South Bend, Indiana, to meet powerful Notre Dame, and then to Charlottesville, Virginia, to meet the University of Virginia. By the time Cahill got to Virginia, there were few healthy players left.

Following that road trip, the Cadets returned home to tangle with Eastern power Penn State. Army then traveled to Boston College, returned home to host Syracuse and Oregon, and then prepared for Navy.

Army finished with a 1-9-1 record in 1970, trimming Holy Cross, 26-0, while managing a 22-22 tie against Oregon. To make matters worse, the Cadets dropped a tough 11-7 decision to Navy. It was the worst season in Army football history.

The schedule wasn't much better in 1971. Stanford, Georgia Tech, Missouri, Penn State, and Air Force comprised the first five games, but surprisingly the Cadets stunned Georgia Tech in Atlanta, 16-13, on a forty-yard field goal by Jim Barclay, a young man from Chattanooga, Tennessee. Barclay was kicking for the first time on the varsity.

The Cadets returned home to upset Missouri, 22-6, behind the efforts of quarterback Kingsley Fink before the largest crowd in history at Michie Stadium. Team captain John Roth led the Cadet defense from his end position, limiting the Big Eight Conference team to just six points.

Road trips to Penn State and Air Force proved unsuccessful, but the Cadets trimmed Virginia, 14-9, to even their record at 3-3. It was off to Miami, Florida, next, but the Cadets came up short, 24-13.

Coach Cahill's squad then reeled off three straight victories to finish the season 6-4. Army ripped Rutgers 30-17, edged Pittsburgh 17-14 on a last-minute field goal, and then outlasted Navy 24-23 in one of the most exciting games in the series.

Gene Ward, former veteran sportswriter with the New York *Daily News,* described this Army-Navy game as one of the finest he had ever seen.

"This was the greatest Army-Navy game ever played. It was one of the greatest football games I've ever seen. There were no bowl bids hanging on the outcome; not a single player ever will sign a pro contract. But it was tremendous, and 97,047 fans walked away from decrepit, old JFK Stadium, where football is played once a year, talking about a game they'll never forget.

"This had everything. What the Cadets and Midshipmen did here in the rain and the gloom, amid pressures you can't imagine if you've never played in an Army-Navy game, is what it's all about. Life, I mean, and it's what our country is all about, too; the way these young Americans handled themselves is the way other Americans handled themselves when our country was younger and deep in peril. Then their names were Washington, Jefferson, and Adams. . . MacArthur, Halsey, and Eisenhower. Here their names were Fink, Stuvek, and McGuckin. . .Ritacco, Canterna, and Van Loan, melting pot names in a melting pot nation they are helping to keep strong and free."

The 1972 football season proved to be one of extremes, both in winning and losing. The schedule was just as challenging as the previous year with Nebraska, Texas A&M, Penn State, Miami, and Syracuse among the top Division I squads. Of course, there also were Air Force and Navy to contend with during the fall. Despite the difficult challenges, the Cadets forged a 6-4 record, including victories over Air Force and Navy, which earned the inaugural Commander-in-Chief's Trophy, an honor bestowed on the winner of the round-robin football competition between the three service academies. This road to success was filled with a good number of potholes along the way.

Before a regional television audience, Coach Tom Cahill's squad absorbed the worst defeat in Army history, against Nebraska in the 1972 season opener. The numbers were devastating enough, Nebraska 77, Army 7. To have portions of the country witness this debacle on their television screens was embarrassing. Trying to stop Johnny Rodgers, David Humm, and the remainder of the Cornhuskers squad was simply unmanageable.

The next stop for Army was College Station, Texas, for a meeting with Texas A&M. It was easy to accept the role of a thirty-point underdog following the results of the Nebraska encounter. But Cahill lifted his wounded squad to new heights under the lights at Texas A&M.

Prior to the start of this intersectional encounter, Army quarterback Kingsley Fink was made an honorary citizen of Fink, Texas, population eight. The mayor of Fink, Mrs. Patricia Albright, presented the Army quarterback a plaque in recognition of his adopted citizenship in this Texas community. For Fink, who called Eau Gallie, Florida, home, the presentation must have been inspiring because he then spearheaded Army to a stunning 24-14 victory over the Aggies.

Fink, an accurate dropback passer, not only riddled the Texas A&M defense with pinpoint passing, but also ran the ball when called upon. He also received able support from backfield mates Bob Hines and Bruce Simpson. The defense was led by team captain Steve Bogosian, Jim Bryan, Grover Dailey, Mercer Ferguson, Tim Pfister, Bob Souza, and Gary Topping.

Army returned home to Michie Stadium the following week to edge Lehigh, 26-21. The Cadets then bowed to Penn State 45-0, trimmed Rutgers 35-28 in New Brunswick, and then dropped a 28-7 decision to Miami. Army nipped Air Force 17-14, and lost to Syracuse 27-6, before stringing consecutive victories by whipping Holy Cross, 15-13, and Navy, 23-15, in the season finale.

The Army schedule in 1973 would rank with powerful Notre Dame's tough intersectional schedule each season. The Cadets prepared for a season opener against Southeastern power Tennessee. Following the opener, Army tackled California, Georgia Tech in Atlanta, Penn State at University Park, Notre Dame, Miami, and Pittsburgh, which featured Tony Dorsett. Additionally, there were the annual tests with rivals Air Force and Navy, with Holy Cross tossed in as a mid-season breather.

Kingsley Fink was closing out his varsity career at quarterback, and his favorite receiver, Jim Ward, was the team co-captain, but Cahill's squad had been demolished by graduation losses and a poor recruiting season. Consequently, Army suffered through its worst season in history,

dropping all ten of its games.

Army played well in the season opener against Tennessee, bowing 37-18 when the Volunteers rallied in the second half to pull away under Condredge Holloway. In fact, the feeling at the Academy was one of excitement after the strong showing in a losing effort. Tom Cahill was not nearly as euphoric. He, more than anyone else, knew the road ahead would be even more difficult.

It took just one week to find out as California ripped the Cadets 51-6. Georgia Tech trimmed Army 14-10, but Penn State pounded the Black Knights 54-3, and Notre Dame followed by spotting Army a 3-0 first quarter lead before recording a 62-3 victory. To make matters worse, a bruised and battered squad dropped a 17-14 decision to "breather" Holy Cross, the first victory the Crusaders ever recorded in their meetings with Army.

Air Force thrashed Army 43-10 in Colorado before Miami edged the Cadets 19-7. In the final two games Army failed to score, while Pittsburgh ran up thirty-four points and Navy piled up fifty-one. The final insult cost Tom Cahill his job as head coach.

Cahill was the first coach fired in the seventies, but hardly the last. His replacement, Homer Smith, was let go following the 1978 season, and Lou Saban resigned after just one year's residence on the banks of the Hudson. Each time there was a coaching change, West Point also suffered because of adverse publicity.

When Cahill was released *Daily News* sports columnist Gene Ward took issue with the decision. Ward claimed the Athletic Board at the Academy had voted to extend Cahill's contract prior to the 1973 Army-Navy game, but reversed that decision following the 51-0 loss to the Middies.

"In the face of that fifty-one-point minus, all the plusses of the magnificent coaching Tom Cahill had done over a span of seven years counted for nothing," wrote Ward in his column on Dec. 16, 1973. "Forgotten was the fact he had taken over the varsity squad at the close of Paul Dietzel's disastrous stewardship and, in the course of one season, brought Army back to the big time.

"That was in 1966. After spring practice under Cahill, the plebe coach, and while the athletic brass still was interviewing big names, a delegation of players had gone to the 'Supe' with a respectful request that Tom Cahill be made their coach. Whether it swayed the brass or not, Tom was hired and that autumn his first Army varsity squad blanked such clubs as Penn State, Holy Cross, and Pitt on the way to an 8-2 record. And Cahill's peers in the American Coaches Association named him Coach of the Year.

". . . They fired a man who had been a coach at West Point fifteen years . . . who had earned the title, 'A Man for the Corps,' for his understanding of, and rapport with, West Point and West Point cadets. He has a son who is a West Point graduate and played football on his '72 team. West Point had a great football coach, but they let him go."

The 1973 season was a disaster, but it did have some bright spots. Despite the loss to Tennessee in the opener,

Army tight end Clennie Brundidge, co-captain of the 1978 Army football squad, is the career leader in pass receptions at West Point. Brundidge caught 147 passes for 2,278 yards from 1975 to 1978. He had fifty-one receptions in 1977 when Army posted a 7-4 record and added forty-seven receptions in 1976.

Army fullback Bob Hines lettered three years in football while at West Point, 1970-1972. During his final year Hines, from Chester, Pennsylvania, gained 202 yards to lead the Cadets to a 17-14 victory over Air Force. That was the sixth best single game effort in West Point history at that time. He closed out his 1972 season with 844 yards rushing on 202 carries.

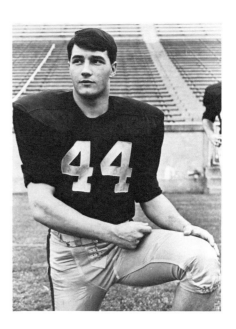

Gen. William C. Westmoreland, chief of staff of the Army, visits Michie Stadium to watch Army tie Oregon 22-22 in 1970.

Army split end Joe Albano of West Caldwell, New Jersey, a class of 1970 graduate, was one of the finest receivers in Army football history. He lettered three years in football (1968-1970) and caught 91 passes for 1,230 yards. He also holds the single game and season records for pass receptions at West Point. He pulled in thirteen passes against Syracuse in 1970, in addition to catching ten passes in games against Baylor and Penn State. Albano also established the season record with fifty-four catches in 1970 for 669 yards.

Kingsley Fink set an Army record by passing for 328 yards. That single game mark was broken three years later by another quarterback of the seventies, Leamon Hall. Like Fink, Hall was a Florida native, calling Apopka his home.

Fink also ranks second in career passing with 3,079 yards on 257 completions, including two straight seasons in which he piled up more than 1,000 yards passing. In 1972, Fink completed 88 passes for 1,139 yards. Then, in 1973, he accumulated 1,141 yards with 101 completions. Teammate Jim Ward caught seventy-six of Fink's passes for 916 yards to rank seventh in career receptions.

Homer Smith, a 1954 graduate of Princeton University, was named Army's twenty-seventh head football coach in January, 1974. He came to West Point from U.C.L.A. where he was an offensive coordinator under Pepper Rodgers. During his two years on the Bruins' staff, U.C.L.A. went 17-5 and led the nation in rushing in 1973. When Rodgers accepted the head coaching position at Georgia Tech, his alma mater, Smith joined him as assistant head coach and offensive coordinator. However, after just two weeks at Georgia Tech, Smith accepted the Army head coaching position.

Coaching at a service academy wasn't strange to Smith. He served four years as an assistant coach under Ben Martin at the Air Force Academy. While there the Falcons met Army once, bowing 14-10 in 1963 at Soldier Field in Chicago, when Ken Waldrop ran seventeen yards for the winning touchdown late in the fourth quarter to erase a 10-7 Air Force lead.

"No one was more anxious to be at West Point than I was," said Smith after accepting the position. "I have always reacted to service academies in a positive way. I am simply inspired by it all even as a tourist.

"I would like to maximize West Point football with young men who are truly representative of the Corps which identifies with them. I want to take advantage of the things Coach Tom Cahill and his staff have developed here. I want to build up the strength levels and skill development of our players as high as they can go. I feel the problems that lie ahead are the kind of problems I have trained myself to handle."

Smith perfected the Wishbone-T offense while at U.C.L.A. and brought that offensive attack to West Point. The question was whether Army had the personnel to run the Wishbone.

Smith's 1974 squad compiled a 3-8 record. The Cadets opened with a 14-7 win over Lafayette, but then dropped five consecutive games to Tulane, California, Penn State, Duke, and Notre Dame. Army carved out a 13-10 win over Holy Cross, bowed to Vanderbilt, but then rallied for a 17-16 victory over Air Force. Army racked up forty-two points against North Carolina, but the Tar Heels piled up fifty-six of their own in the tenth game of the season. Then Navy blanked Army 19-0.

In 1975, things didn't get much better. Army compiled a 2-9 record as Smith tried to run the Wishbone with co-captain Scott Gillogly and toss in a passing attack with Leamon Hall. The season started out well enough with two straight victories over Holy Cross and Lehigh. But then nine consecutive defeats followed, including a 67-14 loss to Stanford, where Smith had earned an M.B.A. degree and two of his brothers, Roy and Dean, graduated after successful track careers. Navy also made things uncomfortable for Smith by whipping the Cadets 30-6.

Army seemed to make strides to right itself in the football world during the 1976 season, compiling a 5-6 record. Coach Smith abandoned the Wishbone to take advantage of the talents of quarterback Leamon Hall. Hall became Army's all-time leading passer under Smith's tutelage and also married the coach's daughter, Kim, following graduation in 1978.

The Cadets won three of their first four games in 1976, defeating Lafayette, Lehigh, and Stanford. The only loss came at the hands of North Carolina, 34-32. In the victory over Stanford the Cadets rallied from a 20-0 deficit in the second half to win, so football appeared on the upswing.

However, after such a good start, Army reversed direction and dropped games to Penn State, Tulane, and Boston College. The Cadets came back and whipped Air Force 24-7 at West Point, bowed to Pittsburgh, and then edged Colgate to level their record at 5-5. A victory over Navy would have put the finishing touches on a solid effort, but it was not to be. The Middies whipped the Cadets for the fourth straight year, 38-10.

News accounts said Smith was given an ultimatum to compile a 7-4 record in 1977 and whip Navy or look for work elsewhere. West Point officials denied those reports, but Smith put together Army's first winning effort since 1972. His squad posted a 7-4 record and defeated Air Force and Navy to win the Commander-in-Chief's Trophy. The Falcons fell to the Cadets 30-6, while the Middies absorbed a 17-14 defeat, which ended their bid to tie a record of five consecutive triumphs over Army. For turning around the Cadet football fortunes, Smith was named Eastern "Coach of the Year" by the New York Football Writers Association.

The 1977 season was significant in other ways. Hall opened by throwing a record five touchdown passes against Massachusetts in a 34-10 victory. Three of those went to split end Mike Fahnestock of Selinsgrove, Pennsylvania, who was making his varsity debut.

Tight end Clennie Brundidge and Hall made up one of the most effective passing combinations in Army history. Before graduation, Hall set nearly all of Army's passing records on single game, season, and career categories. Hall set six single game records, seven season records, and seven career marks. He passed for 5,502 yards during his career on 426 completions, both records. He holds the total offense record with 5,524 yards, and tossed thirty-eight touchdown passes in four seasons.

Likewise, Brundidge also set Army receiving records. He caught 147 passes for 2,279 yards and fourteen touchdowns. The fourteen touchdown receptions surpassed the record of twelve set by Whitey Grove from 1933-1935.

Halfback Greg King rushed for 961 yards on 177 carries,

Army quarterback Dick Atha drops back to look for an open receiver during a 1971 game against Georgia Tech in Atlanta. Bob Hines (44) provides blocking support as defensive end Randy Duckworth of Georgia Tech applies pressure from the outside. The Cadets upset the Yellow Jackets 16-13 and went on to post a 6-4 season record.

It is obvious in this photograph that things are not going well for the Army football team, Coach Tom Cahill, and quarterback Kingsley Fink. This was the scene during the 1972 season opener when Nebraska upended Army 77-7, the worst loss in West Point history.

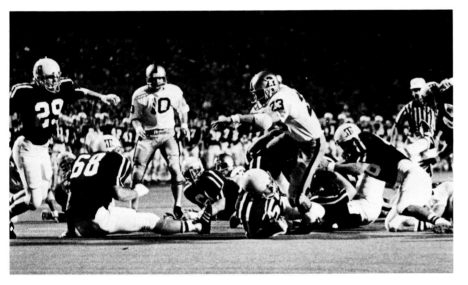

Army halfback Bruce Simpson (23) breaks a tackle while picking up important yardage against Texas A&M in 1972. The Cadets rallied for a 24-14 victory, coming one week after they absorbed a 77-7 defeat at the hands of Nebraska. Looking on is Army quarterback Kingsley Fink (10).

Army quarterback Kingsley Fink holds up a plaque he received prior to the Texas A&M game in 1972. Fink was made an honorary citizen of Fink, Texas, population eight. Each year the populace of Fink invites all those people with the surname Fink to their community for a celebration. The Army quarterback proved a popular name in Fink, but not in College Station.

including a 212-yard rushing effort during a 48-7 victory over Holy Cross. King closed out his career with 1,992 yards to rank sixth on Army's career list.

Despite the success in 1977, Homer Smith's contract was extended for just a single season. The handwriting was on the wall for the Army coach. He knew he would have to produce another winning campaign or hang his hat somewhere else.

Smith's 1978 squad finished 4-6-1 and bowed to Navy 28-0. At one point the Cadets were 1-4-1, but posted consecutive victories over Colgate, Air Force, and Colgate to move to 4-4-1. However, the Cadets bowed to Pittsburgh 35-17 and were blanked by the Middies.

Smith told his squad he "was history." He headed for Cambridge, Massachusetts, to visit the Harvard Divinity School. Two days later, when he returned to the Academy, Smith was informed by family members that his brother, Dean, was killed in an automobile accident in Omaha, Nebraska. While making plans to attend the funeral, he was informed by the West Point Athletic Board that his contract would not be renewed.

Smith, who was the first Army coach since 1940 who had a losing record, planned to quit the Army football program and seek new opportunities. But the Athletic Board informed Smith he was voted out. Torn by the death of his brother, an emotional Smith left the Academy in a chartered plane to be with his family in Omaha.

Two weeks after being fired, a bitter Smith charged that West Point had violated several N.C.A.A. regulations for inequitable distribution of prep school scholarships to favor athletes, for excessive on-campus visits allowed by the N.C.A.A., and the use of athletic department telephone credit cards by players for personal calls.

Lt. Gen. Andrew J. Goodpaster, superintendent at the Academy, issued a statement in response to Smith's charges. He said the allegations had already been investigated and "appropriate action" taken. "If I find that there are additional allegations, they also will be investigated and acted on in a thorough and comprehensive manner," said Gen. Goodpaster. "It is apparent that Coach Smith is greatly disturbed over the decision not to renew his contract and the announcement of the fact as made."

Smith said the Academy had conducted an investigation into the violations after he had suggested there was a problem.

Gen. Goodpaster, in a prepared statement, also referred to the investigation. "I understand that former coach Homer Smith has made a written statement to the press alleging improper recruiting practices on the part of the Military Academy. While I cannot respond in specific terms, not having seen the statement, it appears that these are matters most, if not all, of which he informed us about in December of last year (1977). As a result, we conducted, at my direction, a thorough and extensive internal review of the entire matter, culminating in appropriate action to assure that requirements were being observed properly."

Col. Robert Berry, head of the Department of Law at the Academy, chaired a review board that investigated the allegations leveled by Smith. The N.C.A.A. conducted its review following the completion of the Berry investigation and later reprimanded the Academy for those violations.

When the dust settled after releasing Homer Smith and answering his allegations of N.C.A.A. rules violations at West Point, the athletic department selected Lou Saban, head coach at the University of Miami, to succeed Smith. It was a surprising selection since Saban originally contacted Army athletic director Raymond P. Murphy to recommend one of his Miami assistant coaches. When Saban was told his staff assistant wasn't under consideration, he tossed his name into the ring, and Army pulled it out quickly.

The Academy, obviously seeking a big name for its head coaching position, succeeded. Saban had enjoyed success on both the college and professional levels. He coached the Buffalo Bills twice during his career, winning the Eastern Conference championship in the old American Football League. He also was at the helm when O.J. Simpson was riddling pro defenses en route to an NFL rushing record of over two thousand yards in one season. Saban also coached the Denver Broncos in the NFL. He was at Miami for two years before opting for the banks of the Hudson River in an effort to rejuvenate the Army football program.

Saban had a record of being a football vagabond, jumping from one coaching assignment to another. In fact he once accepted a position at the University of Cincinnati, but left after just two weeks.

While that type of job hopping seemed ill-suited for the Army position, Saban nonetheless stepped in to begin yet another rebuilding effort. An intense football tactician, Saban got off to a flying start in 1979 by winning his first two games. The Cadets edged Connecticut 26-10, and then stunned Stanford 17-13 on a touchdown run by halfback Gerald Walker late in the fourth quarter.

Once again, delusions of grandeur gathered at West Point, only to be dashed by reality. The opening two victories were the only ones Saban's squad was able to chalk up. Eight losses and a 17-17 tie against Duke left Saban with a 2-8-1 record. He also lost his patience and resigned suddenly in July, 1980.

At this time in West Point football history, a name coach obviously didn't turn the football program around, but instead instilled sudden turmoil despite the fact that Saban's top assistant coach, Ed Cavanaugh, was chosen as his replacement.

Saban's departure closed the book on the seventies era of football at West Point. The results were anything but pleasing. The bottom line showed Army with thirty-six victories, sixty-eight defeats, and three ties.

Army quarterback Kingsley Fink rolls to his right looking for an Army receiver to break into open during 1972 Army-Navy game in Philadelphia. Fink guided the Cadets to a 23-15 victory over the Middies.

Some old friends dropped into Michie Stadium, the scene of many of their past triumphs, during the 1973 Army football season. Bill Carpenter, left, the "Lonely End," Al Vanderbush, currently deputy director of athletics at the Academy and former co-captain of the 1960 Army team, and Bob Anderson, former two-time All-America halfback. Anderson was at West Point as a member of Army's radio network.

Army quarterback Kingsley Fink was one of the finest passing quarterbacks in West Point history. Fink ranks second in career passing at the Academy with 3,079 yards on 257 completions.

Army's football team had its difficulties during the 1973 season, but many of those problems came because of the talents of its opponents. Pittsburgh defeated Army 34-0 at Michie Stadium, thanks in part to the efforts of tailback Tony Dorsett, one of the finest runners in college football history. Here Dorsett gains yardage, slipping the tackle by Jim Cisek. Dorsett also had inflicted plenty of damage on the Dallas Cowboys' National Football League opponents for the past decade.

Homer Smith stops briefly by a cannon at West Point's Trophy Point shortly after being named head football coach. Smith was the first to introduce the Wishbone offense to Army football. He utilized that attack for two seasons before reverting to the pro-set with Leamon Hall as his quarterback. Smith had just one winning season at the Academy, that coming in 1977 when Army posted a 7-4 mark and defeated rival Navy.

Army football coach Homer Smith made his West Point coaching debut in 1974, replacing Tom Cahill. Smith compiled a record of twenty-one victories, thirty-three defeats, and one tie during his five seasons at the Academy. He came to West Point after serving as offensive coordinator at UCLA. He remained out of coaching for a year after leaving West Point, returned to UCLA as offensive coordinator, and joined the Kansas City Chiefs as an assistant under head coach Frank Ganz. Ganz served as an assistant coach here at West Point under Smith. Smith recently joined the University of Alabama coaching staff.

Army quarterback Scott Gillogly runs the
Wishbone attack installed by first-year coach
Homer Smith in 1974. Here Gillogly gains
yardage against Penn State. The Cadets
jumped to a 14-0 lead on the Nittany Lions,
but Coach Joe Paterno's squad rebounded to
post a 21-14 victory.

Army coach Homer Smith, left, instructs
quarterback Leamon Hall during final
moments of the Army-Air Force encounter in
1974. Hall rallied the Cadets to a last minute
17-16 victory over the Falcons at Michie
Stadium. It was Hall's first year at West Point.
The Apopka, Florida native went on to
become Army's all-time leading passer.

Army fullback Brad Dodrill (37) follows the
block of Markus Hardy (45) to gain yardage
up the middle during 21-14 loss to Penn State
in 1974. Nittany Lion linebacker Greg Buttle
(67) moves in to make the tackle.

Army's 1974 team captain, Bob Johnson (84),
talks to teammate Rick Conniff (91), a
defensive end, during the season opener
against Lafayette. Army edged the Leopards
14-7 during Homer Smith's debut as head
coach. Johnson was unable to play during
the season because of cancer. He later
recovered and was commissioned following
graduation.

Alexander "Babe" Weyand was inducted in the National Football Foundation Hall of Fame during ceremonies in 1974. Weyand was an outstanding guard and tackle at West Point from 1911 to 1915.

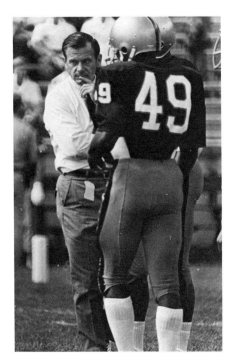

Army coach Homer Smith ponders his next play, which he will give fullback Willie Thigpen (49). Smith was head coach at West Point from 1974 to 1978.

While the seventies were anything but memorable in the annals of Army football history, the year 1972 was one of the most successful as the Cadets posted a 6-4 record and took the measure of Navy, 23-15. Some members of the Rabble Rousers were just as successful, kidnapping the Navy goat and holding it hostage. In this photograph, Bob Sansone holds the Army mascot, while Chuck Hutzler handles the Naval Academy mascot. The goat was eventually returned to the Middies during the eve of the 1972 Army-Navy clash in Philadelphia.

Army tight end Clennie Brundidge (82) leaps high in the air to pull in a touchdown pass against Holy Cross in 1976. Army posted a 26-24 victory over the Crusaders. Brundidge went on to become the finest pass receiver in Army history. He also lettered in basketball.

Army halfback Greg King (43) poses with a Midshipman's cap following the Cadets' 17-14 victory over Navy in 1977. King played an instrumental role in Army's success that season, piling up 961 yards on 177 carries. That ranks as the ninth best single season rushing effort in football history at West Point. He still holds the Army record for the longest run from scrimmage, 97 yards against Holy Cross in 1977. That is also a Michie Stadium record. King's scintillating run against the Crusaders helped propel Army to a 48-7 victory.

Members of the 1977 Army football team gather around the Commander-in-Chief's Trophy presented to the team that wins the round robin football competition each year between Army, Air Force, and Navy. The trophy was initially introduced to service academy football in 1972, and the Cadets won the trophy for the first time that year under the guidance of Coach Tom Cahill. Army won it a second time in 1977 under Coach Homer Smith, and have won it twice since Coach Jim Young has been at the Army football helm, in 1984 and 1986.

Army quarterback Leamon Hall (16) looks downfield for a receiver during a game against Stanford University in 1976 at Michie Stadium. Hall staged one of the most remarkable comebacks in Army history, rallying the Cadets from a 20-0 deficit in the second half to a 21-20 victory. The win, as incredible as it was, proved to be one of the most satisfying to Coach Homer Smith. Just a year earlier he took his 1975 Army team to Palo Alto to meet Stanford only to see Army drubbed by a 67-14 margin.

Army halfback Greg King (43) breaks a tackle and picks up good yardage against Boston College in 1976. King put together his best season in 1977, gaining 961 yards as Army posted a 7-4 record.

Army quarterback Leamon Hall (16) and tight end Clennie Brundidge celebrate after a 17-14 victory over rival Navy in 1977. Hall closed out his career with that victory, setting fifteen Army passing records during his four years at West Point. Brundidge holds Army's career receiving records for most receptions (147), most yards receiving (2,279), and most touchdown receptions (14).

Army's Heisman Trophy winners, left to right, Pete Dawkins, Glenn Davis, and Felix "Doc" Blanchard, wave to appreciative Army football fans during halftime ceremonies at Michie Stadium honoring them for their achievements in 1977.

In 1977, the Military Academy honored its former Heisman Trophy winners. In this photograph are, left to right, Glenn Davis, Army co-captain Chuck D'Amico, Felix "Doc" Blanchard, co-captain and quarterback Leamon Hall, and Pete Dawkins. The three Heisman winners were presented autographed footballs by the 1977 Army football team. The special weekend proved almost prophetic as the Cadets compiled a 7-4 record in 1977 and defeated Air Force 31-6 and Navy 17-14 to win the Commander-in-Chief's Trophy. Blanchard was Army's first Heisman winner, taking the honor in 1945. Davis won the coveted trophy a year later, while Dawkins was honored in 1958, Coach Earl "Red" Blaik's final season.

Lt. Gen. Andrew J. Goodpaster, super-intendent of the Academy, presents the Army Athletic Association Trophy to Clennie Brundidge during graduation.

Coach Lou Saban took over the football coaching reins at West Point in 1979 following the dismissal of Homer Smith. Saban, who enjoyed immense success in professional football with the Buffalo Bills and the Denver Broncos, won his first two games at the Academy. But the Cadets failed to maintain that momentum and dropped eight encounters, while managing a tie in another game against Duke. Saban, who was as well known with moving companies as with college and professional football teams, left during the summer of 1980. His top assistant, Ed Cavanaugh, then took over the coaching assignment.

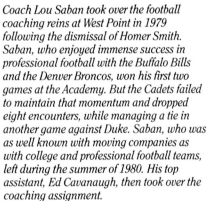

Mike Fahnestock made an auspicious start in his Army football career, corralling three touchdown passes during a 34-10 victory over Massachusetts in 1977. That tied a single game record which was first set by Jim Cain in 1949 against Fordham and equaled by Dick Stephenson against Colgate in 1956. Fahnestock, from Selinsgrove, Pennsylvania, lettered four years in football while at the Academy. He was also an outstanding hurdler on Army's track team.

Lou Saban trots onto the artificial carpet at Michie Stadium during his coaching debut against Connecticut in 1979. The Cadets edged the Huskies 26-10 and then stunned Stanford a week later in California, 17-13. But it was downhill after that as Army managed only a 17-17 tie against Duke while dropping eight games.

Saban shouts instructions to assistant coach Clarence Shelmon during the 1979 season opener at Michie Stadium. Saban made an auspicious start as Army's head coach, but didn't stay around very long for curtain calls, departing in the summer of 1980.

Resplendent with fall foliage and another capacity crowd is this shot of Michie Stadium, home of the Army football team. Named in honor of Dennis Mahan Michie, the first captain and coach at West Point in 1890, the stadium provides football fans one of the most colorful spectacles in the nation during the fall season. At the left corner of the stadium is the football locker room, a three-story structure that includes weight training facilities as well as locker rooms.

CHAPTER 12

THE LONG ROAD BACK

As the United States Military Academy moves closer to recognizing its 100th year of Army football in 1990, it does so on a very positive note. When Coach Jim Young's squad prepared for the 1987 season the immediate goal was a fourth consecutive winning season, something that has not been accomplished at West Point since the 1960-1963 period. When the eighties decade began, the Army football program was looking for its first winning season since the days of Leamon Hall in 1977.

In 1980, the Academy re-examined the football program, questioning why the Naval Academy and Air Force Academy were succeeding when Army was in the midst of a frustrating struggle to turn the corner on success.

One answer to the problem was stability, both in the coaching staff and in the athletic administration. Not since Earl Blaik was head football coach and athletic director had the Academy stabilized its multi-sport program. Athletic directors from all walks of the Army would come and go every three years. It is difficult to evaluate a program's strengths and weaknesses in so short a span of time.

That changed in 1980. When Maj. Gen. (Ret.) Raymond Murphy stepped down from the position of director of athletics, West Point decided to civilianize the director's position in order to establish more continuity in the program. It was a decision that has proved successful.

Frustrated at suffering losses to Navy on the gridiron, the Military Academy tapped a former assistant athletic director at Navy, Carl Ullrich, to administer the twenty-six-sport athletic program. Ullrich was serving as athletic director at Western Michigan University when the Army position opened, and he jumped at the opportunity to return to a service academy athletic program.

"I was very happy at Western Michigan," said Ullrich after accepting the directorship at West Point. "I would not have left had it not been for this opportunity to return to a service academy. My eleven years at the Naval Academy were most enjoyable, both professionally and for my family. That is why I look forward to this opportunity at West Point."

Ullrich certainly had the proper credentials to head the Army program. A 1950 graduate of Cornell University who also holds a master's degree in public administration from the University of Baltimore, Ullrich spent eleven successful years at the Naval Academy as an assistant athletic director and coach of the Navy crew team. He joined the Naval Academy staff in 1968 and supervised the areas of admissions, counseling, recruiting, eligibility and Congressional liaison. He coached the varsity crew for six seasons, winning the Eastern Intercollegiate title in 1971.

Ullrich began his coaching career on the secondary school level following his graduation from Cornell. He returned to his alma mater in 1955 as freshman crew coach. In five years he led the Big Red to three Eastern Intercollegiate and two national championships. Ullrich also coached one year at Boston University (1968). In between he served two years as assistant commandant of the Sanford Naval Academy in Florida. He left Boston University for the Naval Academy.

During his one year at Western Michigan, Ullrich began a revitalization of the Broncos athletic program, which faced competition in the Mid-American Conference. His efforts were successful.

Upon assuming his position at West Point, Ullrich faced an immediate problem, replacing a short-term and unhappy football coach, Lou Saban. Coming so late in the summer, Ullrich tapped Ed Cavanaugh, Saban's most experienced assistant.

Cavanaugh, whose only college head coaching assignment was at Idaho State from 1968-1971 (where he was 20-19), was on vacation in Cape Hatteras, North Carolina, when he was summoned to replace his close friend, Saban.

"If I had known anything like this was going to happen, I might have given the office an address," quipped Cavanaugh. "I knew Lou was unhappy, but I had no inkling he would leave. I am just very happy and proud officials at the Academy offered me the opportunity to become head coach."

Cavanaugh was given three years to continue Saban's efforts to rebuild the football program. He was unable to accomplish the mission. His best season was his last when the Cadets were 4-7, and the most positive showing in the Army-Navy game was a 3-3 deadlock in 1981.

Despite the slow improvement, the Academy was frustrated by five consecutive years of losing football. West Point went searching again high and low for a new football leader. Their search was successful.

Jim Young, former head coach at Purdue and Arizona, had been serving as an assistant athletic director at Purdue when the Army job became vacant. He left coaching to determine whether or not he should change career directions, but missed the on-field competition and the player-coach relationships he had for so many years.

"I enjoyed that year," said Young, "but I did miss certain aspects of coaching. I wasn't interested in coaching at any place. This job appealed to me more than any would have, but why I don't know.

"There was a personal challenge to meet, to make it a successful program, and the individuals I'd work with appealed to me."

After compiling an overall record of 69-32-1 after four years at Arizona and five years at Purdue, he was anxious to begin his new assignment as Army's thirtieth football coach. West Point, likewise, was anxious.

"Jim Young brings to us the ingredients that we feel are needed in order to build a winning football program," said Ullrich while introducing Young to the media at West Point in January, 1983. "He has been a highly successful coach at two first rate institutions, and we are very pleased to have Jim become a key member of our coaching staff."

Young's track record was impressive. In five seasons at Purdue, 1977-1981, he compiled a 38-19-1 record and guided the Boilermakers to three post-season bowl appearances. Purdue was 9-2-1 in 1978 and earned a spot in the Peach Bowl, defeating Georgia Tech 41-21. A year later Young's squad was 10-2, including victories over Notre Dame and Michigan. They earned a spot in the Bluebonnet Bowl, defeating Tennessee 27-22. Then in 1980 Purdue was 9-3, went to the Liberty Bowl, and upended Missouri 28-25.

As head coach at Arizona (1973-76) Young was 31-13. During his first year the Wildcats shared the Western Athletic Conference championship, and during each of his first three years his teams were ranked in the Top 20.

Young received some excellent coaching lessons from Bo Schembechler of Michigan. He joined Schembechler as an assistant coach at Miami of Ohio in 1964 and remained there five years. When Schembechler left for Michigan in 1969, Young went along as defensive coordinator. In four years the Wolverines compiled records of 8-3, 9-1, 11-1, and 10-1; won or shared the Big Ten Conference championship in 1969, 1971, and 1972; and twice represented the conference in the Rose Bowl, first in 1969 and again in 1971.

When he took over as head coach at West Point, Young said emphatically he expected to win. "I don't believe in rebuilding," he said. "When you say that you are telling the players that are here the wrong thing. These are the young

men you are going to work with, and you must convince them they can win. I fully expect to have a winning season this fall."

During his coaching career, Young has been very successful adapting to his personnel. At Arizona he opted to run the Veer offense, option-oriented football. At Purdue he had an outstanding freshman passer, Mark Herrmann, so he ran the pro offense with success.

During his first season at West Point, Young ran the I-formation, but the Cadets finished with just two victories and nine defeats, including a 42-13 loss to Navy in the first service classic to be played in the Rose Bowl. Once again, Young re-evaluated his personnel. He also saw how successful the Air Force Academy had been utilizing the Wishbone-T offense, and felt that type of attack might prove suitable to his personnel at the Academy.

"I realized we didn't have the offensive line ability or the great size to keep doing what we were doing," said Young in an article in the Atlanta *Constitution* in 1985. "I knew we had to go to an option attack. Air Force obviously had success running it and that was a factor.

"But I also believe it's a very good academy offense. It requires great discipline and teamwork. And all eleven men get hit. There is no star system in the Wishbone."

Young's change of direction brought immediate results, an 8-3-1 record in 1984, including a tie against Tennessee and victories over Air Force and Navy. Additionally, the Cadets earned and accepted their first bowl bid in West Point history. They celebrated by edging Michigan State 10-6 in the inaugural Cherry Bowl in Pontiac, Michigan. Their Wishbone was also the best rushing offense in the country.

In 1985, Army continued its resurgence by compiling a 9-3 record. Coach Young's squad also received a second consecutive bowl bid, defeating Illinois in the Peach Bowl, 31-29. If there was a disappointment, it would be in the 17-7 loss to Navy, an unexpected but not unusual event during a service academy clash.

In 1986, the Army team suffered three straight losses midway through the season to Holy Cross, Rutgers, and Boston College to slip to 3-5, but the Cadets reeled off victories over Air Force, Lafayette, and Navy to finish 6-5. Coach Young's squad upset Air Force 21-11, and then trounced Navy 27-7 to win the Commander-in-Chief's Trophy for the second time in four years.

Why is success in football important at the United States Military Academy?

Young easily responds to that question. "Whether it's correct or not, winning football games is important to the image people have of West Point," says the Army coach. "I mean, people look out on the football field and see future leaders of our country there. You should be winners at Army. It might not be right to think that way, but that's the way it is."

A football player's life at a service academy contrasts dramatically with football players at other colleges and universities. Getting up at 5:30 a.m., attending class at all

Coach Ed Cavanaugh observes action at Michie Stadium during his first season as Army head coach in 1980. Cavanaugh succeeded Lou Saban as head coach at West Point. During his three years at the helm, 1980-1982, the Cadets won ten games, lost twenty-one, and tied two.

Cadet Stan March served as First Captain of the Corps of Cadets, the highest position in the cadet chain-of-command, and also was elected captain of the 1980 Army football team. He was the first player since Pete Dawkins in 1958 to serve in both positions. Dawkins was also president of his class.

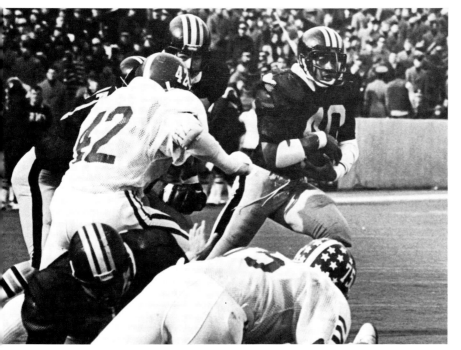

Army halfback Gerald Walker (40) looks for running room against Holy Cross during the 1981 football season. Walker lettered four years in football while at West Point, 1979-1982, and closed out his career as the second leading rusher in Army history with 2,700 yards. Glenn Davis is the career leader with 2,957 yards. Walker had an outstanding year in 1981, rushing for 1,053 yards, the third best season effort in Army history.

times, even on Saturday, drills and ceremony, military courtesy, and academic challenges are a far cry from the recruiting pitch many "blue chip" athletes receive from other institutions. Yet, Coach Jim Young seems to thrive in this environment.

"There's more of a pro-American attitude in the country," says Young. "That doesn't mean we're going to get the kid who can play in the National Football League. But more people are looking favorably on military academies now and from that group you can find some football players."

While the discipline and heavy academic and physical training schedules provide anything but the typical recruiting assets, Young accepts them for the right reasons.

"All the rules at West Point have a purpose," says Young. "It can be demanding here. But if you can't handle stress here, how are you going to handle a lot of stress on the battlefield when everything is on the line. I don't think people in the United States want generals who can't handle the pressure."

While Young's coaching success has somewhat dominated the football picture at West Point, it is also his success in developing players during this span that has proved instrumental in turning the Army football program around.

When Army went to the Wishbone in 1984, Young handed the ball to quarterback Nate Sassaman and told him to get the job done. Sassaman, from Portland, Oregon, had minimal success during his football career at West Point. In high school he was an option quarterback, and he did see duty at quarterback during his first two seasons. However, he did not possess a strong arm, so Young moved him to the defensive backfield.

Sassaman accepted the change with reluctance, but played well nonetheless. When Army switched to the Wishbone, Sassaman volunteered and won the job. The timing could not have been more perfect.

Sassaman was just the type of quarterback Young needed. He possessed quickness, a good command of the game, and a willingness to take the hard knocks. All Sassaman did was gain 1,002 yards, the first time an Army quarterback had rushed for over a 1,000 yards.

Sassaman's backfield mates included Doug Black, Bill Lampley, Jarvis Hollingsworth, Dee Bryant, and Clarence Jones. Black, cut from the football squad during his first two years at West Point, refused to give up and went out again during the spring of his sophomore year. He was listed eighth on the roster of fullbacks, but by the time spring practice was over he was alternating at the starting position.

Black became the Cinderella story of the 1984 season. He rushed for a season record 1,148 yards, surpassing Charlie Jarvis' old record of 1,110 yards which was set in 1968. The native of Salado, Texas, teamed up with Sassaman to make Army's rushing attack the most potent in the nation. It also marked the first time in history two Army backs had rushed for over 1,000 yards in a single season.

Black continued his exceptional running during the 1985 season when Army was 9-3. He led the squad with 950 yards

for a 4.8-yard average per carry. He received able support from quarterbacks Rob Healy and Tory Crawford. Crawford racked up 657 yards. Jones had 604 yards and Lampley another 578 as Army's wishbone continued to roll.

The other success stories came on the offensive line where Pete Edmonds, Karl Heineman, Church Matthews, and Vince McDermott did yeoman duty during the 1984 season. In 1985, there was tight end Rob Dickerson, center Ron Rice, Joe Manausa, and Ed Schultz.

During both those winning seasons there was one lineman who stood out among them all, Don Smith, a 270-pound guard from Fredericktown, Ohio. Smith was named to the Kodak All-America team following the 1985 season, the first Army player to gain first-team All-America recognition since 1968, when linebacker Ken Johnson of nearby Newburgh, New York, was recognized.

"He is the best offensive lineman I have ever been around, either as a head coach or as an assistant, on the college level," said Jim Young on the subject of his best offensive lineman.

Young's solid assessment was supported by Army's opponents.

"He's a premier lineman," said Rick Lantz, defensive line coach at Notre Dame in an Associated Press story. "He could play for any team on our schedule. He could play for us, and he would play well, not just be a squad member. He has the ability for scramble blocking, but he could play a pro-type offense."

Smith shined off the field as well during his West Point career. He was a Rhodes Scholarship candidate before withdrawing his name from consideration. He also was a regimental commander in the Corps of Cadets, overseeing a staff of ten and 1,100 cadets.

There were other noteworthy achievements during the eighties. In 1980, Army football captain Stan March received a National Football Foundation Scholar-Athlete award and an NCAA Scholarship. March also was first captain of the Corps of Cadets, the highest military position a cadet can hold in the chain-of-command during his four years at West Point.

Sassaman was the co-recipient of the Exemplary Player Award in 1984, presented by Football Roundup magazine. He shared that honor with Heisman Trophy winner Doug Flutie of Boston College.

In 1985, Doug Black received a National Football Foundation Scholar-Athlete award and an NCAA scholarship, while Don Smith also was the recipient of an NCAA scholarship.

During the eighties, team captain George Mayes (1980) and Doug Pavek (1985) participated in the East-West Shrine Game in San Francisco. Army participants in the Hula Bowl included defensive back Dave Charest (1980), center Dan Enright (1982), defensive back Mike Williams (1983), defensive end Larry Carroll (1984), linebacker Jim Gentille and defensive back Eric Griffin (1985), and Doug Black and Don Smith (1986). In 1980, wide receiver Mike Fahnestock

Army quarterback Rob Healy (7) looks for running room during a 33-11 victory over Harvard in 1984. Healy was an understudy to Nate Sassman in 1984, but turned in a solid effort during a 24-12 victory over Air Force. In that game Healy was the starter because Sassaman was sidelined with bruised ribs. Healy was the starter at quarterback during the 1985 season when Army finished 9-3 and defeated Illinois in the Peach Bowl.

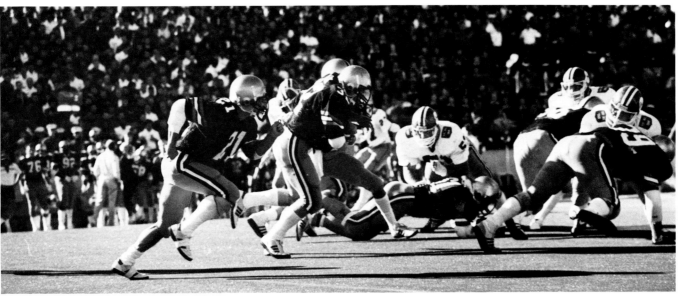

Army fullback Doug Black (32) takes a handoff from quarterback Nate Sassman, follows the blocking of guard Don Smith (79), and gains good yardage against Harvard in 1984. Halfback Dee Bryant (21) also provides blocking support. Black proved to be the "Cinderella" story during the 1984 season. Cut twice during his first two years at the Academy, Black, from Salado, Texas, earned a spot on the varsity during spring practice in 1984. When the 1984 season concluded Black set an Army record for yards rushing with 1,148 yards, surpassing the old record of 1,110 yards set by Charlie Jarvis in 1968.

Army fullback Doug Black looks for running room during a game against Yale in 1985.

played in the Blue-Gray Classic, while Dan Enright and Larry Carroll played in the Japan Bowl in Tokyo in 1982 and 1984, respectively.

On the field, Fahnestock set a single game record in 1980 for yards receiving, piling up 186 against Lehigh. He also set season records for yards receiving, 937, and touchdowns caught, 7.

In 1984, Black set season records for yards rushing, 1,148, and number of rushes, 264.

Placekicker Craig Stopa of Prospect, Kentucky, set numerous Army records on game, season and career categories. He holds the record for the longest field goal, 53 yards against Yale in 1985. He also kicked five field goals against Air Force in 1984. Stopa established a new season record for field goals made in 1984 with fifteen. On the career level, Stopa holds the record for points after touchdown made, 106; field goals attempted, 76; and field goals made, 48. He holds the Army record for most consecutive PATs with 61, including a perfect 44-for-44 in 1985. Stopa also set an NCAA record for the highest percentage of field goals made between 40-49 yards, converting seventeen of twenty-one attempts for 81 percent during his four-year career.

During the eighties, halfback Gerald Walker became the second leading rusher in Army history with 2,700 yards, falling shy of Glenn Davis' career mark of 2,957 yards. Walker rolled up his offensive totals from 1979-1982. He also ranked fourth in season rushing with 1,053 yards for 1981.

Perhaps the most significant accomplishments during the eighties were the performances by Jim Young's 1984 and 1985 squads in their post-season bowl appearances. The Cadets, hungry at the opportunity to participate in a bowl game for the first time in history, were not about to be outdone by any opponent.

In both the Cherry Bowl and the Peach Bowl, Army was a decided underdog. Some questioned their remarkable turn-around, coming against perhaps a less difficult schedule than their Big Ten opponents, Michigan State and Illinois, faced during their regular season.

However, Young's two squads were undaunted by such talk, and produced upset victories during the Cherry Bowl and the Peach Bowl.

Nate Sassaman, the Cherry Bowl's most valuable player, gained over 100 yards in leading the Cadets to a 10-6 triumph over Michigan State. The Army defense held the Spartans' outstanding running back Lorenzo White in check.

Sassaman also led Army to its 28-11 victory over Navy in 1984, undoubtedly the most important of the 1984 season because of all the past frustrations in the Army-Navy game. It was in that service clash that Sassaman went over the 1,000-yard mark before he was relieved of his duties later in the fourth quarter by Young after an outstanding effort.

Perhaps the experience of playing in one bowl game paid off for the Cadets the second time around. Of course, the Army Wishbone did its job on the ground during a 31-29 victory over Illinois on New Year's Eve in 1985. But it was the unexpected that turned the game around for the Cadets.

Defensively, Peel Chronister, who was starting for only the second time during the 1985 season, intercepted two Illinois passes and then batted away a two-point conversion attempt in the final thirty seconds to preserve the Army lead. Unlikely as it seemed before the game, Chronister was selected the outstanding defensive player at the conclusion of matters.

Offensively, the Cadets turned four Illini turnovers into points during the Peach Bowl. Additionally, Army simply did not rely on the rushing attack. They threw the football, from, of all places the halfback position. In the second quarter, halfback William Lampley tossed a 33-yard scoring pass to split end Benny Wright to boost Army's lead to 21-10. With Illinois storming back to take a 23-21 lead in the third quarter, Army pulled off more trickery after moving to the Illinois twenty-six. Jones took a pitch from quarterback Rob Healy, who scored earlier in the game, and ran to his left. Suddenly, he pulled up and heaved a pass to Scott Spellmon in the end zone to put Army back on top, 28-23. A 39-yard field goal by Craig Stop pushed the Cadet lead to 31-23, and they needed that for the win.

Illinois missed a field goal when Chris White's kick ricocheted off the goal post, but Jack Trudeau came back to hit David Williams for a fifty-four-yard touchdown with thirty-four seconds to play. Trudeau then went for the two-point conversion to gain a tie, but Chronister knocked his pass away to preserve Army's second consecutive bowl victory over a Big Ten opponent.

Today, Army's football history remains in Jim Young's hands. There is no better success story.

A football season would not be a total success without a victory over Navy, and Army accomplished that task in 1984, whipping the Middies 28-11 at Veterans Stadium in Philadelphia. The win left Coach Jim Young's squad with a 7-3-1 record and a spot in the inaugural Cherry Bowl against Michigan State. Army concluded the campaign by trimming the Spartans 10-6 to finish 8-3-1. In this photograph Young, left, and members of the squad celebrate the victory over Navy in the locker room. It was the first win over the Middies since 1977.

Army quarterback Nate Sassaman looks downfield for an open receiver during the Cherry Bowl game against Michigan State. Sassaman led the Cadets to a 10-6 upset victory in the first bowl appearance by an Army football team. Sassaman lettered in football for three years, first as a quarterback, then a defensive back, before being relocated back to quarterback in 1984, when Coach Jim Young installed the Wishbone formation.

Army halfback Clarence Jones (40), who provided outside speed for Coach Jim Young's squad during the 1984 season, gains short yardage against Michigan State during the first Cherry Bowl.

Army quarterback Nate Sassaman is interviewed by CBS prior to the 1984 Army-Navy game in Philadelphia. Sassaman led the Cadets to a 28-11 victory over the Middies. He gained 1,366 yards in total offense during the 1984 season, the fifth best season total in Army history. He received the Exemplary Player Award presented by Football Roundup *magazine, sharing the honor with Heisman Trophy winner Doug Flutie of Boston College.*

Army guard Don Smith, a class of 1986 graduate of West Point, earned first team All-America honors following the conclusion of the 1985 season. He was named to the Kodak All-America team. A four-year letterman in football, Smith is the first Army player to gain first team All-America recognition since linebacker Ken Johnson of Newburgh, New York gained All-America honors in 1968.

Army fullback Doug Black (32) follows the blocking of All-America guard Don Smith (79) while picking up good yardage against Syracuse in 1985. The Cadets dropped a decision to the Orangemen.

Carl Ullrich, second from left, director of athletics at West Point, accepts the Cherry Bowl Trophy following Army's 10-6 victory over Michigan State.

The 1984 Army football team compiled an 8-3-1 record. Coach Jim Young's squad defeated both Air Force and Navy to win the Commander-in-Chief's Trophy, and then whipped Michigan State 10-6 in the Cherry Bowl in Pontiac, Michigan. It was the first time an Army football team appeared in a post-season bowl game.

Army kicking specialist Craig Stopa (1) finds the footing somewhat unusual during the game against Memphis State at Michie Stadium in 1985. Snow blanketed the field during the game as the Cadets buried the Tigers by a 49-7 margin. Obviously the snow didn't bother the Cadets.

187

Army placekicking specialist Craig Stopa of Prospect, Kentucky. Stopa is a 1986 graduate of West Point who holds all of Army's career placekicking records. He booted a fifty-three-yard field goal against Yale in 1985 at Michie Stadium for an Army record for the longest field goal in history. That was also a Michie Stadium record. Additionally, Stopa converted five field goals for a single game record against Air Force in 1984. He also holds career records for points after touchdown scored, 106, field goals attempted, 76, and field goals made, 48. Stopa holds the Army record for most PATs in succession, 61, including a perfect forty-four for forty-four in 1985. The holder is quarterback Nate Sassaman.

Army fullback Doug Black, a walk-on who lettered in 1984 and 1985, helped pave the way for the Cadets' first two post-season bowl appearances in West Point history. In 1984, Black rushed for a season record 1,148 yards for the Cadets, who led the nation in the ground gaining department during the first year Coach Jim Young installed the Wishbone offense. His efforts helped Army gain a berth in the inaugural Cherry Bowl, where they trimmed Michigan State, 10-6. A year later Black rushed for 950 yards as Army fashioned a 9-3 record, including a 31-29 victory over Illinois in the Peach Bowl.

Former Heisman Trophy winner Pete Dawkins returns to his alma mater to check on the propects for the Army football team in 1985. Dawkins retired from the Army at the rank of brigadier general, and joined Shearson Lehman in New York. Dawkins teamed up with Bob Anderson and Bill Carpenter in 1958 to lead Army to an undefeated 8-0-1 record, the last time the Cadets finished with an unblemished record on the gridiron. Dawkins is now running for the U.S. Senate in New Jersey.

Coach Jim Young has directed Army's dramatic turnaround in college football, guiding the Cadets to a composite 29-26-1 mark during the past five years. Since assuming the head coaching position in 1983, Young led the Cadets to their first bowl appearance in history in 1984. Army earned a berth in the inaugural Cherry Bowl and dispatched Michigan State 10-6 to complete an 8-3-1 season. A year later, Young's Army squad received a bid to the Peach Bowl after posting an 8-3 record during the regular season. Once again, the Cadets upset a Big Ten representative, edging Illinois, 31-29.

President Ronald Reagan holds up a cadet parka which was presented to him during his visit to the U.S. Military Academy in October 1987. It was a good year to wear a "Beat Navy" parka since Army prevailed in its annual clash with the Midshipmen, 17-3.

Army quarterback Tory Crawford (9) finds an opening in the Navy defense to pick up yardage during a 27-7 victory over the Middies in 1986. Crawford became the second quarterback in Army history to gain over 1,000 yards during a season, racking up 1,078 yards in 1986. The Cadets notched their third consecutive winning season, defeating Air Force, Lafayette, and Navy in their final three games to finish 6-5.

Halfback Clarence Jones lettered three years in football at West Point. He ranked third in rushing during the 1985 season with 604 yards as Army posted a 9-3 record and a 31-29 victory over Illinois in the Peach Bowl.

The Corps of Cadets takes time to blow their horns during a victory over Navy in 1986. The Cadets have had a good deal to cheer about since Jim Young took over the head coaching job in football—three straight winning seasons—the first time that has happened at West Point since 1966-1968. Photograph by Charles W. Kelley.

A Saturday in the fall at the United States Military Academy means much more than just a football game. Tailgate picnics are a sight to see for unfamiliar visitors to the Academy grounds. Cadets, families, and friends get together frequently during the picturesque fall season in the Hudson Valley. Photograph by Charles W. Kelley.

Army quarterback Tory Crawford (9) tries to cut back during the 1987 Army-Navy game at Veterans Stadium in 1987. The Cadets trimmed the Middies 17-3, and Crawford closed out his career by scoring one touchdown. The veteran quarterback finished with a career rushing total of 2,313 yards, placing him fifth in Army football history. He also ranks tenth in career passing with 1,636 yards.

No, this is not a member of the alumni at West Point, or for that matter a weekend visitor. It is just a roof ornament of an energetic member of the tailgate picnic set at West Point during the fall. Things have been looking up in football during the past three years, despite the glum look of this attraction. Photograph by Charles W. Kelley.

The Army football team and the Corps of Cadets rally behind the sounds of the Cadet Pep Band. During the past three seasons there has been much to crow about with three consecutive winning efforts and two bowl games in football. The beat of the band has been loud and clear at Michie Stadium and elsewhere. Photograph by Charles W. Kelley.

A cadet rings the victory bell at Michie Stadium. The bell tender has been rather busy at Michie Stadium during the past three years since the Cadets of Coach Jim Young have posted successive records of 8-3-1, 9-3, and 6-5.

Quarterback Tory Crawford (9) slips a Navy tackle, just enough to pitch the ball to senior halfback Andy Peterson (47) who scampered into the end zone with Army's first touchdown against Navy in 1987. The Cadets whipped the Middies 17-3 to finish the season with a 5-6 record.

193

Gary Winton scored 2,296 points to lead the Army basketball team from 1974 to 1978, setting a career record until 1987 when Kevin surpassed Winston with 2,325 points.

Mike Silliman is the fifth leading scorer in Army history with 1,342 points in 68 games from 1963 to 1966. He also was captain of the United States Olympic team that won a gold medal.

Dale Hall is shown here as captain of the 1945 Army basketball team. Hall, who lettered in football while playing in the shadows of Doc Blanchard and Glenn Davis, later served as an assistant football coach under Earl "Red" Blaik. He succeeded Blaik as head football coach at West Point in 1959. Hall was Army's first All-America basketball selection in history.

In 1903, a group of West Point cadets met a team from the Yonkers Y.M.C.A. in the first game of basketball at the U.S. Military Academy. The game was played in the Old Cadet Gymnasium, which was located at a site now occupied by Washington Hall. It was called an exhibition because it introduced basketball, a game that was invented by Dr. James Naismith, to West Point post personnel who were totally unfamiliar with the sport.

The Army team, organized by cadet Joseph Warren Stilwell, defeated the visitors from Yonkers by a 54-10 margin. That first game achieved its desired results as basketball then took its place among the established sports at the Military Academy.

In a news release prepared at West Point on January 27, 1944, Stilwell's place in the history of West Point basketball was catalogued. The news release described Stilwell as "a pioneer of the game, and a smart, aggressive player with a keen eye for the basket." At the time of the news release Stilwell held the rank of lieutenant general and was commanding in China and Burma.

Stilwell was not only responsible for the institution of basketball at West Point, but he was a regular on the basketball team, as well as manager and coach. During his four years at the Academy, Stilwell lettered in football for two seasons, 1902-1903, and served as captain of the first Army cross country team. Two years after his graduation in 1904, Stilwell was assigned to the Military Academy as an instructor where he again became involved with the basketball program. He served as officer-in-charge and coach of the Army team. Stilwell guided the Army basketball fortunes for another four years, 1907-1911, and compiled an overall record of forty-nine victories and just seventeen defeats.

A copy of the 1910 *Howitzer* yearbook states that Army claimed themselves Eastern Champions following the 1909-1910 season, after compiling a 14-1 record. The lone setback came at the hands of Swarthmore by a 27-26 margin in four overtimes. "At the close of the previous season the outlook was rather dark, for Devers, Beardslea, and Catron all were lost from the team," the yearbook states. "But when the practice began last fall under Lt. Stilwell, whom we were fortunate again to have as a coach, a wealth of material was discovered."

One year later the *Howitzer* yearbook stated the basketball team's greatest setback was the loss of Lt. Stilwell, the coach, after receiving another assignment. Quoting the *Howitzer*: "The severest setback was the loss, early in the season of Lt. Stilwell as coach, his detail at the Academy having expired. This officer played as a cadet on the team which introduced the game here, and by his untiring efforts as representative and coach in the last four seasons, West Point has risen to its high position in intercollegiate basketball."

The first intercollegiate basketball game an Army team participated in was during the 1904-1905 season when the Cadets hosted Princeton. The Tigers prevailed in that encounter by a 14-5 margin. Since Stilwell helped introduce the American sport of basketball at West Point, a tradition of success has been built during the past eighty-five years. The efforts of Joseph Stilwell and many others have contributed to that colorful history.

Army teams have compiled a record of 912 victories and 654 losses during the past eighty-five years. In addition to Stilwell's first team, which was 1-0, there have been two other undefeated Army basketball teams. The 1922-1923 squad was 17-0, while the 1944 team registered a 15-0 record. Dale Hall, who played in the shadows of Blanchard and Davis on Army's football team, led that 1944 squad and a year later became Army's first basketball All-America selection.

During the past eighty-five years Army basketball teams have compiled winning seasons fifty-five times and finished at the break-even mark on three other occasions.

One of the most successful coaches in Army basketball history was Leo Novak, a member of the athletic staff at the Academy from 1926 through 1949. He coached the Army basketball squad, as well as serving as an assistant football coach and head track and cross country coach. Novak coached the basketball team from 1927 to 1939, compiling a record of 126 victories and just 61 losses. In thirteen years he did not have a losing season. His last Army squad in 1939 compiled the best record during his coaching tenure, winning thirteen of fifteen games. Three other teams won twelve or more games under Novak's leadership. No other Army basketball coach has won as many games as Novak.

One of the most successful individual players during the twenties was John Roosma, a graduate of the class of 1926. Roosma not only served as captain of the 1926 squad that finished with an 11-6 record and a 21-12 victory over Navy, but he was named to the Naismith Basketball Hall of Fame in 1961, and the Citizens Savings Athletic Foundation Hall of Fame.

The Academy has had seven players receive All-America recognition. Dale Hall was the first in 1945, followed by Mike Silliman in 1965, Jim Oxley in 1970, Gary Winton in 1978, and Kevin Houston in 1987. Honorable mention All-America honors were accorded Matt Brown in 1979, Randy Cozzens in 1985, and Kevin Houston in 1986.

Houston, a 1987 graduate from Pearl River, New York, became Army's all-time leading scorer during the 1986-1987 season. He finished his four-year career with 2,325 points, eclipsing the old record of 2,296 set by Winton from 1974-1978. Houston moved past Winton by scoring 953 points during his final season, becoming the first Army player to lead the nation in scoring and free throw shooting. He averaged 32.9 points during the 1986-1987 season and converted 268 of 294 free throws for a 91.2 percent accuracy rate.

Houston's season total of 953 points was an Army record. He also set Army season records for most free throws, 268, and most field goals, 311. His free throw percentage, .912, was the highest in history. Houston also holds career records for field goal attempts (1,698), free throws (650), free throw percentage (.869) and free throw attempts (748). The Army guard also set the single game scoring record, connecting for 53 points against Fordham to surpass the old mark of 51 points set by Mark Binstein during the 1955-56 season against Rhode Island.

Three Army players—Ed Mueller, '72, Bob Sherwin, '73, and Randy Cozzens, '85—received NCAA post-graduate scholarships following the completion of their Army basketball careers. Sherwin also was the recipient of the Naismith Award in 1973 as the nation's outstanding player under six feet tall.

Mike Silliman, captain of the 1966 Army basketball team, served as captain of the 1968 United States Olympic basketball team that won a gold medal. Silliman currently ranks fifth among Army's all-time scorers with 1,342 points scored from 1963-1966. He averaged 19.7 points per game during his career and ranks third among the all-time rebounders with 784 or 11.1 per game.

Silliman, a 6-foot-6 center from Louisville, was joined on the Olympic team by such top players as Pete Maravich of Louisiana State University (the nation's leading scorer that year), Charlie Scott of North Carolina, Jo Jo White of Kansas, and Bill Hosket of Ohio State University, the first draft choice of the New York Knickerbockers that year.

Among those who did not make the squad that year were Calvin Murphy of Niagara, Rick Mount of Purdue, and Don Issel of Kentucky, three players who gained spots in the National Basketball Association. Silliman did play some professional basketball following completion of his military obligation, seeing limited duty with Buffalo and the Knicks.

Silliman was considered one of the finest basketball players at West Point in modern times. He led the Cadets to three appearances in the National Invitation Tournament, including two trips when Army finished third in the tourney (1964 and 1965).

Army basketball teams did not participate in tournaments until the 1955-1956 season, when the Cadets competed in the Holiday Festival. West Point defeated Rhode Island but bowed to Richmond and Virginia. The Cadets appeared in the N.I.T. for the first time in 1961, and through the 1968-1969 season, earned berths in the N.I.T. field seven times, reaching the semifinals five times. Army was third on three occasions and finished fourth twice. The Cadets also gained a berth in the N.I.T. in 1978 under Coach Mike Krzyzewski, but dropped a two-point decision to Rutgers in the opening round.

The lone tournament victory that an Army basketball team achieved came in 1976 when the Cadets captured the Vermont Classic, defeating Florida State and Yale.

Coach Taylor "Tates" Locke, head coach at West Point from 1963-1965, changed Army's poor tournament record history. During his two years at the helm the Cadets placed third in the N.I.T. twice, placed third in the Hurricane Classic, and fourth in the Far West Classic.

When Locke departed, young Bob Knight took over the head coaching assignment. At the time he signed on as head coach, he was completing an enlisted tour of duty as Locke's assistant coach. Knight spent six years at the Academy before leaving for the head coaching position at Indiana University. It took this Ohio State graduate just four years to lead the Hoosiers to the N.C.A.A. championship. In sixteen seasons at Indiana, Knight has produced three national championship teams, the latest this past 1986-1987 season.

During his six years at the Academy Knight suffered just one losing season, his last year when Army was 11-13. The Cadets led the nation in defense for three consecutive years. Four of his Army teams earned berths in the N.I.T., reaching the semifinal round three times. While at Ohio State, Knight played three years of varsity basketball. During that time the Buckeyes won three Big Ten championships and captured the national championship in 1960. Ohio State also finished second in the N.C.A.A. tournament in 1961 and 1962, Knight's final year.

Knight is considered an outstanding tactician, an excellent leader, and a master of getting the most from his

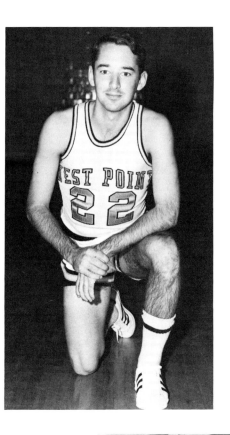

Bob Sherwin, captain of the 1972-1973 basketball team, received the Naismith Award as the nation's best player under six feet tall. Sherwin ranked ninth in career scoring with 1,253 points in 71 games, averaging 17.7 points per game.

Bill Schutsky served as captain of the 1967-1968 Army team that finished with a 20-5 record. Schutsky ranks seventh on Army's all-time scoring list with 1,292 points from 1965-1968, averaging 18.2 points per game.

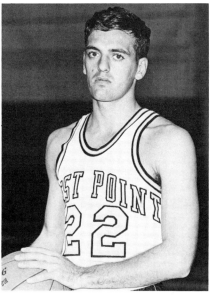

Jim Oxley captained the 1969-1970 Army team that compiled an 18-10 record under coach Bob Knight. Oxley ranks sixteenth on Army's career scoring with 953 points in eighty-one games from 1967 to 1970. Oxley also gained All-America honors in 1970.

Dennis Schlitt, who scored 800 points during his basketball career at West Point from 1980 to 1985, connects for a driving layup against Siena College in 1982. Schlitt, a guard, battled back from an internal infection which nearly claimed his life to finish out his West Point career.

material. The former Army coach has gotten into hot water because of his temperament. He is one of the most intense coaches in college basketball, but also one of the most successful in the history of the college game.

Perhaps the most notorious of Knight's temper difficulties came during the 1979 Pan American Games in San Juan, Puerto Rico. Knight was arrested for assaulting a police security officer during the end of a practice session. A *New York Times* reporter, Neil Amdur, reported that Knight claimed the American team had ten minutes remaining in its allotted practice time when a Brazilian women's team arrived and created a commotion. Knight demanded the Brazilian team either leave or remain quiet. He said the security officer, Jose Silva, ordered the Brazilian team to remain.

Knight claimed that Silva shook his hand at him three times. The fourth time Knight said Silva's finger caught him in the side of the eye. Knight reacted instinctively and hit Silva in the face.

Knight was charged with assault and battery and resisting arrest. He then filed countercharges of assault and battery, violation of civil rights and incarceration in jail without knowledge of the charges.

Following the U.S. victory in the Pan American Games that year, Knight refused to return to Puerto Rico for the trial on advice from his attorney.

Most recently, a book on Indiana basketball entitled *A Season on the Brink* was a best seller, chronicling Knight's dealings with his Indiana squad throughout the 1985 season. Knight charged that author John Feinstein of the *Washington Post* failed to follow an agreement to write specifically about the Indiana team. Knight also criticized the colorful language the author used throughout the book.

Despite these difficulties, Knight remains one of the most respected basketball coaches in the nation.

Unfortunately, when Knight left the Academy the Army basketball program went into a tailspin despite the efforts of Coach Dan Dougherty. Dougherty, an assistant coach under Jack Kraft at Villanova University, took over the Army helm in 1971. He joined the Villanova staff in 1966 as freshman coach and two years later was elevated to the varsity staff. During his time at Villanova the Wildcats appeared in the N.C.A.A. tournament three times and twice in the N.I.T.

Despite his success there and on the high school level, Dougherty suffered through four frustrating seasons at the Academy. His first two squads compiled 11-13 records, but his 1973-1974 squad was only 6-18. The following year things went from bad to worse as Army was just 3-22.

Dougherty was replaced by Mike Krzyzewski, captain of Bob Knight's 1968-1969 team which compiled an 18-10 record. Krzyzewski was head coach at the USMA Preparatory School prior to accepting the head coaching position at West Point.

Krzyzewski spent five seasons at the Academy, resurrecting the Army basketball program. He compiled a record of 73

victories and 59 defeats before leaving for the head coaching position at Duke University. During his tenure at his alma mater, Krzyzewski's teams twice appeared in the Eastern College Athletic Conference Metro playoffs and once earned a berth in the N.I.T. He also guided the Cadets to their first tournament victory in the Vermont Classic.

Two of Krzyzewski's mainstays while coaching at the Academy were Gary Winton and Matt Brown, two of Army's all-time scoring leaders. Winton became Army's career scoring leader at the conclusion of his four years at West Point, tallying 2,296 points. That record stood until the 1986-1987 season when Kevin Houston surpassed that mark by scoring 953 points during the season. He finished with 2,325 points. Matt Brown ranks fourth on Army's all-time scoring list with 1,511 points.

When Krzyzewski departed for Durham, North Carolina, and the Duke University campus, his top assistant, Pete Gaudet, took over the head coaching assignment at the Academy. Gaudet was unable to re-establish Army's winning form during two seasons, winning just 12 games.

Les Wothke, head coach at Western Michigan University, was named Army's basketball coach prior to the 1982-1983 season. Just prior to the start of his coaching tenure, West Point joined the Metro Atlantic Athletic Conference which includes Fordham University, Manhattan College, Fairfield University, St. Peter's College, Holy Cross College, Iona College, and LaSalle University. The Cadets have been very competitive in the conference, earning many individual honors.

Kevin Houston was named Rookie of the Year in the Metro Atlantic Athletic Conference in 1984, as well as All-Metropolitan Rookie of the Year. He also was All-MAAC for three consecutive years, 1985-1987. Randy Cozzens was an All-Metro selection four straight years and was named MAAC "Player of the Year" in 1985. Houston duplicated that honor in 1987. Coach Les Wothke also gained a share of the conference accolades. He was named "Coach of the Year" in 1985 when Army posted a 16-13 record.

The Army basketball program has come a long way since its first game in the Old Cadet Gymnasium. The Cadets play and practice in the Multi-Purpose Sports Complex adjacent to Michie Stadium. The basketball arena has a capacity of more than five thousand, while the hockey rink holds just over twenty-eight hundred.

There have been many outstanding basketball coaches who were not only successful at West Point, but at other colleges and universities. When John Mauer was named head coach in 1948, he came from the University of Tennessee where he guided the Volunteers to a record of 128 victories and just 42 defeats. His Tennessee teams also won the Southeastern Conference championship twice, in 1940-1941 and in 1942-1943.

A graduate of the University of Illinois where he gained prominence as a blocking back for the legendary Harold "Red" Grange, Mauer was captain of the Illini squad and won All-Big Ten honors. His record at West Point was 33-35,

Coach Bob Knight instructs his 1966 Cadet squad during a game against Fordham. Knight, one of the most successful coaches in basketball, left the head coaching assignment at West Point to accept a similar position at Indiana University. Knight has led the Hoosiers for sixteen years, winning three National Collegiate Athletic Association championships.

Dick Murray was captain of Coach Bob Knight's first Army basketball team, the 1965-1966 squad that finished with an 18-8 record. Murray ranks twenty-fourth on Army's career scoring list with 658 points from 1963 to 1966.

Kevin Houston goes high in the air to sink a jump shot during a game against Fairfield University during the 1986-1987 season. Houston scored a team record 953 points during the season to lead the nation in scoring and free throw shooting. That effort pushed him to the top of Army's all-time scoring list with 2,325 points.

Coach Bob Knight is pictured with Bill Schutsky, captain of the 1967-1968 basketball team which compiled a 20-5 record. Schutsky ranks seventh on the career scoring list with 1,292 points in 71 games for an 18.2 average. Schutsky also ranks sixteenth among Army's career rebounding leaders.

posting consecutive 9-8 records during his final two seasons at the Academy. He left West Point for the head coaching assignment at the University of Florida.

Veteran college coach Elmer Ripley replaced Mauer and stayed at West Point for two seasons before leaving for a position in the Harlem Globetrotters organization. Ripley was responsible for developing young players for positions on the Globetrotter squad.

Ripley came to the Academy with outstanding credentials. He served head coaching assignments at Georgetown University three different times, at Yale, at Columbia, at Notre Dame, and at John Carroll University. His collegiate coaching record after leaving West Point included 285 victories and 218 defeats.

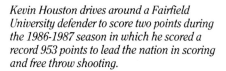

Kevin Houston drives around a Fairfield University defender to score two points during the 1986-1987 season in which he scored a record 953 points to lead the nation in scoring and free throw shooting.

A LOOK INTO THE PAST

Year	Coach	Captain	Won	Lost
1903	Joseph Stilwell	Horatio Hackett	1	0
1904	Joseph Stilwell	Horatio Hackett	2	1
1904-05	Self Coached	Harold Hetrick	3	4
1905-06	Self Coached	Harold Hetrick	7	4
1906-07	Harry Fisher	Lewis Rockwell	9	5
1907-08	Joseph Stilwell	Harvey Higley	9	3
1908-09	Joseph Stilwell	Jacob Devers	9	2
1909-10	Joseph Stilwell	John Millikin	14	1
1910-11	Joseph Stilwell	Carl McKinney	9	3
1911-12	Harvey Higley	Archibald Arnold	8	4
1912-13	Harvey Higley (19-6)	John VanVliet	11	2
1913-14	Joseph Stilwell (49-17)	John MacTaggart	5	7
1914-15	Jacob Devers	Frederic Boye	11	2
1915-16	Jacob Devers (16-9)	Louis Hibbs	5	7
1916-17	Arthur Conard (3-8)	John Cole	3	8
1917-18	Ivens Jones	William Gerhardt Leo Kreber	8	4
1918-19	Ivens Jones (11-9)	Joseph Cranston	3	5
1919-20	Joseph O'Shea	Maurice Daniel	12	2
1920-21	Joseph O'Shea (30-7)	Alfred Kessler	18	5
1921-22	Harry Fisher	Ernest Pfeiffer	17	2
1922-23	Harry Fisher	Clement Dabezies	17	0
1923-24	John Van Vliet (16-2)	Leo Vichules	16	2
1925	Harry Fisher (55-10)	William Wood	12	2
1926	Ernest Blood (11-6)	John Roosma	11	6
1927	Leo Novak	Dudley Strickler	11	3
1928	Leo Novak	John Mills	10	5
1929	Leo Novak	Philip Draper	12	5
1930	Leo Novak	Richard Hutchinson	9	6
1931	Leo Novak	Orrin Krueger Dean Strother	12	3
1932	Leo Novak	Raymond Stecker	10	5
1933	Leo Novak	Robin Epler	5	5
1934	Leo Novak	John Hills	8	7
1935	Leo Novak	Wright Hiatt	10	5
1936	Leo Novak	Kenneth Dawalt	7	7
1937	Leo Novak	Charles Meyer	7	6
1938	Leo Novak	Harris Rogner	12	2
1939	Leo Novak (126-61)	John Samuel	13	2
1940	Valentine Lentz	Alvan Gillem	11	4
1941	Valentine Lentz	Richard Reinbold	5	11
1942	Valentine Lentz	Ernest White	10	6
1943	Valentine Lentz	George Rebh Jammie Philpott	5	10
1944	Edward Kelleher	Edward Christl	15	0
1945	Edward Kelleher (29-1)	Dale Hall	14	1
1946	Stuart Holcomb	John Nance	9	6

The 1968-1969 Army basketball team coached by Bob Knight compiled an 18-10 record. Pictured are, front row, left to right, Bob Freeman, Dave Kremenak, Rich Castleman, Mike Krzyzewski, Wade Urban, Jim Oxley, Doug Clevenger, and Steve Lewis; standing, Tom Miller, Alan Fenty, Dick Simmons, Steve Hunt, Max Miller, Mike Gyovai, and Paul Franke.

The 1971-1972 Army basketball team, the first under Coach Dan Dougherty, compiled an 11-13 record. Pictured are, front row, left to right, Doug Crewse, Gary Anderson, John O'Maley, Bob Sherwin, Pete Jackson, Frank Weiss, manager George Devine; second row, Maj. Larry Gunderman, the officer representative, Dave Dlugolenski, Ned Bumgarner, Chris Petersen, Ed Mueller, the team captain, Nick Combs, Skip Loucks, Wally Wojdakowski, and Coach Dan Dougherty. Sherwin was the recipient of the Naismith Award the following year, an award presented to the nation's top basketball player under six feet tall.

1947	Stuart Holcomb (18-13)	Arnold Tucker	9	7
1948	John Mauer	James Rawers	8	9
1949	John Mauer	James Rawers	7	10
1950	John Mauer	Arnold Galiffa	9	8
1951	John Mauer (33-35)	Edward Tixier	9	8
1952	Elmer Ripley	William Ritter	8	9
1953	Elmer Ripley (19-17)	Clarence Hannon	11	8
1953-54	Robert Vanatta (15-7)	Clarence Hannon	15	7
1954-55	Orvis Sigler	Jerry Gilpin	9	9
1955-56	Orvis Sigler	Norris Harbold	10	13
1956-57	Orvis Sigler	Robert McCoy	7	13
1957-58	Orvis Sigler (39-47)	Donald DeJardin	13	12
1958-59	George Hunter	Charles Darby	14	10
1959-60	George Hunter	George Kaiser	14	9
1960-61	George Hunter	Lee Sager	17	7
1961-62	George Hunter	Stewart Sherard	10	11
1962-63	George Hunter (63-48)	Robert Foley	8	11
1963-64	Taylor Locke	Richard Chilcoat	19	7
1964-65	Taylor Locke (40-15)	Joseph Kosciusko	21	8
1965-66	Robert Knight	Richard Murray	18	8
1966-67	Robert Knight	Daniel Schrage	13	8
1967-68	Robert Knight	William Schutsky	20	5
1968-69	Robert Knight	Michael Krzyzewski	18	10
1969-70	Robert Knight	James Oxley	22	6
1970-71	Robert Knight (102-50)	Douglas Clevenger	11	13
1971-72	Daniel Dougherty	Edward Mueller	11	13
1972-73	Daniel Dougherty	Robert Sherwin	11	13
1973-74	Daniel Dougherty	Peter Jackson	6	18
1974-75	Daniel Dougherty (31-66)	David Thomas	3	22
1975-76	Michael Krzyzewski	Thomas Valerio	11	14
1976-77	Michael Krzyzewski	Gary Winston	20	8
1977-78	Michael Krzyzewski	Gary Winton	19	9
1978-79	Michael Krzyzewski	Matthew Brown	14	11
1979-80	Michael Krzyzewski (73-59)	Robert Vaughn	9	17
1980-81	Peter Gaudet	Robert Brown, Martin Coyme	7	19
1981-82	Peter Gaudet (12-41)	Michael Spencer	5	22
1982-83	Les Wothke	Paul Mongan	11	18
1983-84	Les Wothke	Pete Popovich	11	17
1984-85	Les Wothke	Randy Cozzens & Scott Milliren	16	13
1985-86	Les Wothke	Mike Ellis & Mark Michaelsen	9	18
1986-87	Les Wothke (61-81)	Kevin Houston & Ron Steptoe	14	15

The 1957-1958 Army basketball team under Coach Orvis Sigler compiled a 13-12 record. It was Sigler's final year at the helm as he compiled a record of thirty-nine victories and forty-seven defeats. The team captain was Don DeJardin (holding ball). Coach Sigler is in the top row, far right.

The 1941 Army basketball team was Coach Valentine Lentz' second squad during a four-year coaching stint at the Academy. Pictured are, front row, left to right: John W. Guckeyson; Charles H. Schilling; Robert C. Borman; Raymond P. Murphy; team captain Richard D. Reinbold; Ernest J. White, Jr.; Joseph W. Benson; Paul R. Kemp; Richard J. Rastetter; and trainer John Diehl; second row: Coach Valentine Lentz; manager Robert M. Tuttle; Harold W. Rice; Charles M. Fergusson, Jr.; George D. Hughes; Lawrence Y. Greene; Harold K. Roach; Samuel W. Koster, Jr.; Paul R. Larson; Charles E. Hardy; Jack F. Clark; George A. Rebh; and Capt. Edwin J.

Messinger, the officer representative; third row: Donald W. Thompson; James B. Cobb; James F. Frakes; James D. Moore; James R. Anderson; Richard W. Maffry; Henry J. Mazur; Frederick Spann; and William J. Hovde; top row: John J. Courtney, Jr.; Robert V. Whitlow; Kenneth F. Hanst, Jr.; Truman E. Deyo; and Thomas P. Iuliucci. Koster earned the rank of general during his military career and served as superintendent of the Academy from June 1968 to March 1970. Murphy also earned the rank of major general during his career and served as director of athletics on two occasions during his career.

The 1962-1963 Army team was coached by George Hunter, who closed out his West Point coaching stint with a 63-48 record. The team captain was center Bob Foley (44).

Cadet Joseph Stilwell became the first coach and founder of basketball at the United States Military Academy.

Army head basketball coach Mike Krzyzewski, left, yells out instructions to his squad. Krzyzewski, who played under Bob Knight here at the Academy and served as captain of the 1968-1969 squad, was head coach for five years. He started during the 1975-1976 season and compiled an overall record of seventy-three victories and fifty-nine defeats. His finest season was the 1976-1977 campaign when Army posted a 20-8 record. The young Army coach left West Point to take over as head basketball coach at Duke University. Krzyzewski has continued his coaching success at Duke, leading the Blue Devils to the National Collegiate Athletic Association finals. Duke also gained a berth in the NCAA tournament in 1987. At right is his assistant coach, Pete Gaudet. Gaudet took over as Army's head coach when Krzyzewski left for Duke. He held the position for two seasons, and has rejoined Krzyzewski at Duke.

Matt Brown, captain of the Army basketball team during the 1978-1979 season, goes up for two points against Seton Hall. Brown, 6-foot-5, played both guard and forward for Coach Mike Krzyzewski's squad. He currently is fourth on Army's career scoring list.

Army guard Matt Brown (30) goes up to sink a two-pointer during a 76-73 victory over Seton Hall at the West Point Field House in 1977. Brown teamed with All-America Gary Winton and company to compile a 20-8 record during the 1976-1977 season. Coach Mike Krzyzewski's quintet also won the Vermont Classic, the first Army team to win a tournament title, and finished second in the Birmingham Classic. The Cadets also earned a berth in the ECAC Metropolitan playoffs, bowing to Seton Hall 77-71 in the opening round before trimming Manhattan College 64-62 in the consolation game at Madison Square Garden. Army also trimmed rival Navy 54-53 at Annapolis.

Army forward Clennie Brundidge (20) drives in for two points during a game against Iona in 1977. Brundidge, who holds all of Army's football career records for pass receiving, proved adept on the hardwood as well. His efforts during the 1976-1977 season helped Army finish with a 20-8 record, the best under head Coach Mike Krzyzewski.

John Roosma, a graduate of the class of 1926, receives a special award from Col. Jack Schuder, director of athletics, during halftime of an Army basketball game in 1973. Roosma, captain of the Cadet basketball squad in 1926, was selected to the Naismith Basketball Hall of Fame in 1961.

John Roosma, a graduate of the class of 1926, was elected to the Naismith Basketball Hall of Fame in 1961. He is the only Army basketball player to be so honored. Roosma was captain of the 1926 team that won twelve games and lost just three.

Army All-America basketball player Mike Silliman goes up for a hook shot during a practice session. Silliman gained All-America honors in 1966. He also was selected as captain of the 1968 United States Olympic basketball team and helped lead the United States to a gold medal.

Bill Helkie is a class of 1966 graduate who played under Coach Taylor "Tates" Locke and Coach Bob Knight, during his three years with the varsity. Army was 19-7 during his first year and finished third in the National Invitation Tournament. In 1964-1965 the Cadets were 21-8 and repeated their third-place finish in the N.I.T., while Army was 18-8 during Knight's first season in 1965-1966. The Cadets took third-place honors in the Eastern College Athletic Conference Holiday Festival and the Vanderbilt Invitational, while finishing fourth in the N.I.T.

The 1906 Army basketball team, which was self-coached, won seven games and lost four. Harold Hetrick served as team captain. The Cadets defeated Manhattan, the Second Signal Corps, Troy, Rutgers (60-0), Seventh Regiment, Yale Graduates, and Pratt Institute.

The Army basketball team won eight of twelve games during the 1911-1912 winter season. The squad was coached by Harvey Higley, while Archibald V. Arnold served as team captain.

FORMER BASKETBALL CAPTAIN

Maj. Robert Foley, captain of the 1962-1963 Army basketball team under Coach George Hunter, receives a National Collegiate Athletic Association commemorative plaque from NCAA president Harry M. Cross during a ceremony honoring former Medal of Honor winners.

Army's 1914-1915 basketball team, under Coach Jacob L. Devers, won eleven of thirteen games during the winter season. The Cadets opened the year with victories over Fordham, St. Lawrence, and Georgetown, but then dropped consecutive games to Pennsylvania, 23-17, and Union College, 21-12. The Cadets rebounded by winning their final eight games. Frederic Boye served as team captain. Members of the class of 1915 who earned basketball letters included Boye, Leland S. Hobbs, Reese M. Howell, John S. MacTaggert, and Albert W. Waldron. Elmer Oliphant, third row at left, also lettered. He was an outstanding Army football player, gaining All-America honors.

Coach Harry Fisher guided the 1921-1922 Army basketball team to a 17-2 record. Among those seventeen victories was a 21-17 decision over Navy. The Cadets' only losses in 1922 came against Connecticut Agricultural College and Pennsylvania. Ernest Pfeiffer was the Army team captain. Fisher guided West Point's basketball fortunes for three seasons, compiling an outstanding record of fifty-five victories and just ten defeats. In 1923, his Army team finished with a 17-0 record and defeated Navy by a 37-29 count.

The 1922-1923 Army basketball team, under Coach Harry Fisher, compiled a 17-0 record. It was the second Army team to finish an unbeaten season. Ernest H. Pfeiffer served as team captain. Pictured are, first row, left to right, John Roosma, Clement H. Dabezies, team captain Pfeiffer, William R. Forbes, and William H. Wood; second row, team manager Albert R. Dowling, Leo D. Vichules, Donald G. Storck, Alfred A. Kessler, Jr., Walter E. French, and D. F. J. DeBardeleban, an assistant manager who lettered later in basketball; third row, Charles R. Bonnett, Ernest A. Merkle, Aubrey S. Newman, and John H. Fite.

The 1927 Army basketball squad won eleven games and lost just three under the direction of Coach Leo Novak. The Cadets defeated the likes of St. John's, Clarkson, Delaware, Massachusetts Agricultural College, Lehigh, Manhattan, Yale, St. Stephen's, Columbia, New York University, and Union College. Army dropped a 32-25 decision to Navy. The team captain was Dudley Strickler.

The Army basketball team won ten and lost five during the 1928 season. The Cadets defeated McGill University, Dickinson, Massachusetts Agricultural College, Pennsylvania, Manhattan, Colgate, St. Stephens, Columbia, Massachusetts Institute of Technology, and Delaware. Unfortunately, Army bowed to Navy, 29-17. John S. Mills was the team captain.

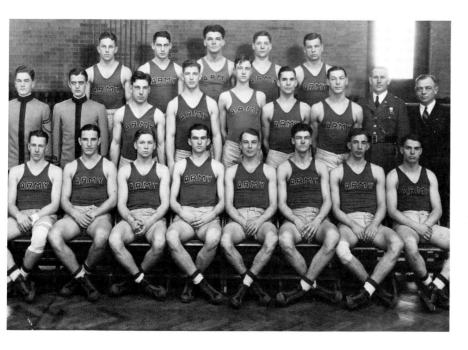

The 1931 Army basketball team, coached by Leo Novak, won twelve games and lost just five during the winter season. Novak's squad opened the season with nine consecutive victories, including wins over Harvard, Princeton, Pennsylvania, Georgetown, and Ohio State, before bowing to Columbia in New York City, 53-31. The Cadets then won three of their final five games, whipping New Hampshire, Carnegie Tech, and West Virginia to finish up the season.

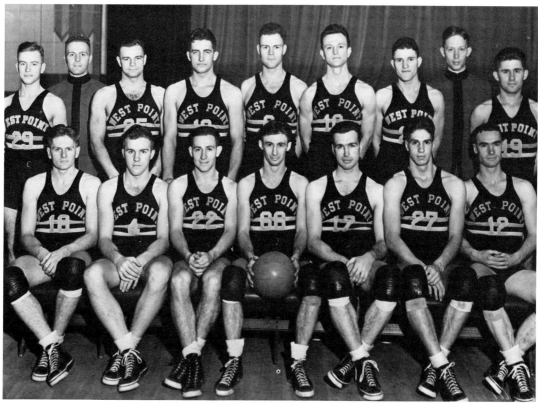

The 1937 basketball team won seven games and lost six. One of those losses was a 42-40 defeat against Navy. Coached by Leo Novak, the Cadets trimmed Lehigh, Yale, Johns Hopkins, Dickinson, Colgate, Providence, and Syracuse.

The 1938 Army basketball team opened the season with seven straight victories en route to a 12-2 record. Coached by Leo Novak, the Cadets also whipped Navy, 44-36. Yale handed Army its first loss in New Haven, 31-25, and Syracuse tripped up the Cadets later by a 36-31 margin. The team captain was Harris E. Rogner.

The 1958-1959 Army basketball team, coached by George Hunter, compiled a 14-10 record. Front row, left to right, are Capt. Hubbard, officer representative; Harold Hannon; David Gleichenhaus; George Kaiser; team captain Charles Darby; Darryle Kouns; Joseph Bobula; and Coach Hunter. Back row, George Joulwan; Michael Brady; Lee Sager; Lee Anderson; Robert H. Strauss, Jr.; James Klosek; Ross Gagliano; Ronald Barick; and Otto Everbach.

The 1959-1960 basketball team, under Coach George Hunter, compiled a 14-9 record. Serving as team captain was George Kaiser. Pictured in the first row are Thomas Culver, David Gleichenhaus, Kaiser, Alan R. DeJardin, and Stewart Sherard. In the second row are Coach Hunter, Ross Gagliano, Robert Chelberg, Lee Anderson, Michael Brady, Robert H. Strauss, Jr., Harold Hannon, Lee Sager, Sylvain Loupe, Lawrence Crane, and manager Edward Bierman.

The first truly organized sport at the Military
Academy was baseball, which started in 1890,
playing a three-game schedule against the
Riverton Club of Philadelphia, the Sylvans
Club of New York, and the Atlantics from
Governors Island. The first game against
Riverton ended in an 8-8 deadlock, but Army
won the other two, whipping the Sylvans 7-1
and the Atlantics 17-14. Pictured above are
members of that first team. Back row: Frank
Webster (1), Samuel Burkhardt (2), Walter
Bethel (3), Sydney Cloman (4), Charles
Rhodes (5), and Edward Winston (6). Front
row includes Alexander Piper (7), catcher
Clement Flagler (8), and Francis Lacey (9),
the pitcher.

CHAPTER 14

BASEBALL

The game of baseball has had a long and rich tradition at the United States Military Academy, starting perhaps with the often controversial claims that the originator of our national pastime is Abner Doubleday, a class of 1842 graduate.

Doubleday, it is said, devised the game while on leave from West Point in Cooperstown, New York, in 1839, drawing out the diamond and the rules of the game. He called the game "Base Ball," but it was patterned after a game called rounders which was played by boys and girls in England. In rounders a player would hit a ball and run to post. It is similar to the English game of cricket.

Controversy arose about describing baseball as an offshoot of rounders. In an article by Robert W. Henderson in the *Bulletin* of The New York Public Library, he explains that in 1880, nationalistic feelings ran high on the American origin of baseball. James Montgomery Ward defended the American origin which credited Doubleday as the game's founder, saying "The assertion that base-ball is descended from rounders is a pure assumption, unsupported even by proof that the latter game antedates the former, and unjustified by any line of reasoning based upon the likeness of the games."

Albert G. Spalding, patron of the game and founder of the sporting goods company, also defended the American origin and suggested a commission be organized to officially determine baseball's origin. The commission consisted of seven men who were very knowledgeable of the game, headed by A. G. Mills, the third president of the National League. Collecting evidence over three years, the commission decided that baseball had its origin in the United States and the "the first scheme for playing it, according to the best available evidence obtainable to date, was devised by Abner Doubleday, Cooperstown, New York, in 1839."

Testimony provided the Spalding commission supporting Doubleday as baseball's founder came from Abner Graves, a fellow pupil of Doubleday's at Green's Select School in Cooperstown. Graves said he was present when Doubleday outlined the playing field with a stick, showing the position of the players. Graves said Doubleday later drew the diamond shape on paper.

"Doubleday then improved Town Ball, to limit the number of players, as many were hurt in collisions," said Graves in testimony that was released by the commission. "From twenty to fifty players took part in the game I have described. He also designed the game to be played by definite teams or sides. Doubleday called the game Base Ball, for there were four bases in it. Three were places where the runner could rest free from being put out, provided he kept his foot on the flat stone base. The pitcher stood in a six foot ring. The ball had a rubber center overwound with yarn to a size somewhat larger than the present day sphere, and was covered with leather or buckskin. Anyone getting the ball was entitled to throw it at a runner between bases, and put him out by hitting him with it. . ."

Henderson, in his article, claims Doubleday could not have invented the game. He says Doubleday undoubtedly played baseball, but he never claimed to be the inventor of the game himself, nor was it mentioned in his obituary appearing in the *New York Times* in January 28, 1893.

Henderson cited other examples showing Doubleday could not have invented the sport. In 1787, students at Princeton were prohibited from playing "with balls and sticks in the back common of the College" because it "is in itself low and unbecoming gentlemen students." Dr. Oliver Wendell Holmes, in his later years, said that he played baseball at Harvard, and he graduated in 1829, a decade before Doubleday is credited with devising the national pastime.

While the origin of baseball can be argued between one historian and another, Doubleday nonetheless is still given credit and the baseball field at the Military Academy was dedicated in his honor in May, 1939, the centennial year of baseball.

Despite the controversy, Doubleday distinguished himself throughout his military career, earning the rank of major general. He served in the Mexican and Civil wars. As a captain he fired the first gun for the Union side in the Civil War at Fort Sumter. On November 29, 1862, he was made a major general of the volunteers. He retired from the U.S. Army in 1873 and died January 26, 1893 in New Jersey at the age of seventy-four.

Baseball did not catch on quickly at the Military Academy. In fact, cricket clubs were formed in 1847, but interest vanished within a year's time. During the Civil War a sophomore (yearling) class at West Point requested permission to purchase baseball equipment. Four years later, games were held at the Academy between respective classes.

Baseball began formally at West Point in 1890 when cadets formed a team and played the Riverton Club of Philadelphia, the Sylvans of New York, and the Atlantics of Governor's Island. The Army squad played an 8-8 tie against Riverton, but trounced the Sylvans 7-1 and the Atlantics by a 17-14 margin.

The baseball team was self-coached during the early days. The Academy sports record book cites only the names of team captains until 1895 when Abraham G. Lott was listed as both coach and captain. He served in that position for two years, leading the Cadets to a 3-2 record in 1895 and a 1-5 record in 1896. Lott later earned the rank of brigadier general in 1927, and served as Commandant of the Cavalry School from 1926-1935 before retiring. He died at the age of seventy-three on January 21, 1945.

The captain of the first Army baseball team in 1890 was George Phillip White, a graduate of the class of 1891. As mentioned previously, White's team was 2-0-1.

The second person listed in the records as baseball coach was Charles Irvine. He held the position for two years, 1901-1902. One of Irvine's players was Douglas MacArthur, a 1903 West Point graduate who returned later as superintendent from 1919 to 1922.

In all there have been fifteen baseball coaches at the Academy. Eric Tipton held the position for twenty years, the longest tenure among the former baseball coaches. He compiled a record of 234-201-5 from 1958 until his retirement in 1977. Tipton, a graduate of Duke University where he was famed as a "coffin corner" punter for the Blue Devils football team, also was the 150-pound football coach at West Point.

The best record, percentage-wise, was compiled by S. Strang Nicklin from 1909 until 1917. His Army teams won 112 games, lost just forty-five, and tied two times. He also was the first Army coach to hold that position for more than three seasons.

Nicklin coached some of Army's most outstanding athletes. Leland Devore, a class of 1913 graduate, lettered in baseball under Nicklin's guidance. He also was an All-America tackle and captain of the 1912 football team which posted a 5-3 record.

Omar Bradley, Louis Merillat, Vernon Prichard, Robert Neyland, and Elmer Oliphant all lettered in baseball while also playing key roles on Army's football team. Merillat was a first team All-America end in 1913. Prichard was Army's top passing quarterback at the time and earned some All-America notice; Oliphant was a two-time All-America in football in 1916 and 1917.

Earl H. Blaik, the winningest football coach in Army history, also was successful on the diamond while at West Point. He lettered under coach J. B. Lobert. Lobert served as baseball coach for eight seasons, compiling a record of eighty victories, fifty-two defeats and three ties.

Other notable names in West Point sports annals who lettered in baseball included William Wood, a class of 1925 graduate who would later serve as head football coach. Russell P. "Red" Reeder, captain of the 1926 Army team, became a fixture at the Academy, serving as an assistant football coach, and later as a baseball assistant coach and athletic administrator following World War II. John Roosma, also a 1926 graduate, lettered in baseball after starring in basketball while at the Academy. Roosma was later inducted into the Helms Foundation Basketball Hall of Fame.

One interesting note in Army baseball history is that Christy Mathewson, one of the finest pitchers in baseball history who played for John J. McGraw's New York Giants, served a three-week tour as an assistant baseball coach in 1908.

The late Kenneth Rapp, former archivist at the U.S. Military Academy, uncovered this piece of historical information and included it in his book on West Point, published by North River Press, Inc., in 1978.

Rapp uncovered a record revealing that Mathewson did, indeed, tutor the Army pitchers prior to the beginning of his spring training in 1908. On January 15, 1908, Lt. Joseph Barnes, secretary of the Army Athletic Association, reported an expenditure authorizing a payment of $75.00 per week and expenses (board and quarters) for Mathewson. He instructed the cadets in the gymnasium before leaving for pre-season training in February of that year.

Rapp writes that Mathewson was chosen by the Athletic Council at West Point for two reasons. First, Mathewson was recognized throughout the nation because of his three shutout performances as a Giants starting pitcher against the Philadelphia Athletics in the 1903 World Series. Additionally, the council chose Mathewson because he was a college man, "that he had exhibited traits of the perfect gentleman, and that he possessed superb natural athletic talent." The Athletic Council felt he would provide an outstanding role model for the cadets.

Mathewson's association with the Academy first occurred on November 17, 1900. Mathewson was a member of the Bucknell football team that met Army that season. When Bucknell moved to the Army 35, Mathewson was sent in to attempt a 35-yard field goal. He made good on his attempt, but Army went on to win the game 18-10 behind the efforts of All-America Paul Bunker.

MacArthur, then a cadet, watched Mathewson play fullback for Bucknell and was impressed by his performance, so much so that he related his feelings to John McGraw when the two met. MacArthur told McGraw that Mathewson

Although football is considered the first organized sport that launched the West Point athletic program, baseball was one of the first sports played on an informal basis when a ball and bat could be found, according to the Howitzer *yearbook. The 1891 Army team pictured here played a two-game schedule, losing to the Manhattan Athletic Club twice by scores of 9-8 and 11-7.*

The 1896 baseball team ran into tough times during the spring season, managing to win just a single game. The Cadets whipped Rutgers 13-4 for its only victory in six games.

played the strongest game at fullback he had ever seen on The Plain at that time. McGraw backed those remarks by saying he felt Mathewson was not only the finest throwing pitcher, but the finest fielding hurler as well.

While Mathewson's short stint as an assistant baseball coach may have been the first experience the cadets had with professional baseball, Army played an exhibition game with the New York Giants in 1914. It was the first of twenty-one meetings with the Giants until they moved to San Francisco in 1978. The Giants won the first encounter 7-2 as well as nineteen others. There was one tie, that coming in 1946 by a 2-2 score.

Army baseball teams also have played exhibition games against the New York Yankees, the Brooklyn Dodgers, the Montreal Royals, the New York Mets, and the Detroit Tigers. The Cadets and Yankees met for the first time in 1927 with the American League champions posting a 2-0 victory. Babe Ruth and Lou Gehrig were members of that famed Yankee team which rightfully had the nickname, the Bronx Bombers.

The Brooklyn Dodgers played at West Point eight times from 1943-1949, winning six of those encounters. The Cadets were victorious in 1945, winning both exhibitions that year 5-4 and 4-0.

The Mets and Cadets first played in 1963. The legendary Casey Stengel brought his "Metsies" to the banks of the Hudson. Among those players who have visited West Point are Yogi Berra, Mickey Mantle, Willie Mays, Duke Snyder, Elston Howard, Tom Seaver, Wes Westrum, Ralph Houk, and many, many more.

On the college level of competition, Army and Navy first met in baseball in 1901 with the Cadets producing a 4-3 victory. After the first undefeated season in 1890, Army waited until 1945 to record another unblemished record, posting a perfect 15-0 mark under Maj. Paul Amen. Amen spent twelve years at West Point, 1943-1954, and compiled an overall record of 133-76-7. During all but three of his twelve seasons at the Academy, Amen's squads posted winning records. Ironically, in 1949 when the Cadets finished with a 6-13 record, cadet Jim Stuff led the Eastern Intercollegiate Baseball League in batting with a .429 average. Additionally, Amen's 1950 team rebounded with a 14-4 record, tied for the Ivy League championship (Eastern Intercollegiate Baseball League).

Army's renowned soccer coach, Joe Palone, coached the varsity baseball team for three seasons, 1955-1957, and recorded an overall record of thirty-two victories, twenty-seven losses, and four ties. During Palone's first season, pitcher Rod Vitty tossed a no-hitter in a 3-0 victory over Swarthmore. Two years later, in 1957, Jon Rindfleisch hurled Army's second no-hitter, also coming against Swarthmore. The Cadets won that game by an 8-0 margin.

When Tipton took over as Army coach in 1958, he had a 10-11-1 record, and then followed with eleven straight winning seasons. His 1960 squad was the first Army team to win the Eastern League championship outright with an overall record of 18-5-1. That squad was led by pitcher Bob Kewley, selected the top player in the East, and third

A LOOK INTO THE PAST

Year	Coach	Captain	Won	Lost	Tied	Year	Coach	Captain	Won	Lost	Tied
1890	None Listed	George P. White	2	0	1	1914	S. Strang Nicklin	Charles M. Milliken	10	5	0
1891	None Listed	Jay J. Morrow	0	2	0	1915	S. Strang Nicklin	Louis A. Merillat	18	3	0
1892	None Listed	Harry H. Pattison	5	1	0	1916	S. Strang Nicklin	Robert R. Neyland, Jr.	10	8	1
1893	None Listed	John H. Rice & Harry H. Pattison	3	2	0	1917	S. Strang Nicklin (118-44-2)	Charles H. Gerhardt	8	1	0
1894	None Listed	John C. Gilmore, Jr.	1	5	0	1918	J.B. Lobert	Elmer Q. Oliphant & Norman McNeil	14	7	0
1895	Abraham G. Lott	Abraham G. Lott	3	2	0						
1896	Abraham G. Lott	Abraham G. Lott	1	5	0	1919	J.B. Lobert	Lt. Foster J. Tate & William S. Murray	10	7	0
1897	None Listed	Thomas A. Roberts	2	5	0						
1898	None Listed	Arthur S. Cowan	1	5	1	1920	J.B. Lobert	George Honnen	7	6	2
1899	None Listed	Arthur S. Cowan & Lewis Brown, Jr.	4	2	0	1921	J.B. Lobert	Glenn C. Wilhide	11	5	0
						1922	J.B. Lobert	Glenn C. Wilhide	11	5	0
1900	None Listed	Lewis Brown, Jr.	3	4	0	1923	J.B. Lobert	Donald G. Storck	11	5	1
1901	Charles Irvine	Stephen Abbott & Frank P. Lahm	6	2	1	1924	J.B. Lobert	George W. Smythe	10	6	0
						1925	J.B. Lobert (80-52-3)	Harry O. Ellinger	6	11	0
1902	Charles Irvine (16-8-1)	Stephen Abbott	10	6	0	1926	H.E. McCormick	Russell P. Reeder, Jr.	6	8	0
1903	Mr. Steinwender	Ephraim F. Graham	5	5	0	1927	H.E. McCormick	Arthur L. Cobb	9	4	0
1904	Mr. Summersgill	Horatio B. Hackett, Jr.	4	4	1	1928	H.E. McCormick	William W. Browning	9	2	0
1905	Walter Clarkson	Patrick H. Winston	5	7	0	1929	H.E. McCormick	Don Z. Zimmerman	5	8	0
1906	Dennis Houle	Charles K. Rockwell	11	3	0	1930	H.E. McCormick	Charles E. Beauchamp	9	5	1
1907	Dennis Houle	Edwin E. Pritchett	7	7	1						
1908	Dennis Houle (23-20-2)	Frederick A. Mountford & Homer McL. Groninger	5	10	1	1931	H.E. McCormick	Charles E. Hoy	7	6	0
						1932	H.E. McCormick	Edward E. Farnsworth, Jr.	11	2	0
						1933	H.E. McCormick	Stephen O. Fuqua, Jr.	5	6	0
1909	S. Strang Nicklin	Charles B. Meyer	8	7	0	1934	H.E. McCormick	Travis T. Brown	9	4	0
1910	S. Strang Nicklin	William C. Harrison	14	6	0	1935	H.E. McCormick	J. Hart Caughey	9	5	0
1911	S. Strang Nicklin	Alexander D. Surles	16	5	1	1936	H.E. McCormick	William R. Grohs	4	9	0
1912	S. Strang Nicklin	Houston L. Whiteside	12	4	0		(83-59-1)				
1913	S. Strang Nicklin	Otis K. Sadtler	16	6	0	1937	Walter E. French	Robert W. Griffin	9	2	0

Army's 1899 baseball team won four games and lost two, claiming decisions over Trinity, Wesleyan, Columbia, and the 7th Regiment of the New York National Guard. Lewis Brown, Jr., and Arthur Cowan served as team captains.

baseman Wayne Williams, who were both named to the All-League team.

Tipton's teams also won back-to-back Eastern League titles in 1965 and 1966. The 1965 team had an overall record of 15-6, while the 1966 squad was 16-4. Pitcher Barry DeBolt was an All-League selection both years, while third baseman Kenny Smith earned All-League honors in 1965 and outfielder John Boretti was an All-League pick in 1966 and 1967. DeBolt is the only Army player to receive All-League honors three straight years, 1964 to 1966.

Ed Haydash, an All-League selection in 1963 and 1964,

was also an All-District selection both years. DeBolt was an All-District selection in 1966 and was joined by shortstop Kenny Smith. Today, Dan Roberts coaches Army's baseball team. He is the son of pitcher Robin Roberts, who led the Philadelphia Phillies for so many years in the 1950s.

The Cadets have almost rewritten the record book during the eighties because the number of games scheduled has nearly doubled since the sport was played on a collegiate level at West Point. During 1981, for example, Army set a season record for most victories, twenty-one, but the overall record was 21-20.

1938	Walter E. French	Robert J. Kasper	9	4	0	1961	Eric Tipton	Wayne Williams	12	7	1
1939	Walter E. French	Samuel G. Kail	8	6	0	1962	Eric Tipton	John L. Schmidt	15	6	0
1940	Walter E. French	Charles G. Esau	5	7	0	1963	Eric Tipton	William Boice	12	10	1
1941	Walter E. French	Richard B. Polk	8	6	0	1964	Eric Tipton	Bob Michela	13	6	0
1942	Walter E. French	William C. Garland	10	4	1	1965	Eric Tipton	Anthony P. Pyrz	15	6	0
	(49-29-1)					1966	Eric Tipton	Eugene Atkinson	16	4	0
1943	Paul J. Amen	Edward F. McCabe &	10	3	0	1967	Eric Tipton	John Boretti	10	8	0
		John C. Stahle				1968	Eric Tipton	Paul T. Krieger	12	9	1
1944	Paul J. Amen	Jerry G. Capka	11	1	0	1969	Eric Tipton	Roger A. Vandenberg	15	7	0
1945	Paul J. Amen	Claude K. Josey	15	0	0	1970	Eric Tipton	Peter B. McCall	7	14	0
1946	Major Paul J. Amen	Richard M. Kinney	9	7	0	1971	Eric Tipton	Thomas A. Pyrz	10	14	0
1947	Major Paul J. Amen	Glenn W. Davis	17	1	1	1972	Eric Tipton	Howard S. Etheridge	8	16	0
1948	Paul J. Amen	Norman L.	16	7	0	1973	Eric Tipton	Gary D. Newsom	10	13	0
		Robinson, Jr.				1974	Eric Tipton	Carl B. McNutt	11	10	0
1949	Paul J. Amen	Richard H. Wagner	6	13	0	1975	Eric Tipton	Brent L. Clark	9	15	0
1950	Paul J. Amen	James V. Irons	14	4	0	1976	Eric Tipton	Michael R. Sloan	14	11	0
1951	Paul J. Amen	Theodore W.	8	14	1	1977	Eric Tipton	Warren C. Chellman	6	19	0
		Griesinger, Jr.					(234-201-5)				
1952	Paul J. Amen	Thomas E. Fitzpatrick	10	10	2	1978	Bill Permakoff	Patrick G. Landry	10	17	0
1953	Paul J. Amen	John B. Oblinger, Jr.	6	9	3	1979	Bill Permakoff	Paul H. Taylor	19	16	0
1954	Paul J. Amen	Walter F. LeCates, Jr.	11	7	0	1980	Bill Permakoff	Ronald D. Schiefer	15	20	0
	(133-76-7)					1981	Bill Permakoff	Paul J. Divis	21	20	0
1955	Joseph M. Palone	Richard G. Cardillo	10	8	2	1982	Bill Permakoff	Kevin F. DeHart,			
1956	Joseph M. Palone	Dennis L. Butler	9	10	0			Timothy J. Morris	19	19	0
1957	Joseph M. Palone	Leonard S. Marella	13	9	2	1983	Bill Permakoff	Kevin M. Batule	12	25	1
	(32-27-4)					1984	Bill Permakoff	Arthur L. Hartman	10	27	0
1958	Eric Tipton	Nels O. Conner	10	11	1	1985	Bill Permakoff	Michael T. Brown	17	21	1
1959	Eric Tipton	Frederick M. Franks	11	10	0	1986	Dan Roberts	Lawrence Tubbs	23	13	1
1960	Eric Tipton	Ned Loscuito	18	5	1	1987	Dan Roberts	Erik Everton	22	20	0

The 1901 Army baseball team is pictured here, a team which compiled a 6-2-1 record. The six victories were the most recorded in a season at that time since the sport was started at West Point in 1890. The coach of the team was Charles Irving, while Stephen Abbott and Frank P. Lahm served as team captains. The photo was presented to the Academy by the family of Leon Kromer, who served as manager of the team.

The Army baseball team won four games, lost four, and tied another during the 1904 season. Coached by Mr. Summersgill, the Cadets claimed victories over Penn State, Williams, New York University, and Navy by an 8-2 margin. Horatio Hackett, Jr., was the team captain.

The senior members of the 1905 Army baseball team, coached by Walter Clarkson, won five games and lost seven. The team captain was Patrick H. Winston who served during World War I before being honorably discharged in 1918. He then became a professor of law at the University of North Carolina.

The 1910 Army baseball team won fourteen games and lost six during the spring season. The fourteen victories were the most ever recorded by an Army squad up to that point. S. Strang Nicklin served as head coach, while William Harrison was the team captain. The Cadets got off to a good start with five straight victories, coming over Berkeley Hall, Seton Hall, Manhattan, Vermont, and Union College. Tufts nipped Army 4-3 for their first loss. Lettermen in the class of 1910 included David Byars, Charles Haverkamp, and David McCoach, Jr.

The 1912 Army varsity baseball team turned in an outstanding season, winning twelve of sixteen games, including an 8-7 victory over Navy. The Cadets, captained by Houston L. Whiteside, closed out the season with six consecutive victories. S. Strang Nicklin coached the Army squad.

The 1916 baseball squad pictured here only managed to compile a 10-8-1 record, but trounced rival Navy by a 13-3 count. Robert R. Neyland, Jr., served as team captain. Neyland would go on to complete a distinguished military and athletic career. He served as an aide de camp to Gen. Douglas MacArthur and eventually retired from the Army at the rank of major. After serving as professor of military science at the University of Tennessee from 1925 to 1930, Neyland became head football coach there in 1936. He returned to active duty in 1941 during the start of World War II, distinguishing himself before retiring at the rank of brigadier general. He returned to Knoxville and the University of Tennessee to become director of athletics, developing one of the finest athletic programs in the nation. The football stadium at Tennessee is named in his honor. Other lettermen from the class of 1916 included William E. Coffin, Jr., William H. Britton, Craigie Krayenbull, Robert E. Lee, Horace L. McBride, Hugh Mitchell, and William G. Patterson.

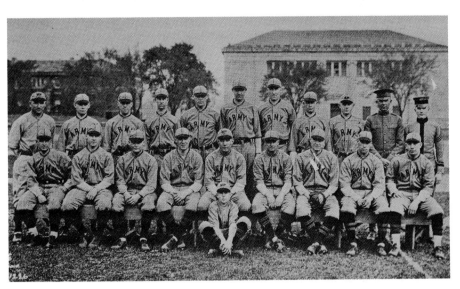

Army's 1918 baseball squad had a successful season under Coach S. Strang Nicklin, winning fourteen times, while losing seven games. The team co-captains were Elmer Oliphant and Norman McNeil. Oliphant, third from right, was an All-America halfback for the Army football team in 1916 and 1917. Among the lettermen from the class of 1918 were William N. Davis, Robert T. Foster, Dorr Hazlehurst, Hugh A. Murrill, Elmer Oliphant, Thomas W. Munford, and William S. Murray.

Coach J. B. Lobert's 1921 Army baseball team won eleven games and lost just five. Team captain Glenn C. Wilhide and his teammates defeated rival Navy that year by an 8-7 margin.

J. B. Lobert was Army's eighth baseball coach since the sport was played competitively starting in 1890. He spent eight years at the Academy, posting a record of eighty victories, fifty-two defeats, and three ties from 1918 until 1925. One of his team captains was All-America football star Elmer Oliphant, co-captain of Lobart's first team that compiled a 14-7 record.

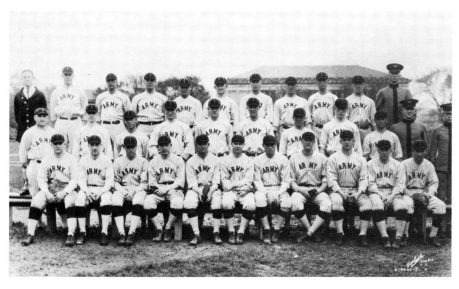

The 1924 Army baseball team compiled a 10-6 record. J. B. Lobert coached the Cadet squad, his seventh year at the helm. He began coaching the varsity nine in 1918 and remained through 1925. He had just one losing season, that coming during his final year as head coach. Team captain of the 1924 squad was George W. Smythe.

This picture shows the Army-Navy baseball game played at Annapolis on May 21, 1925. The Middies were victorious by a 13-7 margin.

The 1928 Army baseball team recorded nine victories and just two defeats under the coaching guidance of H. E. McCormick. The Cadets closed out the season with seven straight victories, whipping Columbia, Swarthmore, Springfield, Catholic, Bucknell, Union, and rival Navy, 9-6. The team captain was William W. Browning.

The 1931 baseball team, slumping with three consecutive losses to close the season, finished with a 7-6 record. The squad was coached by H. E. McCormick, while Charles Hoy served as team captain.

The 1938 Army baseball team, pictured here, won nine games and lost four under Coach Walter E. French.

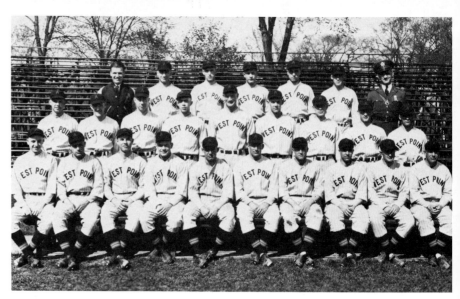

Army's 1938 baseball squad won nine games and lost four under Coach Walter French, who was in his second season as head coach. The team captain was Robert J. Kasper. Among the squad members was John R. Jannerone, first row, second from left, who would return to West Point later in his military career to serve as dean of the Academic Board from 1965 to 1973.

Leo Durocher, who visited West Point as manager of the New York Giants, made an earlier visit to the Academy as a player for the Brooklyn Dodgers. The Dodgers and Cadets met in an exhibition game for eight straight years from 1943 until 1949. In this photo, Durocher is batting in the first encounter against Army in 1943. The Brooklyn "Bums," as they were affectionately called, defeated the Cadets 12-8 in 1943.

New York Giants manager Leo "The Lip" Durocher chats with Academy superintendent, Maj. Gen. Bryant E. Moore, during the National League team's visit to West Point in 1950. The Giants beat the Cadets in an exhibition game 8-0.

New York Giant manager Leo Durocher, left, takes a few moments to talk to Army head football coach Earl "Red" Blaik during a visit to the Academy in 1950. Durocher was nicknamed "Leo the Lip" by members of the New York City news media, while Blaik was sometimes described as a martinet. Despite those characterizations, both were highly successful at their professions.

Leo Durocher, right, chats with members of the Army baseball team prior to the start of an exhibition game between the Cadets and the New York Giants baseball club. The exhibition series with the Giants began in 1914. In this meeting in 1950, the New Yorkers prevailed by an 8-0 margin.

Getting away from his normal duties as Army's head soccer coach, Joe Palone, second row, far right, coached the Army baseball team to a 13-9-2 record in 1957. Leonard S. Marella, first row, fifth from left, was the team captain, while Col. Russell P. "Red" Reeder, next to Coach Palone, a fixture in Army's Athletic Department, served as an assistant coach. One of the thirteen victories was a 3-2 win over Navy. Additionally, pitcher Jon Rindfleisch hurled a no-hitter against Swarthmore, winning 8-0.

Under Coach Eric Tipton, Army's baseball team compiled a 12-7-1 record during the 1961 spring season. Among those squad members was Tom Blanda, who lettered three years in football as a quarterback and participated in the North-South Shrine Game in Miami. Two other three-year football lettermen, Frank Gibson and George Kirschenbauer, played on the 1961 varsity nine, while Bill Sipos (missing from the photograph) also lettered one year in football. Pictured are, front row, left to right, Ron Borrello, the team manager, Bob Kewley, Bill Boice, Manny Scivoletto, Wayne Williams, Dan DiCarlo, Frank Gibson, Roger Zailskas, Martin Zaldo, Walt Downey, the team manager; second row, Coach Eric Tipton, Col. Red Reeder, assistant coach, Wilton McRae, George Kirschenbauer, John Schmidt, Al DeJardin, Jack Shepard, Ralph Fox, Jim Caywood, Gordon Dopslaff, Steve Buchheim, Maj. J. S. Wierings, Officer-in-Charge; third row, Ray LoPresto, Tom Blanda, Mike Boyle, Tom Eccleston, John Grimshaw, Larry Crane, Jeff Davis, Bill Eckert, Terry Hartnett, Bob Parker. Seated in the front is batboy Curt Evans.

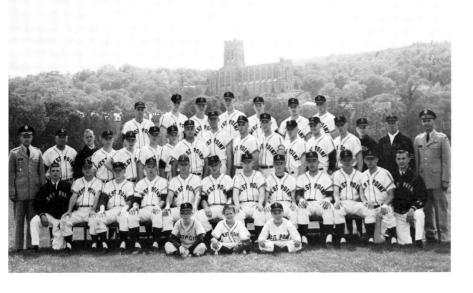

The 1962 baseball team, coached by Eric Tipton, the renowned "coffin corner" kicker from Duke University football fame, compiled a 15-6 record. Tipton is pictured in the second row, second person in. The team captain during the 1962 spring season was John L. Schmidt, while Col. Red Reeder, second from the right in the second row, served as an assistant coach.

Coach Eric Tipton, left, and New York Mets manager Wes Westrum chat with a member of the Cadet varsity squad prior to an exhibition game in 1967. Westrum is the former New York Giants catcher. The Mets shut out the Cadets 4-0 in this meeting.

Coach Eric Tipton coached baseball at the U.S. Military Academy from 1958 until 1977, compiling a record of 234 victories, 201 defeats, and 5 ties. His Army teams also won four Eastern Baseball League championships, sharing the title in 1950, while winning it outright in 1960, 1965, and 1966. Additionally, Coach Tipton guided the Army 150-pound football team from its inception in 1957 until 1976, winning thirteen Eastern Intercollegiate Lightweight Football League championships. His overall record as 150-pound football coach was an incomparable 104 victories, just 14 defeats, and 1 tie. Coach Tipton is a graduate of Duke University where he was an All-America in football under Coach Wallace Wade. Coach Tipton is remembered at Duke for his "coffin corner" kicks that proved crucial throughout his football career.

Army's young pitchers receive some advice from two of the Mets' young hurlers in 1967, Gary Gentry, left, and Tom Seaver, right. Two years later Seaver and Gentry played key roles in leading the Mets to their first pennant and World Series championship.

New York Mets first baseman Ed Kranepool autographs a ball for Army's All-America basketball player Mike Silliman during lunch prior to an exhibition game in 1967. Silliman also lettered in baseball while at West Point.

New York Yankee manager Yogi Berra, in his first year as manager, talks to Coach Eric Tipton prior to an exhibition between the Yankees and the Cadets in 1964.

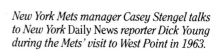

Casey Stengel walks to the dugout at West Point in 1963 after giving the starting lineup to umpires prior to the start of an exhibition game between the fledgling New York Mets and the Army varsity baseball team. After his first year as manager of the "Metsies," Stengel authored a book on the historic first year of the Mets, entitled Can't Anyone Here Play This Game? While the Mets had difficulty beating their National League opponents, they managed to trim the Cadets by a 3-0 margin.

New York Mets manager Casey Stengel talks to New York Daily News reporter Dick Young during the Mets' visit to West Point in 1963.

The legendary Casey Stengel, a man of many words who few could understand, visited West Point as manager of the New York Mets in 1963. He was joined by former Brooklyn Dodger great Duke Snyder and cadet Bill Boice. Stengel, who authored the zany book, Can't Anyone Here Play This Game? about the first year existence of the New York Mets, is recognized for his outstanding tenure as manager of the New York Yankees. He guided the Bronx Bombers to numerous American League pennants and World Series championships.

New York Yankee manager Ralph Houk and Coach Eric Tipton, far right, receive instructions on ground rules at West Point's Doubleday Field before the start of the Yankees' exhibition with the Cadets. The New Yorkers prevailed by an 8-2 margin in 1963.

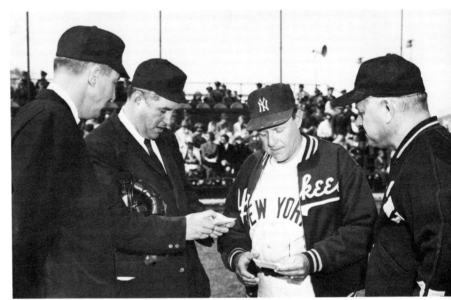

Center fielder Duke Snyder, in the twilight of his career as a member of the New York Mets, is escorted by a cadet during the Mets' visit to the Academy in 1963.

Coach Eric Tipton and New York Mets manager Casey Stengel listen to umpires give ground rules prior to the start of an exhibition game between the Cadets and the Mets in 1963.

Mickey Mantle, New York Yankees' slugger and center fielder, chats with cadets during a spring visit to West Point in the early 1960s. The Yankees began the exhibition series with the Army baseball squad in 1927. With the exception of just one game in the forties and fifties, the Bronx Bombers normally played every other year at the Academy, a traditional visit enjoyed by cadets, Yankee players, and their families.

Yogi Berra chats with Army sports information director Joe Cahill prior to an exhibition game between the New York Yankees and the Army baseball team in 1961. The Bronx Bombers won the game by a lopsided 14-0 margin and thoroughly enjoyed the visit to the scenic Hudson Valley.

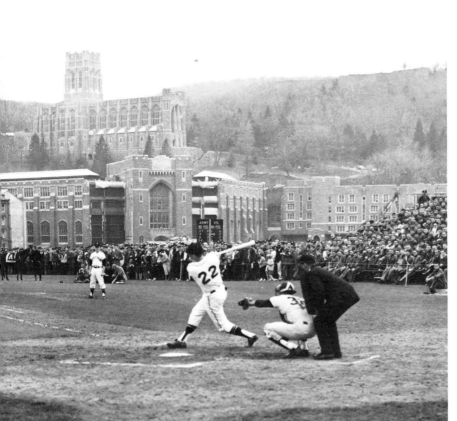

An Army batter swings at a pitch during an exhibition game with the New York Yankees in 1966. Elston Howard (32) is the Yankee catcher. In the background, construction is being done on the Washington Hall complex, adding more barracks to house cadets following the expansion of the Corps of Cadets.

An animated Coach Jack Riley holds arms aloft after Army scores a goal during 1975 game against the University of Connecticut.

Tom Rost (16), the second leading point scorer in Army history, takes a shot in close during a game against New England College in 1976. Rost accounted for 287 points during his four years at West Point, trailing only his brother, Dave, who accounted for 330 points.

CHAPTER 15

Hockey has had a long and distinguished eighty-four-year history at West Point. It started in 1904 when Coach Edward King led the Army team to a 5-1 record, posting victories against such foes as the Newburgh Academy, the Newburgh Alumni, Holbrook, Kingston M.A., and the Riverview Athletic Club.

The lone defeat for the first Army team came at the hands of Mohegan Lake School by a 4-1 margin. LeRoy Bartlett served as captain of the first Army team, and also was team captain in 1905 when the Cadets won seven of eight encounters under captain Richard Foy. Foy remained at the helm for three seasons, compiling an overall record of 15-8-0.

When hockey began, games and practices were determined by the winter cold since The Plain served as a rink after being flooded with water, hardly suitable for an expanding athletic program. Consequently a season schedule consisted of eight to ten games.

Smith Rink was built in 1928 and served as the home of the Army hockey team for fifty-five years before the new Multi-Purpose Sports Complex was completed in time for the start of the 1985-1986 season. Smith Rink proved a distinct advantage for Army hockey teams since it had one of the largest ice surfaces in the country. It originally measured over 230 feet before being shortened to 215 feet to accommodate more seating in the early 1980s. The new ice arena is 200 feet long by 90 feet in width with seating for over 2,500.

Members of the staff and faculty coached Army hockey teams when the sport began, but that changed in 1921 when Talbot Hunter became coach. Hunter coached three seasons at the Academy, climaxed by a 7-7 campaign in 1923, his last season. The seven victories represented the most in Army history at that time.

Ray Marchand assumed the coaching responsibilities in 1924 and remained at that position for twenty years. During that span his Army teams won 74 games, lost 101, and tied 8 times.

After Marchand stepped down after the 1943 season, Lt. Col. John B. R. Hines coached the 1944 squad to a 5-4 record. Henry "Hal" S. Beukema, son of a distinguished department head at the Academy, served as team captain of that squad. Beukema became a pilot after graduating, serving overseas in Berlin and at Barksdale Air Force Base in Louisiana. He died in a crash near Langley Air Force Base in Virginia on January 19, 1954. In 1955, a memorial award was made in his honor and is presented to the Most Valuable Player on the hockey squad each year.

In 1945, Maj. Robert R. Lutz handled the coaching duties, guiding the Cadets to a 7-2-1 mark before Len Patten took over as head coach a year later. Patten coached five seasons at West Point. His best year was 1948 when Army was 11-4-1.

In 1949 hockey was elevated to major sport status at the Military Academy, and that decision helped turn the sport into one of the most popular and successful teams at West Point. However, it took three or four years and a change in coaches to put the hockey program on solid footing.

That foundation was finally established when Earl "Red" Blaik offered the head coaching position in 1951 to a fiery Irishman who starred at Dartmouth College, Jack Riley. He agreed to take the job for one season, commuting from his Medford, Massachusetts, home each fall to prepare his team for the winter campaign.

One year led to thirty-six years as Riley became a college hockey legend because of his success at the Academy. However, looking at his first two seasons, even Riley wondered whether it was worth it. His first two teams managed to win just five games, lost twenty-two, and tie one game.

That statistic would change quickly. In 1953, Army finished at an even .500, splitting sixteen games. During the next thirty-three years Army teams would win twenty or more games eight times. The first team to win twenty games was the 1963-1964 squad, led by team captain Gary Johnson. That feat was duplicated in 1968-1969 when high scoring forward Dave Merhar, the team captain, carried much of the load.

Army set a record with twenty-eight victories during the 1983-1984 season with Robbie Craig serving as team captain. The record of success has followed the affable but volatile Riley throughout his career.

Riley ranks second among the most successful hockey coaches in history with 535 victories. He is currently one of four college hockey coaches ever to win over 500 games. John McInnes of Michigan Tech is the leader with 555 wins.

Riley was selected National Collegiate Athletic Association Coach of the Year twice during his career. He gained the honor initially following the 1956-1957 season when Army finished 14-4, and in 1959-1960 when the Cadets were 16-5-1.

The Army head coach guided the 1960 United States Olympic team to its first Gold Medal in history at Squaw Valley. One of the youngest men to ever direct a U.S. Olympic team, he led the Americans to seven straight victories, including a 9-4 win over Czechoslovakia for the gold medal. The U.S. team also trimmed Canada 2-1 and nipped the Soviet Union, 3-2. The victory over the U.S.S.R. was watched by millions on national television.

A 1947 graduate of Dartmouth College, Riley led the Big Green skaters to three straight Ivy League championships and a forty-six-game unbeaten streak, a record which still stands in the Eastern College Athletic Conference. He was captain of the 1947 squad that tied the University of Toronto for the North American championship.

Following graduation from Dartmouth, Riley earned a berth on the 1948 U.S. Olympic hockey team which competed at St. Moritz, Switzerland. He also served as player-coach of the 1949 United States team that participated in the World Championships at Stockholm, Sweden. In that

tournament, Riley scored both goals in a 2-0 win over Czechoslovakia, the eventual champion.

In November 1979, the Army coach was inducted into the United States Hockey Hall of Fame at Eveleth, Minnesota. His legacy remains intact at West Point since his son, Robbie Riley, is now guiding the Army hockey program. After graduating from Boston College in 1978 where he was co-captain of the Eagles hockey team, he served three years as an assistant coach at St. Lawrence University.

Rob's first head coaching assignment was at Babson College, where he proved an instant success. He led the Beavers to a 27-5-1 record, an ECAC Division II championship, and a National Collegiate Athletic Association Division III championship. The following season Babson posted a 22-9 record, finished second in the ECAC, and reached the quarter-finals of the NCAA Division III tournament. For his efforts Riley was named NCAA Division III Coach of the Year. Obviously, the Army hockey program is in very good hands.

The illustrious history of Army hockey under Jack Riley included outstanding individual records, some of which still stand. In 1968-1969 Dave Merhar set an NCAA Division I scoring record with his fifty-seven goals. He also added thirty-eight assists for ninety-five points.

When Army competed in Division II competition there were other noteworthy accomplishments. George Clark was the high scorer in Division II during the 1973-1974 season, connecting for forty-seven goals and thirty-one assists for seventy-eight points. Dave Rost made his presence felt in 1974-1975 when he had twenty goals and sixty-six assists for eighty-six points. The sixty-six assists are the most in a season in Division II. Two years later Rost had forty-three goals and sixty-five assists for 108 points. The point total represents the most in a season in Division II competition.

The Rost family remained in the forefront of Army hockey

A LOOK INTO THE PAST

Year	Coach	Captain	Won	Lost	Tied
1904	Edward L. King	LeRoy Bartlett	5	1	0
1905	Richard C. Foy	LeRoy Bartlett	7	1	0
1906	Richard C. Foy	Richard Park	5	1	0
1907	Richard C. Foy (15-8-0)	Richard Park	3	6	0
1908	George M. Russell	Philip Gordon	5	2	0
1909	George M. Russell	Philip Hayes	0	1	1
1910	George M. Russell (5-7-4)	Meade Wildrick	0	4	3
1911	LeRoy Bartlett	Millard F. Harmon	1	3	0
1912	LeRoy Bartlett (3-4-1)	Millard F. Harmon	2	1	1
1913	Phillip Gordon	Joseph W. Viner	5	1	0
1914	Phillip Gordon (6-7-0)	Ralph Royce	1	6	0
1915	Frank L. Purdon	Robert W. Strong	1	4	0
1916	Frank L. Purdon	Latham L. Brundred	2	1	1
1917	Frank L. Purdon (9-10-1)	Elbert L. Ford, Jr.	6	5	0
1918	Joseph W. Viner	Henry B. Nichols	6	3	0
1919	Phillip S. Day	Henry B. Nichols	2	2	0
1920	Phillip S. Day (6-4-0)	Henry P. Burgard, II	4	2	0
1921	Talbot Hunter	Harry H. Stout, Jr.	0	2	1
1922	Talbot Hunter	J.D. O'Connell	5	3	1
1923	Talbot Hunter (12-12-1)	Kevin O'Shea	7	7	0
1924	Ray Marchand	Lindsay P. Caywood	3	5	0
1925	Ray Marchand	Henry R. Wesphalinger	3	3	1
1926	Ray Marchand	Willet J. Baird	3	6	0
1927	Ray Marchand	Mark K. Lewis	0	3	1
1928	Ray Marchand	Tito G. Moscatella	1	8	0
1929	Ray Marchand	Normando A. Costello	3	9	0
1930	Ray Marchand	Roy E. Lindquist	6	3	2
1931	Ray Marchand	John K. Waters	4	6	0
1932	Ray Marchand	Thomas C. Darcy	5	4	0
1933	Ray Marchand	David Wagstaff	5	4	0
1934	Ray Marchand	Thomas A. O'Neil	4	6	0
1935	Ray Marchand	James M. Donohue	4	5	1
1936	Ray Marchand	William R. Grohs	5	4	0
1937	Ray Marchand	Maxwell A. Tincher	5	5	0
1938	Ray Marchand	William H. Blanchard	5	4	1
1939	Ray Marchand	Richard D. Curtin	6	4	0
1940	Ray Marchand	George T. Larkin	6	2	2
1941	Ray Marchand	Willard R. Gilbert	4	6	1
1942	Ray Marchand	Frederic H.S. Tate	11	1	0
1943	Ray Marchand	Sidney C. Peterman	3	8	0

history when younger brother Tom connected for forty goals and fifty-seven assists for ninety-seven points, the second highest season point total in Division II.

Merhar's performance was one of the finest in history in Division I competition. He set ECAC record for most goals in a seasons (57), most consecutive games scoring a goal (15), and most consecutive games scoring a point (53).

Dave Rost also holds two ECAC records for most points, 108, and most assists, 66, in a season. Brother Tom also holds the mark for the fastest hat trick, scoring three goals in a twenty-five-second span against Plattsburgh in 1976.

Army hockey teams have competed in the ECAC Division I tournament three times, 1962-1964. They have also earned berths in the Division II tournament in the ECAC six times.

The seventies were dominated by George Clark and Dave Rost. Clark was one of the finest pure goal scorers since the departure of Merhar in the sixties. During three of his four seasons at the Academy, Army earned tournament berths. He scored six goals against New Haven in 1973-1974. A year later he set a record with seven goals against Wesleyan in a 13-2 victory. He closed out his career as the all-time career goal scorer with 153 goals and ranks third in points with 266.

Dave Rost is Army's all-time point scoring leader with 330. He ranks fourth in goals scored with 104 and is the assist leader with 226. That, too, is an ECAC Division II record. He also holds Army season records for points and assists. His brother Tom ranks second with 287 points. George Clark, a 1975 graduate, is third with 266 points, while Jim Knowlton, a 1982 graduate, ranks fourth with 262 points and Merhar is fifth with 229 points. It must be noted that Merhar's record as career scoring leader was surpassed by players who played four years of varsity competition. Merhar was allowed just three varsity seasons under NCAA rules at that time.

There have been many outstanding hockey players at West Point. Pete Dawkins, the Heisman Trophy winner in 1958 while leading the football team to an 8-0-1 record, was considered one of the finest defensemen in the East. Goalie Larry Palmer, who still holds the Army record for most saves in a single game, sixty-three, earned a berth on the 1960 Olympic team. Another goalie, Ron Chisholm, a 1962 West Point graduate, holds the season and career record for best goals against average. The season record is 2.21 goals per game, while his career record is 2.53 goals per game.

Edward Crowley, a 1946 graduate, is the only other hockey player to participate in Olympic competition. Crowley was a teammate of Jack Riley's on the 1948 U.S. team that competed at St. Moritz.

Among former Army defensemen, Ed Hickey is considered one of the finest. He set a record for most assists by a defenseman, thirty-one, in 1956-1957. Toby Lyon equaled that mark during the 1977-1978 season. Hickey also was the first winner of the Beukema Award as the Most Valuable Player in 1955. There have been many other notable winners of that award including Dirk Leuders, Larry Palmer, Neil Mieras, and Ron Chisholm. Those four all played the goalie position.

Mike Thompson and Mike Palone were selected during the 1965 and 1966 season, respectively. Only three players have won the award twice during their hockey careers at West Point: Dave Merhar, Dave Rost, and George Clark.

Army returned to Division I competition during the 1984-1985 season, after competing in Division II since 1974. That decision also revitalized some of the old rivalries with such traditional hockey powers as Harvard, Cornell, Dartmouth, Clarkson, and R.P.I.

Year	Coach	Captain	W	L	T		Year	Coach	Captain	W	L	T
	(71-105-8)	William J. Ray					1965-66	John P. Riley	Laurence Hansen	17	7	1
1944	J.B.R. Hines	Henry Beukema	5	4	0		1966-67	John P. Riley	Parker Anderson	15	12	0
1945	R.R. Lutz	George W. Casey	7	2	1		1967-68	Jack Riley	Michael Palone	14	10	0
1946	Len Patten	Edward F. Crowley	7	6	0		1968-69	Jack Riley	David M. Merhar	20	7	1
1947	Len Patten	Patrick J. O'Connell	4	9	1		1969-70	Jack Riley	David Young	13	12	0
1948	Len Patten	Arthur Snyder, Jr.	11	4	1		1970-71	Jack Riley	Daniel Scioletti	8	14	1
1949	Len Patten	Albert M. Austin	8	7	0		1971-72	Jack Riley	Geoffrey Champion	11	14	0
1950	Len Patten (33-35-2)	Charles F. Kuyk	3	9	0		1972-73	Jack Riley	Edward J. Roubian	9	17	1
1951	John P. Riley	William L. Depew	2	10	1		1973-74	Jack Riley	George D. Clark	20	7	1
1952	John P. Riley	All 1st Classmen	3	12	0		1974-75	Jack Riley	George D. Clark	18	11	0
1953	John P. Riley	David Pistenma	8	8	1		1975-76	Jack Riley	Patrick T. Sullivan	18	9	1
1954	John P. Riley	Victor J. Hugo	10	7	0		1976-77	Jack Riley	Thomas H. Garver	22	6	1
1955	John P. Riley	George L. Monahan	8	8	0		1977-78	Jack Riley	Kevin P. Walsh	13	12	1
1956	John P. Riley	Ralph J. Chesnauskas	11	5	0		1978-79	Jack Riley	Kenneth A. Hawes	7	21	0
1956-57	John P. Riley	Edward I. Hickey	14	4	0		1979-80	Jack Riley	Thomas P. Rost	19	12	1
1957-58	John P. Riley	Leonard R. McCormick	15	4	1		1980-81	Jack Riley	Matthew S. Bradley	20	13	1
1958-59	John P. Riley	Laurence J. Palmer	9	10	1		1981-82	Jack Riley	James A. Knowlton	24	11	0
1959 60	John P. Riley	Edward M. Crowley	16	5	1		1982-83	Jack Riley	Daniel Cox	25	10	1
1960-61	John P. Riley	John D. Dewar	17	8	0		1983-84	Jack Riley	Robert J. Craig	28	5	1
1961-62	John P. Riley	Paul J. Dobbins	18	6	1		1984-85	Jack Riley	Marc Kapsalis	17	13	0
1962-63	John P. Riley	Gerald F. Stonehouse	17	6	2		1985-86	Jack Riley	Edward Moran	18	11	1
1963-64	John P. Riley	Gary R. Johnson	20	8	0			(541-342-21)				
1964-65	John P. Riley	Michael Thompson	17	7	0		1986-87	Robbie Riley	Kevin Keenan	9	19	1

Army forward Tom Rost, the second leading point scorer in history, is shown as he prepared for the 1977-1978 season.

Coach Jack Riley is photographed prior to practice in 1974.

Dan Scioletti, the Most Valuable Player on the Army hockey team in 1971, shares the goalie record for most career shutouts. Scioletti had eight shutouts during his career. Ron Chisholm set the record in 1962.

Coach Jack Riley holds up the Gold Medal he received after leading the United States Olympic team to its historic victory in the 1960 Olympics at Squaw Valley. The hockey victory was the first by the Americans in Olympic history, defeating Canada, the Soviet Union, and Czechoslovakia en route to the Gold Medal.

Army's new home, the Multi-Purpose Sports Complex, gets a workout when the Cadets tangle with Cornell. Here Army players battle for the puck behind the Big Red net. The new facility holds the hockey arena, which seats 2,500, and a basketball arena that seats more than five thousand. The Multi-Purpose Sports Complex cost $16 million; it took two years to complete construction. The opening of the new facility coincided with the close of the Jack Riley coaching era.

Coach Jack Riley is flanked by Dave Merhar, the Army team captain during the 1968-1969 season. Merhar also set a career scoring record at that time with 229 points and 112 goals during his three years on the varsity.

Defenseman Toby Lyon (20) uncorks a slap shot from the point during a game againsts North Adams State College in 1977. Lyon equaled an Army record for most assists in a season by a defenseman, piling up thirty-one. The record was held by Ed Hickey who had thirty-one assists during the 1956-1957 season.

Army defenseman Toby Lyon (20) feeds the puck out front to set up a shot by a teammate during the 1978 game against Norwich University.

The Army hockey team pictured here compiled an 11-4-1 record under Coach Len Patten, his best season during a five-year coaching stint at West Point. A year later hockey was granted major sport status at the Academy.

Coach Jack Riley is flanked by members of his squad after racking up his 400th career victory as a coach. Riley went on to win over 500 games in hockey, all of them here at West Point, before retiring after the 1985-1986 season.

The 1957-1958 Army hockey team, pictured here, compiled a 15-4-1 record, the best record by a Cadet squad under Coach Jack Riley at that time. Among the squad members is goalie Larry Palmer (1), who earned a spot on Jack Riley's United States Olympic hockey squad in 1960. Pete Dawkins, Army's Heisman Trophy winner in football, is wearing No. 3. Dawkins was one of the best defensemen in the East, even though he did not play competitive hockey until coming to West Point. Coach Jack Riley is at the far right. Next to Riley is assistant trainer Gene Benner. Benner left the Academy, but now is back serving as head trainer for the athletic department.

Coach Jack Riley's 1955-1956 Army hockey team, including the leading members pictured here, won eleven games and lost just five during the season.

Army center Jim Knowlton scores a goal against the Royal Military College during a 12-4 victory 1979. The Army-RMC hockey series is one of the most colorful of international college rivalries. It began in 1923 and was called the "Hands Across the Border" series for its international flavor of competition between the United States and its neighbor to the north, Canada. In the early games, there were no penalties called, but that changed during Coach Jack Riley's tenure since the games became too rough.

Army goalie Ron Chisholm was one of the finest goaltenders in history. Chisholm holds records for best goals-against average on season and career categories. His 2.21 goals against average during the 1961-1962 season is the best in West Point history, while his 2.53 career average is also tops.

Army's record-setting goal scorer, George Clark (9), connects from up close during a game against Lowell University in 1974.

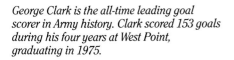

George Clark is the all-time leading goal scorer in Army history. Clark scored 153 goals during his four years at West Point, graduating in 1975.

The 1923 Army hockey team won seven games, equaling the record for most victories in a season at that time. Additionally, five members of that team achieved the rank of major general: John J. Binns '23 (top row, first on left), Royal B. Lord '23 (bottom row, first on left), Charles G. Stevenson (bottom row, third from left), Elnar B. Gjelsteen (bottom row, second from right), and Henry R. Westphallinger '25 (bottom row, far right).

Army wing Tom Rost (16) flips a pass to his brother Dave Rost (14) during a game against North Adams State College in 1977. The Cadets trimmed North Adams, 6-4. The Rost brothers proved to be one of the most prolific scoring combinations in Army history. Dave established new Army career scoring marks with 330 points, coming on 104 goals and 226 assists. The assist total is also a career record. Rost also set a season record for most points scored with 108, coming on 43 goals and 65 assists in 1976-1977. He also set a season assist record in 1974-1975 with sixty-six.

In 1941, the hockey team at West Point, under Coach Ray Marchand, won four games, lost six, and tied one. The Cadets defeated Lehigh, Cornell, Hamilton, and Middlebury. Pictured are, front row, left to right, Frederic H. S. Tate, team captain Willard R. Gilbert, Joseph S. Tate, Joseph S. Grygiel, Roscoe B. Woodruff, and Lloyd R. Salisbury; second row, Coach Marchand, Sidney C. Peterman, James O. Frankosky, John F. Phelan, Arthur R. King, Robert V. Elsberry, Charles H. Garvin, Stephen V. Plume, and team manager Harry H. Ellis; back row, Edward A. Munn, Howard L. Lambert, Thomas H. Ray, Benjamin Norris, and Edward L. Corcoran.

Army center Dave Rost (14) whips a shot past the Royal Military College goalie during the annual skirmish with the Canadian military school during a 1977 encounter. The Cadets routed the visiting Redmen by an 11-2 count. Army compiled a record of twenty-two victories, just six losses, and one tie during the 1976-1977 season. Coach Riley's squad also earned a berth in the ECAC Division II playoffs, trimming American International College 7-6 in overtime before bowing to Union College 11-4 in the semi-finals.

Army center Dave Rost (14) battles for the loose puck behind the net during a game against Princeton in 1977. The Cadets took the measure of the Tigers by a 6-2 count. Rost is Army's career scoring leader with 330 points.

The 1922 hockey team at West Point, coached by Talbot Hunter, compiled a 5-3-1 record. James D. O'Connell was the team captain. O'Connell went on to a very successful career in the U.S. Army, attaining the rank of lieutenant general before retiring in 1959. He also was a vice president of General Telephone and Electronics Labs, and served as a special assistant to President Lyndon B. Johnson from 1964 to 1969.

Billy Cavanagh, born in Lawrence, Massachusetts, on July 7, 1886, learned the sport of boxing from a very young age. He had his first professional bout at fourteen and went on to win the middleweight championship of Canada. The only thing Cavanaugh liked more than boxing was teaching boxing, and the Academy provided such an opportunity in 1918. He organized the first USMA boxing team in 1921 and coached through 1948. He had a record of 129 wins, 38 losses, and 13 ties at West Point, coaching seven undefeated teams. His boxers won twenty-nine individual titles and four tournament team championships during his West Point coaching career.

The history of boxing at the Military Academy can be traced simply to the success of William J. Cavanagh, a native of Lawrence, Massachusetts, where he learned to box at a very young age. Cavanagh fought his first professional bout at the age of fourteen and later went on to win the middleweight championship of Canada.

It seemed the only thing Cavanagh liked as much as boxing was teaching boxing, and the Military Academy provided that option to him in 1918. It took Cavanagh just three years to organize the first intercollegiate boxing team at West Point in 1921, and he guided that program through 1948. During that span, Cavanagh compiled a record of 129 victories, just 38 losses, and 13 ties.

Seven of his Army teams posted unbeaten records and 29 of his boxers won individual championships. Additionally, Army won four tournament team championships under Cavanagh's guidance.

In an article written by Robert Degen in the spring of 1967 for *Assembly* magazine, an official publication of the Association of Graduates at West Point, a most appropriate description of Cavanagh was presented.

A LOOK AT THE PAST

Year	Coach	Captain	Won	Lost	Tied
1921	William J. Cavanagh	None Listed	1	0	0
1922	William J. Cavanagh	Howard G. Davidson	4	0	0
1923	William J. Cavanagh	John W. Harmony	3	1	0
1924	William J. Cavanagh	William H. Maglin	1	3	0
1925	William J. Cavanagh	John I. Brosnan	5	0	0
1926	William J. Cavanagh	Harry McN. Grizzard	5	1	1
1927	William J. Cavanagh	John R. Lovell	4	2	1
1928	William J. Cavanagh	Carl F. Fritzsche	5	2	1
1929	William J. Cavanagh	Jacob G. Reynolds	5	2	0
1930	William J. Cavanagh	Ludlow King	7	1	0
1931	William J. Cavanagh	Eugene L. Brown	7	0	1
1932	William J. Cavanagh	John G. Coughlin	6	1	1
1933	William J. Cavanagh	Joseph A. Remus	4	0	1
1934	William J. Cavanagh	Robert H. Bennett	5	1	1
1935	William J. Cavanagh	John S. B. Dick & John F. Rhoades	3	2	1

Born on July 7, 1886, Cavanagh was slated to fight Kid Hope in his first bout. According to lore, Kid Hope heard some of Cavanagh's friends boasting of his talents for fisticuffs, and failed to show up for the fight. Cavanagh, more confident than ever, accepted another bout the following week. He fought six rounds to a draw, and came out with a broken hand. Before the hand healed, boxing was outlawed in Boston and a whole year passed before Cavanagh fought again.

Billy returned to the ring, fighting as "Kid Glover." Under that name he fought many of the top welterweights in the country, but the championship always eluded him. In 1907, he quit the ring to get married and became a boxing instructor in New York City. In time he invested in his own gymnasium, where he conducted boxing and gym classes for New Yorkers who wanted to reduce weight or keep fit.

That career wasn't enough for Cavanagh, so he returned to the ring, fighting as a middleweight. He culminated his career by winning the middleweight championship of Canada.

In 1918, he had an opportunity to come to West Point as boxing instructor and coach and he accepted. That is when boxing came to life at the Academy. More than sixteen thousand cadets passed through Cavanagh's classes at West Point. He was described as "tough" and "authoritative" while at the Academy.

"When I say 'on guard,' step right out on guard...On Guard!" yelled Cavanagh. It was one of the early commands plebes learned at West Point, and they weren't likely to forget it.

When Cavanagh ended his coaching career in 1948, Herbert J. Kroeten took over as head coach. Kroeten coached the boxing team for the next seven years, before the sport was discontinued on an intercollegiate basis in 1955. His record was 19-20-5. Kroeten is still very much in tune to boxing today. He is a member of the Department of Physical Education at West Point, instructing plebes in boxing.

While no longer involved in intercollegiate competition, boxing is still very popular at West Point. The brigade championships, held each spring, always draw an enthusiastic gathering in the cadet gymnasium.

Year	Coach	Captain	W	L	T
1936	William J. Cavanagh	William F. Meany	3	2	1
1937	William J. Cavanagh	Battle M. Barksdale	4	1	1
1938	William J. Cavanagh	Bertram C. Harrison	6	0	0
1939	William J. Cavanagh	Doishard F. Hall	5	1	0
1940	William J. Cavanagh	Walter W. Lavell	4	1	2
1941	William J. Cavanagh	Harry N. Rising, Jr.	5	2	0
1942	William J. Cavanagh	Frank B. Clay	6	0	0
1943	William J. Cavanagh	Robert McN. Peden & Donald C. Pense	2	3	1
1944	William J. Cavanagh	William C. McGlothlin	2	3	1
1945	Major H. P. Pillsbury	David Fink	5	2	0
1946	William J. Cavanagh	Steven L. Conner, Jr.	8	0	0
1947	William J. Cavanagh	Harry P. Ball	5	2	1
1948	William J. Cavanagh (121-33-13)	Thomas W. Hazard, Jr.	6	2	0
1949	Herbert J. Kroeten	Ralph Puckett, Jr.	2	4	0
1950	Herbert J. Kroeten	William H. Kellum & Peter H. Monfore	3	3	1
1951	Herbert J. Kroeten	Stanley S. Scott	3	3	0
1952	Herbert J. Kroeten	James E. McInerney, Jr.	2	4	1
1953	Herbert J. Kroeten	James J. McGee	3	4	0
1954	Herbert J. Kroeten	Andrew J. Maloney, Jr.	2	2	2
1955	Herbert J. Kroeten (19-20-5)	Don P. Rundle	4	1	1

Cadet Richard Shea was one of the finest track performers in Army history, winning sixteen major intercollegiate middle distance and cross country championships before graduating from the Academy in 1952. Shea set seven indoor and outdoor track records and captained both the indoor and outdoor track teams in 1952. He was killed in action in Korea on July 8, 1953, and was posthumously awarded the Medal of Honor for valor during wartime. The outdoor track facility at West Point was dedicated in his honor on May 10, 1958.

Steve Kreider demonstrates the form that helped him set an Academy record in the javelin with a toss of 264 feet, 2 inches during the 1979 Penn Relays in Philadelphia's Franklin Field. In these photographs, Kreider is competing against an Oxford-Cambridge track team in 1977.

CHAPTER 17

TRACK

Track and field competition began at the United States Military Academy in the spring of 1893, three years after baseball and football were established as official athletic activities for the Corps of Cadets in 1890.

The importance of the first Army-Navy football game in developing athletics—and certainly track and field—at West Point should not be underestimated. In fact, losing to the Midshipmen in the opening game also served a purpose, since it made members of the Corps and the staff and faculty work that much harder to change the result.

Thus, the stage was set for the establishment of other sports at the Academy. However, in 1893 it was called Field Day. Competition was held in track and field between classes. At first, Field Day consisted of teams of five competitors from each class, and the class of 1896 was the winner, receiving a banner from the Army Officers Athletic Association.

The A.O.A.A. was organized in 1892, along with the U.S.M.A. Athletic Association. The Army Officers Athletic Association was formed to encourage athletics at the Military Academy and throughout the Army. The U.S.M.A. Athletic Association was formed to directly control the athletic program.

One year after the first Field Day was held, the rules of the competition were changed, allowing two competitors from each class in each event. During the first Field Day all competitors were required to compete in all events. The change brought instant improvement in the performances.

A spring Field Day remained very much a part of the athletic schedule at West Point, but a second Field Day was established during the winter months later.

Intercollegiate competition did not begin in outdoor track until 1921 when Army defeated Tufts, 93-33. The first coach was Lt. Elmer Q. Oliphant, a former two-time All-America halfback in football at West Point (1916-1917) and a National Football Foundation Hall of Fame selection in 1955.

Oliphant coached the track team for two years, leading them to an unblemished 3-0 record the second season.

Lt. Eugene L. Vidal took over the coaching assignment in track in 1923 and coached for two seasons, compiling a 7-1 record. Then the Athletic Association selected Leo Novak to establish a solid program. Novak, who also coached basketball at West Point, developed Army's traditional strong outdoor program.

Novak began quickly, leading the Cadet track squad to twenty-two straight victories over the course of four seasons. He spent twenty-five years at the Academy, compiling a record of ninety-six victories and twenty-four defeats in outdoor track before resigning at the close of the 1949 season. He also established an indoor track program in 1942 and was 11-2 before closing out his coaching career.

Novak's outdoor squads won four Heptagonal championships, one Nonagonal title, and finished first in the IC4A Track and Field championship three times. His Army teams also had two second-place finishes at the IC4A competition, along with a second and third at the national A.A.U. championships.

Jess Mortensen succeeded Novak and served as cross country and track coach in 1950 and 1951. His 1950 cross country squad finished with a 7-1 record, won the Heptagonal Cross Country championship and took runner-up honors in the annual IC4A Cross Country championship. Mortensen's indoor track teams posted identical 4-0 records during his two years. His 1951 squad also won the indoor Heptagonal championship, while his outdoor team was third in the Heptagonals.

Mortensen was an outstanding track performer at the University of Southern California. He won the NCAA javelin throw championship while there, and also finished fifth in the Olympic tryouts for the decathlon in 1928. Mortensen won the National Decathlon championship in 1931, setting a new world record. He was track and cross country coach at the University of Denver before accepting the same position at West Point.

Carleton Crowell succeeded Mortensen as track and cross country coach and built a solid string of successes. Crowell guided Army teams to 351 victories and a dozen Heptagonal championships—five in indoor track, four in cross country, and three in outdoor track. Every indoor and outdoor Academy track record was shattered during his twenty-five years at the helm, with the exception of a single record.

Crowell suffered a fatal heart attack on September 5, 1975, at the age of sixty-two.

The venerable Army coach came to the Academy in 1947 from the University of Tennessee where he was head track coach and freshman basketball coach. It took Crowell just two years to bring the Volunteers their first Southeastern Conference cross country championship, and he repeated that performance in 1950.

Crowell guided the Army indoor teams to a composite record of 139 victories, just 50 defeats, and one tie. In outdoor track, his teams won 87 meets and lost 57, while in cross country his teams won 125 and lost 53.

Captain Mel Pender, a former Olympian serving as an assistant track coach at West Point, coached the 1975-1976 indoor team and the 1976 outdoor team. Then John Randolph, former head track and cross country coach at the College of William and Mary, was named head coach. Randolph remained at West Point for three seasons before accepting a similar position at the University of Florida. While at the Academy, Randolph compiled a 28-2-1 record in indoor track and a 14-3 outdoor mark.

Ron Bazil, head track coach at Adelphi University, succeeded Randoloph and has guided the Cadet track fortunes for the past eight years. The Army coach has an overall track record of 52-19, while he is 46-21 in cross country.

In addition to the success of Army teams in both indoor and outdoor track, there have been many outstanding individual performers throughout the long history of this sport.

One of the finest was Richard Shea, a 1952 graduate of West Point. Shea enlisted in the Army in 1944 and served as a staff sergeant in the 53rd Constabulary Regiment in Nuremberg, Germany. A native of Portsmouth, Virginia, Shea did not compete in cross country until entering the Army, but he went on to win the European 1,500 and 5,000-meter championships.

Shea entered West Point in 1948, served as a cadet captain and was the recipient of the Army Athletic Association Trophy presented to the senior who has provided outstanding service to athletics during his Academy career. He won sixteen major intercollegiate middle distance and cross country championships, and set seven indoor and outdoor Academy track records. He also was captain of the 1953 indoor and outdoor track squads.

Shea was assigned to Korea following graduation and died in action on July 8, 1953, at Sokkogae, trying to repel Communist "suicide attacks" during the Korean Conflict. He was awarded the Medal of Honor posthumously for wartime bravery, the 77th Medal of Honor awarded during the Korean War.

A LOOK INTO THE PAST

Outdoor Track

Year	Coach	Captain	Won	Lost	Tied	Year	Coach	Captain	Won	Lost	Tied
1921	Lt. Elmer Q. Oliphant	David J. Crawford	1	0	0	1950	Jess Mortensen	Richard G. Bastar	4	1	0
1922	Lt. Elmer Q. Oliphant	David J. Crawford	3	0	0	1951	Carleton Crowell	James W. Cain	3	1	0
1923	Lt. Eugene L. Vidal	Herbert R. Campbell	4	0	0	1952	Carleton Crowell	Richard T. Shea	2	1	0
1924	Lt. Eugene L. Vidal	Lewis C. Barkes	3	1	0	1953	Carleton Crowell	Joseph P. Perlow	3	1	0
1925	Leo Novak	Aubrey S. Newman	2	3	0	1954	Carleton Crowell	Charles S. Brown	3	2	0
1926	Leo Novak	Tyler Calhoun, Jr.	3	1	0	1955	Carleton Crowell	Lewis C. Olive	3	2	0
1927	Leo Novak	Joseph H. Gilbreth	6	0	0	1956	Carleton Crowell	Alan L. Thelin	2	4	0
1928	Leo Novak	Roy H. Guertler	5	0	0	1957	Carleton Crowell	Stanley T. Johnson	3	4	0
1929	Leo Novak	William E. Hall	5	0	0	1958	Carleton Crowell	Jerry W. Bells	5	2	0
1930	Leo Novak	James S. Luckett	4	1	0	1959	Carleton Crowell	Gilbert E. Roesler	2	5	0
1931	Leo Novak	Ernest Moore	4	1	0	1960	Carleton Crowell	William G. Hanne	3	4	0
1932	Leo Novak	Norman H. Lankenau	4	1	0	1961	Carleton Crowell	Howard H. Roberts	2	5	0
1933	Leo Novak	Winton S. Graham	5	0	0	1962	Carleton Crowell	Gary L. Brown	5	2	0
1934	Leo Novak	Ronald C. Martin	3	1	1	1963	Carleton Crowell	Joseph A. Almaguer	4	3	0
1935	Leo Novak	William G. Proctor	4	1	0	1964	Carleton Crowell	William J. Straub	5	1	0
1936	Leo Novak	Clyde L. Layne	5	0	0	1965	Carleton Crowell	Harold A. Jenkins	2	4	0
1937	Leo Novak	Richard P. Klocko	3	2	0	1966	Carleton Crowell	Henry R. Farrell	5	1	0
1938	Leo Novak	David O. Byars	4	1	0	1967	Carleton Crowell	John M. W. Graham	6	0	0
1939	Leo Novak	Mahlon W. Caffee	6	0	0	1968	Carleton Crowell	Daniel B. Seebart	5	0	0
1940	Leo Novak	Frank A. de Latour	5	1	0	1969	Carleton Crowell	Sheridon H. Groves	3	2	0
1941	Leo Novak	Stanton C. Hutson	5	3	0	1970	Carleton Crowell	James A. Osman	4	1	0
1942	Leo Novak	Ralph J. White	6	0	0	1971	Carleton Crowell	William F. Diehl	2	2	0
1943	Leo Novak	Edward W. Cutler & Robert J. Walling	2	1	0	1972	Carleton Crowell	Stephen G. Hannan	3	2	0
						1973	Carleton Crowell	Ronnie E. Madera	4	2	0
1944	Leo Novak	Carl B. Anderson	2	1	0	1974	Carleton Crowell	Marshall L. Best	4	3	0
1945	Leo Novak	Jared W. Morrow	2	1	0	1975	Carleton Crowell	John F. Craven	4	3	0
1946	Leo Novak	Bernard E. Conor	1	3	0		(87-57)				
1947	Leo Novak	James B. Egger	1	2	0	1976	Capt. Mel Pender	Keith E. Simms	4	3	0
1948	Leo Novak	Charles D. Nash	4	0	0	1977	John Randolph	Ivory D. Carson	5	1	0
1949	Leo Novak (96-24-0)	John A. Hammack	5	0	0	1978	John Randolph	David M. Wiener	7	1	0

The outdoor track facility at West Point is dedicated in his honor.

Edwin E. "Buzz" Aldrin, Jr., the former NASA astronaut, competed in track at West Point. During his last year, 1951, Aldrin finished second in the pole vault during the IC4A championship, clearing 13-6. His career best was 13-8, just ⅛ of an inch shy of the Academy record at that time.

Aldrin joined NASA in 1963 and became an astronaut in 1964. He was the pilot for the Gemini 12 mission in November of 1966. Aldrin served as the Command Module Pilot back-up for the Apollo 8 mission, the first flight to the moon, and then was the Lunar Module Pilot for the Apollo 11 flight, the first manned landing on the Moon on July 20, 1969.

Another one of Army's outstanding competitors was Bill Straub, a 1964 graduate. Straub shared the 5,000-meter run championship at the National Collegiate Athletic Association Outdoor Track Championship in 1964. The native of Mt. Kisco, New York, finished in a dead head with Jim Murphy of the Air Force Academy at Eugene, Oregon.

It took twenty-five minutes to decide the finish of the race, but it didn't faze Straub. "I wanted to run fourteen minutes," said Straub in a *New York Times* article, "and I expected it would be worth fifth place. But we went out slowly, and it became my type of race."

Straub and Murphy were timed in 14 minutes, 12.3 seconds, a meet record. Straub is the only Army runner who has won an NCAA individual track championship.

Curt Alitz, son of former Army wrestling coach LeRoy Alitz, is considered another one of Army's finest cross country and track performers. An All-America in cross country, Alitz also was successful during the indoor and outdoor track seasons. During the 1978 outdoor season he won the 10,000-meter event at the Heptagonal championships, and the two-mile event at the IC4A championship. In 1977, Alitz won the 10,000-meter race at the Penn Relays in 28:44, while winning the 3,000-meter steeplechase and the 5,000-meter run at the Heptagonals. The Army distance runner gained All-America honors twice in indoor track in the 3,000-meter run. He is a three-time All-America in outdoor track, gaining those honors twice in the 10,000-meter run and once at the 5,000-meter distance. Army's Dennis Trujillo also earned All-America recognition in the two-mile run indoors and the three-mile run outdoors.

1979	John Randolph (14-3)	Michael B. Willis	2	1	0
1980	Ron Bazil	Stephen D. Kreider	3	0	0
1981	Ron Bazil	James Daly	2	2	0
1982	Ron Bazil	Jeffrey A. Scott	0	1	0
1983	Ron Bazil	Todd Kulik	1	2	0
1984	Ron Bazil	Derric Anderson & Robert Muska	3	2	0
1985	Ron Bazil	Kendrick Kahler & Christopher McPadden	4	1	0
1986	Ron Bazil	Thomas Szoka	0	1	0
1987	Ron Bazil (14-9-0)	Eric Tuggle	1	1	0
1942	Leo Novak	Francis H. Bonham	0	1	0
1943	Leo Novak	Edward W. Cutler & Robert J. Walling	1	1	0

Indoor Track

1944	Leo Novak	Carl B. Anderson	3	0	0
1945	Leo Novak	Jared W. Morrow	1	0	0
1946	Leo Novak	Bernard E. Conor	0	0	0
1947	Leo Novak	James B. Egger	1	0	0
1948	Leo Novak	Charles D. Nash	2	0	0
1949	Leo Novak (11-2)	John A. Hammack	3	0	0
1950	Jess Mortensen	Richard C. Bastar	4	0	0
1951	Jess Mortensen (8-0)	James W. Cain	4	0	0
1952	Carleton Crowell	Richard T. Shea	3	1	0
1953	Carleton Crowell	Joseph P. Perlow	3	1	0
1954	Carleton Crowell	Charles S. Brown	3	2	0
1955	Carleton Crowell	Lewis C. Olive	3	2	0
1956	Carleton Crowell	Alan L. Thelin	2	3	1
1957	Carleton Crowell	Stanley T. Johnson	4	3	0
1958	Carleton Crowell	Jerry W. Betts	4	3	0
1959	Carleton Crowell	Gilbert E. Roesler	7	0	0
1960	Carleton Crowell	William G. Henne	7	0	0
1961	Carleton Crowell	Howard H. Roberts	3	3	0
1962	Carleton Crowell	Gary L. Brown	6	1	0
1963	Carleton Crowell	Joseph A. Almaguer	6	1	0
1964	Carleton Crowell	William J. Straub	6	2	0
1965	Carleton Crowell	Harold A. Jenkins	7	2	0
1966	Carleton Crowell	Henry R. Farreell	6	3	0
1967	Carleton Crowell	John M. W. Graham	8	0	0
1968	Carleton Crowell	Gregory C. Camp	7	1	0
1968-69	Carleton Crowell	Larry Lemaster	9	0	0
1969-70	Carleton Crowell	George Forsythe	10	1	0
1970-71	Carleton Crowell	Kevin James	9	2	0
1971-72	Carleton Crowell	Tony L. Dedmond	6	5	0
1972-73	Carleton Crowell	John L. Cerny	9	4	0
1973-74	Carleton Crowell	Allen L. Sample	5	5	0
1974-75	Carleton Crowell (139-50-1)	Jesse F. Owens & John F. Craven	6	5	0
1975-76	Capt. Mel Pender	Glenn H. Hulse	7	2	0
1976-77	John Randolph	Scott A. Leishman	9	0	0
1977-78	John Randolph	Michael J. Schaefer	9	2	1
1978-79	John Randolph (28-2-1)	Lloyd R. Darlington	10	0	0
1979-80	Ron Bazil	Gary B. Hopper	3	2	1
1980-81	Ron Bazil	Robert A. Payne	8	2	0
1981-82	Ron Bazil	Kevin Kullander	7	1	0
1982-83	Ron Bazil	Charles Babers	6	0	0
1983-84	Ron Bazil	Derric Anderson	7	1	0
1984-85	Ron Bazil	John Zornick	4	1	0
1985-86	Ron Bazil	Wendell Champion	2	1	0
1986-87	Ron Bazil (38-10)	Karl Harrison	1	2	0

Ron Madera, second from left, competes in the Heptagonal Track and Field championships in 1971 at Franklin Field in Philadelphia. Madera was a sprinter and relay specialist while at the Academy. Madera helped Army win a Heptagonal title in the 440-yard relay in 1972, while running legs on two winning Heptagonal relays and one winning relay at the Penn Relays in 1973.

Army track coach Mel Pender, right, an Olympic Gold Medal winner at the age of thirty-one, talks with three of his sprinters in 1971, left to right, Marshall Best, Tony Dedmond, and Bob Patton. Pender earned his gold medal during the 1968 Olympics at Mexico City in the 400-meter relay. He joined the Army coaching staff in 1970 and worked with the sprinters, taking over as head coach in 1975-1976 after the sudden death of veteran coach Carleton Crowell. Pender guided the Army indoor team to a 7-2 record and the outdoor team to a 4-3 mark. Twice during his competitive track career Pender won berths on the United States Olympic team as a sprinter. He qualified for the first time in 1964, but suffered a pulled muscle in the quarter-final heats at Tokyo, Japan. After medication he was still able to compete in the semi-finals and finals, but finished in sixth place after a heroic effort. Four years later he qualified again, avoided injuries in the 100-meter dash, but still finished a disappointing sixth. Some of that disappointment was eliminated when he helped the United States win the gold in the 400-meter relay.

Curt Alitz, son of former Army wrestling coach LeRoy Alitz, proved to be one of the finest distance runners in Army track history. In this photo, he is competing in the 3,000-meter run against rival Navy in 1978. During the 1978 outdoor track season, Alitz won the 10,000-meter title in the annual Heptagonal championships which consist of track competition between the eight Ivy League schools and Navy. In 1977, he won the 10,000-meter event at the Penn Relays with a time of 28:44.4, while capturing the 3,000-meter Steeplechase and the 5,000-meter run at the Heptagonal championships. During the indoor track season in 1978 he won the IC4A three mile title, while in 1977 he was victorious in the two-mile event at the IC4A meet.

Hurdler Mike Willis gives the high sign after hitting the tape at the finish of the 110-meter high hurdles during the annual Heptagonal Outdoor Track championships held at West Point in 1978. Willis won the title with a time of 14.35 seconds. He set an Academy record in the high hurdles in 1978, being clocked in 13.9 seconds in Louisiana. He set another Army mark in the 200-meter dash that same season with a time of 21.79 seconds.

Army distance runner Dennis Trujillo of Pueblo, Colorado, takes the lead in the 10,000-meter run during the annual Heptagonal Outdoor Track and Field championships held at West Point in 1976. Trujillo earned his Heps title with a time of 29:36.0.

Army sprinter Marshall Best gets set to cross the finish line while anchoring the 440-yard relay team in 1972. Later that season, Best anchored the same relay that won the Heptagonal championship title with a time of 41.3 seconds. The other members of that winning contingent were Tony Dedmond, Jack Craven, and Ron Madera.

Army's veteran coach Carleton Crowell congratulates a Pennsylvania competitor and makes a special presentation during the 1975 outdoor Heptagonal Track and Field championships held at West Point. The Heptagonal track event includes competitors from the eight Ivy League colleges and Army and Navy.

247

Curt Alitz rolls to victory in the two-mile run to help lead Army to a 68-50 victory over rival Navy during their indoor confrontation at the West Point Field House in 1977. The victory put the finishing touches on Army's undefeated 9-0 season under the guidance of first-year coach John Randolph, former track coach at the College of William and Mary. Alitz went on to win the two-mile run at the Heptagonal Indoor championships and the indoor IC4A meet, setting an Army record in the latter with a time of 8:37.6. A year later the Army distance specialist won the one-mile run at the Heptagonals and the three-mile event during the IC4A meet. He set another Army record in the three-mile run with a time of 13:23.8. Alitz also gained All-America honors twice indoors in the 3,000-meter run.

The 1966 outdoor track team won five of six meets under Coach Carleton Crowell. Among the five victories was a 78-76 win over Navy. The only loss was to Harvard by a 79-75 margin. The Cadets did win the Heptagonal track championships for the sixth time in history. The Heptagonal track competition includes all eight Ivy League colleges and universities, in addition to Army and Navy. Team members included, seated left to right, team captain Rance Farrell, Bill Clinton, Bob McDonald, and John Nolan; second row, Coach Carleton Crowell, Mark Spelman, John Cochran, Tom Almojuela, Dave Linder, Greg Camp, Mike Oshel, John Phillips, Jim Jenkins, John Douglas, Bob Adams, and assistant coach R. Trahan; third row, Bob Clarke, Hugh Shaffer, Chris Iaconis, Jim

Black, Leroy Outlaw, Dan Seebart, Larry Hart, Jack Norris, Tom Vollrath, Dan Linbaugh, and Major Nick Terzopoulos, the officer representative; back row, Bob Hayes, John Armstrong, Bob Keller, Bob Rettig, Mark Edelman, Paul Haseman, Jim Siket, Joe Finley, Mike Warren, Jim Warner, and Paul DeCoursey. Missing from the team picture were Bob Ramsay, Dick Black, John Graham, Steve Kujawski, Mike Delleo, and Tim Jeffrey. During the Heptagonals, Seebart and Warner were double winners. Seebert finished first in the shot put (54-6¾) and the discus (170-1), while Warner was first in the mile (4:09.7) and the two mile run (9:04.8). Hart won the hammer throw (184) and Kujawski took the pole vault event (14-6).

Coach Carleton Crowell, third row far left, guided his Army outdoor track team to a 3-1 record in 1951. One of those victories was a 68⅔-61⅓ victory over Navy. The Cadets' only loss was to Manhattan, 77½-62½. Richard Shea, second row fourth from left, was a key performer for Army in 1951, winning the two mile run at the Heptagonal championships in 9:15. He also won the two mile event at the Penn Relays, setting a meet record with a time of 9:11.9.

Leo Novak, second row at left, coached the 1932 Army track team to a 4-1 record. The Cadets defeated Boston College, Holy Cross, West Virginia, and Penn State. Notre Dame handed the Cadets their only loss of the season by a 68⅓ to 57⅔ score. The Army team captain was Norman Lankenau.

In 1931, the men's track team at West Point won four of five meets under Coach Leo Novak. The Cadets defeated Bowdoin, Boston College, Pittsburgh, and West Virginia. The only loss was to New York University. The team captain was Ernest Moore. One of the team's most outstanding efforts came in the Penn Relays where John T. Malloy, Carl E. Green, John L. Innskeep, and team captain Moore won the half-mile relay in 1:28.6.

Army's 1926 track team, pictured here, opened the season with a loss to Columbia, but then bounced back to win their final three meets, including a 69⅖-65⅗ victory over Navy. Leo Novak served as head coach.

Army's outdoor track team completed the spring season in 1928 with an unblemished 5-0 record. Coach Leo Novak's squad also took the measure of Navy by a score of 84½-41½. The five victories pushed a consecutive meet winning streak to fifteen. The Cadets also defeated Columbia, Marquette, Virginia, and Springfield. The team captain was Ray H. Guertler.

THE SQUAD

Army's undefeated 1927 track team won six meets during the season under Coach Leo Novak. The team captain was Joseph H. Gilbreth. The Cadets claimed victories over Columbia, Virginia, Colgate, Georgetown, Springfield, and Navy by a 103½-31½ score.

The Army track program began competing on an intercollegiate level in 1921, defeating Tufts 93 to 33. Lt. Elmer Q. Oliphant, an All-America in football at West Point, was the first coach. Oliphant was also at the helm in 1922. This is a photograph of the 1922 squad which won all three of its meets, defeating Columbia, Pittsburgh, and Springfield. Oliphant is in the third row center in uniform. The team captain was David J. Crawford, the sixth from the left at the top row.

Army cross country runner Dennis Trujillo (158) is in good position during the early stages of a cross country meet against St. John's and Fairleigh Dickinson University at West Point in 1974. For Trujillo, the 1974 cross country season proved highly successful as he captured both the Heptagonal and IC4A championships. He was the first Army cross country runner to capture both the Heptagonal championship and the ICAA championship since Richard Shea accomplished the same feat three straight years from 1949-1951.

The sport of cross country began at the United States Military Academy in 1922 when Army defeated New Hampshire State College and Hamilton College. There was little fanfare and no team championship competition as there is today.

Robert Heber Van Volkenburgh, a class of 1913 graduate, served as the first coach, while John R. Noyes was the team captain. Army defeated New Hampshire State by a 21-33 margin, and then trimmed Hamilton 29-31.

Van Volkenburgh coached just one season. Born in Michigan in February of 1890, he served with the Coast Artillery Corps, earned a master of science degree at Massachusetts Institute of Technology and served on the War Department General Staff during World War II, attaining the rank of brigadier general. Brig. Gen. Van Volkenburgh was commanding general of the 40th Cavalry Brigade in the Southwest Pacific and Philippines theatres during World War II.

Following the initial season in 1922, six years passed before Army resumed competition in cross country. Leo Novak took over the coaching chores in 1928 and immediately put the program on sound footing. He compiled a record of ninety-three victories and just twenty-eight defeats during twenty-two years of coaching at the Academy.

Four of Novak's cross country squads went undefeated and two won team championships. The Army coach registered unblemished records in 1928, 1935, 1945, and 1948. Additionally, his 1944 squad won the Heptagonal Cross Country championship.

The 1945 Army cross country team won the IC4A Cross Country championship, along with a second Heptagonal title.

One of the top Army performers developed by Novak was Arthur H. Truxes who won the individual title at the Heptagonals in 1943 and 1944, the first Army competitor to register that type of success in intercollegiate competition. Others would follow.

Army has had thirteen individual champions in Hepta-gonal competition. In addition to Truxes' back-to-back triumphs in 1943 and 1944, Heptagonal champions included Frederick J. Knauss (1946), Richard Shea three times (1949-1951), Lewis C. Olive (1952), Richard McDonald Greene (1959), William J. Straub (1963), Paul A. DeCoursey (1965), Dennis R. Trujillo (1974), and Curtis J. Alitz (1976, 1977).

Greene and Alitz are the only All-America selections in the history of the sport. Greene was named in 1959 while Alitz, son of former Army wrestling coach LeRoy Alitz, earned All-America honors in both 1975 and 1976. He finished fifteenth in the 1975 NCAA Cross Country championship meet, and came back the following year to finish twenty-seventh among all competitors entered.

There have been just eight cross country coaches in history. When Novak departed in 1949, he was replaced for one season by Jess Mortensen, who compiled a 7-1 record. He left after his first season in 1950. Nathaniel Cartmell took over and posted a 17-4 record in three seasons before Carleton Crowell became coach in 1953.

Crowell became Army's most successful cross country coach by posting a record of 145 victories and just 52 losses during a span of 22 years at West Point. Crowell died unexpectedly in 1975. His coaching responsibilities were handled by Col. Harold Beal.

John Randolph, former track and cross country coach at William & Mary, took over the assignment in 1976 and recorded twenty-one victories, twelve defeats and a tie.

Ron Bazil assumed the coaching duties in 1979 after Randolph accepted a position as head track and field coach at the University of Florida. Randolph is now back at William & Mary in the athletic director position. Bazil has been very successful during his seven years at West Point. He has been particularly effective in developing the women's cross country program at the Academy.

Cross country competed on several courses at West Point. At one time, cross country meets were held near the Howze Field area adjacent to Michie Stadium. They are currently using the West Point Golf Course.

Dennis Trujillo holds the course record with a time of 24 minutes, 14 seconds. This former Heptagonal champion from Pueblo, Colorado, set the record on October 11, 1974.

Army also has competed regularly at Van Cortlandt Park in New York City. Curt Alitz set the most recent Army record at Van Cortlandt Park in 1976. He was timed in 23 minutes, 58.1 seconds.

Curt Alitz, a two-time All-America in cross country while at West Point, is joined by Coach John Randolph prior to a workout in 1976. Alitz finished fifteenth at the NCAA Cross Country championship in 1975 and came back a year later to take the twenty-seventh spot among all competitors. Alitz also won Heptagonal and IC4A championships during 1976.

A LOOK INTO THE PAST

Year	Coach	Captain	Won	Lost	Tied
1922	Robt. H. Van Volkenburgh	John R. Noyes	2	0	0
1928	Leo Novak	Kai E. Rasmussen	4	0	0
1929	Leo Novak	George W. Lermond	3	1	0
1930	Leo Novak	Orrin C. Krueger	4	1	0
1931	Leo Novak	Allen F. Clark, Jr.	3	1	0
1932	Leo Novak	Alfred D. Starbird	3	1	0
1933	Leo Novak	William F. Northam	3	1	0
1934	Leo Novak	Durward E. Breakefield	3	1	0
1935	Leo Novak	Howard M. McManus	4	0	0
1936	Leo Novak	William H. Lewis	3	2	0
1937	Leo Novak	John C.F. Tillson III	3	3	0
1938	Leo Novak	Robert H. Schellman	4	2	0
1939	Leo Novak	Frank A. deLatour	4	2	0
1940	Leo Novak	George B. Moore	5	1	0
1941	Leo Novak	Fred E. Rosell, Jr.	3	1	0
1942	Leo Novak	Frederick M. King	2	2	0
1943	Leo Novak	William E. Hensel Harold J. Saine	4	1	0
1944	Leo Novak	Arthur H. Truxes	4	1	0
1945	Leo Novak	Frank B. Tucker	7	0	0
1946	Leo Novak	Frederick J. Knauss	5	3	0
1947	Leo Novak	William F. Trieschmann, Jr.	5	3	0
1948	Leo Novak	Thomas P. Strider	8	0	0
1949	Leo Novak (93-28-0)	Richard H. Lewandowski	9	1	0
1950	Jess Mortensen (7-1-0)	Harold G. Marsh	7	1	0
1951	Nathaniel Cartmell	Louis M. Davis	6	0	0
1952	Nathaniel Cartmell	Robert G. Day	6	2	0
1953	Nathaniel Cartmell (17-4-0)	Billy J. Cory	5	2	0
1954	Carleton Crowell	Robert O. Wray	3	4	0
1955	Carleton Crowell	Ralph W. Stephenson	3	5	0
1956	Carleton Crowell	Louis S. Quatannens	3	3	0
1957	Carleton Crowell	Jerome C. Lewis	2	5	0
1958	Carleton Crowell	David R. Carroll	10	0	0
1959	Carleton Crowell	Richard W. Healy, Jr.	8	1	0
1960	Carleton Crowell	Lynn A. Bender	8	1	0
1961	Carleton Crowell	John W. Jones, Jr.	8	1	0
1962	Carleton Crowell	Carl E. Chickedantz	8	3	0
1963	Carleton Crowell	William J. Straub	5	4	0
1964	Carleton Crowell	John R. Malpass, Jr.	10	2	0
1965	Carleton Crowell	Fred W. Barnes	12	0	0
1966	Carleton Crowell	James Warner	9	1	0
1967	Carleton Crowell	Paul A. DeCoursey	9	2	0
1968	Carleton Crowell	Jimmy R. Lucas	6	3	0
1969	Carleton Crowell	James A. Kee	5	4	0
1970	Carleton Crowell	Jeffrey A. McNally	7	3	0
1971	Carleton Crowell	Robert J. Curran	6	3	0
1972	Carleton Crowell	Lelie R. Alm	9	1	0
1973	Carleton Crowell	Dale A. Fletcher	7	4	0
1974	Carleton Crowell	Norman F. Reinhardt	6	6	0
1975	Carleton Crowell (145-52-0)	Dennis R. Trujillo	1	1	0
	Harold Beal		4	6	0
1976	John Randolph	Wayne A. Chiusano	7	4	0
1977	John Randolph	Curtis J. Alitz	6	5	0
1978	John Randolph (21-12-0)	John J. Enright	8	3	0
1979	Ron Bazil	Robert A. Thomas	6	6	0
1980	Ron Bazil	Robert A. Payne	8	5	0
1981	Ron Bazil	Robert J. Afridi & Thomas A. Wuchte	7	2	0
1982	Craig Sherman	Cardell Williams & Christopher Mozina	4	4	0
1983	Ron Bazil	Joseph M. Malloy	8	3	0
1984	Ron Bazil	John J. Muller	8	1	0
1985	Ron Bazil	David Fleece	5	3	0
1986	Ron Bazil (46-21)	Mica Comstock	4	1	0

Army distance specialist Curt Alitz, son of former wrestling coach LeRoy Alitz, crosses the finish line ahead of the pack during a 1975 cross country meet at West Point. Alitz finished fifteenth during the NCAA Cross Country championship that year to earn All-America recognition for the first time. A year later, Alitz won the Heptagonal and IC4A cross country championships and finished twenty-seventh in the NCAA meet to regain his All-America recognition. He is the only Cadet cross country competitor to gain All-America recognition twice. Alitz also set the Cadet record at the Van Cortlandt Park cross country park with a time of 23:58.1 on November 15, 1976.

Curt Alitz (131) and Dennis Trujillo (158) cross the finish line together during a 1974 cross country meet at West Point. Alitz and Trujillo are considered two of the finest distance runners in Academy history.

The scenic West Point Golf Course serves as the home for Army's cross country team. An Army runner takes the lead after circling a portion of the fairway on the seventh hole.

Bob Sears, a 1939 graduate, performs on the parallel bars. Sears is considered one of the finest gymnasts to attend West Point. He won Eastern championships on the parallel bars in 1938 and 1939, captured the horizontal bar and the all-around title in 1939. Additionally, he won National Intercollegiate Championships in the rope climb (1938), the horizontal bar (1938) and the parallel bars (1939). He also won National AAU championships in the long horse (1947) and the parallel bars (1947). Sears was a member of the Army Air Corps during World War II, earning the Distinguished Flying Cross and two Air Medals. He was a prisoner of war during World War II, but escaped from his German captors. He later served in Korea, 1953-1954, and eventually retired from active duty at the rank of colonel in 1962.

CHAPTER 19

The Army gymnastics program has had a long and successful intercollegiate history, beginning in 1926. The first West Point coach was Francis Dohs, who got off to a rather inauspicious start when his 1928 West Point squad won just one of five meets.

The Cadets opened the season with a 37-17 loss to Dartmouth, but then edged the Massachusetts Institute of Technology, 29-25, for its only victory. Army then dropped decisions to Princeton, Temple, and Pennsylvania to finish with a 1-4 record.

Coach Dohs saw his team rebound during its second season of intercollegiate competition, winning four of six meets. Dohs coached the gymnastics squad for nearly six years, resigning after six meets in 1931 with an overall record of 19-18.

Thomas E. Maloney took over the coaching duties from Dohs and quickly turned the West Point gymnastics program into one of the most successful in the East. During thirty-six years of coaching at the Academy from 1931 until the opening of the 1965-1966 season, Maloney's teams won 210 intercollegiate meets, lost just thirty-three and tied in six others. Nine of his teams won Eastern championships outright and two others shared Eastern titles.

Maloney, the winningest gymnastics coach in Army history, guided his teams to twenty-eight straight triumphs after assuming the coaching duties before Temple ended the streak with a 35-19 win over the Cadets in 1936.

A total of eleven of Maloney's Army teams completed unbeaten seasons, and two others were unbeaten with one tie. His 1934 Army team was the first to win an Eastern championship, and duplicated that effort a year later. Army also won a share of the Eastern title in 1937 and another outright championship in 1938.

One of the most successful gymnasts developed by Maloney was Robert C. Sears, captain of the 1939 Army team. He was the first Army gymnast to win a national championship, accomplishing that achievement in 1938-1939 when he won the horizontal bar event and the rope climb event both years. The only other Army gymnast to win a national title is John H. Claybrook, who won the rope climb event

in 1952.

All of Army's Eastern championships came when Maloney was head coach, the last in 1962 when the Cadets finished the regular season with a 7-0-1 record.

Army has had numerous individual Eastern champions beginning in 1928 when Francis H. Falkner won the parallel bars event. Falkner was captain of the 1928 Army team.

Sears was the most successful Army competitor during Eastern competition, winning five titles. He finished first in the parallel bar and the horizontal bar events in 1938, and then came back a year later to claim titles as the top all-around gymnast, as well as firsts on the parallel bars and the horizontal bar.

There has been one Army gymnast who qualified for Olympic competition. Garland D. O'Quinn, Jr., a 1958 West Point graduate, competed in the 1960 Olympics held in Rome.

Following Maloney's successful tenure as gymnastics coach at West Point, he was succeeded by Frank Wells. Wells guided the gymnastics program for seven years, compiling a 35-28 record.

In 1972-1973 Ned Crossley, a Springfield College graduate, succeeded Wells and authored a highly successful ten-year tour. Crossley's Army teams won eighty-nine meets and lost just thirty-five. Additionally, the Cadets garnered runner-up honors in the Eastern Intercollegiate Gymnastics League championships three times. Army finished second in 1977-1978, and accomplished the same achievement during the next two years.

Crossley's finest team was the 1978-1979 squad which won fourteen of fifteen meets, while his 1975-1976 and 1979-1980 squads posted 13-1 records. The Army coach also developed three Eastern champions, Scott Shorr in vaulting in 1978, George Rhynedance a share of the floor exercise title in 1980, and Chris J. Adams in vaulting in 1982.

Crossley stepped down as Army coach following the 1981-1982 season, but remains in the Department of Physical Education at the Academy. Larry Butler, a Penn State graduate, succeeded Crossley.

A LOOK INTO THE PAST

Year	Coach	Captain	Won	Lost	Tied
1926	Francis Dohs	Malcolm D. Jones, Jr.	1	4	0
1927	Francis Dohs	Harold S. Wood	4	2	0
1928	Francis Dohs	Francis H. Falkner	4	2	0
1929	Francis Dohs	John K. Poole	4	3	0
1930	Francis Dohs	Anthony E. Curcio	5	2	0
1931	Francis Dohs	Donald N. Yates	3	5	0
	(19-18-0)				
	Thomas E. Maloney				
1932	Thomas E. Maloney	John C. Steele	7	0	0
1933	Thomas E. Maloney	Alden K. Sibley	5	0	0
1934	Thomas E. Maloney	Austin W. Betts	5	0	0
1935	Thomas E. Maloney	Frederick B. Hall	5	0	0
		Herbert C. Gee			
1936	Thomas E. Maloney	Beverley E. Powell	4	1	1
1937	Thomas E. Maloney	Don R. Ostrander	5	1	0
1938	Thomas E. Maloney	Allen D. Hulse	6	0	0
1939	Thomas E. Maloney	Robert C. Sears	5	1	0
1940	Thomas E. Maloney	Paul H. Krauss	5	1	0
1941	Thomas E. Maloney	Wadsworth P. Clapp	4	1	0
1942	Thomas E. Maloney	Wallace B. Frank	2	1	1
1943	Thomas E. Maloney	George M. Eberle	2	3	0
		Edward M.			
		Watkins, Jr.			
1944	Thomas E. Maloney	Wallace D. Moore	4	1	0
1945	Thomas E. Maloney	Donald E. Gross	6	0	0
1946	Thomas E. Maloney	Paul J. Quinn	7	2	0
1947	Thomas E. Maloney	William B. Cronin	4	4	0
1948	Thomas E. Maloney	Lewis M. Jamison	6	3	0
1949	Thomas E. Maloney	Thomas R. Mackenzie	7	1	0
1950	Thomas E. Maloney	Carl L. Brunson	7	0	1
1951	Thomas E. Maloney	Thomas B. Horgan	7	0	0
1952	Thomas E. Maloney	Jack C. Kleberg	8	0	0
1953	Thomas E. Maloney	George A. Haas	6	2	0
1954	Thomas E. Maloney	William M. Charles	5	1	2
1955	Thomas E. Maloney	Robert D. Carpenter	7	1	0
1956	Thomas E. Maloney	William C. Haponski	8	0	0
1957	Thomas E. Maloney	Willis Thomson	7	1	0
1958	Thomas E. Maloney	Garland D. O'Quinn	11	0	0
1959	Thomas E. Maloney	Jimmy C. Hill	8	1	0
1960	Thomas E. Maloney	Richard Seaward	10	0	0
1961	Thomas E. Maloney	Jonathan Aaronsohn	5	2	0
1962	Thomas E.. Maloney	Philip A. Costain	7	0	1
1962-63	Thomas E. Maloney	Stephen J. Best	8	2	0
1963-64	Thomas E. Maloney	Michael J. Gray	6	2	0
1964-65	Thomas E. Maloney	Tadahiko Ono	7	2	0
1965-66	Thomas E. Maloney	Howard S. Pontuck	6	3	0
	(210-33-6)				
	Frank Wells				
1966-67	Frank Wells	John R. Ouellette	7	3	0
1967-68	Frank Wells	Charles Beckwith	4	5	0
1968-69	Frank Wells	Donald E. Warner	6	3	0
1969-70	Frank Wells	John Senor	4	5	0
1970-71	Frank Wells	Robert C. Harvey	6	3	0
1971-72	Frank Wells (35-28-0)	Theodore F. Leger	4	6	0
1972-73	Ned Crossley	John W. Rutherford	4	8	0
1973-74	Ned Crossley	William Pierce	2	7	0
1974-75	Ned Crossley	James C. Johns	7	4	0
1975-76	Ned Crossley	Richard L. Bogusky	13	1	0
1976-77	Ned Crossley	Matthew M. Holm	12	2	0
1977-78	Ned Crossley	Scott H. Shorr	10	2	0
1978-79	Ned Crossley	Robert M. Caliva	14	1	0
1979-80	Ned Crossley	George H.	13	1	0
		Rhynedance			
1980-81	Ned Crossley	Christopher T. Fulton	6	5	0
1981-82	Ned Crossley	Scott A. Francis	8	4	0
1982-83	Ned Crossley	Richard G. Gesing	7	6	0
1983-84	Larry Butler	Douglas A. Garmer	12	4	0
1984-85	Larry Butler	Daniel Kelly	6	6	0
1985-86	Larry Butler	Jeffrey Baum	9	3	0
1986-87	Larry Butler	Anthony Cariello	4	7	0

Army's 1934-1935 gymnastics team won the Eastern Intercollegiate Gymnastics League championship under the direction of Coach Thomas J. Maloney. Maloney took over the coaching responsibilities at West Point late in the 1931 season and led Army teams to twenty-eight consecutive victories before being beaten by Temple in 1936 to end the streak. The 1935 team won all five of its meets, defeating Penn State, Massachusetts Institute of Technology, Dartmouth, Princeton, and Temple before winning the Eastern championship. Pictured are, first row, left to right, Milton C. Taylor, Lt. Raymond E. Bell, Officer-in-Charge, co-captain Frederick B. Hall, Jr., co-captain Herbert C. Gee, Coach Tom Maloney, and Beverley E. Powell; second row, team manager Daniel J. Murphy, Clifford F. Cordes, Jr., William S. Steele, Robert Van Roo, Seward W. Hulse, Monte J. Hickok, Jr., Turner C. Rogers, and assistant manager William G. Lee, Jr.; third row, James T. Willis, Eldred G. Robbins, Jr., Howard P. Persons, Carroll D. Wood, Horace Greeley, William C. Haneke, and Lamar F. Woodward; top row, Leroy H. Rook, Oliver G. Haywood, Jr., William B. Travis, and Don R. Ostrander. Hall won an Eastern championship in the side horse event in 1933 and 1934.

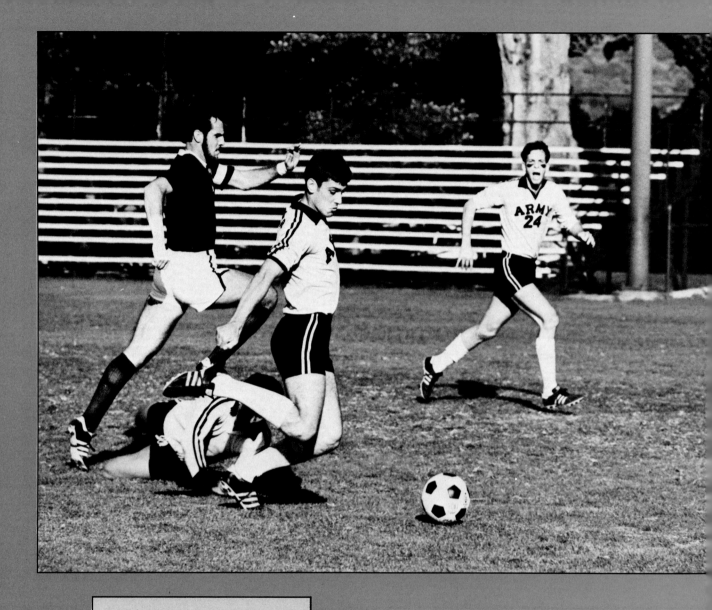

Army forward Rick Rodemers chases down the ball during a match at West Point's Clinton Field.

Intercollegiate competition in soccer began in 1921 at West Point when the Cadets trimmed Dartmouth by a 4-3 margin. Army also met Princeton, Colgate, Springfield, Syracuse, and Amherst during that first season, finishing with a 3-2-1 record.

This marked the beginning of the sixty-six-year history of the sport heading into the 1987 fall season. During that span, Army soccer teams have only recorded eight losing seasons.

S. C. MacDonald coached the first Army team in 1921, while Oscar L. Beal was the team captain.

MacDonald is the first of nine coaches who have guided the fortunes of the West Point soccer program. The most successful mentor was Joe Palone, a native of Belmont, New York who joined the Military Academy staff in 1943 and became head soccer coach in 1947.

With the exception of a three-year break from 1955-1957 when he served as head baseball coach, Palone led the program for twenty-nine years and compiled a record unmatched in the history of the sport at West Point. His soccer teams won 227 games, lost just 80, and played 35 ties.

Only two of Palone's teams had losing records, the last coming in 1949 when the Cadets were 2-5-1 during his third season at the Academy. From that point the worst Army ever did was 5-5 in 1961. Two of his teams were undefeated. The 1950 Army squad compiled an 8-0-1 record, while the Cadets were 9-0-1 the following year. Additionally, his soccer teams won Eastern Intercollegiate championships from 1950-1952.

The veteran coach was at the helm when soccer was elevated to major sport status in 1954. In 1965, Palone won his 100th game at West Point when the Cadets trounced the U.S. Merchant Marine Academy by a 10-0 margin in the season opener.

Eleven years later, in 1976, the Army coach won his 200th game when the Cadets edged Rutgers, 4-1. Two years later Palone retired to devote more time to improving his golf game year round. He split his time between Myrtle Beach, South Carolina, and his home in New Windsor, New York, just a short fifteen-minute ride from the Academy.

Palone's responsibility at West Point was not simply coaching the soccer team. He was a member of the Department of Physical Education and taught thousands of cadets over the years. Additionally, he was well known throughout the Hudson Valley region as a basketball official and baseball umpire.

When he closed out his career in 1978, Army provided him with a proper sendoff with a 1-0 victory over rival Navy on a blustery November day at Clinton Field. If there was ever a frustration in Palone's career, it might be the lack of luck he had during games against Navy.

One example of that frustration occurred in 1963 when Palone fielded one of his finest Army teams. The Cadets reeled off ten consecutive victories during the regular season, including overtime victories over Yale and Maryland, and received a berth in the National Collegiate Athletic Association tournament.

The Cadets opened tourney play with a 4-2 win over Adelphi and a 3-1 decision over Brown. But Navy jolted Palone's squad with a 4-0 win to knock Army out of the tournament.

Palone's teams qualified for the NCAA tournament in 1964-1966, 1968, 1970-1973, and 1975. In 1964 and 1965, the Cadets won their first two games in the tournament, only to be eliminated by Michigan State on both occasions. The Spartans trimmed Army 3-2 in overtime in 1964 and 3-1 the following year. In 1966, Army again won its first two tourney contests, only to be eliminated by the University of San Francisco, 2-0. In 1968, Army defeated Harvard and Brockport State during the NCAA playoffs, but then bowed to Brown by a 3-1 margin.

When Palone ended his career at the conclusion of the 1978 season, there was no better way to complete the final chapter of his success story with a victory over the U.S. Naval Academy. A penalty kick provided the margin of difference in that encounter, a kick that Palone will never forget.

Ray Marchand, the third soccer coach at West Point,

enjoyed a similar period of longevity at West Point. He guided the Army soccer program for nineteen years, taking over in 1924. He remained at that position until 1942, compiling a record of ninety-four victories, thirty-four defeats, and twenty ties. Marchand also coached Army's hockey team from 1924 until 1943. His overall record was 78-101-8.

When Palone stepped down in 1978, Dick Edell took over the coaching chores while also guiding the Army lacrosse team back to prominence. Edell served as head soccer coach for just three seasons, compiling a 20-14-8 record. He turned over the coaching responsibilities to Army's current coach Joe Chiavaro, a former Army assistant soccer coach, under both Palone and Edell.

Chiavaro, a Cortland State graduate, has led Army during the past five years. His Cadet teams have won forty-six games, lost thirty-five, and tied eight. Chiavaro has upgraded the schedule during the past five years, providing the Cadets an opportunity to meet nationally ranked teams two or three times during the season.

There have been many outstanding players at West Point throughout the years. Some of those have been outstanding performers in other sports at the Academy. One such example is John Roosma, who starred on Army's basketball teams, and was later inducted into the Helms Foundation Hall of Fame. A graduate of the class of 1926, Roosma also lettered in soccer.

Thomas Truxton, one of the finest lacrosse players in Army history, also lettered in soccer. He is a graduate of the class of 1937. Astronaut Edward White, the first man to walk in space in June, 1965, lettered in soccer while at the Academy. He was a 1952 graduate who served with the National Aeronautics and Space Administration from 1962-1967. Lt. Col. White was tragically killed with two other astronauts when fire erupted in the Apollo spacecraft at Cape Kennedy (Canaveral), Florida, on January 27, 1967.

West Point's former athletic director, Col. William J. Schuder, a 1947 graduate, also lettered in soccer as a member of Palone's first team.

A LOOK INTO THE PAST

Year	Coach	Captain	Won	Lost	Tied
1921	S.C. MacDonald	Oscar L. Beal	3	2	1
1922	H.J. Ratican	John G. Wilson	6	2	0
1923	H.J. Ratican (10-5-1)	Leonard G. Bingham	4	3	1
1924	Ray Marchand	Raymond B. Oxrieder	5	1	1
1925	Ray Marchand	Malcolm R. Kammerer	6	1	1
1926	Ray Marchand	William J. Glasgow	3	2	1
1927	Ray Marchand	James E.. Briggs	6	1	1
1928	Ray Marchand	Fred W. Sladen	4	2	2
1929	Ray Marchand	Harry B. Packard	2	3	3
1930	Ray Marchand	Edward K. Purnell	6	2	0
1931	Ray Marchand	George D. Campbell	6	1	0
1932	Ray Marchand	Gerald L. Roberson	6	2	0
1933	Ray Marchand	Jack L. Neely	5	2	1
1934	Ray Marchand	Julius D. Stanton	6	2	0
1935	Ray Marchand	Charles B. Tyler	5	1	2
1936	Ray Marchand	Robert M. Stegmaier	6	0	2
1937	Ray Marchand	Frederick C. Lough	5	1	2
1938	Ray Marchand	John G. Pickard	7	2	0
1939	Ray Marchand	Charles B. Hazeltine	1	5	1
1940	Ray Marchand	Ken O. Dessert	6	2	0
1941	Ray Marchand	John W. Guckeyson	6	1	1
1942	Ray Marchand (94-34-20)	Henry J. Ebrey	3	3	2
1943	Col. G.L. Roberson	Ralph J. Sciolla	5	2	0
1944	Col. G.F. McAneny	Stanley G. Calder	6	2	0
1945	Col. G.F. McAneny	Calvert R. Benedict	7	1	1
1946	Col. G.F. McAneny (20-5-5)	Frederick G. Hudson	7	2	4
1947	Joseph Palone	John W. Brennan	6	5	3
1948	Joseph Palone	John T. Marley	8	8	2
1949	Joseph Palone	Don G. Novak	2	5	1
1950	Joseph Palone	Daniel H. Wardrop	8	0	1
1951	Joseph Palone	Douglas A. Slingerland	9	0	1
1952	Joseph Palone	Fred L. Smith	8	1	1
1953	Joseph Palone	James J. Fraher	8	1	1
1954	Joseph Palone	Francis J. Adams	6	2	2
1955	John B. Kress	John H. Oakes	2	8	0
1956	John B. Kress	Albert H. Krapf	3	5	2
1957	John B. Kress (9-19-2)	Robert W. Puff	4	6	0
1958	Joseph Palone	Fred Manzo	4	1	4
1959	Joseph Palone	Phillip E. Chappell	7	1	2
1960	Joseph Palone	Dominador B. Bazan	8	2	0
1961	Joseph Palone	Arthur S. Brown	5	5	0
1962	Joseph Palone	Gerald F. Stonehouse & Frank J. Kelly	7	3	1
1963	Joseph Palone	Wayne R. Wheeler	12	1	0
1964	Joseph Palone	John M. Deems	10	3	0
1965	Joseph Palone	James Kriebel	12	1	1
1966	Joseph Palone	Joseph C. Casey	10	3	2
1967	Joseph Palone	Edward Milinski	9	4	0
1968	Joseph Palone	Robert Behncke	10	3	1
1969	Joseph Palone	John A. Veenstra	7	3	2
1970	Joseph Palone	Daniel Scioletti	9	3	0
1971	Joseph Palone	James Moran	9	4	0
1972	Joseph Palone	Lawrence A. Saksa	8	3	1
1973	Joseph Palone	Roman Ciupak	9	2	3
1974	Joseph Palone	P. Randolph Nelson	7	3	2
1975	Joseph Palone	Richard Morales	10	3	1
1976	Joseph Palone	James S. Johnson	8	4	1
1977	Joseph Palone	Jose R. Olivero	9	2	2
1978	Joseph Palone (228-80-35)	Deryl P. Smoak	11	4	0
1979	Dick Edell	John K. Stoner	5	5	3
1980	Dick Edell	Edward J. Apgar	6	6	1
1981	Dick Edell (20-14-8)	Alex G. Sung	9	3	4
1982	Joe Chiavaro	Timothy Miller & Timothy McDonald	11	4	2
1983	Joe Chiavaro	David Shimkus & Harold Prantl	9	7	3
1984	Joe Chiavaro	Richard Machovina	8	8	1
1985	Joe Chiavaro	John McHugh	8	9	1
1986	Joe Chiavaro (46-35-7)	James Lowery	10	7	0

Army's venerable soccer coach, Joe Palone, watches his squad play during a 1978 Army-Navy match. The Cadets tripped the Middies 1-0 on a penalty kick to give Palone a proper sendoff in his final game as a head coach. Palone's Army teams won 227 games in 29 years at West Point.

Army halfback Jose Olivero leaps to head the ball away from a Yale opponent during the 1975 game at West Point's Clinton Field. The Cadets blanked Yale 4-0 in this game en route to a 10-3-1 season. Coach Joe Palone's booters also gained a berth in the National Collegiate Athletic Association championships, bowing to perennial power Hartwick by a 2-1 margin in overtime.

Army soccer coach Joe Palone

Coach Joe Palone is surrounded by members of his 1978 team following a 1-0 victory over rival Navy. The victory was number 227 and his last as head soccer coach at West Point, an emotional ending to one of the most outstanding coaching records in Army history.

Coach Joe Palone, right, observes his Cadet squad during his final game as head coach in 1978. The Army squad provided a good sendoff, whipping rival Navy, 1-0. Palone became head soccer coach at West Point in 1947, and with the exception of three years, 1955-1957, held those coaching responsibilities until his retirement. During his twenty-nine-year tenure as head coach, Army soccer teams compiled a record of 227 victories, just 80 losses, and 35 ties. Palone also was an instructor in the Department of Physical Education at West Point, an avid golfer, and a high school and college basketball official. Joining Palone on the sidelines is assistant coach Col. Corky Henninger.

The Army soccer team won six games and lost just two in 1940 under the guidance of Coach Ray Marchand, who also doubled as the Cadet hockey coach. The winning record was quite an achievement for Army after finishing at 1-5-1 a year earlier. Kenneth Dessert served as team captain. Army claimed victories over Syracuse, Brown, Bucknell, Lehigh, M.I.T., and Navy by a 2-0 count. Team members included, front row, left to right, assistant manager, Richard House, Edward Foote, John Mattina, George Hesselbacher, Rexford Dettre, Allen Frawley, Edwin Marks, Howard Clark, Norman Cota, Theodore White, Benjamin Spiller, and Timothy Pedley; second row, Lawrence Lahm, Matthew Redlinger, Ellwood Claggett, Henry Kozlowski, Francis Myers, Herbert Stern, team captain Kenneth Dessert, George Stillson, Joseph Knowlton, John Guckeyson, Roy Bowling, Edison Walters, and trainer Andrew Pollock; third row, Maurice Miller, Captain T. J. Conway, Clifford Cole, Eugene Weeks, Francis Voegeli, James Frankosky, Hal Crain, Charles Garvin, Alfred Hayduk, Alvin Wilder, Vincent Coates, Henry Ebrey, William Warren, Coach Ray Marchand, and manager John Christensen; top row, Mitchel Goldenthatl, Robert Terry, James Freeman, Miles Gayle, and James Bush.

Rhonda Barush, an All-America second team selection in rifle, is the only woman ever selected as team captain of the rifle team. Barush served in that capacity during the 1985-1986 season.

In 1979, Army set an Academy record for a five-man team in rifle. That record-setting team included, left to right, Dave Moeller, Sam Hutchins, Dan Szarenski, Bob Jacobs, and Bill Schneider. Szarenski was a two-time second team All-America, while Jacobs notched second team All-America honors in 1978.

The 1964-1965 Army rifle team compiled an 8-1 record under the guidance of Sgt. Maj. Al O'Neill. Members of that team included, kneeling left to right, Mike Fuller, a first team All-America in 1966, and Ladd Metzner, a second team All-America in 1964; standing, Capt. Richard Hargrove, officer representative, team captain Bill Bradburn, a three-time first team All-America, Gary Chambers, a 1965 second team All-America, and Coach O'Neill.

Rifle has been a competitive sport at the Military Academy since 1919 and during the past sixty-five seasons Army has never had a losing record. Additionally, eighteen rifle teams have compiled unbeaten records.

One of the finest teams was the 1977-1978 team, coached by Master Sergeant Ken Hamill. That squad compiled a perfect 18-0 record, the most victories ever recorded in a single season. Dan Szarenski and Robert Jacobs set the pace for the Cadets that season, earning second team All-America honors.

Coach Hamill is the most successful coach in the history of the sport at West Point. He has guided Army teams to 165 victories over the past fourteen years. In addition to the one undefeated team, five other teams have lost just a single match during the regular season.

The first Army shooter to gain first team All-America honors was Richard A. Wise in 1942. There has been one three-time All-America at West Point; William J. Bradburn accomplished that achievement from 1963-1965. Four others have been selected for first team All-America honors twice during their West Point careers. They are Amos C. Mathews, 1947-1948, Lucien D. Bolduc, 1948-1949, Gordon P. Rogers, 1956-1957, and David Cannella, 1982-1983.

The list is even longer for Army shooters who have received second team All-America recognition. One of the most notable is Rhonda Barush, who gained second team All-America honors during the 1983 season. She is also the first woman to serve as captain of the rifle team, serving in that capacity during the 1985-1986 season.

David Cannella gained first team All-America honors in 1983 in both smallbore and air rifle. He was also team captain of the 1983-1984 squad that compiled a 16-1 record. The sixteen victories represented the second highest total in history.

The 1975-1976 Army rifle team is pictured here after compiling a 9-3 record during the season and finishing first in the National Rifle Association Sectional championships. Master Sergeant Ken Hamill, far right, coached that Army squad, completing his first year at the Academy.

A LOOK INTO THE PAST

Year	Coach	Captain	Won	Lost	Tied
1919	Capt. P.W. Newgarden	None Listed	2	1	0
1923	None Listed	All 1st Classmen	2	1	0
1924	Maj. C.A. Bagby	Robert V. Lee	7	0	0
1925	Maj. C.A. Bagby	John W. Black	12	0	0
1926	Maj. C.A. Bagby (22-0)	Robert K. McDonough	3	0	0
1927	Lt. R.A. Schow	Barney A. Daughtry	7	1	0
1928	Capt. F.A. Macon	Nathan B. Forrest	4	1	0
1929	Capt. F.A. Macon (10-1)	Herbert Milwit	6	0	0
1930	Capt. H.C. Barnes	Keith H. Ewbank	6	0	0
1931	Capt. H.C. Barnes (8-1)	John W. Hansborough	2	1	0
1932	Lt. F.X. Mulvihill	William R. Huber	5	1	0
1933	Lt. F.X. Mulvihill	Robert W. Hain	5	2	0
1933	Lt. F.X. Mulvihill	John M. Breit	5	0	0*
1934	Lt. F.X. Mulvihill	George B. Dany, III	5	1	0
1935	Lt. F.X. Mulvihill (25-4)	John Williamson	5	0	0
1936	Lt. T.S. Riggs	Charles M. McCorkle	8	1	0
1937-38	Rifle Discontinued				
1939	Lt. O.C. Kromer	John K. Boles	6	2	0
1940	Lt. O.C. Kromer (11-3)	Walter E. Gunster	5	1	0
1941	Capt. R.L. Jewett	Jack C. McClure	9	0	0
1942	Maj. J.L. Throckmorton	Richard A. Wise	8	0	0
1943	Maj. C.F. Leonard	Howard F. Wehrle / Albert R. Shiely	9	1	0
1944	Maj. H.N. Moorman	Joseph R. Waterman	10	0	0
1945	Lt. R.A. Wise	John B. Bennet	4	2	0
1946	Maj. C.E. Mowry	Robert F. Dickson	13	1	0
1947	Col. J.L. Throckmorton	William D. Brown	8	1	0
1948	Col. J.L. Throckmorton (22-4)	Walter W. Plummer	6	3	0
1949	Lt. Col. George J. Murray	Amos C. Mathews	8	1	0
1950	Lt. Col. George J. Murray	Lucien E. Bolduc	7	2	0
1951	Lt. Col. George J. Murray (24-5)	Stewart Paterson	9	2	0
1952	Col. E.T. Miller	Stewart Paterson	8	1	0
1953	Col. E.T. Miller (15-3)	Gilbert A. Volker	7	2	0
1954	J.R. Waterman	John R. Shelter	9	1	0
1955	MSgt. O.L. Gallman	Robert C. Werner	9	1	0
1956	MSgt. O.L. Gallman	Conrad C. Ege	8	1	0
1956-57	MSgt. O.L. Gallman	Gordon B. Rogers	8	1	0
1957-58	MSgt. O.L. Gallman	James H. Jones	12	0	0
1958-59	MSgt. O.L. Gallman	Warren S. Smith	10	0	0
1959-60	MSgt. O.L. Gallman	George R. Stanley	8	0	0
1960-61	MSgt. O.L. Gallman	Louis C. Berra	5	3	0
1961-62	MSgt. O.L. Gallman	Morris E. Brown	5	3	0

Army's 1931 rifle team won four matches and lost two under the direction of Capt. H. C. Barnes. The Cadets defeated George Washington University and Columbia University in a five-team match. They bowed to the U.S. Marines from Quantico, Virginia, and the District National Guard. Army then trimmed the New York Stock Exchange and the Essex Troop of New Jersey in their final two matches. The team captain was John W. Hansborough.

1962-63	SMaj. O.L. Gallman (72-12)	Louis J. Sturbois	7	3	0
1963-64	MSgt. Al J. O'Neill	Michael E. Wikan	7	1	0
1964-65	MSgt. Al J. O'Neill	William J. Bradburn	8	1	0
1965-66	MSgt. Al J. O'Neill	Michael B. Fuller	8	1	0
1966-67	MSgt. Al J. O'Neill	Charles Swanson	10	0	0
1967-68	SFC Kenneth Hamill	John R. Williams	6	3	0
1968-69	SMaj. Al J. O'Neill	James G. Cox	6	3	0
1969-70	SMaj. Al J. O'Neill	Henry Leonard	9	2	0
1970-71	SMaj. Al J. O'Neill	Charles D. Moore	10	2	0
1971-72	SMaj. Al J. O'Neill	Robert A. Strong	10	0	0
1972-73	SMaj. Al J. O'Neill	Dennis Morgenstern	10	2	0
1973-74	SMaj. Al J. O'Neill	Gary Stinnett	8	1	0
1974-75	MSgt. Ken Hamill	Ralph D. Ghent	9	3	0
1975-76	MSgt. Ken Hamill	Jose D. Riojas	6	5	0
1976-77	MSgt. Ken Hamill	John J. Luther	9	1	0
1977-78	MSgt. Ken Hamill	William J. McArdle	18	0	0
1978-79	MSgt. Ken Hamill	Daniel Szarenski	13	1	0
1979-80	MSgt. Ken Hamill	Samuel R. Garza	10	2	0
1980-81	MSgt. Ken Hamill	William Schneider	12	2	0
1981-82	MSgt. Ken Hamill	Brian F. Malloy	15	3	0
1982-83	MSgt. Ken Hamill	James Timmer	11	1	0
1983-84	Ken Hamill	David Cannella	16	1	0
1984-85	Ken Hamill	Al Scott	11	2	0
1985-86	Ken Hamill	Rhonda Barush	15	1	0
1986-87	Ken Hamill (165-29-0)	Paul Arthur	14	4	0

* outdoor

Army's rifle team turned in an exceptional effort during the 1933 season, posting a 6-1 record during the indoor season and an unblemished 5-0 record during the spring outdoor campaign. Lt. F. X. Mulvihill, beginning his second season as head coach, watched his squad open the indoor season by defeating New York University, Brooklyn Polytechnic Institute, Fordham, and Syracuse in dual matches. Army defeated M.I.T. and Columbia in a three-team match, dropped a close decision to the New York Stock Exchange team, and then rebounded to defeat Cornell University and R.P.I. in a three-team match. Robert W. Hain served as captain of the indoor team. During the outdoor season the Cadets defeated the Jersey Rifle Association, the Old Guard of New York, Essex Troop of New Jersey, and the New York Stock Exchange team twice to go undefeated. The captain of the outdoor squad was John M. Breit. Among the lettermen in rifle from the class of 1933 were Breit, Hain, Percival Gabel, Norman L. Mini, Richard E. Myers, and John F. Thorlin.

Capt. F. A. Macon, coach of the Army rifle team in 1928, guided his squad to a 4-1 record. The Cadets opened the season with a four-point loss to Essex Troop of New Jersey, and then rebounded to defeat the 71st Regiment of the New York National Guard, George Washington University, Fort Orange Post, American Legion, and the 102nd Engineers of the New York National Guard. Nathan B. Forrest was Army's team captain that season, while members of the class of 1928 to earn letters in rifle included James E. Briggs, Frederick J. Dau, Forrest, Harry C. Kirby, Benjamin S. Shute, and Emmett F. Yost.

Lacrosse has been one of the most successful varsity sports at the Military Academy since its inception in 1907. This popular Eastern spring sport, developed by the American Indian, is gaining popularity throughout the country. Maryland, Long Island, and upstate New York in the Syracuse area are the hotbeds of high school lacrosse and provide most of the outstanding players for the traditional college lacrosse powers: Johns Hopkins, Maryland, Virginia, the Naval Academy, Syracuse, and Cornell.

West Point gets its fair share of those outstanding high school players, although the history of this sport documents the success Army coaches have had in developing some of their top lacrosse players from among the best athletes from other varsity sports. Bill Carpenter, the "Lonely End" for Coach Earl Blaik in 1958, also was selected the Outstanding Defensive Player in the nation during his final year at West Point.

Among Army's long list of All-America selections since 1928, many are former football players at the Academy: Chuck Born (1928), Milton Summerfelt (1932), Robert Stillman (1934), Clinton True (1935), Woodrow Wilson (1939), Arthur Frontczak (1940), Donaldson Tillar (1958), Carpenter, and Dick Luecke (1969).

West Point has eight players and coaches who have been selected into the Lacrosse Hall of Fame. One of the most renowned is Coach F. Morris Touchstone, who assumed the head coaching position at West Point in 1929. Touchstone served as head coach for twenty-eight years and compiled an outstanding record of 215 victories, just 84 losses and 6 ties.

A native of Baltimore, Touchstone graduated from Baltimore City College (high school) in 1917. While there he played football, baseball, and basketball.

After graduation, Touchstone attended the Chicago YMCA College, now called George Williams College, and majored in physical education. He wanted to enter the coaching profession. He received a bachelor of science degree from the University of Chicago in 1920, and then was appointed an athletic instructor at the Mount Washington Club.

Touchstone moved on to the Maryland State Normal School and then took over as head coach at Yale University. He spent four years there before taking over the coaching responsibilities at West Point. One of the highlights of Touchstone's career was winning the national championship at West Point in 1944. He repeated that achievement in 1945, sharing the title with the Naval Academy. Army also shared the national championship with Princeton in 1951. He was inducted into the Hall of Fame in 1960, the first from West Point to be so honored.

Among the former Army players inducted into the Hall of Fame are Harry E. Wilson, class of 1928; Thomas Truxton, class of 1937; James Hartinger, class of 1949; A. Norman Webb, class of 1964; Robert Miser, class of 1960, and Peter Cramblet, class of 1970. James F. "Ace" Adams joins Touchstone as the only other West Point coach to be inducted.

Touchstone's success typified the success Army lacrosse teams have had throughout the history of the sport. Only three Army teams have ever suffered through a losing season since its inception in 1907.

When Touchstone, a Lacrosse Hall of Fame selectee, stepped down in 1957, James F. "Ace" Adams took over the coaching chores at the Academy. During his twelve years at West Point, Adams' teams won ninety-two games, lost just twenty-four and tied one. Additionally, four of Adams' teams won or shared the national lacrosse championship.

An All-America midfielder and co-captain while at Johns Hopkins, Adams began his coaching career at St. Paul's High School and compiled a 35-3 record. In 1951 his team won the Maryland state championship.

Adams played for the Mount Washington Lacrosse Club in 1953 and became head coach in 1957. He guided the Wolfpack to a 9-0-1 record and shared the National Open championship with Johns Hopkins. A year later he became Army's sixth lacrosse coach.

When Adams accepted the head coaching position at the University of Pennsylvania, Al Pisano was named as his successor. Pisano, head coach at Cortland State College, coached the Army team for seven years. During that time he compiled a record of forty-six victories and thirty-one defeats.

In 1971, Pisano's Cadet squad set an Academy record with eleven victories and just two defeats. The National Collegiate Athletic Association also established its first tournament to determine a collegiate champion. Army was among the top eight teams selected for the tournament. The Cadets thrashed Hofstra 19-3 in the tournament opener, but then bowed to Cornell, 17-16. The Big Red went on to win the first national championship under the NCAA banner.

Pisano's teams qualified for the NCAA Tournament in 1972 and 1973, but then suffered through a 3-7 season in 1974.

Dick Edell, head soccer and lacrosse coach at the University of Baltimore, was named Army's coach in 1977, and quickly rebuilt the West Point lacrosse program. Edell's teams never won less than eight games during his seven years at the helm. In 1983, his final year at West Point, Army finished with an 11-3 record to equal the season mark for victories.

Under Edell's leadership, Army returned to lacrosse prominence, qualifying for the NCAA playoffs during four of his seven seasons. The Cadets gained the playoffs during the final three years of his coaching tenure.

The Army mentor resigned following the 1983 season to accept the head coaching position at the University of Maryland. Edell has had similar success in College Park, leading the Terps to an undefeated regular season in 1987. Maryland was upset by Johns Hopkins in the semi-finals of the NCAA Tournament.

Jack Emmer, head coach at Washington & Lee University and a former Rutgers lacrosse star, succeeded Edell as Army's head coach. During his four years at West Point, he has compiled a 37-18 record. Additionally, the Cadets have participated in the NCAA playoffs three years.

Emmer's first two Cadet teams compiled 11-3 and 10-4 records, respectively, but his 1986 team slipped to 6-6. In 1987, Army rebounded with a 10-5 record, gaining a berth in the NCAA playoffs again.

To say Army has been successful in lacrosse since its inception is somewhat of an understatement. A total of seventy-six players have gained first team All-America recognition. Among the leaders are three-time All-America picks Thomas Truxton (1935-1937), James Hartinger (1947-1949), and Pete Cramblet (1968-1970). Truxton, Hartinger, and Cramblet were inducted into the Lacrosse Hall of Fame.

Ten Army players gained first team All-America recognition twice during their careers. They are Charles Pottenger (1931-1932), Milton Summerfelt (1932-1933), Gene Tibbets (1933-1934), Clinton True (1935-1936), Richard Groves (1944-1945), William Devens (1945-1946), John McEnery (1947-1948), Donaldson Tillar (1958-1959), Tom Sheckells (1964-1965), and Tom Cafaro (1970-1971).

Among Army's individual records, Scott Finlay, a class of 1979 graduate, is the all-time career scoring leader with 186 points as a crease attackman. The Army attackman from Valley Cottage, New York, scored 140 goals and added 46 assists during his four-year career. His 140 goals is also a career record.

A LOOK INTO THE PAST

Year	Coach	Captain	Won	Lost	Tied
1907	Self-Coached	Everett S. Hughes	1	0	0
1909	Self-Coached	Herman Erlenkotter	4	0	0
1910	Mr. O'Rourke	Ivens Jones	5	0	0
1921	Talbot Hunter	Alfred A. Kessler	2	3	0
1922	Talbot Hunter	Alfred A. Kessler	5	2	0
1923	Talbot Hunter (15-6-1)	Lawrence S. Barroll	8	1	1
1924	M. J. Collins	Armand J. Salmon	6	1	0
1925	Frank J. Grace	Frank G. Fraser	6	1	0
1926	Frank J. Grace	Prentice E. Yeomans	9	2	0
1927	Frank J. Grace	Thomas H. Trapnell	8	2	0
1928	Frank J. Grace (31-6-1)	Lyle E. Seeman	8	1	1
1929	F. Morris Touchstone	Stanley H. Ayre	8	2	0
1930	F. Morris Touchstone	Eugene A. Kenny & Richard J. O'Keefe	6	5	0
1931	F. Morris Touchstone	Clyde R. McBride & Joseph B. Zimmerman	9	1	0
1932	F. Morris Touchstone	Thomas C. Darcy	9	1	0
1933	F. Morris Touchstone	Charles H. Pottenger	8	1	0
1934	F. Morris Touchstone	Gene H. Tibbets	5	4	0
1935	F. Morris Touchstone	Robert M. Stillman	8	1	0
1936	F. Morris Touchstone	Clinton U. True	7	1	1
1937	F. Morris Touchstone	Thomas Truxton	9	1	0
1938	F. Morris Touchstone	Charles W. Sherburne	7	3	0
1939	F. Morris Touchstone	James H. Keller	8	2	0
1940	F. Morris Touchstone	Joseph J. Eaton, Jr.	7	3	0
1941	F. Morris Touchstone	Joseph J. Thigpen	8	2	0
1942	F. Morris Touchstone	Thomas T. Galloway	8	1	0
1943	F. Morris Touchstone	Robert C. Marshall & Gabriel A. Ivan	5	4	0
1944	F. Morris Touchstone	John H. Cushman	6	2	0
1945	F. Morris Touchstone	Levin B. Broughton	5	1	1
1946	F. Morris Touchstone	W. George Devens	8	2	0
1947	F. Morris Touchstone	Robert M. Montague	10	2	0
1948	F. Morris Touchstone	John W. McEnery	9	3	0
1949	F. Morris Touchstone	James V. Hartinger & John L. Rust	5	4	0
1950	F. Morris Touchstone	Philo B. Lange	7	4	0
1951	F. Morris Touchstone	Edward C. Meyer	8	2	0
1952	F. Morris Touchstone	Joseph C. Austin	9	2	1
1953	F. Morris Touchstone	John E. Johnson	9	2	0
1954	F. Morris Touchstone	Peter N. Leone	9	2	0

Tom Sheckells holds the career assist mark with eighty, while Tom Cafaro, the Most Valuable Attackman in the country in 1971, holds season records for goals, 51, and points, 85. Paul Cino set a season record for assists in 1982 with forty-two and the single game assist record with eight against Bucknell in 1982.

Joe Austin set a single game record for goals scored in 1952 when he scored ten against Cornell. Russ Bolling holds the single game record for total points, collecting twelve in 1972 against the New York Lacrosse Club on eight goals and four assists. Defensively, goalie Jim Torrence tops all record holders on season and game categories. He made 209 saves in 1955 and 39 saves against Navy in 1954. All-America selection George Slabowski holds the career record for goalie saves with 603.

Army lacrosse teams have won or shared the national championship seven times, the last coming in 1969 when they shared the title with Johns Hopkins.

Jim "Ace" Adams coached the Army lacrosse team from 1958 until 1969, compiling a 92-24-1 record. His teams won or shared the national championship four times, winning the outright national and open championship in 1958, his first year at the Academy. Adams left West Point to accept the head coaching position at the University of Pennsylvania, and later accepted the head coaching position at the University of Virginia.

1955	F. Morris Touchstone	Alexander R. MacDonald	5	6	0
1956	F. Morris Touchstone	John H. Higgins	7	4	0
1957	F. Morris Touchstone (215-84-6)	Benedict E. Glyphis	6	5	0
1958	James F. Adams	Raymond B. Riggan	9	0	0
1959	James F. Adams	Stephen W. Fertig	8	2	0
1960	James F. Adams	Robert S. Miser	8	2	0
1961	James F. Adams	Samuel D. Wilder	8	2	0
1962	James F. Adams	Charles C. Darrell	8	2	0
1963	James F. Adams	Paul D. Stanley	7	3	0
1964	James F. Adams	Roy C. Buckner	8	1	0
1965	James F. Adams	Thomas R. Sheckells	8	3	0
1966	James F. Adams	Frank J. Kobes	6	3	0
1967	James F. Adams	Thomas C. Pettit	6	3	0
1968	James F. Adams	Donald R. Workman	6	2	1
1969	James F. Adams (92-24-1)	Francis D. Boyle	10	1	0
1970	Al Pisano	John T. Connors	7	3	0
1971	Al Pisano	Steven Wood	11	2	0
1972	Al Pisano	Frank J. Eich	8	3	0
1973	Al Pisano	Thomas Fitzsimmons	6	5	0
1974	Al Pisano	Thomas O'Leary	3	7	0
1975	Al Pisano	Walter P. Schaefer	5	5	0
1976	Al Pisano (46-31-0)	Richard P. Bifulco	6	6	0
1977	Dick Edell	Kevin G. Scherrer	8	3	0
1978	Dick Edell	Jose R. Olivero	10	3	0
1979	Dick Edell	Michael C. Gray	10	3	0
1980	Dick Edell	Thomas J. Endres	8	4	0
1981	Dick Edell	Robert J. Henry	10	4	0
1982	Dick Edell	Kenneth R. Dahl	9	4	0
1983	Dick Edell (66-24-0)	Paul Cino	11	3	0
1984	Jack Emmer	Michael Riccardi & George Slabowski	11	3	0
1985	Jack Emmer	P.J. O'Sullivan & Peter Short	10	4	0
1986	Jack Emmer	William Schiffer	6	6	0
1987	Jack Emmer (37-17-0)	Daniel Williams & Thomas Hickman	10	4	0

Army goalie George Slabowski stops a shot by an Air Force attackman during a 19-5 victory over the Falcons in 1981. Slabowski earned second team All-America honors while at the Academy and served as co-captain of the 1984 Army squad. Slabowski holds the career record for saves with 603.

Army coach Dick Edell views the action during a game against Johns Hopkins University in 1978. Edell served as head coach from 1977 to 1983.

Coach Jim Adams is pictured here prior to practice at the Military Academy in 1958, his first year at the helm. Adams guided the Cadets to an unblemished 9-0 record that season, while winning the National Collegiate and National Open championship.

Army attackman Pete Cramblet, another three-time All-America, is pictured here during his playing days at the Academy. Cramblet, now a major serving at Fort Lewis, Washington, was inducted into the Lacrosse Hall of Fame in 1987. In 1970, Cramblet was the recipient of the Jack Turnbull Memorial Trophy as the nation's outstanding attackman, and the 1st Lieutenant Raymond Enners Memorial Award as the outstanding player in the nation.

Lt. Gen. James Hartinger, a three-time All-America while at West Point, is officially inducted into the Lacrosse Hall of Fame during ceremonies at Michie Stadium in 1976. Participating in the ceremony are, left to right, Col. Jack Schuder, director of athletics at the Academy, Thomas Hayes, head coach at Rutgers University representing the Hall of Fame, Lt. Gen. Hartinger, and Col. Gilbert Kirby, chairman of the Athletic Board at that time.

Lt. Gen. James Hartinger is pictured here when he was a member of the Army lacrosse team in 1949. Hartinger was a three-time All-America and was inducted into the Lacrosse Hall of Fame in 1975. He is one of eight former West Point players and coaches who have been inducted into the Hall of Fame.

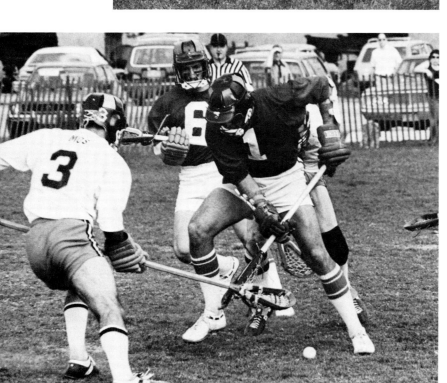

Army defenseman Scott Mos (3) battles for a loose ball during a game against Ohio Wesleyan University in 1976. The Cadets prevailed in this encounter 13-9, but finished with a less than satisfactory 6-6 record.

A. Norman Webb, a first team All-America goalie at West Point in 1964, is one of six Army players to be inducted into the Lacrosse Hall of Fame. Webb was inducted in 1983.

Coach Al Pisano became lacrosse coach at West Point in 1970, succeeding Jim "Ace" Adams. In seven years Pisano's teams compiled an overall record of forty-six victories and thirty-one defeats.

Army attackman Tom Cafaro sits on a bench and chats with a young Army fan prior to the start of game in 1971. Cafaro was voted the Outstanding Attackman in the nation that year, leading Army to an 11-2 record. The Cadets also earned a berth in the first NCAA-sanctioned lacrosse championship playoff, bowing to Cornell 17-16 in the semi-finals at Michie Stadium. Cornell went on to win the NCAA title that season. Cafaro also played in the annual North-South game and gained All-America honors.

Army crease attackman Scott Finlay (30) fires a shot on goal against Johns Hopkins in 1978. Finlay is Army's career scoring leader in lacrosse with 186 points and 150 goals, both records. Finley, who hails from Valley Cottage, New York, in Rockland County, won four letters in lacrosse while at West Point.

Army lacrosse coach Dick Edell instructs his squad during a crucial timeout during the 1981 season. Edell took over the head coaching position at West Point in 1977 and rebuilt a program that had fallen on hard times. During his first season, Army compiled an 8-3 record and from that point on never won less than eight games during Edell's tenure. He compiled a record of seventy-six victories and just twenty-eight defeats in seven seasons, and his teams earned berths in the NCAA lacrosse playoffs four times, qualifying in each of his last three years. Edell, whose West Point teams were nationally ranked every year, left the Academy to accept the head coaching position at the University of Maryland.

The 1928 Army lacrosse team, coached by Frank J. Grace, compiled a record of eight victories, one defeat, and one tie. The only loss came at the hands of Rutgers by an 8-3 margin, while the Cadets played to a 4-4 tie against Navy. Army defeated Hobart, Johns Hopkins, Swarthmore, Colgate, Lafayette, New York University, Harvard, and Penn State. All-America Chuck Born played a key role for the Cadets, while other senior lettermen included Laverne V. G. "Blondie" Saunders, "Lighthorse" Harry Wilson, Norris Harbold, and Lyle Seeman, all football lettermen.

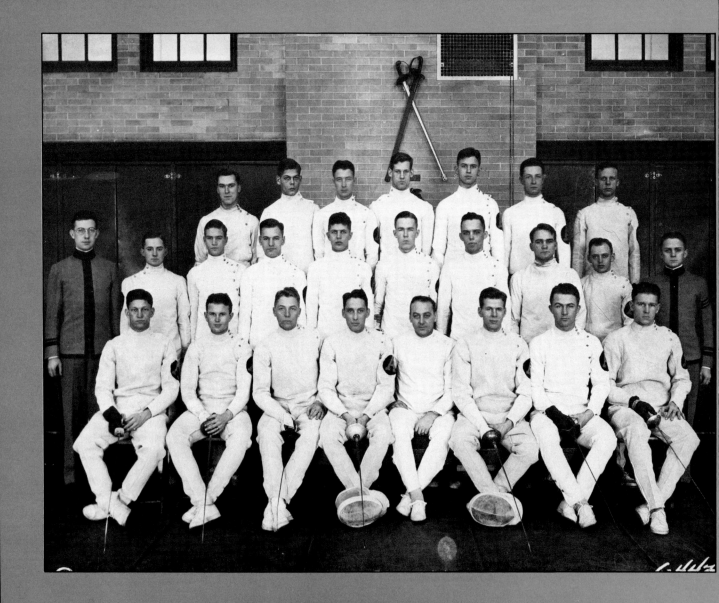

Army's 1931 fencing team was 5-2. Captain of the squad was Gustave M. Heiss, who later qualified for the 1932 and 1936 Olympics. Heiss served during World War II, retiring in 1946 at the rank of colonel because of wounds sustained during the war.

CHAPTER 23

Cadets competed in fencing on an intercollegiate level in 1902, but its history dates back to the 1830s when fencing and riding were both taught at the U.S. Military Academy. Such instruction was required to prepare cadets for their roles as officers in the U.S. Army.

While football and baseball began West Point's sports history on the intercollegiate level, fencing wasn't far behind as one of the original intercollegiate sports. Its start in 1902 was very successful as Coach L.R. Senac's squad won five consecutive matches, defeating Cornell, Harvard, Columbia, Yale, and Pennsylvania before going on to capture the Eastern Intercollegiate Fencing championship.

Edmund Bull served as team captain of the first Army fencing team, and also was named captain in 1903 when the Cadets once again finished with an unblemished 4-0 record under the guidance of Coach Richard Malchien. Malchien's squad also duplicated the victory in the Eastern Intercollegiate Fencing championships.

Bull, a 1904 graduate of West Point, participated in the Expedition against the Moros in 1905 and then returned to West Point to serve in the Tactical Department and then the Modern Languages Department at the Academy until 1919. He retired in 1919 on a disability at the rank of lieutenant colonel.

Army fencing teams were almost invincible at the start. From 1902 until 1911 the Cadets won thirty-one consecutive meets before Harvard defeated the Cadets 6-3 in the final match in 1911 to snap the streak.

Coach Louis Vauthier, who took over the coaching responsibilities in 1904, compiled a 35-1 record as head coach at West Point through the 1912 season. Fencing was discontinued as a varsity sport in 1913 and was not resumed until 1923. When fencing was initiated again in 1923, Vauthier teamed up with John W. Dimond for two seasons, 1923-1924, winning seven of ten matches to close out his coaching tenure with a 42-4 record.

Under Vauthier's guidance, Army fencers performed exceptionally well and earned berths on the United States Olympic

team. Three fencers, Scott D. Breckinridge, George S. Patton, Jr. and Harold M. Rayner competed in the 1912 Olympics in Stockholm. Patton, a 1905 graduate, participated in both fencing and modern pentathlon during the Olympics that year. Breckinridge is not a graduate, but Rayner is a 1912 graduate. He also qualified for the 1920 Olympics held in Antwerp and the 1928 Olympics in Amsterdam. Francis W. Honeycutt, another of Vauthier's fencers who is a 1904 graduate, participated in the 1920 Olympics, while Robert Sears, a 1909 West Point graduate, also qualified for the U.S. squad that year.

Dimond remained at the helm through 1946, compiling a record of 117 victories, 56 defeats and 7 ties. His 1933 and 1934 Army teams finished with undefeated records, while twelve of his Army fencers won Eastern championships.

Several of Dimond's fencers also earned berths on the United States Olympic team. Lawrence V. Castner, captain of the 1923 team, qualified for the 1924 Olympics in Paris. Richard W. Mayo participated in the 1928 Olympics in Amsterdam, competing in fencing and modern pentathlon, and also competed in modern pentathlon during the 1932 Olympics in Los Angeles.

Other former West Point graduates who competed in Olympic fencing competition include: Thomas J. Sands, Frederick R. Weber, and Gustave M. Heiss in the 1936 Olympics in Berlin, and Robert S. Dow, an ex-cadet from the class of 1966 who competed in the 1972 Olympics in Munich.

Servando Velarde assumed the coaching responsibilities at West Point in 1947 and registered a 17-13-1 record. In 1949, the Cadets tied for first place in the National Collegiate Athletic Association championships, led by the efforts of team captain Richard C. Bowman.

Bowman won the Eastern Intercollegiate Fencing title in the epee, and followed that victory up with a championship in the NCAA meet. He is the only Army fencer to ever win an individual title at the NCAA championship.

Bowman served in World War II before entering the U.S. Military Academy. Following graduation in 1949 he entered

Military Academy. Following graduation in 1949 he entered the Air Force and completed pilot training in 1951. From there he was assigned to the 729 Bomber Squadron, 452 Bomber Wing during the Korean War, receiving the Distinguished Flying Cross and three Air Medals during his tour. From 1952 to 1956, he served as an instructor at Vance Air Force Base before being assigned to the Office of the Commandant at the U.S. Air Force Academy.

Bowman earned an M.S. degree from Oklahoma State University, a master of public administration degree, and a doctorate degree from Harvard. He spent four years at the Air Force Academy as an instructor in the Political Science Department. Later assignments saw Bowman elevated to the rank of major general where he was assigned to the Office of the Secretary of the Air Force and the Office of the Assistant Secretary of Defense for Internal Security Affairs.

Fencing was dropped once again from intercollegiate competition following the 1949 season, where upon it was resumed two years later under Coach Marcel Pasche. Pasche started strongly by registering a 7-3 record during his first season, but in four years his overall mark was 20-19-0.

Following the 1954 season, fencing once again was relegated to club status at the Military Academy and not resumed under the intercollegiate banner until the 1967-1968 season. A. John Geraci was named fencing coach and guided the Cadets' fortunes through the 1975-1976 season. During his eight years at the helm, Geraci's Army teams won sixty-three matches and lost forty-three. He also had one All-America fencer, David H. Huntoon, who gained that recognition in saber competition.

Richard Bowman was a two-time All-America in epee, while Chester S. Trubin gained similar honors in 1948 and 1949 in saber. William Schuster gained All-America honors in 1948 in foil. Barnard Cummings was an All-America in foil in 1949. Arthur R. Stebbins was a saber All-America selection in 1952, while Phillip D. Vollmann was an All-America in epee in 1953.

Fencing remained an intercollegiate sport through the 1978-1979 season when it was relegated to club status once again.

A LOOK INTO THE PAST

Year	Coach	Captain	Won	Lost	Tied
1902	L.R. Senac (5-0-0)	Edmund L. Bull	5	0	0
1903	Richard Malchien (4-0-0)	Edmund L. Bull	4	0	0
1904	Louis Vauthier	George V. Strong	4	0	0
1905	Louis Vauthier	Alvin B. Barber	3	0	0
1906	Louis Vauthier	Forrest E. Williford	4	0	0
1907	Louis Vauthier	John A. Holabird	4	0	0
1908	Louis Vauthier	Oliver A. Dickinson	4	0	0
1909	Louis Vauthier	Robert Sears	4	0	0
1910	Louis Vauthier	Oscar N. Sohlbert	5	0	0
1911	Louis Vauthier	Harold M. Rayner	3	1	0
1912	Louis Vauthier	William H. Wilbur	4	0	0
Fencing Discontinued from 1913 to 1922					
1922	Louis Vauthier & John Dimond	Lawrence V. Castner	1	2	0
1923	Louis Vauthier & John Dimond	Lawrence V. Castner	4	1	0
1924	Louis Vauthier & John Dimond Vauthier Record (124-59-7)	Albert K. Stebbins	3	2	0
1925	John W. Dimond	Wilfred P. Champlain	6	2	0
1926	John W. Dimond	Richard D. Mayo	1	4	0
1927	John W. Dimond	Charles P. Bixel	6	1	0
1928	John W. Dimond	John H. Hinrichs	3	1	0
1929	John W. Dimond	Thomas J. Sands	2	4	1
1930	John W. Dimond	Philip C. Wehle	9	1	1
1931	John W. Dimond	Gustave M. Heiss	5	2	0
1932	John W. Dimond	Charles R. Murray	4	2	1
1933	John W. Dimond	Maurice E. Kaiser	6	0	0
1934	John W. Dimond	William M. Gross	5	0	0
1935	John W. Dimond	Charles A. Symroski	2	5	0
1936	John W. Dimond	Robert T. Crowder	6	2	0
1937	John W. Dimond	William H. Lewis	2	3	0
1938	John W. Dimond	Donald W. Thackeray	4	5	1
1939	John W. Dimond	Harry W. Kinnard, Jr.	8	2	0
1940	John W. Dimond	Alan G. Rorick	10	2	0
1941	John W. Dimond	Alfred J. F. Moody	8	5	0
1942	John W. Dimond	Andrew H. Weigel	4	5	0
1943	John W. Dimond	George T. Prior & Christopher J. H. Munch	7	3	1
1944	John W. Dimond	John W. Donaldson	5	4	1
1945	John W. Dimond	Jose L. Carrion	7	1	1
1946	John W. Dimond (117-56-7)	Clyde M. MacKenzie	7	2	0
1947	Servando Velarde	Edson L. Garrabrants	4	6	0
1948	Servando Velarde	William A. Shuster	7	4	0
1949	Servando Velarde (17-13-1)	Richard C. Bowman	6	3	1
1950	Marcel Pasche	John S. Matthews	5	5	0
1951	Marcel Pasche	Bruce H. Robertson	7	3	0
1952	Marcel Pasche	William S. Shields	3	7	0
1953	Marcel Pasche	Clifford J. Landry	5	5	0
1954	Marcel Pasche (20-19-0)	Philip D. Vollmann	5	4	0
Fencing Discontinued After 1954 Season					
1967	A. John Geraci	Steven L. Murphy	11	3	0
1968	Ronald McMahan & A. John Geraci	Thomas D. Watson	10	4	0
1969	Ron McMahan & A. John Geraci	Nicholas Costantino	8	4	0
1970	A. John Geraci	Jerry B. Edelen	7	4	0
1971	A. John Geraci	James E. Lyon	10	4	0
1972	A. John Geraci	George Weightman	11	4	0
1973	A. John Geraci	Edward F. Polom	10	4	0
1974	A. John Geraci	Jay R. Bishop	3	11	0
1975	A. John Geraci (63-43-0)	Gary L. Wingo	4	9	0
1976	CPT Ronald D. Feher	Robert L. Carter	4	9	0
1977	CPT Terry Bresnick	Robert W. Hamilton	8	6	0
1978	CPT Frank Kendall	Robert J. Reed	4	7	0

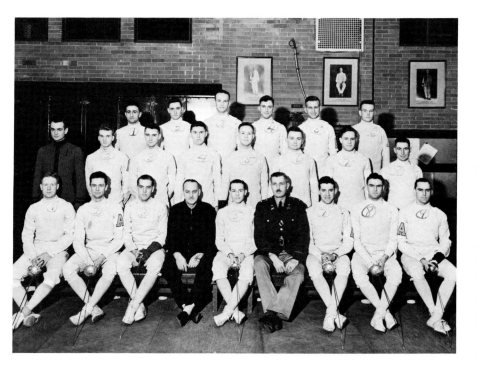

The fencing team at West Point compiled an outstanding 8-2 record during the 1938-1939 season, defeating Princeton twice, Columbia, Yale twice, Harvard, City College of New York, and the New York Fencers Club. John W. Dimond, the second fencing coach at the Academy, led the Cadets to their second highest season victory total at that time. The only losses were to New York University, 5-4, and Navy, 16-11. Two members of the squad, Salvatore E. Manzo and Davisson Dalziel, won Eastern championships. Manzo won in the epee weapon, while Dalziel was an Eastern titlist in saber. Pictured are, front row, left to right, Clark W. Mayne, Ellsworth R Jacoby, John C. Bane, Coach John Dimond, team captain Harry W. O. Kinnard, Lt. Philip C. Wehle, Officer-in-Charge, Salvatore E. Manzo, Paige E. Smith, and Herbert M. Bowlby; second row, team manager Michael S. Davison, Alan G. Rorick, Davisson Dalziel, John E. Schremp, William M. Petre, Raymond P. Campbell, Alan M. Strock, and Marvin L. Jacobs; top row, Alfred J. R. Moody, George R. Adjemian, Harrington W. Cochran, Arthur L. Meyer, Roy J. Clinton, and Willis B. Sawyer.

Coach John W. Dimond, who succeeded Louis Vauthier as Army's fencing coach in 1925, led the 1928 squad to a 3-1 record. Dimond had assisted Vauthier for three seasons, 1922-1924, before taking over sole responsibility for coaching the Army fencing squad. Dimond remained at West Point until 1946. His overall record during that span was 117 victories, 56 losses, and 7 ties in twenty-two seasons. Two of his fencing squads, 1933 and 1934, went undefeated. Team captain of the 1928 team was John H. Hinrichs.

Wrestling began its intercollegiate history at West Point in 1921 when Coach Tom Jenkins guided his Cadet squad to a 22-5 victory over Princeton. The Army squad also took the measure of Washington & Lee University and Springfield College that year to finish with a perfect 3-0 record.

The roots of wrestling, however, go much further back. In 1905, Col. Herman J. Koehler had completed a major expansion to the physical education program at the Academy. He offered the coaching position in wrestling to Jenkins, who was considered one of the finest wrestlers in the world at that time.

Born in Bedford, Ohio on August 3, 1872, Jenkins, at the age of twenty, left a job at a local steel mill to devote his time to his wrestling career. For the next five years Jenkins wrestled anyone who would venture into the ring. He traveled throughout the United States and to Europe as a feature attraction with a vaudeville troupe.

In an article written for *Assembly* magazine in 1967 by Maj. Robert Degen of the Office of Physical Education, it was said there was a standing offer of fifty dollars for anyone who could stay in the ring with Jenkins for more than fifteen minutes. There is no record that anyone ever managed to pocket the money. Jenkins once wrestled a bear as a publicity stunt according to some reports, but Degen says the Army wrestling instructor never spoke of it.

From 1897 until 1906, Jenkins was widely recognized as the world's "catch-as-catch-can" wrestling champion. He was beaten by three different Terrible Turks and Frank Gotch, but he was still at the top of the wrestling world when he accepted the coaching position at West Point. A year later, Jenkins lost his championship to Gotch and decided to devote his life to the "young gents" at the U.S. Military Academy.

In his article Degen remarked: "Cadets who learned their wrestling fundamentals under Tom Jenkins can well remember how lightly Tom regarded differences in size and weight—often considerable—between two potential opponents. By his standards the smaller man just had to fight harder. In almost every class session the occasion would arise when Tom would confront two obviously mismatched cadets and ask them how much they weighed. When they told him, he would invariably order in his gravelly voice, 'Close enough. Wrassle!' Equally well remembered was the classic Jenkins philosphy: 'There ain't no holt but that there's a guard agin' it.'"

Jenkins devoted thirty-seven years to coaching and teaching cadets at West Point. He retired after the 1935 season, compiling an overall record of fifty-four victories, forty-four defeats, and one tie. Army provided him a 21-9 victory over Cornell in his final match. After retiring, Tom and his wife Lavinia moved to a small home in Cornwall-on-Hudson, just a short distance from the Academy. He died in June, 1957.

Lloyd Appleton took over the coaching responsibilities at West Point following the retirement of Jenkins and carried on the respected tradition for the next nineteen years. An undefeated wrestler in college and a Silver Medalist in the 1928 Olympics, Appleton compiled an outstanding record of eighty-six victories, fifty-one losses, and five ties. Army produced thirty-seven Eastern place finishers during his coaching career. Al Paulekas took runner-up honors at the NCAA championships in 1953.

Appleton, who served as an instructor in the Department of Physical Education for another sixteen years and helped establish a wrestling program for Army troops in Europe, was inducted into the National Wrestling Hall of Fame in 1983.

LeRoy Alitz was named head coach in 1955 and remained in that position for the next twenty-three years. An Iowa native, Alitz compiled a record of 146 victories, 134 defeats, and 15 ties. The victory total is the most by any of Army's five wrestling coaches during the history of the sport.

Alitz helped develop Army's only NCAA wrestling champion, Mike Natvig. Natvig won the national title at 147 pounds two consecutive years, 1962 and 1963. A total of ten of Alitz' wrestlers placed in the nationals and seventy-two won Eastern Intercollegiate Wrestling Association recognition.

Alitz has been recognized throughout college wrestling for his efforts on behalf of the sport. He was inducted into the Helms Foundation Hall of Fame in 1972, as well as the New York State Coaches Hall of Fame. Today, Alitz is the director of fourth class wrestling at West Point.

Ron Pifer, an outstanding wrestling coach at State College High School in Pennsylvania, succeeded Alitz and compiled a 31-26-2 record in three seasons, 1978-1980. Eleven of his Army wrestlers also placed in the Eastern Championships.

Ed Steers, a native of Silver Spring, Maryland, assumed the head coaching job at West Point during the 1980-1981 season and has turned the program into one of the finest in the country.

During the past six seasons, Steers has guided the wrestling team to 124 victories, just 26 defeats, and 2 ties, by far the most successful mark in the sport's history. Additionally, four of his wrestlers have garnered All-America recognition. Dennis Semmel, Darrel Nerove, and Dave Rippley gained All-America honors in 1985-1986, while Dan Costigan was an All-America in 1986-1987. Semmel, Nerove, and Costigan gained those honors during NCAA competition. Rippley is the first freshman (plebe) in history to be named an All-America by the *Amateur Wrestling News*.

Steers also guided the 1986-1987 team to its first Eastern Intercollegiate Wrestling Association championship last year.

Among Army's other place finishers and All-Americas in the NCAA championships are Al Rushatz, third at 177 pounds in 1960; Mark Scureman, third at 147 in 1965; Robert Steenlage, third at 123 pounds in 1966; Robert Robbins, fifth at 145 in 1966; Jim Harter, fourth at 177 in 1967; Mike Nardotti, sixth at 160 in 1968, and Bill James, sixth at 134 in 1971.

Al Rushatz is the second Army wrestler to gain All-America recognition. He finished third at 177 pounds during the 1960 NCAA championships to gain those honors. Col. Rushatz is currently deputy director of the Department of Physical Education at West Point.

A LOOK INTO THE PAST

Year	Coach	Captain	Won	Lost	Tied
1921	Tom Jenkins	James E. McDavid	3	0	0
1922	Tom Jenkins	F.M. Greene	3	4	0
1923	Tom Jenkins	Robert M. Smith	2	5	0
1924	Tom Jenkins	Washington M. Ives Jr.	4	2	0
1925	Tom Jenkins	Joseph P. Cleland	5	1	0
1926	Tom Jenkins	Walter Young, Jr.	5	3	0
1927	Tom Jenkins	Ernest G. Schmidt	5	2	0
1928	Tom Jenkins	Arthur W. Meehan	3	5	0
1929	Tom Jenkins	Louis A. Hammack	5	3	0
1930	Tom Jenkins	Harry B. Packard	4	4	0
1931	Tom Jenkins	Merle L. Fisher	2	6	0
1932	Tom Jenkins	Frank G. Jamison	4	2	2
1933	Tom Jenkins	William V. Thompson	3	2	0
1934	Tom Jenkins	Thomas A. McCrary	3	3	0
1935	Tom Jenkins (54-44-3)	John Neiger	3	2	1
1936	Lloyd Appleton	William D. Cairnes	3	3	0
Wrestling Discontinued in 1937 and 1938					
1939	Lloyd Appleton	Harry N. Brandon	3	3	0
1940	Lloyd Appleton	Raymond J. Downey	3	5	0
1941	Lloyd Appleton	George H. Welles	1	7	0
1942	Lloyd Appleton	Joe D. Hennessee	5	3	0
1943	Lloyd Appleton	James S. Changaris & Glenn P. Ingwersen	6	1	0
1944	Lloyd Appleton	David P. Wood	5	1	1
1945	Lloyd Appleton	George C. Fee	7	0	0
1946	Lloyd Appleton	Robert A. Land	5	2	0
1947	Lloyd Appleton	John E. Mock	6	4	0
1948	Lloyd Appleton	Stanley E. Thevenet	7	2	1
1949	Lloyd Appleton	Ralph C. Raabe	7	3	0
1950	Lloyd Appleton	Albert J. Fern	4	3	2
1951	Lloyd Appleton	Dean D. Mulder	5	3	0
1952	Lloyd Appleton	Donald R. Swygert	5	4	1
1953	Lloyd Appleton	Robert C. Karns	7	3	0
1954	Lloyd Appleton (86-51-5)	Gerald A. Lodge	7	4	0
1955	LeRoy Alitz	Gerald D. Tebben	2	6	0
1956	LeRoy Alitz	John W. Nicholson	3	3	2

Robert Steenlage finished third during the 1966 NCAA championships at 123 pounds to gain All-America recognition. A 1966 graduate, Steenlage hailed from Britt, Iowa.

Dennis Semmel gained All-America honors during the 1985-1986 season, joining an elite group of exceptional Army wrestlers.

Al Paulekas was the first Army wrestler ever to gain All-America recognition. He gained those honors in 1953 when he finished second at the NCAA championships at 177 pounds.

Year	Coach	Captain	W	L	T
1957	LeRoy Alitz	Loren D. Reid	3	5	1
1958	LeRoy Alitz	Glenn K. Phillips	7	3	0
1959	LeRoy Alitz	Gerald Weisenseel	4	6	1
1960	LeRoy Alitz	Raymond Andrews	6	4	0
1961	LeRoy Alitz	Warren L. Miller	7	4	0
1961-62	LeRoy Alitz	Alfred S. Rushatz	6	4	0
1962-63	LeRoy Alitz	Cliff M. Natvig	4	5	1
1963-64	LeRoy Alitz	Edwin C. Winborn	2	4	2
1964-65	LeRoy Alitz	Carl R. Arvin	9	2	1
1965-66	LeRoy Alitz	John R. Steenlage	6	3	0
1966-67	LeRoy Alitz	Roger T. Heimann	7	3	1
1967-68	LeRoy Alitz	James M. Harter	8	2	0
1968-69	LeRoy Alitz	John A. Dinger	5	4	2
1969-70	LeRoy Alitz	William McBeth	8	7	0
1970-71	LeRoy Alitz	William D. James	9	5	0
1971-72	LeRoy Alitz	William D. James	13	6	1
1972-73	LeRoy Alitz	Nage L. Damas	9	12	1
1973-74	LeRoy Alitz	Michael J. Campo	6	11	1
1974-75	LeRoy Alitz	John C. Schoonover	6	13	0
1975-76	LeRoy Alitz	Charles M. Allen	7	11	0
1976-77	LeRoy Alitz (146-134-15)	Robert F. Vottero	9	11	1
1977-78	Ron Pifer	Richard R. McPhee	6	11	2
1978-79	Ron Pifer	Thomas E. Coleman	11	8	0
1979-80	Ron Pifer (31-26-2)	Vincent C. Masi	14	7	0
1980-81	Ed Steers	Douglas E. Graham	19	3	1
1981-82	Ed Steers	C. D. Johnson & Michael W. Palzer	18	4	0
1982-83	Ed Steers	Bob Turner & Ed Wohlwender	21	3	0
1983-84	Ed Steers	Whit Gibson & Mike Parietti	12	9	0
1984-85	Ed Steers	Dan Parietti & Dan Sullivan	16	2	1
1985-86	Ed Steers	Dennis Semmel	18	3	0
1986-87	Ed Steers (124-26-2)	Cliff Harris & Dave McCormick	20	2	0

Mike Natvig, a graduate of the class of 1963, earned a National Collegiate Athletic Association championship and All-America honors in wrestling in 1962 and 1963 at 147 pounds. Natvig was commissioned in the Artillery branch of the U.S. Army. He served in Germany and in Vietnam before returning to West Point as an instructor in the Department of Physical Education.

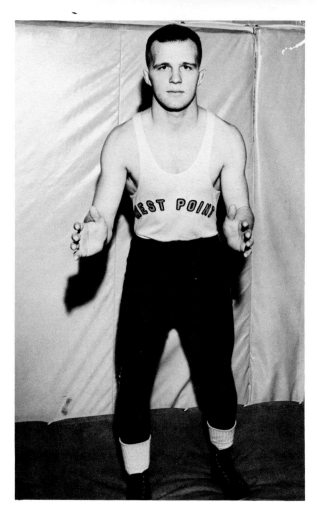

Bill James gained All-America honors in wrestling in 1971 by finishing sixth at the NCAA championships at 134 pounds.

Mike Nardotti finished sixth at the 1968 NCAA championships to gain All-America honors at 160 pounds.

n Harter gained All-America wrestling
nors while at the Academy by finishing
urth at 177 pounds in 1967.

Ron Pifer, a 1962 graduate of Penn State
University, succeeded LeRoy Alitz as head
wrestling coach. He spent three years at the
Academy, compiling a record of thirty-one
victories, twenty-seven defeats. While at Penn
State, Pifer was an Eastern champion at 147
pounds and placed in the NCAA championships three consecutive years. He was an
outstanding high school wrestling coach in
Pennsylvania prior to coming to West Point,
guiding State College High School to an
86-30-2 record in dual meet competition.

LeRoy Alitz, head wrestling coach at West
Point for twenty-three seasons, was inducted
into the Helms Foundation Amateur
Wrestling Hall of Fame in 1972. He guided
Army wrestling teams to 146 victories during
his tenure. He also served as president of the
NCAA and the Eastern Intercollegiate
Wrestling Coaches Association, and
completed six years as chairman of the NCAA
Wrestling Rules Committee. He continues to
instruct cadets in the Department of Physical
Education.

Coach Ed Steers became the fifth wrestling
coach in Army history in 1980. During the
past six seasons he has developed a program
that has gained national prominence. His
record during that span is 124 victories, just
26 defeats, and 2 ties, the finest record percentage-wise in West Point wrestling history.
Steers' 1986-1987 Army squad won its first
Eastern Intercollegiate Wrestling Association
championship in history.

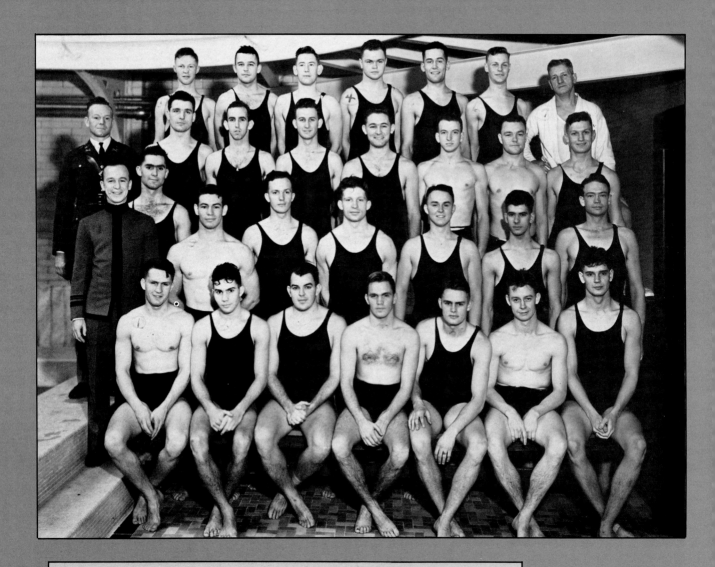

The West Point swimming team, under Coach Joseph N. Nill, won five meets and lost two during the 1938-1939 season. Among the victories was a 48-27 win over Navy. Robert N. Crandall served as team captain. The captain-elect for 1940 was Hank Brewerton, who gained All-America honors a year later in the 220- and 440-yard freestyle. Two other members of the 1939 team, Robert W. Garrett and Charles H. Colwell, won Eastern Intercollegiate Swimming championships. Garrett was first in the 50-yard freestyle with a time of 0:23.8 seconds in 1939. Colwell won the 50-yard freestyle in 0:23.8 and the 100-yard freestyle in 0:52.6 during the 1940 Eastern championships. Nill began coaching at the Academy in 1925 and remained at that position through 1943, compiling a record of 87-49-1. Pictured are, front row, left to right, Charles E. Thomas, Paul F. O'Neil, 1940 captain-elect Henry R. Brewerton, team captain Robert W. Crandall, Hume Peabody, Walter L. Moore, and Charles H. Colwell; second row, team manager William H. Barnett, David G. Gauvreau, Frank G. Forrest, Christopher C. Coyne, Alexander F. Muzyk, John E. Beier, Eugene A. Trahan, and Robert B. Spragins; third row, Lt. Charles B. Duff, Officer-in-Charge, John F. Harris, Robert W. Garrett, Robert M. Williams, Thomas H. Muller, James B. Bonham, Horace G. Foster, and Peter K. Dilts; top row, Richard S. Abbey, Malcolm C. Johnson, Robert M. Coleman, John Dibble, Jr., Arnold T. Phillips, Burdett E. Haessly, and Coach Joseph Nill.

CHAPTER 25

MEN'S SWIMMING

Army swimming coach Jack Ryan began his twenty-ninth year at the U.S. Military Academy in 1988, the dean of the West Point coaching staff. Ryan has guided the swimming program since the 1959-1960 season and has more victories than any other swimming coach since the sport began intercollegiate competition in 1921.

A native of Pawtucket, Rhode Island, Ryan established numerous New England swimming records. The Army coach is a 1947 graduate of Ohio State University where he won Big Ten championship titles in both the 440- and 1,650-yard freestyle events and earned All-America recognition nine times.

He began his coaching career at Highland Park High School, stayed for one season, and then was named head coach at the University of Florida in 1949. He spent eight years at Florida, compiling an outstanding 51-21 record. In addition, his Gators also won the Southeastern Conference championship four times.

Ryan accepted the head coaching position at West Point prior to the 1959-1960 season, succeeding Gordon Chalmers. Since coming to West Point, Ryan has guided the men's swimming program to 253 victories, just 124 defeats, and one tie.

His 1965-1966 Army squad was one of the best in history, completing a perfect 13-0 season to win the Eastern Intercollegiate Swimming League championship. The Cadets also finished second in the Eastern Seaboard Swimming and Diving championships.

Ryan also helped develop the first National Collegiate Athletic Association champion in 1986-1987 when John Van Sant won the 200-yard breaststroke title.

Ryan has helped develop numerous All-America swimmers while at West Point. His first as head coach at the Academy was Anthony Clay, who gained those honors in the 100-yard freestyle event in 1953. That same year, Army's freestyle relay team earned All-America honors. Relay members included Steve Bliss, Jerry Merges, Clay, and William Landgraf.

In 1964, two Army relay teams qualified for All-America recognition. Bliss, Landgraf, Clay, and Paul Bucha earned that honor in the freestyle relay, while Larry Herdegen, Bob Magruder, Frank Pratt, and Jerry Merges qualified for All-America in the medley relay event.

Army relays were successful in national competition in 1965 as well. Warren Trainor, Bucha, Al Clay, and Steve Bliss won All-America honors in the freestyle relay; Kerry O'Hara, John Landgraf, Frank Pratt, and Trainor earned it in the medley relay, while O'Hara was an All-America in the 200-yard backstroke.

A year later Jay Williams was an All-America in three events—200-, 500-, and 1,650-yard freestyle events—and Frank Pratt was an All-America in the 100- and 200-yard butterfly events. O'Hara again made All-America in the 200-yard backstroke, while Charles Gantner was an All-America in the 200-yard individual medley event. Army's medley relay also gained top honors.

Most recently VanSant carried Army's colors very well in national competition. During the 1985-1986 season he gained All-America honors in the breaststroke during the NCAA Swimming and Diving championships, and then topped it off in 1986-1987 by placing first at the nationals.

Swimming at the Military Academy got off on the right foot in 1921 when Coach Alex Maffert led the Cadets to a perfect 4-0 record. Army defeated Lehigh, Columbia, Harvard, and Syracuse during that first season.

Maffert coached for two years, posting a 9-2 record. He was succeeded by Capt. A. Pendleton, who guided the swimming team for two seasons and a 10-4 record.

Joseph H. Nill took over the coaching responsibilities in 1925 and remained at the position until the close of the 1943 winter season. During his nineteen years at West Point, Nill's teams won eighty-nine meets, dropped forty-nine, and tied once.

Capt. R. L. Starr coached three seasons at the Academy, beginning in 1944, and posted a 19-6 record before Gordon Chalmers was named head coach prior to the 1947 season. Chalmers' first team won just four of twelve meets, but his

Army teams never compiled a losing season for the next twelve years. Chalmers ended up with 112 victories, just 56 defeats, and 2 ties. He won his 100th meet at the Academy during his final season when the Cadets defeated Franklin & Marshall by a 78-8 margin.

After Jack Ryan established his swimming program at West Point, he rolled to his 100th victory during the 1968-1969 season when Army defeated Ohio University 70-20. His 200th win came during the 1981-1982 season when the Cadets defeated Monmouth College by a 71-42 margin. His 250th victory was achieved during the 1986-1987 season. Ryan's 1964-1965 and 1965-1966 teams finished second at the Eastern Seaboard Swimming and Diving championships, while his 1966-1967 squad was third.

Coach Ryan has also directed the women's swimming team at West Point since the 1982-1983 season, completing his finest record in 1986-1987 when Army finished at 11-1. In all, the dean of Army coaches needs just four victories from either his men's or women's teams to notch three hundred career triumphs.

A LOOK INTO THE PAST

Year	Coach	Captain	Won	Lost	Tied
1921	Alex Maffert	All 1st Classmen	4	0	0
1922	Alex Maffert (9-2)	Waldemar F. Breidster	5	2	0
1923	CPT A. Pendleton	Waldemar F. Breidster	6	1	0
1924	CPT A. Pendleton (10-4)	George A. Duerr	4	3	0
1925	Joseph H. Nill	Arthur Bliss	3	3	0
1926	Joseph H. Nill	John C. B. Elliott	4	4	0
1927	Joseph H. Nill	Francis E. Howard	4	4	0
1928	Joseph H. Nill	Richard P. O'Keefe	6	1	1
1929	Joseph H. Nill	Charles C. W. Allen	7	1	0
1930	Joseph H. Nill	George G. Garton	6	2	0
1931	Joseph H. Nill	William A. Davis	7	1	0
1932	Joseph H. Nill	Benjamin J. Webster	5	3	0
1933	Joseph H. Nill	Chalmer K. McClelland	2	3	0
1934	Joseph H. Nill	Thomas B. Maury	4	2	0
1935	Joseph H. Nill	Edgar J. Treacy	5	1	0
1936	Joseph H. Nill	Alfred W. Hess	5	0	0
1937	Joseph H. Nill	Kelley Lemmon	3	3	0
1938	Joseph H. Nill	William C. Fite, III	3	3	0
1939	Joseph H. Nill	Robert W. Crandall	5	2	0
1940	Joseph H. Nill	Henry R. Brewerton	5	3	0
1941	Joseph H. Nill	Robert W. Garrett	4	5	0
1942	Joseph H. Nill	Frank C. Scofield	7	2	0
1943	Joseph H. Nill (87-49-1)	George W. Criss & LeRoy W. Wilson, Jr.	2	6	0
1944	CPT. R. L. Starr	Philip S. Grant	5	3	0
1945	MAJ. R. L. Starr	William E. Glynn	9	0	0
1946	LTC. R. L. Starr (19-6)	Raymond E. Thayer	5	3	0
1947	Gordon H. Chalmers	John G. Hayes	4	8	0
1948	Gordon H. Chalmers	James A. Van Fleet	10	3	0
1949	Gordon H. Chalmers	Edwin S. Townsley	12	1	0
1950	Gordon H. Chalmers	James W. Smyly	8	3	0
1951	Gordon H. Chalmers	John H. Craigie	6	6	0
1952	Gordon H. Chalmers	John D. Smith	8	4	0
1953	Gordon H. Chalmers	James C. Pfautz	7	4	1
1954	Gordon H. Chalmers	Peter F. Witteried	9	4	1
1955	Gordon H. Chalmers	William E. Roth	5	8	0
1956	Gordon H. Chalmers	Robert E. Quackenbush	7	6	0
1956-57	Gordon H. Chalmers	Nicholas J. Robinson	9	4	0
1957-58	Gordon H. Chalmers	Gordon L. Goodman & Mahlon Kirk	13	2	0
1958-59	Gordon H. Chalmers (112-56-2)	George D. Kissinger	14	3	0
1959-60	John E. Ryan, Jr.	George P. Bare	9	5	0
1960-61	John E. Ryan, Jr.	Charles Sollohub	8	5	0
1961-62	John E. Ryan, Jr	Robert B. Thomas	11	4	0
1962-63	John E. Ryan, Jr.	Michael W. Kilroy	13	2	0
1963-64	John E. Ryan, Jr.	William H. Landgraf	13	1	0
1964-65	John E. Ryan, Jr.	Paul W. Bucha	10	1	0
1965-66	John E. Ryan, Jr.	Frank Pratt	13	0	0
1966-67	John E. Ryan, Jr.	Kerry L. O'Hara	9	3	0
1967-68	John E. Ryan, Jr.	Kenneth T. Cummings	11	2	1
1968-69	John E. Ryan, Jr.	William B. Kerr	10	3	0
1969-70	John E. Ryan, Jr.	Jon G. Noll	6	7	0
1970-71	John E. Ryan, Jr.	Jack Frink	11	2	0
1971-72	John E. Ryan, Jr.	John D. Ferguson	5	8	0
1972-73	John E. Ryan, Jr.	William Deatherage	7	7	0
1973-74	John E. Ryan, Jr.	Terry R. Youngbluth	6	9	0
1974-75	John E. Ryan, Jr.	Jeffrey H. Boatright	6	9	0
1975-76	John E. Ryan, Jr.	Samuel E. Fogarty	7	7	0
1976-77	John E. Ryan, Jr.	Ted S. Kanamine & Raymond J. Bosse	7	6	0
1977-78	John E. Ryan, Jr.	Timothy P. Glenn	11	2	0
1978-79	John E. Ryan, Jr.	William R. MacHardy	11	2	0
1979-80	John E. Ryan, Jr.	Robert L. Ruck	9	4	0
1980-81	John E. Ryan, Jr.	J. Marc LeGare	4	9	0
1981-82	John E. Ryan, Jr.	Matthew Klingele	8	5	0
1982-83	John E. Ryan, Jr.	Theodore Martin	9	5	0
1983-84	John E. Ryan, Jr.	Norbert Klopsch & Gerald Schlabach	9	5	0
1984-85	John E. Ryan, Jr.	Andrew Martin	11	3	0
1985-86	John E. Ryan, Jr.	John Lazar	9	4	0
1986-87	John E. Ryan, Jr. (253-123-1)	John VanSant	10	3	0

John VanSant became the first Army men's swimmer to win a national title at the National Collegiate Athletic Association Swimming and Diving championships. VanSant accomplished that achievement during the 1986-1987 season, winning the 200-yard breaststroke event in 1:57.64. He also gained All-America honors for that effort.

President Richard M. Nixon presents the Medal of Honor to Capt. Paul Bucha in 1968. Bucha distinguished himself as a member of the Army swimming team while at the United States Military Academy.

Paul W. "Buddy" Bucha, a class of 1965 graduate at the U.S. Military Academy, earned All-America honors twice in swimming as a member of the 400-yard freestyle relay. Bucha teamed up with Steve Bliss, William Landgraf, and Anthony Clay to earn national recognition in 1964, and then repeated that achievement a year later, this time teaming up with Warren Trainor, Anthony Clay, and Steve Bliss. Bucha distinguished himself on a much higher scale following graduation at West Point. After earning a Master of Business Administration degree at Stanford University in 1967, Bucha became a company commander and an S-3 for the 101st Airborne Division in Vietnam from 1967 to 1968. He won a Medal of Honor for valor and bravery, the highest military award, during his tour. He also received two Bronze Star Medals for valor, two Army Commendation Medals, and a Purple Heart for wounds sustained in Vietnam. Bucha returned to the Academy in 1969 as an instructor in the Department of Social Sciences before resigning his commission in 1972 at the rank of captain.

In 1972, the National Collegiate Athletic Association Swimming and Diving championships were held in West Point's Olympic swimming pool, a key meet for the finest men's swimmers in the nation who had hopes for notching a spot on the U.S. Olympic swimming team. Among those competing was Mark Spitz of Indiana University, one of the finest swimmers in the country. Spitz would go on to capture seven Gold Medals in the Olympics.

Mark Spitz of Indiana University receives a congratulatory handshake from Brig. Gen. John R. Jannarone after winning a national title at West Point.

Mark Spitz holds his hands up in triumph after winning a national butterfly championship.

292

Ted Kanamine, right, is joined by other members of Army's freestyle relay in 1976, including Tim Glenn, Ray Bosse, and Mike French. Kanamine is one of the finest swimmers in modern history at West Point. Kanamine won Eastern Seaboard Swimming championships in the 200- and 400-yard individual medley events (backstroke, butterfly, breaststroke and freestyle) in 1976 and 1977. He also was awarded the Phil Moriarty Award as the outstanding swimmer in the Eastern championships both years. As a senior, Kanamine won the 200 individual medley at the Easterns with a time of 1:53.28. In the preliminary heats the Army swimmer set both a meet and Academy record with a time of 1:53.00. Kanamine came back one night later and set meet and Academy records in the 400 individual medley with a time of 4:02.86. He also was third in the 200-yard butterfly event to help lead Army to a fourth place finish with 215 points, trailing Princeton, Harvard, and Yale in that order.

Army fielded an intercollegiate swimming team for the first time in 1921, coached by Alex Maffert. The Cadets won all four of their meets, defeating Lehigh, Columbia, Harvard, and Syracuse. There was no team captain listed for that team, but Waldemar Breidster, first row, far right, a football letterman, was captain of the 1922 and 1923 swimming squads at West Point.

Army swimming coach Jack Ryan closes out a venerable coaching career in 1988 after compiling a record of 253 victories, just 124 defeats, and one tie. Originally from Pawtucket, Rhode Island, Ryan began his coaching career at Highland Park High School. He stayed for one season, and then was named head coach at the University of Florida in 1949. While there he compiled a 51-21 record and won four Southeastern Conference championships in eight seasons before accepting the head coaching position at West Point.

The Army tennis team, coached by Ralph Chambers, won eight matches and lost four during the 1941 season. Chambers was the third tennis coach in West Point history, taking over in 1933. He remained at that position until the conclusion of the 1946 season. During fourteen years at the helm, Chambers compiled a record of 126 victories and just 33 defeats. His Army teams went undefeated three times—1938, 1939, and 1945. The team captain was Richard G. Tindall, Jr. Pictured are, front row, left to right, Andrew J. Evans, Frederic H. S. Tate, John G. Hoyt, team captain Richard G. Tindall, Charles R. Murrah, and Keith E. Canella; back row, Dale E. Buchanan, Coach Ralph E. Chambers, William H. Tucker, Capt. H. E. Brooks, Officer-in-Charge, Donald L. Driscoll, John W. Leonard, and team manager Vincent P. Carlson.

CHAPTER 26

MEN'S TENNIS

Intercollegiate tennis competition began at the U.S. Military Academy in 1921 when the Cadets defeated Villanova, 4-1.

Col. Clayton E. Wheat coached the Army squad and remained at that position until 1928. During his nine years as head coach, Army teams compiled a 24-27-8 record. One of his top players was Edgar Garbisch, a two-time first team All-America in football (1922, 1924) who was inducted into the National Football Foundation Hall of Fame. Garbisch was captain of the 1925 tennis team.

George Ward succeeded Wheat in 1929 and led the Cadets for three seasons. His teams won sixteen matches, lost fifteen, and tied two.

Ralph E. Chambers became head coach in 1933 and became the most successful tennis coach in West Point History. During his fourteen years at the Military Academy, Chambers guided the Cadets to a record of 126 victories and just 30 defeats.

Between 1937 and 1940, Chambers' teams won twenty-seven consecutive matches. The streak began with a 5-4 victory over Dartmouth in 1937 and was ended when Miami University pinned an 8-1 loss on Army in 1940.

Overall, three of Chambers' squads finished with unbeaten records: 1938 (11-0), 1939 (10-0), and 1945 (11-0). In 1944, the Army tennis squad provided Chambers with his 100th victory at the Academy, defeating Columbia 9-0. That unbeaten 1945 squad was led by team captain Doug Kenna, an All-America quarterback for Army's 1944 football team that won the first national championship in history.

Leif Nordlie assumed the head coaching duties in tennis in 1947. Although he was unable to match the success of his predecessor, Nordlie nonetheless won more than 100 matches as head coach at West Point. Overall, he led the Cadets to 136 victories, 128 defeats, and one tie during seventeen years at West Point.

Bill Cullen took over for Nordlie in 1964 and put the tennis program back into prominence in the East. During his seven seasons at West Point, Cullen's teams won eighty-two matches and lost just thirty. He had just one losing season, 1966, when Army won six of fifteen matches. However, the 1967 squad rebounded with a 10-5 mark.

When Cullen left West Point following the 1970 season, former Davis Cup player Ron Holmberg was named as his replacement. The Cornwall-on-Hudson resident was unable to maintain the same consistency, guiding the Cadets to just one winning season during his six-year stay at the Academy, a 9-8-1 mark in 1976, his final season.

Holmberg was more successful in developing the squash program at West Point, winning forty-nine while losing just twenty-six times.

Paul Assaiante became tennis and squash coach following Holmberg's departure. An assistant gymnastics coach at West Point, Assaiante was an outstanding gymnast and net star while at Springfield College.

During his first season as head coach, Assaiante guided the Cadets to a 9-8 record. His teams had only two losing seasons, compiling an overall nine-year record of 116 victories and just 88 losses.

Following the 1985 season Assaiante left West Point to become a tennis professional at a Westchester County tennis club. Robert Detrich succeeded Assaiante and has guided the tennis program for the past two seasons.

A LOOK INTO THE PAST

Year		Captain	Won	Lost	Tied
1920	Clayton E. Wheat	None Listed	1	0	0
1921	Clayton E. Wheat	Maxwell D. Taylor	1	3	0
1922	Clayton E. Wheat	Maxwell D. Taylor	1	4	2
1923	Clayton E. Wheat	Charles W. Stewart	2	2	2
1924	Clayton E. Wheat	Clarence W. Bennett	4	2	2
1925	Clayton E. Wheat	Edgar W. Garbisch	3	6	0
1926	Clayton E. Wheat	Thomas E. Barbour	1	7	1
1927	Clayton E. Wheat	David D. Hedekin	4	1	0
1928	Clayton E. Wheat	Thomas L. Sherburne	7	2	1
	(24-27-8)				
1929	George S. Ward	John N. Stone	6	4	1
1930	George S. Ward	Harold E. Brooks	4	7	1
1931	George S. Ward	John T. Helms	6	4	0
	(16-15-2)				
1932	None Listed	Herbert B. Thatcher	5	5	0
1933	Ralph E. Chambers	Royal Reynolds	8	2	0
1934	Ralph E. Chambers	Lloyd E. Felleng & Edward M. O'Connell	6	3	0
1935	Ralph E. Chambers	Charles J. Daly	7	3	0
1936	Ralph E. Chambers	Charles B. Tyler	6	4	0
1937	Ralph E. Chambers	William C. Chenoweth	8	2	0
1938	Ralph E. Chambers	Gabriel C. Russell	11	0	0
1939	Ralph E. Chambers	Albert F. Rollins	10	0	0
1940	Ralph E. Chambers	Sanford H. Webster	9	3	0
1941	Ralph E. Chambers	Richard G. Tindall	8	4	0
1942	Ralph E. Chambers	Dale E. Buchanan	8	3	0
1943	Ralph E. Chambers	Keith E. Canella & Leo V. Hayes	9	3	0
1944	Ralph E. Chambers	Charles D. Daniel	11	2	0
1945	Ralph E. Chambers	Edgar D. Kenna	11	0	0
1946	Ralph E. Chambers	Richard H. Turner	14	4	0
	(126-30-0)				
1947	Leif Nordlie	Carlton J. Wellborn	15	5	0
1948	Leif Nordlie	William P. Dougherty	15	8	0
1949	Leif Nordlie	Charles W. Oliver	10	6	0
1950	Leif Nordlie	Joseph B. Love	6	6	1
1951	Leif Nordlie	William R. Richardson	5	8	0
1952	Leif Nordlie	Edmund J. Reinhalter	5	9	0
1953	Leif Nordlie	Ralph L. Sanders	7	7	0
1954	Leif Nordlie	George H. Olmsted	4	10	0
1955	Leif Nordlie	Roland H. Nordlie	5	9	0
1956	Leif Nordlie	Elford M. Mayson	7	7	0
1957	Leif Nordlie	Glaudis P. Gaspard	6	7	0
1958	Leif Nordlie	George C. Huff	6	9	0
1959	Leif Nordlie	Rush S. Yelverton	5	12	0
1960	Leif Nordlie	Donald A. Hubbard	9	8	0
1961	Leif Nordlie	Robert S. Cain	6	9	0
1962	Leif Nordlie	James C. Peterson	11	6	0
1963	Leif Nordlie	Didrick A. Voss	14	2	0
	(136-128-1)				
1964	William Cullen	John W. Leyerzaph	13	2	0
1965	William Cullen	Walter H. Oehrlein	13	4	0
1966	William Cullen	Joseph S. Hardin	6	9	0
1967	William Cullen	Joseph S. Hardin	10	5	0
1968	William Cullen	William Gardepe	14	3	0
1969	William Cullen	Rick A. Wilber	13	2	0
1970	William Cullen	Paul T. Krieger	13	5	0
	(82-30-0)				
1971	Ron Holmberg	John Stevenson	5	11	0
1972	Ron Holmberg	Raymond L. Federici	3	13	0
1973	Ron Holmberg	William R. Brown	5	12	0
1974	Ron Holmberg	James E. Armstrong	6	10	0
1975	Ron Holmberg	James E. Armstrong	5	9	0
1976	Ron Holmberg	Zachary L. Smith	9	8	1
	(33-63-1)				
1977	Paul Assaiante	Zachary L. Smith	9	8	0
1978	Paul Assaiante	Daniel R. Hammond	7	9	0
1979	Paul Assaiante	Charles K. Williams	12	9	0
1980	Paul Assaiante	J. S. Todd	13	8	0
1981	Paul Assaiante	Frederick S. Wright	13	9	0
1982	Paul Assaiante	George Geczy	16	9	0
1983	Paul Assaiante	George Geczy	16	11	0
1984	Paul Assaiante	Charles Deal & Christopher Wilson	16	10	0
1985	Paul Assaiante	Theodore Wilson	14	15	0
	(116-88-0)				
1986	Robert Detrich	Scott Poirier	10	17	0
1987	Robert Detrich	Frederick Krawchuk & Jeffrey Vezeau	13	17	0
	(23-34-0)				

Dan Hammond, left, was captain of the 1978
Army tennis team, playing the No. 1 singles
position for the Cadets. He also served as
captain of the squash team during the 1977-78
winter season, gaining All-America honors
under coach Paul Assaiante.

Ron Holmberg, for many years considered
one of the finest tennis players in the world,
served as tennis and squash coach at the U.S.
Military Academy from January 1971 until
June of 1976. He was the sixth tennis coach
in West Point history since the sport was
started at the Academy in 1920 and the fourth
person to hold the head coaching position in
squash since the sport was first played
competitively in 1948.

Holmberg played the international tennis circuit from 1954 until 1971 before taking over the
coaching position at West Point, compiling an
outstanding record. Three times he was a
member of the United States Davis Cup team,
while being ranked in the Top 10 of the
United States men's singles national rankings
for ten years. His highest ranking on the
tennis circuit was No. 7 in the world in 1960.

Holmberg, a native New Yorker, graduated
from Brooklyn's Bishop Loughlin Memorial
High School, and went to Tulane University,
where he turned in a brilliant career on the
intercollegiate circuit. Before graduating in
1960 with a Bachelor of Arts degree,
Holmberg was named to the All-America team
three consecutive years, 1957-1959, was team
captain and the No. 1 player of the Green
Wave squad which captured the NCAA team
championship in 1959, and twice teamed
with Crawford Henry to win the NCAA
doubles championship, first in 1957 and
again in 1959.

As a freshman at Tulane in 1956,
Holmberg was crowned World champion in
the Junior championships at Wimbledon,
England. In later years, he was winner of the
U.S. National Men's Indoor Doubles
championship in 1961, and a finalist in 1962
and again in 1969. He also was a finalist in
the U.S. National Indoor Men's Singles
championship in 1968.

Holmberg won the Canadian Men's
Singles championship in 1965, the Canadian
Men's Doubles championship in 1965 and
1969 and the Interservice Men's Singles and
Doubles championship in 1962 and 1963.

As head tennis coach at West Point his
record was thirty-three victories, sixty-three
losses, and one tie. His best season was 1976
when the Cadets finished at 9-8-1. He
compiled a 41-25 record as squash coach.
The 1971-1972 season was his best when
Army finished 12-4. The following year the
Cadets had an 11-4 record.

Members of the 1972 Army pistol team receive All-America certificates from the National Rifle Association during a ceremony in the Athletic Department. Participating in the ceremony are, left to right, Col. William Schuder, director of athletics, Bill Epley, Lee Pollock, Col. (Ret.) C. J. Shaffer of the N.R.A. staff, Jim Ritter, Phil Neil, and Dave Gallay.

A LOOK INTO THE PAST

Year	Coach	Captain	Won	Lost	Tied
1923	None Listed	Thomas S. Timberman	13	1	0
1924	Capt. S.L. Scott	Richard H. Harrison	10	0	0
1925	Capt. S.L. Scott (21-2)	Carl W. Holcomb	11	2	0
1926	Lt. J.C. Hamilton	Marvin W. Peck	9	2	0
1927	Capt. C.P. Johnson	Frederick Funston, Jr.	4	3	0
1928	Capt. W.A. Dumas	John A. Samford	6	4	0
1929	Lt. G.B. Conrad	Oliver H. Gilbert	5	4	0
1930	Lt. G.B. Conrad (11-7-1)	Philip F. Kromer, Jr.	6	3	1
1931	Maj. F.B. Inglis	Charles F. Densford	7	3	0
1932	Maj. F.B. Inglis (11-7)	George Kumpe	4	4	0
1933	Lt. H.J. John	Carlyle W. Phillips	3	6	0
1934	Lt. H.J. John (3-11)	Karl T. Gould	0	5	0
1935	Lt. W.R. Hensey, Jr.	William W. Lapsley	3	4	0
1939	Lt. H.F. Sykes, Jr.	All 1st Classmen	0	6	0
1940	Capt. L.A. Vickrey	Jodie G. Stewart	6	5	0
1941	Capt. L.A. Vickrey	Mortimer B. Birdseye	16	3	0
1942	Capt. L.A. Vickrey	Ben F. Hardaway	13	3	0
1943	Capt. L.A. Vickrey (42-17)	John A. Hine & William J. Greene	7	6	0
1944	Maj. R.J. Mercer	William H. Walters	7	1	0
1945	Lt. Col. C.F. Leonard	Frederick W. Robinson	6	2	0
1946	Col. D.G. Gilbert	Edwin D. Fraser	9	0	0
1947	Lt. Col. R.B. Spragins	Charles K. Leech	5	1	0

CHAPTER 27

PISTOL

Cadets at the United States Military Academy have been competing in pistol since 1923. The first team compiled a 13-1 record and Army teams have been successful in this sport ever since, suffering only four losing seasons.

Army teams have compiled unbeaten records on fourteen occasions, the last coming during the 1981-1982 season when the Cadets finished with an unblemished 13-0 record.

Master Sergeant Huelet "Joe" Benner was one of the most successful Army pistol coaches, compiling a record of sixty-five victories and just seven defeats during his ten years of coaching at West Point from 1954-1963. During that span, four of his teams (1954, 1955, 1959-1960, 1960-1961) posted unbeaten records.

Huelet was an outstanding shooter in his own right, winning three world championships, six national titles, two Pan American championships, and two Olympic medals (Gold and Silver). Five of his Cadet shooters participated on the All-Army team while another was a Rhodes scholar and was invited to represent Britain in the 1960 Olympics.

Master Sergeant Herbert Roberts succeeded Benner and guided Army during four seasons. His teams won twenty-six consecutive matches from 1963-1964 to 1966-1967. Roberts' overall record was 32-3.

Sgt. Maj. Leonard Ross succeeded Roberts and recorded sixty-three victories and just eight defeats during his six years at the Academy. Two of his teams registered unbeaten records.

Master Sergeant Emil Heugatter guided the pistol team from 1973-1974 to 1975-1976 and was 35-3. Sergeant First Class John Smith coached from 1976-1977 to 1978-1979 and was 27-2, while SFC John McClellan followed with a 43-4 record. Today, Master Sergeant (Ret.) Jack McJunkin guides the pistol team.

Pistol teams at the Academy have won national championships seven times, winning five consecutive titles from 1962 to 1966, in 1968, and most recently in 1986.

Year	Coach	Captain	W	L	T
1948	Lt. Col. A.M. Murray	Charles R. Lehner	9	2	0
1949-1953	Pistol Discontinued				
1954	M. Sgt. Huelet L. Benner	John A. Poteat	8	0	0
1955	M. Sgt. Huelet L. Benner	Leland D. Floyd	5	0	0
1956	M. Sgt. Huelet L. Benner	Anthony J. Ortner	7	1	0
1956-57	M. Sgt. Huelet Benner	George V. Rogers	4	1	0
1957-58	M. Sgt. Huelet Benner	Dick S. Oberg	8	1	0
1958-59	M. Sgt. Huelet Benner	Cuthbert P. Hutton	5	2	0
1959-60	M. Sgt. Huelet Benner	John B. Hubard	8	0	0
1960-61	M. Sgt. Huelet Benner	Donald L. McBee	7	0	0
1961-62	SMaj. Huelet Benner	Charles D. Swick	6	1	0
1962-63	SMaj. Huelet Benner	Miles M. Eberts	7	1	0
1963-64	SMaj. Herbert Roberts (65-7)	Everett D. Grimes	8	1	0
1964-65	SMaj. Herbert Roberts	Calvin G. Kahara	9	0	0
1965-66	SMaj. Herbert Roberts	James A. Dickens	9	0	0
1966-67	SMaj. Herbert Roberts (32-3)	Robert M. Hartley	6	2	0
1967-68	SMaj. Leonard Ross	Robert L. Merritt	10	0	0
1968-69	SMaj. Leonard Ross	James C. Adamson	12	0	0
1969-70	SMaj. Leonard Ross	Victor L. Ross	9	3	0
1970-71	SMaj. Leonard Ross	Paul Drake	9	3	0
1971-72	SMaj. Leonard Ross	James S. Ritter	11	1	0
1972-73	SMaj. Leonard Ross (63-8) And MSgt. Emil Heugatter	William Epley	12	1	0
1973-74	MSgt. Emil Heugatter	Charles Gleichenhaus	11	1	0
1974-75	MSgt. Emil Heugatter	Cary Mehlenbeck	13	1	0
1975-76	MSgt. Emil Heugatter (35-3)	Robert G. Crosby	11	1	0
1976-77	SFC John Smith	Eric W. Stanhagen	7	1	0
1977-78	SFC John Smith	Patrick O. McGaugh	10	0	0
1978-79	SFC John Smith (27-2-0)	Louis B. Anderson	10	1	0
1979-80	SFC John McClellan	David J. Dinon	8	0	0
1980-81	SFC John McClellan	David B. Lemauk	9	0	0
1981-82	SFC John McClellan	Alan C. Guarino	13	0	0
1982-83	SFC John McClellan (43-4-0)	Edward H. Wentworth	13	4	0
1983-84	MSgt. Jack McJunkin	Leon Moores	11	5	0
1984-85	MSgt. Jack McJunkin	Stephen Witkowski	13	1	0
1985-86	MSgt. Jack McJunkin	Richard Shelton	8	1	0
1986-87	MSgt. Jack McJunkin (38-8-0)	Dominic Perriello	6	1	0

Army's 1965-1966 pistol team completed an unbeaten 9-0 record. Pictured are, left to right, Bob Merritt, a three-time All-America, Jim Stanley, another All-America, Sgt. Maj. Herbert Roberts, Pete Hanely, three-time All-America Jim Dickens, the team captain, and Ted Sendak.

Sergeant First Class John Smith, second row top right, guided the Army pistol team to an outstanding 11-1 record during his first year at West Point in 1975-1976. The only loss came at the hands of the Air Force by a 74-point margin. The Cadets defeated Navy by a comfortable margin, 7814 to 7757, and finished first in the National Rifle Association sectionals.

CHAPTER 28

Golf joined the intercollegiate sports family at West Point when Gen. Douglas MacArthur was superintendent. The first intercollegiate match was held in 1922 against Columbia. The Lions edged the Cadets by a 5-4 margin that day, but Army responded by trimming Rensselaer Polytechnic Institute and Syracuse University later in the season to finish at 2-1.

Fred Canausa coached the Army squad, while Mark McClure was the team captain. Canausa held the head coaching job for the longest period in history, remaining at the helm for twenty-one years before leaving following the 1942 season. During that span Army golf teams won sixty-one matches, lost forty-five and tied ten.

Although golf was discontinued for three years after the 1942 season, the West Point team won the Eastern Intercollegiate championship playing informally in 1944. The sport was resumed in 1945, coached by Lt. Col. Dan Chandler. The Cadets tied in matches against Sleepy Hollow Golf Club and the Naval Academy, but won the Eastern Intercollegiate championship.

William J. Schuder served as captain of the 1947 Army golf team which compiled a 1-4 record. Schuder returned to West Point to serve as director of intercollegiate athletics in 1971.

Bert Yancey, one of the most consistent golfers on the Professional Golf Association tour in the seventies, lettered in golf at West Point in 1961, but resigned from the Academy.

The West Point Golf Course was completed in the late forties and remains one of the most picturesque of college golf courses. However, the course is noted for its hills, along with its winding and narrow fairways which place a premium on hitting the ball straight rather than long distances.

Perhaps the most successful period in Army golf history occurred when Walter Browne took over as head coach in 1953. Brown remained at the helm until 1966 in which he compiled a record of eighty-nine victories, just thirty-one defeats, and one tie during his thirteen seasons at West Point. His 1960 Army team finished with an unblemished 9-0 record and won the Eastern Intercollegiate champion-

ship, while his last two squads (1964, 1965) finished with 11-1 and 13-1 records, respectively.

Denny West took over the reins from Browne in 1966 and was 22-5 during his two seasons. Nick Karl served as head coach for five seasons and led Army teams to a composite 37-25 record.

Chris Gurry replaced Karl in 1973 and was 18-11 in two seasons, while John Fox served as head coach in 1975, guiding Army to a 12-2 mark during his one season at West Point.

Maj. Paul Kirkegaard took over as head coach in 1976 and led Army to a 14-1 record and an 18-1 mark a year later before being reassigned. David Yates was selected as his replacement and quickly kept the Army program on top. Yates was 15-2 during his first season, and then compiled a 21-0 mark a year later. The twenty-one victories represents the most ever recorded by an Army team during a season.

When Yates left the Academy following the 1979 season, LTC Ed Temple, an associate professor in the Department of Foreign Languages, coached the varsity for one season and compiled a 20-6 record. Then John Means, former Colorado State coach, took over the head coaching responsibilities in 1981 and remains in that position today. Means started his coaching career on the right foot, leading the Cadets to an unblemished 16-0 record.

Army has won two Eastern Intercollegiate championships during its golf history. The 1945 team was the first to win an Eastern title, while the 1960 squad followed. Stanley G. Calder, captain of that 1945 team, also won the Eastern medalist championship in 1945, while Donald A. Johnson won the Eastern medalist title in 1966 as a sophomore. Johnson also served as team captain of the 1968 Army team.

Army golf teams were most consistent on their home course from 1974 to 1980 when they won seventy-eight straight matches.

The Cadets joined the Metro Atlantic Athletic Conference in 1982 and promptly won the conference championship against Manhattan, Fordham, Fairfield, St. Peter's College, and Iona College. LaSalle and Holy Cross joined the conference later. The Cadets have dominated the MAAC competition, winning every team championship since the start in 1982.

Army qualified for competition in the National Collegiate Athletic Association championships as a team on just one occasion under Coach John Means. However, several Army golfers have earned the right to compete in that national competition at the close of the spring season.

A LOOK INTO THE PAST

Year	Coach	Captain	Won	Lost	Tied
1922	Fred Canausa	Mark McClure	2	1	0
1923	Fred Canausa	James F. Early	4	0	1
1924	Fred Canausa	Emil Pasolli, Jr.	2	2	1
1925	Fred Canausa	William B. LeFavour	3	2	0
1926	Fred Canausa	Charles D. Sugrue	1	1	2
1927	Fred Canausa	Herman W. Schull	3	0	2
1928	Fred Canausa	Robert S. Isreal	1	4	0
1929	Fred Canausa	George E. Keeler	5	1	0
1930	Fred Canausa	Paul W. Blanchard	4	2	0
1931	Fred Canausa	Theodore W. Parker	3	2	1
1932	Fred Canausa	Frederick R. Young	4	2	0
1933	Fred Canausa	Franklin G. Smith	3	3	0
1934	Fred Canausa	Arthur F. Meier	2	4	0
1935	Fred Canausa	John J. Duffy	4	2	0
1936	Fred Canausa	David McCoach, III	4	1	1
1937	Fred Canausa	Wilbur E. Davis	4	0	2
1938	Fred Canausa	James H. Lynch	1	5	0
1939	Fred Canausa	William A. Garnett	2	4	0
1940	Fred Canausa	Joseph S. Hardin	2	4	0
1941	Fred Canausa	Ben I. Mayo	3	3	0
1942	Fred Canausa (61-45-10)	Thomas J. Hanley	4	2	0
Golf Discontinued 1943-1944					
1945	Lt. Col. Dan Chandler	Stanley G. Calder	0	0	2
1946	Al Collins	Fred W. Knight	2	3	0
1947	James E. Deal	William J. Schuder	1	4	0
1948	Dennis J. Lavender	William B. Caldwell	2	4	0
1949	Dennis J. Lavender	Clayton L. Moran	2	5	0
1950	Dennis J. Lavender	Thomas O. Brandon	1	5	0
1951	Dennis J. Lavender	Ernest G. Rose	2	6	0
1952	Dennis J. Lavender (13-21-0)	James N. Walter	6	1	0
1953	Walter Browne	Raymond F. Allen	4	3	0
1954	Walter Browne	Gerald E. VanValkenburg	5	3	1
1955	Walter Browne	Eugene A. Auer	5	2	0
1956	Walter Browne	James L. Stroope	5	2	0
1957	Walter Browne	Charles B. Stone	3	3	0
1958	Walter Browne	William R. Parks	2	5	0
1959	Walter Browne	Rand Edelstein	8	2	0
1960	Walter Browne	Rand Edelstein	9	0	0
1961	Walter Browne	James E. Jenz	7	3	0
1962	Walter Browne	John M. Woods	9	3	0
1963	Walter Browne	Warren B. Battis	8	3	0
1964	Walter Browne	Stephen B. Pembrook	11	1	0
1965	Walter Browne (89-31-1)	Harry N. Joyner	13	1	0
1966	Denny West	Freddy E. McFarren	10	4	0
1967	Denny West (22-5-0)	Andrew J. Nusbaum	12	1	0
1968	Nick Karl	Donald A. Johnson	7	5	0
1969	Nick Karl	John T. D. Casey	8	5	0
1970	Nick Karl	Gregory H. Knight	7	3	0
1971	Nick Karl	Charles Swannack	8	7	0
1972	Nick Karl (37-25-0)	Gordon R. Jaehne	7	5	0
1973	Chris Gurry	David Rodarte	10	5	0
1974	Chris Gurry (18-11-0)	David Rodarte	8	6	0
1975	John Fox (12-2)	Gregory A. Stone	12	2	0
1976	Maj. Paul Kierkegaard	Gregory A. Stone	14	1	0
1977	Maj. Paul Kierkegaard	John J. Powers	18	1	0
1978	Dave Yates	John W. Bressler	15	2	0
1979	Dave Yates (36-2-0)	Charles H. King	21	0	0
1980	Lt. Col. Edward Temple	Stephen E. Galing	20	6	0
1981	John Means	Michael J. Lessel	16	0	0
1982	John Means	Michael C. Smith	3	1	0
1983	John Means	Robert P. Smith	6	1	0
1984	John Means	John N. Schuster & David L. Goodling	6	1	0
1985	John Means	David L. Goodling	5	0	0
1986	John Means	Rob Lott	8	0	0
1987	John Means	Randy Chavez	4	0	0

The Army golf team in 1940 won matches over Fordham and Swarthmore, but dropped four other decisions during a period when the world was thinking about war. Team members included, first row, left to right, Robert Young, Earle W. Brown II, Frank Smiley, Coach Fred Canausa, and James Harper; back row, Walter Short, Miles Gayle, John Linderman, Thomas Hanley, and George MacMullin, Jr. Coach Canausa was the first golf coach at West Point, guiding the intercollegiate program from 1922 until 1942 when the sport was discontinued for two years. Army nonetheless played informally in 1944 and won the Intercollegiate championship. Coach Canausa's best year was 1929 when the Cadets won five of six matches.

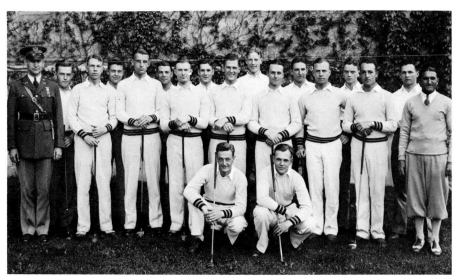

The Army golf team compiled a 3-2-1 record during the 1931 season, defeating Swarthmore, Massachusetts Institute of Technology, and Amherst. The Cadets also played to a 3-3 tie against Penn State, while dropping matches to Princeton and Lafayette. Pictured are, front row, left to right, James Cain and Sherburne Whipple, Jr.; second row, Lt. H. M. Jones, Officer-in-Charge, Robert W. Meals, George Mather, Frederick Young, Theodore W. Parker, Robert A. Stunkard, Sidney Giffin, Franklin G. Smith, and Coach Fred Canausa; back row, Frederick Weis, Charles Meade, David Pressnell, Robert Turner, Arthur F. Meier, William Yarbrough, Hugh Cary, and J. Paul Craig.

The 1927 Army golf team won three matches and tied two under the guidance of Coach Fred Canausa, far left. This is a photograph of some members of that squad for use in the Howitzer yearbook. The team captain was Herman W. Schull, Jr.

Army squash and tennis coach Bill Cullen, right, congratulates Cadet Walter Oehrlein after he won an International Squash Intercollegiate championship in 1965. Coach Cullen compiled an outstanding record at West Point. His tennis teams posted a record of eighty-two victories and just thirty defeats during seven seasons, 1964-1970, while his squash teams won seventy matches and lost just twenty-seven during the same span. Oehrlein is the only intercollegiate squash champion in West Point history.

A LOOK INTO THE PAST

Year	Coach	Captain	Won	Lost	Tied
1948	Leif O. Nordlie	Russell C. Ball	8	3	0
1949	Leif O. Nordlie	Charles W. Oliver	7	3	0
1950	Leif O. Nordlie	John A. Magee	4	6	0
1951	Leif O. Nordlie	Kermit D. Johnson	7	3	0
1952	Leif O. Nordlie	Robert B. King	10	1	0
1953	Leif O. Nordlie	Clifford Worthy	10	2	0
1954	Leif O. Nordlie	Rufus D. Hutcheson	8	3	0
1955	Leif O. Nordlie	Leon E. McKinney	7	4	0
1956	Leif O. Nordlie	Garrett V. Sidler	9	2	0
1956-57	Leif O. Nordlie	George W. Bailey	9	3	0
1957-58	Leif O. Nordlie	Donald R. Williams	8	4	0
1958-59	Leif O. Nordlie	Orthus K. Lewis	10	3	0
1959-60	Leif O. Nordlie	Henry B. Fisher	7	6	0
1960-61	Leif O. Nordlie	Richard McNear	9	5	0
1961-62	Leif O. Nordlie	James F. McQuillen	8	5	0
1962-63	Leif O. Nordlie (132-56)	Stephen Silvasy	11	3	0
1963-64	William C.B. Cullen	Richard V. Oehrlein	12	2	0
1964-65	William C.B. Cullen	Thomas C. Genoni	9	4	0
1965-66	William C.B. Cullen	Henry Langendorf	8	5	0
1966-67	William C.B. Cullen	James B. Allen	8	6	0
1967-68	William C.B. Cullen	Charles A. Vehlow	12	3	0
1968-69	William C.B. Cullen	Kenneth Fleming	11	3	0
1969-70	William C.B. Cullen	George Alcorn	10	4	0

Squash is a relatively new sport at the U.S. Military Academy, beginning intercollegiate competition in 1948. Leif O. Nordlie served as Army's first coach and developed a solid foundation for the squash program.

Nordlie held the coaching position for fifteen years, compiling a record of 132 victories and just 56 defeats. During his first season, Army won eight of eleven matches. One of Nordlie's finest seasons was in 1952 when the Cadets finished with a 10-1 record. The most victories his squash teams recorded in a season was eleven, that coming during his final year of coaching in 1962-1963. Army was 11-3 that year. Nordlie collected his 100th victory as Army's coach in 1959-1960 when the Cadets shut out Wesleyan 9-0.

William "Bill" C. B. Cullen replaced Nordlie in 1963-1964 and was an instant success as head coach. He led the Army team to a 12-2 record during the season and finished second in the National Intercollegiate championships, sharing that spot with Princeton.

Cullen spent seven years at West Point, compiling a record of seventy victories and just twenty-seven defeats. One of the highlights of his coaching tenure came in 1965 when Walter Oehrlein won an International Squash Intercollegiate championship in 1965. He is the only intercollegiate squash champion in Army history.

When Cullen resigned, assistant coach Ron Davis was elevated to the head coaching position for one season. Shortly after, the Academy named former Davis Cup star Ron Holmberg as the tennis and squash coach. Holmberg served five years as head squash coach, guiding the Cadets to a record of forty-nine victories and twenty-six defeats.

Lt. Col. John H. Bradley coached the squash team for one season, 1976-1977, before Paul Assaiante, a Springfield College graduate and an assistant gymnastics coach at the Academy, was named head tennis and squash coach. Assaiante, a native of Pearl River, New York, was an outstanding tennis and gymnastics competitor at Springfield.

Assaiante's first Army team won just four of ten matches, but during the remainder of his eight-year coaching tenure the Cadets never suffered a losing season. One of his best efforts came in 1980-1981 when Army finished with an 18-5 record, the most victories recorded in a season. Assaiante developed three squash All-America selections, Dan Hammond (1977-1978), a first-team selection, and second-team selections Dan Kellas (1982-1983) and Richard Clarke (1983-1984).

	(70-27)				
1970-71	Robert Davis & Ronald E. Holmberg	Gerald S. Petersen	4	8	0
1971-72	Ronald E. Holmberg	William D. James	12	4	0
1972-73	Ronald E. Holmberg	Joseph P. Cyr	11	4	0
1973-74	Ronald E. Holmberg	Geary O. Bauman	7	7	0
1974-75	Ronald E. Holmberg	Michael A. Killham	9	5	0
1975-76	Ronald E. Holmberg	Justin S. Huscher	10	6	0
	(49-26)				
1976-77	LTC. J.H. Bradley	Brian E. Smith	5	6	0
1977-78	Paul Assaiante	Daniel R. Hammond	4	6	0
1978-79	Paul Assaiante	Tracy H. Freeman	12	7	0
1979-80	Paul Assaiante	Robert J. Davis	15	6	0
1980-81	Paul Assaiante	Louis G. Yuengert	18	5	0
1981-82	Paul Assaiante	Terry A. Harmanson	13	9	0
1982-83	Paul Assaiante	Daniel B. Kellas	12	5	0
1983-84	Paul Assaiante	Richard Clarke	14	8	0
1984-85	Paul Assaiante	James Hamilton	10	8	0
	(98-54)				
1985-86	Satinder Bajwa	Brian Snell	8	10	0
1986-87	Satinder Bajwa	Robert Fancher	9	10	0
	(17-20)				

Army quarterback Warren Chellman hands off to a teammate during a 150-pound football game at West Point's Shea Stadium during the mid-seventies. The Cadets joined the Eastern Intercollegiate Lightweight Football League in 1957.

CHAPTER 30

LIGHTWEIGHT FOOTBALL

Lightweight football is an Eastern sport that was born in 1934 and affiliated with the Eastern College Athletic Conference in 1939. The sport provides an opportunity for young men who played high school football to continue their pursuits on the college level, though they may not have the size or strength to compete on the varsity level.

George E. Little of Rutgers pioneered the start of the 150-lb. Football League, and was joined by Pennsylvania, Princeton, Rutgers, Villanova, Yale, Cornell, and Lafayette. Rutgers won the first league championship in 1934, and repeated that feat the following season.

Although the league halted competition from 1943-1945 because of World War II, it resumed in 1946 and accepted the U.S. Naval Academy as its newest member. Navy took command, winning the league title during its first three seasons and nine championships during its first eleven years.

The U.S. Military Academy joined the league in 1957. Coach Earl "Red" Blaik asked Eric Tipton to join the West Point athletic department staff to handle the coaching responsibilities for both the 150-pound football team and the baseball squad. Blaik could not have selected a more knowledgeable coach.

Those who remember college football in the 1930s say Eric Tipton was one of the greatest punters to ever play the college game. He was an All-America tailback while at Duke from 1936-1938. He lettered three years and helped the Blue Devils compile an outstanding 25-4-1 record during his career in Durham, North Carolina.

Tipton's outstanding achievements as a college player and coach were detailed in an article written by Bob Kinney, sports information director at West Point. Kinney, who joined the West Point staff in 1963, worked with this veteran coach until he retired in 1977 after winning 338 games at the Academy.

"His record of athletic achievement surpasses a level that many would dare even to dream of, much less reach," wrote Kinney. Most would agree.

Tipton not only gained All-America honors at Duke in football, but he was enshrined in the National Football Foundation Hall of Fame. He also played professional baseball with the Philadelphia Athletics and the Cincinnati Reds. He played baseball for fifteen seasons, none ever below the Triple-A level.

When a fractured kneecap ended Tipton's playing days, he joined the College of William and Mary football staff as an assistant coach. He spent five years in Williamsburg, Virginia, as an offensive backfield coach and head baseball coach before accepting the position at West Point.

Tipton was an instant success, leading the lightweight football team to a league championship in its first year with a 5-0-1 record. Tipton repeated that success a year later when the Cadets compiled a 6-0 record.

During his twenty years as head coach, Tipton guided the 150-pound team to 104 victories, just fourteen defeats, and one tie. His Army teams won or shared thirteen league championships during that span. Since his departure the Cadets have won six other league titles, the last in 1986 when they shared the championship with Navy and Cornell.

During lightweight football's thirty years of history at the Academy, Army has had twenty-nine winning seasons. Only the 1963 squad, which won just two of five games, failed to record a winning campaign.

When Tipton departed in 1977, George Storck coached the Army lightweight team from 1977 through 1980. Coach Storck compiled a 16-5 record and won two league titles, in 1979 and 1980.

Maj. Larry Henly coached the 1981 squad to a 4-1 record and a share of the Eastern championship. Lt. Col. Bob Knapp took over in 1982 and guided the Cadets for two seasons, posting an 11-2 record and one league title.

In 1984, Tim Mingey took over the coaching chores and was 5-2 in each of his two seasons. When Mingey accepted a position to serve as the Army football recruiting coordinator, he relinquished his lightweight football coaching responsibilities to Bob Thompson. During his first season in 1986,

Thompson led the Cadets to a 5-2 record and a share of the Eastern championship with Navy and Cornell. It was Army's nineteenth title.

One of the unique aspects of lightweight football is that players weigh in two days prior to each game, and must not weigh more than 158 pounds. Teams cannot begin workouts until three weeks before their first game and scouting is not permitted.

An added attraction was added to the Army lightweight football schedule, thanks to the kindness of the residents of Pottsville, Pennsylvania. This coal mining town demonstrated its enthusiasm for our nation's service academies by inviting Army and Navy lightweight teams to compete in a bowl game, called none other than the Anthracite Bowl.

Pottsville residents rolled out the red carpet to the Army and Navy lightweight teams for the first time in 1983. The two teams were hosted at a Friday afternoon luncheon and then toured the Pottsville elementary schools. Each class supported either Army or Navy and demonstrated their enthusiasm throughout the visit.

Players from both teams are hosted by town families, play the game on Saturday, attend an awards banquet following the game, and then attend church services on Sunday. Some players even teach Sunday school.

Army and Cornell squared off in the 1986 Anthracite Bowl. It remains one of the most enjoyable trips of the season.

An Army running back picks up yardage during a 150-pound football game during the seventies. Players must weigh no more than 158 pounds two days before each game in the Eastern Lightweight Football League, and are weighed in just as wrestlers are weighed in for a match. No scouting is permitted in the league and practice sessions are limited.

A LOOK INTO THE PAST

Year	Coach	Captain	Won	Lost	Tied
1957	Eric Tipton	Bradley J. Johnson	5	0	1
1958	Eric Tipton	Richard D. Welch	6	0	0
1959	Eric Tipton	Herman T. Eubanks	5	1	0
1960	Eric Tipton	Eugene Witherspoon	5	1	0
1961	Eric Tipton	Walter R. Browne	5	1	0
1962	Eric Tipton	Eugene Blackwell	6	0	0
1963	Eric Tipton	William T. DiNeno	2	3	0
1964	Eric Tipton	Charles F. Shaw	6	0	0
1965	Eric Tipton	Thomas F. Hayes	5	1	0
1966	Eric Tipton	Gary W. Atkins	6	0	0
1967	Eric Tipton	John Throckmorton	4	2	0
1968	Eric Tipton	Kenneth M. Bevis	6	0	0
1969	Eric Tipton	John Lovelace	4	2	0
1968	Eric Tipton	John Lovelace	4	2	0
1970	Eric Tipton	Benjamin George	6	0	0
1971	Eric Tipton	Michael Scisco	5	1	0
1972	Eric Tipton	William L. Moore	6	0	0
1973	Eric Tipton	Royce Richardson	6	0	0
1974	Eric Tipton	Jay Gruskowski	6	0	0
1975	Eric Tipton	Bruce L. Weyrick	4	2	0
1976	Eric Tipton	Kenneth F. Miller	6	0	0
1977	George Storck	Thomas P. Bostick	3	2	0
1978	George Storck	Ronald Bonesteel	3	2	0
1979	George Storck	Game Captains	4	1	0
1980	George Storck	Alfred A. Coppola	6	0	0
1981	Maj. Larry Henly	Robert E. Scurlock	4	1	0
1982	Bob Knapp	Leonard McWherter	3	2	0
1983	Bob Knapp	Jeffrey D. Bertocci	8	0	0
1984	Tim Mingey	Anthony J. English & Thomas M. DeBerardino	5	2	0
1985	Tim Mingey	Ernest Marcone & Chris Townley	5	2	0
1986	Bob Thompson	Scott Andrews & James Yacone	5	2	0

*Army quarterback uncorks an accurate pass
during a 150-pound football game against
Pennsylvania at West Point's Shea Stadium in
1986. The Cadets compiled a 5-2 record that
season. Army has participated in lightweight
football since 1957.*

CHAPTER 31

WOMEN'S SPORTS AT WEST POINT

When President Gerald Ford signed legislation in 1975 to permit women to enter our nation's service academies, it created a near revolution among some West Point graduates and a revelation within the women's movement in the United States.

The first class entered in July of 1976, breaking uncharted territory in the history of West Point, the oldest service academy. It was difficult for everyone at first. Now, more than a decade has passed since the first group of women entered the U.S. Military Academy, and despite an occasional grumble from an old alumnus, the Corps of Cadets and the West Point community have adapted.

When women entered West Point they had to prove themselves. They had to succeed in academics and military training before being accepted. It took a good deal of time, patience, and some hard knocks, but women have succeeded and will continue to do so.

With women at the Military Academy, the Army athletic program also began a modest expansion. Basketball provided the outlet for the first women's competitive team. Nicknamed the "Sugar Smacks," the women's basketball squad began competition on a club basis. Dennis Van Fossen served as head coach.

Smack is a cadet slang term for a plebe or freshman at the Academy. Obviously, the "sugar" portion of the nickname referred to the feminine gender now residing within the Gothic gray walls of West Point.

The women's quintet was elevated to varsity status in 1977. Coach Joe Ciampi was named head coach and guided the "Lady Knights" to an 18-5 record. It was the start of a very successful history. During the past ten years the Army women's basketball team has won 179 games and lost 109.

During the first season, Carol Barkalow and Dena Caradimitropoulo led the squad, both with 13.8 scoring averages. Barkalow also set the pace with a season high thirty-point effort against Long Island University.

Coach Ciampi guided the Lady Knights to further success during the 1978-79 season. Army was 21-5 and finished second in the New York State Association for Intercollegiate Athletics for Women (AIAW) championships. The Lady Knights also finished third in the Princeton Invitational Tournament.

Two records were set that year. The Lady Knights scored 111 points during a win over the State University of New York at New Paltz, hammering the visitors by a seventy-two point margin. The latter record still stands, although the former record for most points was shattered in 1986-1987.

During the past ten years the women's basketball team has had eight winning seasons, including an 18-14 mark under Coach Harold Johnson in 1986-87. Johnson held the head coaching position longest, serving from 1980-81 until the conclusion of the 1986-87 campaign. He compiled a record of 123 victories and 86 defeats during his seven years at the helm.

Ciampi coached two years, compiling a 39-10 mark, before accepting the head coaching position at Auburn, where he has consistently led the Lady Tigers into the Top Twenty in Division I competition.

Elizabeth Cousins guided the Lady Knights during the 1979-1980 season, posting a 17-13 record.

During the history of women's basketball, three players have gained All-America recognition and six have scored over 1,000 points during their careers.

Pam Pearson was selected Army's first second-team All-America following the 1983-1984 season when the Lady Knights compiled a 25-3 rcord. Pearson received similar honors in 1984-1985. Julie DelGiorno gained second-team All-America honors following the 1985-1986 season, while guard Laurie Goetz gained third-team All-America recognition at the conclusion of the 1986-87 season.

Kim Hall was the first Army player to surpass 1,000 points during her career. She accomplished that during the 1980-1981 season, finishing with 1,106 points. Pat Walter was the second to break 1,000 points a year later when she finished with 1,108. Two years later, 1983-1984, Melody Smith set a career mark with 1,420 points. Pam Pearson became the fourth 1,000-point scorer in 1984-1985 with 1,010, and also set a career record with 881 rebounds.

Julie DelGiorno scored 1,270 points during her four-year career to become the fifth in history to break the 1,000-point plateau, while Laurie Goetz accomplished the same feat during the 1986-1987 season, scoring 1,331 points.

Competition began in women's indoor track during the 1978-1979 season. Capt. Chuck Hunsaker served as head coach. He remained in that position for three seasons, compiling an overall record of 28-9. The 1980-1981 season was one of the best as Hunsaker's squad finished first in the Eastern AIAW Division III Indoor championship. A year later the Lady Knights finished second.

Craig Sherman was head women's coach in 1981-1982, compiling a 5-5 mark, before Ron Bazil took over the women's and men's coaching responsibilities. Bazil has been at the helm for the past five seasons, producing a 13-1-1 record.

Women's swimming began varsity competition during the 1978-1979 season and has compiled an overall record of seventy-three victories and thirty-seven defeats during that span.

Susan Tendy was the first Army women's swimming coach, handling those chores four seasons. Her teams compiled an overall record of 30-15, including a 12-0 mark during the first year.

Jack Ryan, head coach of the men's team, assumed the women's coaching responsibilities as well in 1982-1983. The success continued. During the last five years, Ryan's squads have an overall record of forty-three victories and twenty-two defeats. He has developed several All-America swimmers as well.

The first All-America in women's swimming was Shelby Calvert. She gained those honors in 1980 in five events—the 100, 200, 500, and 1,650-yard freestyle events, and the 100-yard butterfly event. Katie Lunsford gained All-America honors in the 50-yard butterfly in 1982 and Tracy Garcia was an All-America in 1983 in the 50 breaststroke event.

Clare Hramiec gained All-America recognition four consecutive years. In 1984, she qualified for those honors in the 100 and 200-yard breaststroke events. She duplicated that effort a year later and also received that recognition in the 400-yard medley relay. In 1986, Hramiec again was an All-America in the 200 breaststroke, while last year she gained those honors in the 100 breaststroke event.

Jackie Haug and Jeanne Britanisky were All-Americas in the 100-yard backstroke event in 1985, while in 1986 Ann Marie Wycoff was an All-America in the 200 butterfly, the 200 individual medley, and the 400 individual medley.

In 1986-1987, Wycoff became the first Army women's national champion. She finished first in the 400-yard individual medley event and second in the 200-yard individual medley event at the NCAA Division II national championships. She also gained All-America honors in the 500-yard freestyle and the 200-yard butterfly.

Kathy Pierce was an All-America selection in the 200 and 400-yard individual medley events. Meg Martin gained All-America honors in the 100 and 200-yard breaststroke, Hramiec won All-America honors in the 100-yard breaststroke, and Carol Ann Heller was an All-America in the 500-yard freestyle.

The women's outdoor track team began competition in 1979, compiling a 6-2 record that first season. Susan Kellett served as team captain, while Capt. Hunsaker handled the coaching responsibilities. Hunsaker served for three seasons, registering a 14-3 record.

Craig Sherman was head coach for one season, 1982, guiding the Lady Knights to a perfect 6-0 record. Ron Bazil assumed the head coaching duties in 1983 and is 11-2.

During their first season the Army women's squad finished third at the New York State championships. Army won the New York State AIAW Division III title in 1981 and took runner-up honors a year later. That same year, 1982, Army finished first in the Division III championships and third at the nationals.

Army has had seven All-America selections. Tracy Hanlon and Alma Cobb gained All-America honors in 1981. Hanlon finished sixth in the long jump at the nationals with a jump of 17-8½ to gain All-America recognition, while Cobb was fourth in the shot put with a toss of 42 feet, 6 inches.

Hanlon and Cobb repeated those successes in 1982. Cobb was fifth in the discus event (132-3) and first in the heptathlon (4,895 points), while Hanlon won the long jump event with a leap of 19 feet, 3 inches, an Academy and meet record. Ann Buckingham took a third in the high jump, while Teresa Southworth, Buckingham, Michelle Walla, and Mary List qualified for All-America recognition in the mile relay with a time of 4:01.12.

In 1983, Hanlon gained All-America honors at the NCAA Division II championships by finishing second in the Heptathlon with 5,402 points. She also was second in 1984 and fifth in the Division I Heptathlon with 5,560 points.

In 1986, Pam Pearson gained All-America honors in the long jump and triple jump, while Teresa Sobiesk was fourth in the 5,000-meter run to gain her All-America honors. This past season, Diana Wills was third in the triple jump at the nationals to gain All-America recognition.

Women's cross country began competition in 1978 and compiled a 6-3 record under Capt. Chuck Hunsaker. His squad also finished twentieth at the Eastern championships. Hunsaker's final two seasons produced unblemished 8-0 and 6-0 records. In 1979 the Cadets finished second at the Eastern AIAW championships and ninth at the NAIA Division III national championships. In 1980, Hunsaker's squad won the Easterns and finished ninth at the nationals. Teresa Sobiesk gained All-America honors in women's cross country in 1986, the only woman to accomplish that honor.

Women's volleyball began competition in the fall of 1978, and Coach Bob Bertucci led the Lady Knights to a 17-9 record. Wendy Teach served as head coach in 1979, guiding her squad to a 16-11 record.

In 1980, Gail Bennett was named head coach and

remained at that position for three seasons. Bennett's best season was the 1982 campaign when Army finished 35-17-2.

Bob Gambardella became head coach in 1983 and has led the Lady Knights to four straight winning seasons, including a 40-12 record a year ago, the most victories in a season.

Army began intercollegiate competition in women's softball in 1979 under the guidance of Coach Dennis Helsel. Helsel's squad finished 14-9 and placed second in the New York State AIAW championship. A year later, Helsel led his team to a 10-7 record.

The best season for the women's softball squad was in 1986 when Coach Al Arceo led the Cadets to a 27-7 record, the most victories in a season. Jill Schurtz, a hard-throwing pitcher, was the team captain. Arceo had more success in 1987 when Army finished at 23-18.

Chris Batjer coached the first intercollegiate women's tennis team at West Point, posting a 7-4 mark in her first season. Steve Medoff coached the women's team for two years, finishing with an outstanding record of thirty victories and just three defeats.

When Medoff left the Academy, Pete Castellano took over and coached the women's team to a composite 69-36 record over the next five seasons. He was replaced by Maggie Morris last year, but the Lady Knights slipped to 9-14. Most recently the women's tennis program was taken over by Jim Worthington.

The newest of the women's intercollegiate sports is soccer. Gene Ventriglia, an outstanding high school soccer coach from the mid-Hudson region, guided Army to a 9-6-3 mark in 1986. Natalie Conroe served as team captain.

Army forward Kim Hall sinks a basket on a driving layup against St. John's at the Army Field House in 1981. Hall was the first woman player to score more than 1,000 points in her career, finishing with 1,106.

Army forward Julie DelGiorno is congratulated by Lt. Gen. Willard W. Scott, superintendent of the U.S. Military Academy, after scoring her 1,000th career point during the 1985-1986 season. DelGiorno also was selected a Division II second team All-America following the conclusion of her final season. She finished with 1,270 points to finish third on the all-time Army career list.

313

Army forward Pam Pearson (30) sinks a jump shot during a game in 1985. Pearson is the first woman to receive All-America honors in basketball. She was selected a second team All-America during the 1983-1984 season when Army finished 25-3 and won the NCAA Eastern Regional Division II championship. She received similar honors at the conclusion of the 1984-1985 season, closing out her career with 1,010 points and a career record 881 rebounds.

Laurie Goetz closed out her women's basketball career at West Point following the 1986-1987 season. She became the second leading scorer in Army history with 1,340 points. She also was selected a third team All-America.

The first Army women's intercollegiate basketball team is pictured here prior to the start of the 1977-1978 season. Coach Joe Ciampi, currently the head women's basketball coach at Auburn University, is kneeling at the far left. Christi Stevens, holding the ball, is the first team captain, a position she held during her four years at the Academy. Kim Hall (42) went on to become the first woman player at West Point to score over 1,000 points.

The 1986-1987 Army women's basketball team is pictured here. Coach Harold Johnson is at the far left. Assistant coach Lynn Chiavaro is to the right of Johnson. She was elevated to the head coaching position for the 1987-1988 season.

Shelby Calvert is the first Army women's swimmer to gain All-America honors. She achieved those honors in 1980 in six events— the 100, 200, 500, and 1,650-yard freestyle events and the 100 and 200-yard butterfly events.

Ann Marie Wycoff, a 1986 All-America swimmer in the 400 and 200-yard individual medley events and the 200-yard butterfly, is the first Army women's national champion. Wycoff won a national title during the 1986-1987 season, finishing first in the 400-yard individual medley at the NCAA championships.

Tracy Garcia won All-America honors in 1983 in the 50-yard breaststroke event.

Tracy Hanlon gained All-America honors in women's track during the 1982 season, finishing sixth in the long jump at the nationals with a jump of 17 feet, 8 inches. She repeated that honor a year later, winning the long jump event at the nationals with a leap of 19 feet, 3 inches, both Academy and meet records.

Julie DelGiorno (32) looks for the open player during a women's basketball game in the Central Gymnasium in 1986. DelGiorno scored 1,270 points during her four years at the Academy, the fifth women's player to score over 1,000 points during her career.

Julie DelGiorno goes up for a jump shot during a game against C. W. Post in 1986 at the Multi-Purpose Sports Complex.

Kim Hall is pictured here prior to a practice session in 1981.

Pat Walter is the second women's basketball player to score more than 1,000 points during her career. She moved past Kim Hall as the career leader with 1,108 points. Hall had 1,106 points.

Kim Hall receives congratulations from Lt. Gen. Andrew J. Goodpaster, superintendent, after scoring her 1,000th point during a game against C. W. Post in 1981. Hall was the first women's player to score more than 1,000 points, finishing with 1,106.

The Army women's basketball team elected co-captains during the 1983 season, Alma Cobb and Melody Smith. Cobb (24) and Smith (42) flank Coach Harold Johnson. Smith is Army's all-time career scorer in women's basketball, finishing with 1,420 points.

Kim Hall (42) goes high in the air to deflect a shot taken by a Fordham player during a game in the Central Gymnasium in 1977.

A LOOK INTO THE PAST— WOMEN'S TENNIS

Year	Coach	Captain	Won	Lost	Tied
1979	Chris Batjer	Sandra Nikituk	7	4	0
1979-80	Steve Medoff	Sandra Nikituk	13	3	0
1980-81	Steve Medoff	Bonny Epstein & Kathryn Carlson	17	0	0
1981-82	Pete Castellano	Gail Petty	14	7	0
1982-83	Pete Castellano	Kathy Spaulding & Kim Dee	7	12	0
1983-84	Pete Castellano	Susan Meckfessel	16	8	0
1984-85	Pete Castellano	Lelia True	19	1	0
1985-86	Pete Castellano (69-36)	Kristen Powell	13	8	0
1986-87	Maggie Morris	Tanja Shipman & Aimee Lenz	9	14	0

A LOOK INTO THE PAST— WOMEN'S SOFTBALL

Year	Coach	Captain	Won	Lost
1979	Dennis Helsel	Diane Stoddard	10	7
1980	Dennis Helsel (20-14)	Diane Stoddard	10	7
1981	Lorraine Quinn	Lori Utchel	9	11
1982	Suzie Horne	Mandy Fulshaw	9	11
1983	Lorraine Quinn	Eileen Mulholland	6	16
1984	Harold Johnson	Marcia Ganoe	18	14
1985	Harold Johnson (28-36)	Lori Stocker	10	22
1986	Al Arceo	Jill Schurtz	27	7
1987	Al Arceo (50-25)	Tresa LaCamera	23	18

A LOOK INTO THE PAST— WOMEN'S VOLLEYBALL

Year	Coach	Captain	Won	Lost	Tied
1978	Bob Bertucci	Claire Kirby & Karen Kinsler	17	9	0
1979	Wendy Teach	Jane Perkins	16	11	0
1980	Gail Bennett	Yvonne Doll	13	18	0
1981	Gail Bennett	Cindy Glazier	29	26	1
1982	Gail Bennett	Joyce Schossau	35	17	2
1983	Bob Gambardella	Brigite Wahwassuck	21	14	0
1984	Bob Gambardella	Michelle Walla	27	9	0
1985	Bob Gambardella	Wilma Larsen	23	10	0
1986	Bob Gambardella	Shelly Dye	40	12	0

A LOOK INTO THE PAST— WOMEN'S OUTDOOR TRACK

Year	Coach	Captain	Won	Lost	Tied
1979	Capt. Charles Hunsaker	Susan P. Kellett	6	2	0
1980	Capt. Charles Hunsaker	Susan P. Kellett	4	1	0
1981	Capt. Charles Hunsaker (14-3)	Diane L. Pittman	4	0	0
1982	Craig Sherman	Roberta B. Baynes	6	0	0
1983	Ron Bazil	Marianne O'Brien	2	0	0
1984	Ron Bazil	Amy S. McDonald & Tracy S. Hanlon	5	0	0
1985	Ron Bazil	Corine R. Hall	3	1	0
1986	Ron Bazil	Marilyn Gibbs	0	0	0
1987	Ron Bazil (11-2)	Maria Smith	1	1	0

A LOOK INTO THE PAST— WOMEN'S SOCCER

Year	Coach	Captain	Won	Lost	Tied
1986	Gene Ventriglia	Natalie Conroe	9	6	3

A LOOK INTO THE PAST— WOMEN'S SWIMMING

Year	Coach	Captain	Won	Lost	Tied
1978-79	Susan Tendy	Bobbi L. Fiedler	12	0	0
1979-80	Susan Tendy	Bobbi L. Fiedler	6	3	0
1980-81	Susan Tendy	Nancy L. Harmon	7	5	0
1981-82	Susan Tendy (30-15)	Meet Captains	5	7	0
1982-83	John L. Ryan, Jr.	Judy Cain	5	7	0
1983-84	John L. Ryan, Jr.	Chris Gayagas	7	9	0
1984-85	John L. Ryan, Jr.	Debra Lane	12	2	0
1985-86	John L. Ryan, Jr.	Molly Hagan	8	3	0
1986-87	John L. Ryan, Jr. (43-22)	Clare Hramiec	11	1	0

A LOOK INTO THE PAST— WOMEN'S INDOOR TRACK

Year	Coach	Captain	Won	Lost	Tied
1978-79	Capt. Charles Hunsaker	Denise I. Dawson	6	4	0
1979-80	Capt. Charles Hunsaker	Terry J. Tepper	11	3	0
1980-81	Capt. Charles Hunsaker	Diane L. Pittman	11	2	0
1981-82	Craig Sherman	Harlene A. Nelson	5	5	0
1982-83	Ron Bazil	Kathleen Schmidt	2	1	0
1983-84	Ron Bazil	Ann Buckingham	4	0	0
1984-85	Ron Bazil	Mary List	3	0	0
1985-86	Ron Bazil	Michelle Collins	2	0	0
1986-87	Ron Bazil (13-1-1)	Regina Weinpahl	2	0	1

A LOOK INTO THE PAST— WOMEN'S BASKETBALL

Year	Coach	Captain	Won	Lost
1977-78	Joseph Ciampi	Christi L. Stevens	18	5
1978-79	Joseph Ciampi (39-10)	Christi L. Stevens	21	5
1979-80	Elizabeth Cousins	Christi L. Stevens	17	13
1980-81	Harold Johnson	Melissa Miles & Magdaline C. Caradimitropoulo	21	13
1981-82	Harold Johnson	April M. Hughlett	15	14
1982-83	Harold Johnson	Melody Smith & Alma Cobb	11	16
1983-84	Harold Johnson	Alma Cobb & Melody Smith	25	3
1984-85	Harold Johnson	Karen Short	14	15
1985-86	Harold Johnson	Julie DelGiorno	19	11
1986-87	Harold Johnson (123-86)	Laurie Goetz	18	14

A TRIBUTE TO THE 1988 COACHING STAFF

The United States Military Academy has had a long and illustrious athletic history since intercollegiate competition began in 1890 when Army and Navy met in football on The Plain. Since that time cadet athletes have been trained, nurtured, and developed through an ever-expanding athletic program.

The importance of this athletic training and the success it brings on the "fields of friendly strife" plays an important role in developing officer-leaders to defend our national heritage. Gen. Douglas MacArthur felt very strongly about the purpose of athletics by orchestrating a major expansion of this program that has been carried forward by superintendents who followed.

Today, the Military Academy fields twenty-eight intercollegiate teams that play a regional and national schedule. The importance of the professionalism of those men and women who carry the responsibility of training these young men and women cannot be underestimated.

The Army coaching staff today plays an integral role in the development of the cadet-athletes, just as their predecessors did in carving out West Point's sports history. We present the Army head coaching staff:

Al Arceo
Women's Softball

Satinder Bajwa
Squash

Ron Bazil
Men & Women's
Cross Country & Track

Andy Bowers
Water Polo

Larry Butler
Gymnastics

Lynn Chiavaro
Women's Basketball

Joe Chiavaro
Men's Soccer

Bob Detrich
Men's Tennis

Jack Emmer
Lacrosse

Bob Gambardella
Women's Volleyball

Ken Hamill
Rifle

Jack McJunkin
Pistol

John Means
Golf

Rob Riley
Hockey

Dan Roberts
Baseball

Jack Ryan
Men & Women's Swimming

Ed Steers
Wrestling

Bob Thompson
Lightweight Football

Gene Ventriglia
Women's Soccer

Jim Worthington
Women's Tennis

Les Wothke
Men's Basketball

Jim Young
Football

CHAPTER 32

A SPECIAL TRIBUTE

There is little doubt in anyone's mind that personalities such as Gen. Douglas MacArthur, Earl "Red" Blaik, Glenn Davis, Doc Blanchard, and Pete Dawkins dominated the history of sports at the United States Military Academy.

However, there are two gentlemen whose love of West Point, interest in cadets, and a special dedication to the Academy motto—Duty, Honor, Country—have made them giants among these exceptional athletes. Coming at different times, and from different places, Marty Maher, a friendly immigrant Irishman, and Russell P. "Red" Reeder, a World War II hero, have carved out an indelible historical spot among those who have touched West Point.

Marty Maher came to West Point in 1896 and went to work in the Cadet Mess as a waiter. He spoke of his job in the Cadet Mess in an article written by the late Joe Cahill, former sports information director, in 1946.

"I'll niver forget the first table I set, either," chortled Marty. "They had a knife, a fork and two spoons. When they told me the second spoon was fer dessert, I wus wunderin' what that would be. Parsnips was another funny dish to be havin' on the table. We used to throw them to the hogs in Ireland."

Marty found the work difficult at first, but he learned quickly. He received thirteen dollars a month with "breakage" out. After he dropped a full tray of dishes on a waxed floor one time, he thought it was time to make a change.

Maher enlisted in the Army, and his first assignment was in the West Point gymnasium. There he remained for most of his thirty years. He went from being a custodian to becoming a swimming instructor, and finally a trainer for the football team.

Marty built a saga around his technique as a swimming instructor, even though he hated the water. In his article, Cahill recalled that Maher guaranteed to teach anyone to swim in five lessons, but did all of his strokes from the deck of the pool.

After thirty years of service, Maher retired from the Army at the rank of technical sergeant. The next day he joined the Military Academy staff as a civilian, never even leaving his office in the gymnasium. When he retired again in 1946, he was given a full dress review by the Corps of Cadets.

Gen. Jacob L. Devers, the chief of army ground forces at that time, wrote to Marty regarding his retirement in 1946: "You are one of the great men of your time—always full of enthusiasm and a burning desire to get your job done more quickly and better than anyone else. You came all the way up through the ranks and by your example, sound advice, your wealth of historical facts, and your great loyalty to the United States Military Academy and the things it stood for, you influenced more young leaders for good at the starting point of their careers than almost any other man known to me."

Another article written in the *New York Times* by the late Arthur Daley dealt with the legendary sergeant from West Point, and attests to the profound influence this Irish immigrant had during his fifty years at West Point.

In 1986 when the Army football team defeated Air Force and Navy to win the Commander-in-Chief's Trophy, President Ronald Reagan made the presentation in the White House. Coach Jim Young and many senior members of the squad journeyed to Washington, D.C. for the ceremony. Joining the football team for the award presentation was Col. Russell P. "Red" Reeder. At the age of eighty-six it takes a good deal of effort to get around, but he was not about to miss this historic occasion. It is perhaps symbolic of Reeder's love of West Point and this great nation.

Reeder was assigned to command the Twelfth Infantry Regiment in 1944 by Gen. Omar Bradley. He led his regiment ashore on D-Day, June 6, 1944, at Utah Beach. For his efforts Reeder received the Distinguished Service Cross, the first awarded during the invasion of Europe. On the sixth day of the Normandy invasion, Reeder was severely wounded in both legs, hip, elbow, and back by a German .88 millimeter shell. He was hospitalized for a month and then flown to Walter Reed Hospital where his left leg was amputated below the knee.

After suffering the agony of losing a leg, Reeder was retired from the Army in the fall of 1945. However, he was placed on active duty the next day and transferred to the Military Academy where he commanded the Second Regiment of the Corps of Cadets. He helped initiate a leadership course at West Point at the direction of Maj. Gen. Maxwell D. Taylor.

In 1947, he retired from the Army again and joined the Army Athletic Association as an assistant athletic director. Reeder was responsible for the maintenance operation of the physical plant. He also coached the Plebe baseball team and assisted with the varsity for twelve years. He served two tours on the Board of Trustees of the Association of Graduates.

At the age of sixty-five, Reeder became an author, writing a book entitled *The Mackenzie Raid*. He also collaborated with his sister, Nardi Reeder Campion, to write *The West Point Story, Born at Reveille,* and *Bringing Up the Brass,* a story on none other than Marty Maher.

Reeder retired from the Army Athletic Association on June 15, 1967, but he resides in nearby Garrison, New York to keep close tabs on the Academy.

At the age of seventy-seven, Reeder was given a "day" at West Point during the Army-Duke football game. Al De-Santis, a columnist for the *Middletown Times Herald Record,* wrote a tribute to this gentleman of sports and his big "day."

APPENDIX

USMA OLYMPIC COMPETITORS

1912 Stockholm

Guy V. Henry, Jr.	1898	Riding
John C. Montgomery	1903	Riding
Ephrain F. Graham	1903	Riding
Scott D. Breckinridge	X1904	Fencing
George S. Patton, Jr.	1905	Fencing, Modern Pentathlon
Harold M. Rayner	1912	Fencing

1920 Antwerp

John B. A. Barry	X1902	Riding
Francis W. Honeycut	1904	Fencing
Berkely T. Merchant	1905	Riding
William W. West	1905	Riding
Sloan Doak	1907	Riding
Robert Sears	1909	Fencing, Modern Pentathlon
Harry D. Chamberlain	1910	Riding
Karl C. Greenwalt	1912	Riding
Harold M. Rayner	1912	Fencing, Modern Pentathlon
Alexander M. Weyand	1916	Wrestling
Eugene L. Vidal	Nov. 1918	Track
Thomas R. Denny	Nov. 1918	Track
Joseph A. Cranston	1919	Boxing
Henry I. Szymanski	1919	Wrestling
Perry Allen	X1911	Polo

1924 Paris

Sloan Doak	1907	Riding
Edgar W. Taulbee	1916	Riding
Ernest N. Harmon	Apr. 1917	Modern Pentathlon
Frank L. Carr	Aug. 1917	Riding
Frederick R. Pitts	1920	Modern Pentathlon
Sidney R. Hinds	1920	Shooting
George H. Bare	1920	Modern Pentathlon
Lawrence V. Castner	1923	Fencing
John V. Grombach	1923	Boxing
Chan F. Coulter	1925	Track
George W. Lermond	1930	Track

1928 Amsterdam

Sloan Doak	1907	Riding
Harry D. Chamberlain	1910	Riding
Harold M. Raymer	1912	Fencing
Frank L. Carr	Aug. 1917	Riding
Edward Y. Argo	X June 1918	Riding
Charles J. Barrett	1922	Modern Pentathlon
Peter C. Hains, III	1924	Modern Pentathlon
Aubrey S. Newman	1925	Modern Pentathlon
Richard W. Mayo	1928	Fencing, Modern Pentathlon
Louis A. Hammack	1929	Wrestling

1932 Los Angeles

Harry D. Chamberlain	1910	Riding
John T. Cole	Apr. 1917	Riding
Edward Y. Argo	X June 1918	Riding
John W. Wofford	1920	Riding
Leroy J. Stewart	1922	Riding
Earl F. Thomson	1922	Riding
Andrew A. Frierson	1924	Riding
Carl W. A. Raguse	1924	Riding
Richard W. Mayo	1928	Modern Pentathlon
Brookner W. Brady	1928	Modern Pentathlon
Raymond W. Curtis	1927	Riding
Clayton J. Mansfield	1928	Modern Pentathlon
Gustave M. Heiss	1931	Fencing

1936 Berlin

Dean Hudnutt	1916	Shooting
Cornelius C. Jadwin	June 1918	Riding

Earl F. Thomson	1922	Riding
Carl W. A. Raguse	1924	Riding
C. Stanton Babcock	1925	Riding
Milo H. Matteson	1925	Riding
John M. Willems	1925	Riding
Raymond W. Curtis	1927	Riding
Thomas J. Sands	1928	Fencing
Frederick R. Weber	1930	Fencing, Modern Pentathlon
Gustave M. Heiss	1931	Fencing
Alfred D. Starbird	1933	Modern Pentathlon
Charles F. Leonard, Jr.	1935	Modern Pentathlon

1948 London

Earl F. Thomson	1922	Riding
Andrew A. Frierson	1924	Riding
Franklin F. Wing, Jr.	1930	Riding
Frank S. Henry	1933	Riding
Charles A. Symroski	1935	Riding
Charles H. Anderson	1938	Riding
George B. Moore	1941	Modern Pentathlon
John W. Donaldson	1944	Modern Pentathlon
Hale Baugh	1946	Modern Pentathlon
Richard L. Gruenther	1946	Modern Pentathlon

1948 Saint Moritz

Edward F. Crowley	1946	Hockey

1952 Helsinki

Guy K. Troy	1946	Modern Pentathlon
Frederick L. Denman	1951	Modern Pentathlon
Harlan W. Johnson	1951	Modern Pentathlon
John E. B. Wofford	X1953	Riding

1960 Rome

Garland D. O'Quinn, Jr.	1958	Gymnastics
Edward Bagdonas	1959	Track
Ronald L. Zinn	1962	Track

1960 Squaw Valley

Laurence J. Palmer	1959	Hockey

1964 Tokyo

Joseph B. Amlong	1961	Rowing
Ronald L. Zinn	1962	Track

1968 Mexico City

Maurice T. Lough	1964	Modern Pentathlon
Maurice B. Silliman	1968	Basketball

1972 Munich

Robert S. Dow	X1966	Fencing
Lyle B. Nelson	1971	Biathlon

1976 Innsbruck

Lyle B. Nelson	1971	Biathlon

1980 Lake Placid

Lyle B. Nelson	1971	Biathlon

1984 Sarajevo

Lyle B. Nelson	1971	Biathlon

1988 Calgary

Lyle B. Nelson	1971	Biathlon

X—Attended but did not graduate

BIBLIOGRAPHY

Primary Sources:

Historical files from the Sports Information Office at the U.S. Military Academy, the Association of Graduates, and the Archives of the U.S. Military Academy Library. Additional information was obtained from the *Howitzer* class yearbooks from 1894 until 1986, and photographs from the Associated Press, International News Organization, and the Archives of the USMA Library.

Books:

Cohane, Tim, *Gridiron Grenadiers, The Story of West Point Football,* New York, 1948.

Cohane, Tim, *You Have to Pay the Price,* New York, 1959.

Cohane, Tim, *Great College Football Coaches of the Twenties and Thirties,* New Rochelle, N.Y., 1973.

Danzig, Allison, *The History of American Football,* Englewood Cliffs, N.J., 1956.

Hill, Dean, *Football Through the Years,* New York, N.Y., 1940.

Edson, James S., *The Black Knights of West Point,* New York, N.Y., 1954.

Koger, Jim, *National Champions (History of Football 1900-1969),* New York, N.Y., 1970.

Schoor, Gene, *The Army-Navy Game, A Treasury of the Football Classic,* New York, 1967.

Reeder, Red, and Nardi Reeder Campion, *The West Point Story,* New York, N.Y., 1956.

Photographic Credits:

Acme Newspictures
Press Association Inc.
Salvatore Palazzo, U.S. Army Photographer
Sean Brogan, U.S. Army Photographer
Dave Meyer, U.S. Army Photographer
Vince Guariglia, U.S. Army Photographer
Mike Fusco, U.S. Army Photographer
Al Murphy, U.S. Army Photographer
Charles W. Kelley Jr., New York, N.Y.
United Press International
Diane Sheridan, U.S. Army Photographer
John J. Tierney
The White House Photographic Staff
Gary Betush, U.S. Army Photographer
Ron Dixon, U.S. Army Photographer
U.S. Navy Photographs
Robert Johnson, The *Tennessean*
Steve Petrak, U.S. Army Photographer
Wide World Photos, New York, N.Y.
Frank Jurkoski, International News Photos

INDEX

Sylvans of New York, 14, 212, 214
Szarenski, Dan, 266
Szvetecz, Ed, 139

T
Tandy, Fremont S., 54
Tate, Danny, Lt., 20
Tate, Frederic H. S., 238, 294
Tatum, Mary Elizabeth, 89
Taylor, Maxwell, Maj. Gen., 93
Taylor, Milton C., 259
Temple, Ed, 301
Tendy, Susan, 312
Tennis—A Look into the Past, 296
Terrible Turks, 283
Terzopoulos, Nick, 248
Thayer, Sylvanus, 14, 160
Thigpen, Willie, 172
Thomas, Charles E., 288
Thompson, Bob, 307, 308
Thompson, Donald W., 202
Thompson, Mike, 233
Thorlin, John F., 270
Thorpe, Jim, 37
Tibbets, Gene, 272
Tillar, Donaldson, 271, 272
Tim Cohane, 87
Timberlake, Ed, 20, 23
Timberlake, Patrick, 54
Tindall, Richard G., 294
Tipton, Arthur, 32
Tipton, Eric, 214, 225, 226, 228, 307
Toczylowski, Stephen, 110
Topping, Gary, 164
Torney, Henry, 32, 34
Torrence, Jim, 273
Touchstone, F. Morris, 271
Town Ball, 213
Track—A Look into the Past, 244
Trahan, Eugene, A., 288
Trahan, R., 248
Trainor, Warren, 289, 291
Tranchini, Joe, 144
Travis, William B., 259
Trent, John, 97, 131
Trevor, George, 91
Trice, Harley, 66
Triplet, William S., 54
Trubin, Chester S., 280
Trudeau, Jack, 184
True, Clint, 68, 271, 272
Trujillo, Dennis, 247, 252-255
Truman, Bess, 117
Truman, Harry S., President, 94, 117, 118
Truman, Margaret, 117
Truxes, Arthur H., 253
Truxton, Thomas, 262, 271, 272
Tucker, Arnold, 89, 91, 93-96, 113, 114, 116
123-126
Tucker, William H., 294
Turner, Robert, 303
Tuttle, Robert, 202

U
U.S. Hockey Hall of Fame, 232
Uberecken, Hank, 150
Uebel, Pat, 136, 139
Ullrich, Carl, 179, 187
Ulrich, Bill, 146, 148
Urban, Wade, 201
Usry, Don, 140, 144

V
Van Fleet, James, 15, 45, 52
Van Fossen, Dennis, 311
Van Roo, Robert, 259
Van Sant, John, 289, 291
Van Volkenburgh, Robert Heber, 253
Vanderbush, Al, 140, 156, 169
Vaughan, Gwynn, 148
Vauthier, Louis, 279, 281
Velarde, Servando, 279
Ventriglia, Gene, 313
Vichules, Leo D., 207
Vidal, Eugue, 39, 156, 243
Vidal, Felix, 66

Violations, N.C.A.A., 168
Vitty, Rod, 216
Vollmann, Phillip D., 280
Vollrath, Tom, 248

W
Waldron, Albert W., 207
Waldrop, Ken, 148, 166
Walker, Gerald, 181, 184
Walker, Kirby, 20, 23
Walla, Michelle, 312
Walsh, Bill, 121
Walter, Pat, 311, 317
Walterhouse, Dick, 122
Ward, Gene, 163, 164
Ward, James Montgomery, 213
Ward, Jim, 164, 166
Warmath, Murray, 147
Warner, Jim, 248
Warren, John W., 54
Warren, Mike, 248
Washington Hall, 229
Watkins, James 102
Watkins, Jim, 88
Watkins, Paul, 157
Webb, A. Norman, 271, 276
Webb, Bill, 122
Webb, William, 110
Weber, Frederick R., 279
Webster, Frank, 212
Wehle, Phillip, 281
Weis, Frederick, 303
Weiss, Frank, 201
Wells, Frank, 257
Welsh, George, 136
Wendel, Martin, 110
Wesson, Charlie, 26
West, Denny, 301
West, William, 122
Westmoreland, William C., Gen., 165
Westphallinger, Henry R., 238
Westrum, Wes, 216, 226
Weyand, Alexander, 37, 39, 40, 156, 172
Wheat, C. E., 295
Whipple, Sherburne, Jr., 303
White, Chris, 184
White, Ernest J. Jr., 202
White, George Phillip, 214
White, Jo Jo, 196
White, Walter C., 54
Whiteside, Houston L., 219
Whitlow, Robert V., 202
Whitson, Wallace E., 54
Wierings, J. S., 225
Wightkin, Bill, 129
Wilby, Francis B., Maj. Gen., 88
Wilhelm, Walter M., 34
Wilhide, Glenn, 54, 220
Williams, David, 184
Williams, Harry L., 20, 22
Williams, Jay, 289
Williams, Mike, 182
Williams, Pete, 96
Williams, Robert M., 288
Williams, Wayne, 216, 225
Willis, James T., 259
Willis, Mike, 247
Wills, Diana, 312
Wilson, Harry "Lighthorse," 47, 52, 58
Wilson, Harry E., 271
Wilson, John W., Col., 19
Wilson, Willard, 105
Wilson, Woodrow, 271
Winston, Edward, 212
Winston, Patrick H., 218
Winton, Gary, 194, 196, 198, 204
Woessner, Carl, 150
Wojdakowski, Wally, 201
Women's Sports—A Look into the Past, 319
Wood, Carroll D., 259
Wood, William, 214
Wood, William, 65, 69, 79, 92, 207
Woodruff, Bob, 98
Woodruff, Roscoe, B., 238
Woods, William B., 54
Woodward, Charles G., 23

Woodward, Lamar F., 259
Woodward, Stanley, 134
Worthington, Jim, 313
Wothke, Les, 198
Wrestling —A Look into the Past, 284
Wright, Benny, 184
Wycoff, Ann Marie, 312, 315

Y
Yablonski, Ventan, 97
Yancey, Bert, 301
Yanelli, Sylvio, 94
Yarbrough, William, 303
Yarnell, Steve, 150
Yates, Dave, 301
Yeoman, Bill, 96, 98
Yerges, Howard, 94
Yonakur, Johnny, 107
Yost, Emmett F., 270
"You Have to Pay the Price," 138
Young, Dick, 227
Young, Frederick, 303
Young, Jim, 173, 179, 180, 182, 184, 185
Young, Robert, 303
Young, Terry, 150, 154

Z
Zailskas, Roger, 225
Zaldo, Martin, 225
Zastrow, Bob, 134
Zeigler, Lewis, 132
Zilly, Jack, 107, 121
Zontini, Louis, 181